iPhone 3D Programming

iPhone 3D Programming

Developing Graphical Applications
with OpenGL ES

Philip Rideout
foreword by Serban Porumbescu

O'REILLY®

Beijing · Cambridge · Farnham · Köln · Sebastopol · Tokyo

iPhone 3D Programming
by Philip Rideout

Published by O'Reilly Media, Inc., 1005 Gravenstein Highway North, Sebastopol, CA 95472.

O'Reilly books may be purchased for educational, business, or sales promotional use. Online editions are also available for most titles (*http://my.safaribooksonline.com*). For more information, contact our corporate/institutional sales department: 800-998-9938 or *corporate@oreilly.com*.

Editor: Brian Jepson
Production Editor: Loranah Dimant
Copyeditor: Kim Wimpsett
Proofreader: Teresa Barensfeld
Production Services: Molly Sharp

Indexer: Ellen Troutman Zaig
Cover Designer: Karen Montgomery
Interior Designer: David Futato
Illustrator: Robert Romano

Printing History:
May 2010:   First Edition.

ISBN: 978-0-596-80482-4

[LSI]   [2011-02-04]

1296485125

Frank and Doris Rideout
1916–1998 and 1919–2007

Table of Contents

Foreword

I'm sitting at my kitchen table writing this foreword on the eve of yet another momentous occasion for Apple. Today, February 23, 2010, marks the day the 10-billionth song was downloaded from the iTunes Music Store. Take a moment to really think about that number and keep in mind that the iTunes Music Store was launched just shy of seven years ago back in April 2003. That's right. Ten billion songs downloaded in just under seven years.

The news gets even better. If you're holding this book, you're probably interested in iPhone application development, and the next number should really get you excited. On January 5, 2010, Apple announced that 3 billion applications had been downloaded from its App Store in just under 18 months. Phenomenal!

Months before I was asked to review this book, I had started putting together an outline and researching material for my own iPhone graphics book. When I was asked whether I was interested in being a technical reviewer for a book that seemed so similar to what I was planning, I definitely hesitated. But I've always been a big fan of O'Reilly books and quickly changed my mind once I realized it was the publisher backing the book.

Philip has done a fantastic job of focusing on the content most crucial to getting you productive with OpenGL ES on the iPhone as quickly as possible. In the pages that follow you'll learn the basics of using Xcode and Objective-C, move through the fixed function (OpenGL ES 1.1) and programmable (OpenGL ES 2.0) graphics pipelines, experiment with springs and dampeners, and learn advanced lighting techniques. You'll even learn about distance fields and pick up a bit of Python along the way. By the end of this book, you'll find yourself resting very comfortably on a solid foundation of OpenGL ES knowledge. You'll be well-versed in advanced graphics techniques that are applicable to the iPhone and beyond.

I knew from the moment I read the first partial manuscript that this was the book I wish I had written. Now that I've read the book in its entirety, I'm certain of it. I'm confident you'll feel the same way.

— Serban Porumbescu, PhD
Senior Gameplay Engineer
Tapulous Inc.

Preface

How to Read This Book

"It makes programming fun again!" is a cliché among geeks; all too often it's used to extol the virtues of some newfangled programming language or platform. But I honestly think there's no better aphorism to describe iPhone graphics programming. Whether you're a professional or a hobbyist, I hope this book can play a small role in helping you rediscover the joy of programming.

This book is *not* an OpenGL manual, but it does teach many basic OpenGL concepts as a means to an end, namely, 3D graphics programming on the iPhone and iPod touch. Much of the book is written in a tutorial style, and I encourage you to download the sample code and play with it. Readers don't need a graphics background, nor do they need any experience with the iPhone SDK. A sound understanding of C++ is required; fluency in Objective-C is useful but not necessary. A smidgen of Python is used in Chapter 7, but don't let it scare you off.

I tried to avoid making this book math-heavy, but, as with any 3D graphics book, you at least need a fearless attitude toward basic linear algebra. I'll hold your hand and jog your memory along the way.

If you're already familiar with 3D graphics but haven't done much with the iPhone, you can still learn a thing or two from this book. There are certain sections that you can probably skip over. Much of Chapter 2 is an overview of general 3D graphics concepts; I won't be offended if you just skim through it. Conversely, if you have iPhone experience but are new to 3D graphics, you can gloss over some of the Objective-C and Xcode overviews given in Chapter 1.

In any case, I hope you enjoy reading this book as much as I enjoyed writing it!

Conventions Used in This Book

The following typographical conventions are used in this book:

Italic

> Indicates new terms, URLs, email addresses, filenames, and file extensions. It also indicates the parts of the user interface, such as buttons, menus, and panes.

`Constant width`

> Used for program listings, as well as within paragraphs to refer to program elements such as variable or function names, databases, data types, environment variables, statements, and keywords.

`Constant width bold`

> Shows commands or other text that should be typed literally by the user.

`Constant width italic`

> Shows text that should be replaced with user-supplied values or by values determined by context.

 This icon signifies a tip, suggestion, or general note.

 This icon indicates a warning or caution.

Using Code Examples

This book is here to help you get your job done. In general, you may use the code in this book in your programs and documentation. You do not need to contact us for permission unless you're reproducing a significant portion of the code. For example, writing a program that uses several chunks of code from this book does not require permission. Selling or distributing a CD-ROM of examples from O'Reilly books does require permission. Answering a question by citing this book and quoting example code does not require permission. Incorporating a significant amount of example code from this book into your product's documentation does require permission.

We appreciate, but do not require, attribution. An attribution usually includes the title, author, publisher, and ISBN. For example: "*iPhone 3D Programming* by Philip Rideout. Copyright 2010 Philip Rideout, 978-0-596-80482-4."

If you feel your use of the code examples falls outside fair use or the permission given here, feel free to contact us at *permissions@oreilly.com*.

Safari® Books Online

Safari Books Online is an on-demand digital library that lets you easily search over 7,500 technology and creative reference books and videos to find the answers you need quickly.

With a subscription, you can read any page and watch any video from our library online. Read books on your cell phone and mobile devices. Access new titles before they are available for print, and get exclusive access to manuscripts in development and post feedback for the authors. Copy and paste code samples, organize your favorites, download chapters, bookmark key sections, create notes, print out pages, and benefit from tons of other time-saving features.

O'Reilly Media has uploaded this book to the Safari Books Online service. To have full digital access to this book and others on similar topics from O'Reilly and other publishers, sign up for free at *http://my.safaribooksonline.com*.

How to Contact Us

Please address comments and questions concerning this book to the publisher:

O'Reilly Media, Inc.
1005 Gravenstein Highway North
Sebastopol, CA 95472
800-998-9938 (in the United States or Canada)
707-829-0515 (international or local)
707-829-0104 (fax)

We have a web page for this book, where we list errata, examples, and any additional information. You can access this page at:

http://oreilly.com/catalog/9780596804831

To comment or ask technical questions about this book, send email to:

bookquestions@oreilly.com

For more information about our books, conferences, Resource Centers, and the O'Reilly Network, see our website at:

http://www.oreilly.com

Acknowledgments

Harsha Kuntur planted the seed for this book by lighting up every dinner conversation with his rabid enthusiasm for the iPhone. Equally important are Stephen Holmes (who unintentionally made me into an Apple fanboy) and David Banks (who inspired me to get into graphics).

I'd also like to thank my editor and personal champion at O'Reilly, Brian Jepson. Much thanks to both John T. Kennedy and Jon C. Kennedy for their valuable suggestions (can't the Irish be more creative with names?). I was joyous when Serban Porumbescu agreed to review my book—I needed his experience. I'm also supremely grateful to Alex MacPhee and David Schmitt of Medical Simulation Corporation, who have been accommodating and patient as I tried to juggle my time with this book. Thanks, Alex, for catching those last-minute bugs!

Finally, I'd like to thank Mona, who had 1-800-DIVORCE on speed dial while I was having an affair with this book, but she managed to resist the temptation. In fact, without her limitless support and encouragement, there's absolutely no way I could've done this.

## CHAPTER 1

Quick-Start Guide

Rumors of my assimilation are greatly exaggerated.

—Captain Picard, *Star Trek: First Contact*

In this chapter, you'll plunge in and develop your first application from scratch. The goal is to write a HelloArrow program that draws an arrow and rotates it in response to an orientation change.

You'll be using the OpenGL ES API to render the arrow, but OpenGL is only one of many graphics technologies supported on the iPhone. At first, it can be confusing which of these technologies is most appropriate for your requirements. It's also not always obvious which technologies are iPhone-specific and which cross over into general Mac OS X development.

Apple neatly organizes all of the iPhone's public APIs into four layers: Cocoa Touch, Media Services, Core Services, and Core OS. Mac OS X is a bit more sprawling, but it too can be roughly organized into four layers, as shown in Figure 1-1.

At the very bottom layer, Mac OS X and the iPhone share their kernel architecture and core operating system; these shared components are collectively known as *Darwin*.

Despite the similarities between the two platforms, they diverge quite a bit in their handling of OpenGL. Figure 1-1 includes some OpenGL-related classes, shown in bold. The NSOpenGLView class in Mac OS X does not exist on the iPhone, and the iPhone's EAGLContext and CAEGLLayer classes are absent on Mac OS X. The OpenGL API itself is also quite different in the two platforms, because Mac OS X supports full-blown OpenGL while the iPhone relies on the more svelte OpenGL ES.

The iPhone graphics technologies include the following:

Quartz 2D rendering engine
Vector-based graphics library that supports alpha blending, layers, and anti-aliasing. This is also available on Mac OS X. Applications that leverage Quartz technology must reference a *framework* (Apple's term for a bundle of resources and libraries) known as *Quartz Core*.

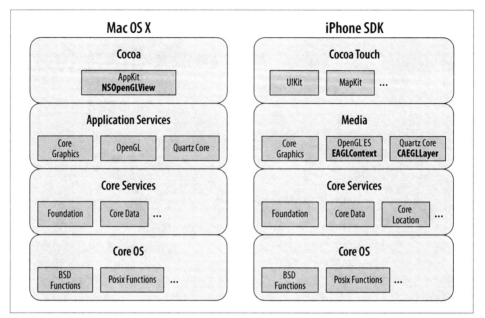

Figure 1-1. Mac OS X and iPhone programming stacks

Core Graphics
> Vanilla C interface to Quartz. This is also available on Mac OS X.

UIKit
> Native windowing framework for iPhone. Among other things, UIKit wraps Quartz primitives into Objective-C classes. This has a Mac OS X counterpart called *AppKit*, which is a component of *Cocoa*.

Cocoa Touch
> Conceptual layer in the iPhone programming stack that contains UIKit along with a few other frameworks.

Core Animation
> Objective-C framework that facilitates complex animations.

OpenGL ES
> Low-level hardware-accelerated C API for rendering 2D or 3D graphics.

EAGL
> Tiny glue API between OpenGL ES and UIKit. Some EAGL classes (such as `CAEGLLayer`) are defined in Quartz Core framework, while others (such as `EAGLContext`) are defined in the OpenGL ES framework.

This book chiefly deals with OpenGL ES, the only technology in the previous list that isn't Apple-specific. The OpenGL ES specification is controlled by a consortium of companies called the *Khronos Group*. Different implementations of OpenGL ES all support the same core API, making it easy to write portable code. Vendors can pick and choose from a formally defined set of extensions to the API, and the iPhone supports a rich set of these extensions. We'll cover many of these extensions throughout this book.

Transitioning to Apple Technology

Yes, you do need a Mac to develop applications for the iPhone App Store! Developers with a PC background should quell their fear; my own experience was that the PC-to-Apple transition was quite painless, aside from some initial frustration with a different keyboard.

Xcode serves as Apple's preferred development environment for Mac OS X. If you are new to Xcode, it might initially strike you as resembling an email client more than an IDE. This layout is actually quite intuitive; after learning the keyboard shortcuts, I found Xcode to be a productive environment. It's also fun to work with. For example, after typing in a closing delimiter such as), the corresponding (momentarily glows and seems to push itself out from the screen. This effect is pleasant and subtle; the only thing missing is a kitten-purr sound effect. Maybe Apple will add that to the next version of Xcode.

Objective-C

Now we come to the elephant in the room. At some point, you've probably heard that Objective-C is a requirement for iPhone development. You can actually use pure C or C++ for much of your application logic, if it does not make extensive use of UIKit. This is especially true for OpenGL development because it is a C API. Most of this book uses C++; Objective-C is used only for the bridge code between the iPhone operating system and OpenGL ES.

The origin of Apple's usage of Objective-C lies with NeXT, which was another Steve Jobs company whose technology was ahead of its time in many ways—perhaps too far ahead. NeXT failed to survive on its own, and Apple purchased it in 1997. To this day, you can still find the NS prefix in many of Apple's APIs, including those for the iPhone.

Some would say that Objective-C is not as complex or feature-rich as C++, which isn't necessarily a bad thing. In many cases, Objective-C is the right tool for the right job. It's a fairly simple superset of C, making it quite easy to learn.

However, for 3D graphics, I find that certain C++ features are indispensable. Operator overloading makes it possible to perform vector math in a syntactically natural way. Templates allow the reuse of vector and matrix types using a variety of underlying numerical representations. Most importantly, C++ is widely used on many platforms, and in many ways, it's the *lingua franca* of game developers.

A Brief History of OpenGL ES

In 1982, a Stanford University professor named Jim Clark started one of the world's first computer graphics companies: Silicon Graphics Computer Systems, later known as SGI. SGI engineers needed a standard way of specifying common 3D transformations and operations, so they designed a proprietary API called IrisGL. In the early 1990s, SGI reworked IrisGL and released it to the public as an industry standard, and OpenGL was born.

Over the years, graphics technology advanced even more rapidly than Moore's law could have predicted.* OpenGL went through many revisions while largely preserving backward compatibility. Many developers believed that the API became bloated. When the mobile phone revolution took off, the need for a trimmed-down version of OpenGL became more apparent than ever. The Khronos Group announced OpenGL for Embedded Systems (OpenGL ES) at the annual SIGGRAPH conference in 2003.

OpenGL ES rapidly gained popularity and today is used on many platforms besides the iPhone, including Android, Symbian, and PlayStation 3.

All Apple devices support at least version 1.1 of the OpenGL ES API, which added several powerful features to the core specification, including vertex buffer objects and mandatory multitexture support, both of which you'll learn about in this book.

In March 2007, the Khronos Group released the OpenGL ES 2.0 specification, which entailed a major break in backward compatibility by ripping out many of the fixed-function features and replacing them with a *shading language*. This new model for controlling graphics simplified the API and shifted greater control into the hands of developers. Many developers (including myself) find the ES 2.0 programming model to be more elegant than the ES 1.1 model. But in the end, the two APIs simply represent two different approaches to the same problem. With ES 2.0, an application developer needs to do much more work just to write a simple Hello World application. The 1.*x* flavor of OpenGL ES will probably continue to be used for some time, because of its low implementation burden.

Choosing the Appropriate Version of OpenGL ES

Apple's newer handheld devices, such as the iPhone 3GS and iPad, have graphics hardware that supports both ES 1.1 and 2.0; these devices are said to have a *programmable graphics pipeline* because the graphics processor executes instructions rather than performing fixed mathematical operations. Older devices like the first-generation iPod touch, iPhone, and iPhone 3G are said to have a *fixed-function graphics pipeline* because they support only ES 1.1.

---

* Hart, John C. *Ray Tracing in Graphics Hardware*. SPEC Presentation at SIGGRAPH, 2003.

Before writing your first line of code, be sure to have a good handle on your graphics requirements. It's tempting to use the latest and greatest API, but keep in mind that there are many 1.1 devices out there, so this could open up a much broader market for your application. It can also be less work to write an ES 1.1 application, if your graphical requirements are fairly modest.

Of course, many advanced effects are possible only in ES 2.0—and, as I mentioned, I believe it to be a more elegant programming model.

To summarize, you can choose from among four possibilities for your application:

- Use OpenGL ES 1.1 only.
- Use OpenGL ES 2.0 only.
- Determine capabilities at runtime; use ES 2.0 if it's supported; otherwise, fall back to ES 1.1.
- Release two separate applications: one for ES 1.1, one for ES 2.0. (This could get messy.)

Choose wisely! We'll be using the third choice for many of the samples in this book, including the HelloArrow sample presented in this chapter.

Getting Started

Assuming you already have a Mac, the first step is to head over to Apple's iPhone developer site and download the SDK. With only the free SDK in hand, you have the tools at your disposal to develop complex applications and even test them on the iPhone Simulator.

The iPhone Simulator cannot emulate certain features such as the accelerometer, nor does it perfectly reflect the iPhone's implementation of OpenGL ES. For example, a physical iPhone cannot render anti-aliased lines using OpenGL's smooth lines feature, but the simulator can. Conversely, there may be extensions that a physical iPhone supports that the simulator does not. (Incidentally, we'll discuss how to work around the anti-aliasing limitation later in this book.)

Having said all that, you do not need to own an iPhone to use this book. I've ensured that every code sample either runs against the simulator or at least fails gracefully in the rare case where it leverages a feature not supported on the simulator.

If you do own an iPhone and are willing to cough up a reasonable fee ($100 at the time of this writing), you can join Apple's iPhone Developer Program to enable deployment to a physical iPhone. When I did this, it was not a painful process, and Apple granted me approval almost immediately. If the approval process takes longer in your case, I suggest forging ahead with the simulator while you wait. I actually use the simulator for most of my day-to-day development anyway, since it provides a much faster debug-build-run turnaround than deploying to my device.

The remainder of this chapter is written in a tutorial style. Be aware that some of the steps may vary slightly from what's written, depending on the versions of the tools that you're using. These minor deviations most likely pertain to specific actions within the Xcode UI; for example, a menu might be renamed or shifted in future versions. However, the actual sample code is relatively future-proof.

Installing the iPhone SDK

You can download the iPhone SDK from here:

http://developer.apple.com/iphone/

It's packaged as a *.dmg* file, Apple's standard disk image format. After you download it, it should automatically open in a Finder window—if it doesn't, you can find its disk icon on the desktop and open it from there. The contents of the disk image usually consist of an "about" PDF, a *Packages* subfolder, and an installation package, whose icon resembles a cardboard box. Open the installer and follow the steps. When confirming the subset of components to install, simply accept the defaults. When you're done, you can "eject" the disk image to remove it from the desktop.

As an Apple developer, Xcode will become your home base. I recommend dragging it to your Dock at the bottom of the screen. You'll find Xcode in */Developer/Applications/ Xcode*.

 If you're coming from a PC background, Mac's windowing system may seem difficult to organize at first. I highly recommend the Exposé and Spaces desktop managers that are built into Mac OS X. Exposé lets you switch between windows using an intuitive "spread-out" view. Spaces can be used to organize your windows into multiple virtual desktops. I've used several virtual desktop managers on Windows, and in my opinion Spaces beats them all hands down.

Building the OpenGL Template Application with Xcode

When running Xcode for the first time, it presents you with a *Welcome to Xcode* dialog. Click the *Create a new Xcode project* button. (If you have the welcome dialog turned off, go to File→New Project.) Now you'll be presented with the dialog shown in Figure 1-2, consisting of a collection of templates. The template we're interested in is *OpenGL ES Application*, under the *iPhone OS* heading. It's nothing fancy, but it is a fully functional OpenGL application and serves as a decent starting point.

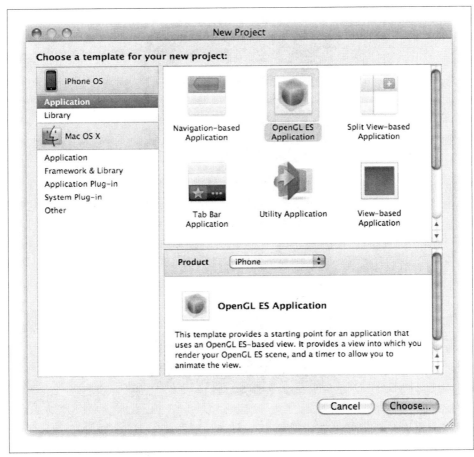

Figure 1-2. New Project dialog

In the next dialog, choose a goofy name for your application, and then you'll finally see Xcode's main window. Build and run the application by selecting *Build and Run* from the *Build* menu or by pressing ⌘-Return. When the build finishes, you should see the iPhone Simulator pop up with a moving square in the middle, as in Figure 1-3. When you're done gawking at this amazing application, press ⌘-Q to quit.

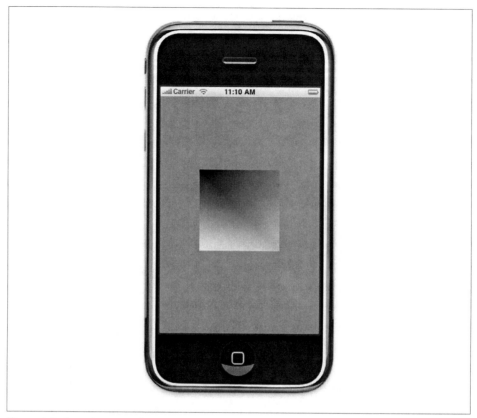

Figure 1-3. OpenGL ES Application template

Deploying to Your Real iPhone

This is not required for development, but if you want to deploy your application to a physical device, you should sign up for Apple's iPhone Developer Program. This enables you to provision your iPhone for developer builds, in addition to the usual software you get from the App Store. Provisioning is a somewhat laborious process, but thankfully it needs to be done only once per device. Apple has now made it reasonably straightforward by providing a *Provisioning Assistant* applet that walks you through the process. You'll find this applet after logging into the iPhone Dev Center (*http://developer.apple.com/iphone/*) and entering the iPhone Developer Program Portal.

When your iPhone has been provisioned properly, you should be able to see it in Xcode's *Organizer* window (Control-⌘-O). Open up the *Provisioning Profiles* tree node in the left pane, and make sure your device is listed.

Now you can go back to Xcode's main window, open the *Overview* combo box in the upper-left corner, and choose the latest SDK that has the *Device* prefix. The next time you build and run (⌘-Return), the moving square should appear on your iPhone.

HelloArrow with Fixed Function

In the previous section, you learned your way around the development environment with Apple's boilerplate OpenGL application, but to get a good understanding of the fundamentals, you need to start from scratch. This section of the book builds a simple application from the ground up using OpenGL ES 1.1. The 1.*x* track of OpenGL ES is sometimes called *fixed-function* to distinguish it from the OpenGL ES 2.0 track, which relies on shaders. We'll learn how to modify the sample to use shaders later in the chapter.

Let's come up with a variation of the classic Hello World in a way that fits well with the theme of this book. As you'll learn later, most of what gets rendered in OpenGL can be reduced to triangles. We can use two overlapping triangles to draw a simple arrow shape, as shown in Figure 1-4. Any resemblance to the *Star Trek* logo is purely coincidental.

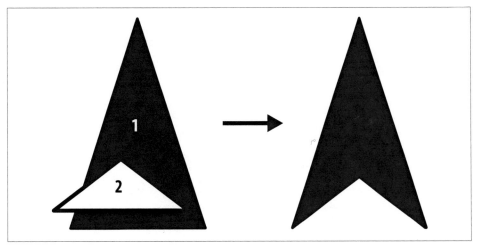

Figure 1-4. Arrow shape composed from two triangles

To add an interesting twist, the program will make the arrow stay upright when the user changes the orientation of his iPhone.

Layering Your 3D Application

If you love Objective-C, then by all means, use it everywhere you can. This book supports cross-platform code reuse, so we leverage Objective-C only when necessary.

Figure 1-5 depicts a couple ways of organizing your application code such that the guts of the program are written in C++ (or vanilla C), while the iPhone-specific glue is written in Objective-C. The variation on the right separates the application engine (also known as *game logic*) from the rendering engine. Some of the more complex samples in this book take this approach.

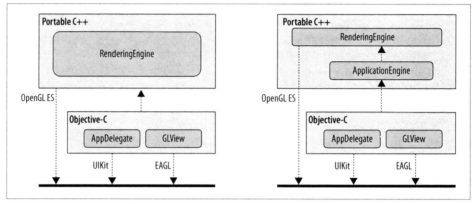

Figure 1-5. Layered 3D iPhone applications

The key to either approach depicted in Figure 1-6 is designing a robust interface to the rendering engine and ensuring that any platform can use it. The sample code in this book uses the name IRenderingEngine for this interface, but you can call it what you want.

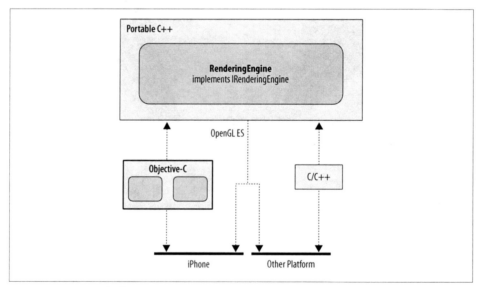

Figure 1-6. A cross-platform OpenGL ES application

The IRenderingEngine interface also allows you to build multiple rendering engines into your application, as shown in Figure 1-7. This facilitates the "Use ES 2.0 if supported, otherwise fall back" scenario mentioned in "Choosing the Appropriate Version of OpenGL ES" on page 4. We'll take this approach for HelloArrow.

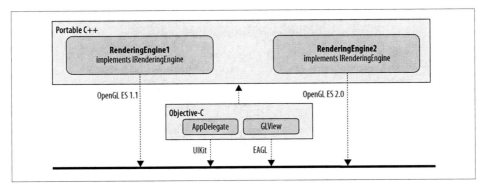

Figure 1-7. An iPhone application that supports ES 1.1 and 2.0

You'll learn more about the pieces in Figure 1-7 as we walk through the code to HelloArrow. To summarize, you'll be writing three classes:

RenderingEngine1 and RenderingEngine2 (portable C++)
> These classes are where most of the work takes place; all calls to OpenGL ES are made from here. RenderingEngine1 uses ES 1.1, while RenderingEngine2 uses ES 2.0.

HelloArrowAppDelegate (Objective-C)
> Small Objective-C class that derives from NSObject and adopts the UIApplication Delegate protocol. ("Adopting a protocol" in Objective-C is somewhat analogous to "implementing an interface" in languages such as Java or C#.) This does not use OpenGL or EAGL; it simply initializes the GLView object and releases memory when the application closes.

GLView (Objective-C)
> Derives from the standard UIView class and uses EAGL to instance a valid rendering surface for OpenGL.

Starting from Scratch

Launch Xcode and start with the simplest project template by going to File→New Project and selecting Window-Based Application from the list of iPhone OS application templates. Name it *HelloArrow*.

Xcode comes bundled with an application called *Interface Builder*, which is Apple's interactive designer for building interfaces with UIKit (and AppKit on Mac OS X). I don't attempt to cover UIKit because most 3D applications do not make extensive use of it. For best performance, Apple advises against mixing UIKit with OpenGL.

For simple 3D applications that aren't too demanding, it probably won't hurt you to add some UIKit controls to your OpenGL view. We cover this briefly in "Mixing OpenGL ES and UIKit" on page 310.

Optional: Creating a Clean Slate

The following steps remove some Interface Builder odds and ends from the project; this is optional, but it's something I like to do to start from a clean slate.

1. Interface Builder uses an XML file called a *xib* for defining an object graph of UI elements. Since you're creating a pure OpenGL application, you don't need this file in your project. In the *Groups & Files* pane on the left, find the folder that says *Resources* (or something similar such as *Resources-iPhone*). Delete the file ending in *.xib*. When prompted, move it to the trash.

2. The xib file normally compiles to a binary file called a *nib*, which is loaded at runtime to build up the UI. To instruct the OS not to load the nib file, you'll need to remove an application property. In the *Resources* folder, find the *HelloArrow-Info.plist* file. Click it and then remove the property called *Main nib file base name* (toward the bottom of the Information Property List). You can remove a property by clicking to select it and then pressing the Delete key.

3. The template application normally extracts the name of the application delegate from the nib file during startup; since you're not using a nib file, you need to pass in an explicit string. Under *Other Sources*, open *main.m*, and change the last argument of the call to `UIApplicationMain` from `nil` to the name of your application delegate class (for example, `@"HelloArrowAppDelegate"`). The `@` prefix means this is a proper Objective-C string rather than a C-style pointer to `char`.

4. The template includes a property in the application delegate that allows Interface Builder to hook in. This is no longer needed. To remove the property declaration, open *HelloArrowAppDelegate.h* (in the *Classes* folder), and remove the `@property` line. To remove the implementation, open *HelloArrowAppDelegate.m*, and remove the `@synthesize` line.

Linking in the OpenGL and Quartz Libraries

In the world of Apple programming, you can think of a *framework* as being similar to a library, but technically it's a *bundle* of resources. A bundle is a special type of folder that acts like a single file, and it's quite common in Mac OS X. For example, applications are usually deployed as bundles—open the action menu on nearly any icon in your *Applications* folder, and you'll see an option for *Show Package Contents*, which allows you to get past the façade.

You need to add some framework references to your Xcode project. Pull down the action menu for the *Frameworks* folder. This can be done by selecting the folder and clicking the *Action* icon or by right-clicking or Control-clicking the folder. Next choose Add→Existing Frameworks. Select *OpenGLES.Framework*, and click the Add button. You may see a dialog after this; if so, simply accept its defaults. Now, repeat this procedure with *QuartzCore.Framework*.

 Why do we need Quartz if we're writing an OpenGL ES application? The answer is that Quartz owns the layer object that gets presented to the screen, even though we're rendering with OpenGL. The layer object is an instance of `CAEGLLayer`, which is a subclass of `CALayer`; these classes are defined in the Quartz Core framework.

Subclassing UIView

The abstract `UIView` class controls a rectangular area of the screen, handles user events, and sometimes serves as a container for child views. Almost all standard controls such as buttons, sliders, and text fields are descendants of `UIView`. We tend to avoid using these controls in this book; for most of the sample code, the UI requirements are so modest that OpenGL itself can be used to render simple buttons and various widgets.

For our HelloArrow sample, we do need to define a single `UIView` subclass, since all rendering on the iPhone must take place within a view. Select the *Classes* folder in Xcode, click the *Action* icon in the toolbar, and select Add→New file. Under the *Cocoa Touch Class* category, select the Objective-C class template, and choose *UIView* in the *Subclass of* menu. In the next dialog, name it *GLView.mm*, and leave the box checked to ensure that the corresponding header gets generated. The *.mm* extension indicates that this file can support C++ in addition to Objective-C. Open *GLView.h*. You should see something like this:

```
#import <UIKit/UIKit.h>

@interface GLView : UIView {
}

@end
```

For C/C++ veterans, this syntax can be a little jarring—just wait until you see the syntax for methods! Fear not, it's easy to become accustomed to.

`#import` is almost the same thing as `#include` but automatically ensures that the header file does not get expanded twice within the same source file. This is similar to the `#pragma once` feature found in many C/C++ compilers.

Keywords specific to Objective-C stand out because of the @ prefix. The `@interface` keyword marks the beginning of a class declaration; the `@end` keyword marks the end of a class declaration. A single source file may contain several class declarations and therefore can have several `@interface` blocks.

As you probably already guessed, the previous code snippet simply declares an empty class called GLView that derives from UIView. What's less obvious is that data fields will go inside the curly braces, while method declarations will go between the ending curly brace and the @end, like this:

```
#import <UIKit/UIKit.h>

@interface GLView : UIView {
    // Protected fields go here...
}

// Public methods go here...

@end
```

By default, data fields have protected accessibility, but you can make them private using the @private keyword. Let's march onward and fill in the pieces shown in bold in Example 1-1. We're also adding some new #imports for OpenGL-related stuff.

Example 1-1. GLView class declaration

```
#import <UIKit/UIKit.h>
#import <OpenGLES/EAGL.h>
#import <QuartzCore/QuartzCore.h>
#import <OpenGLES/ES1/gl.h>
#import <OpenGLES/ES1/glext.h>

@interface GLView : UIView {
    EAGLContext* m_context;
}

 - (void) drawView;

@end
```

The m_context field is a pointer to the EAGL object that manages our OpenGL context. EAGL is a small Apple-specific API that links the iPhone operating system with OpenGL.

 Every time you modify API state through an OpenGL function call, you do so within a *context*. For a given thread running on your system, only one context can be current at any time. With the iPhone, you'll rarely need more than one context for your application. Because of the limited resources on mobile devices, I don't recommend using multiple contexts.

If you have a C/C++ background, the drawView method declaration in Example 1-1 may look odd. It's less jarring if you're familiar with UML syntax, but UML uses - and + to denote private and public methods, respectively; with Objective-C, - and + denote instance methods and class methods. (Class methods in Objective-C are somewhat similar to C++ static methods, but in Objective-C, the class itself is a proper object.)

Take a look at the top of the *GLView.mm* file that Xcode generated. Everything between @implementation and @end is the definition of the GLView class. Xcode created three methods for you: initWithFrame, drawRect (which may be commented out), and dealloc. Note that these methods do not have declarations in the header file that Xcode generated. In this respect, an Objective-C method is similar to a plain old function in C; it needs a forward declaration only if gets called before it's defined. I usually declare all methods in the header file anyway to be consistent with C++ class declarations.

Take a closer look at the first method in the file:

```
- (id) initWithFrame: (CGRect) frame
{
    if (self = [super initWithFrame:frame]) {
        // Initialize code...
    }
    return self;
}
```

This is an Objective-C initializer method, which is somewhat analogous to a C++ constructor. The return type and argument types are enclosed in parentheses, similar to C-style casting syntax. The conditional in the if statement accomplishes several things at once: it calls the base implementation of initWithFrame, assigns the object's pointer to self, and checks the result for success.

In Objective-C parlance, you don't call methods on objects; you *send* messages to objects. The square bracket syntax denotes a message. Rather than a comma-separated list of values, arguments are denoted with a whitespace-separated list of name-value pairs. The idea is that messages can vaguely resemble English sentences. For example, consider this statement, which adds an element to an NSMutableDictionary:

```
[myDictionary setValue: 30 forKey: @"age"];
```

If you read the argument list aloud, you get an English sentence! Well, sort of.

That's enough of an Objective-C lesson for now. Let's get back to the HelloArrow application. In *GLView.mm*, provide the implementation to the layerClass method by adding the following snippet after the @implementation line:

```
+ (Class) layerClass
{
    return [CAEAGLLayer class];
}
```

This simply overrides the default implementation of layerClass to return an OpenGL-friendly layer type. The class method is similar to the typeof operator found in other languages; it returns an object that represents the type itself, rather than an instance of the type.

The + prefix means that this is an override of a class method rather than an instance method. This type of override is a feature of Objective-C rarely found in other languages.

Now, go back to `initWithFrame`, and replace the contents of the `if` block with some EAGL initialization code, as shown in Example 1-2.

Example 1-2. EAGL initialization in GLView.mm

```
- (id) initWithFrame: (CGRect) frame
{
    if (self = [super initWithFrame:frame]) {
        CAEAGLLayer* eaglLayer = (CAEAGLLayer*) super.layer; ❶
        eaglLayer.opaque = YES; ❷

        m_context = [[EAGLContext alloc] initWithAPI:kEAGLRenderingAPIOpenGLES1]; ❸

        if (!m_context || ![EAGLContext setCurrentContext:m_context]) { ❹
            [self release];
            return nil;❺
        }

        // Initialize code...
    }
    return self;
}
```

Here's what's going on:

❶ Retrieve the `layer` property from the base class (`UIView`), and downcast it from `CALayer` into a `CAEAGLLayer`. This is safe because of the override to the `layerClass` method.

❷ Set the `opaque` property on the layer to indicate that you do not need Quartz to handle transparency. This is a performance benefit that Apple recommends in all OpenGL programs. Don't worry, you can easily use OpenGL to handle alpha blending.

❸ Create an `EAGLContext` object, and tell it which version of OpenGL you need, which is ES 1.1.

❹ Tell the `EAGLContext` to make itself current, which means any subsequent OpenGL calls in this thread will be tied to it.

❺ If context creation fails or if `setCurrentContext` fails, then poop out and return `nil`.

Memory Management in Objective-C

The alloc-init pattern that we used for instancing `EAGLContext` in Example 1-2 is very common in Objective-C. With Objective-C, constructing an object is always split into two phases: allocation and initialization. However, some of the classes you'll encounter supply a class method to make this easier. For example, to convert a UTF-8 string into a `NSString` using the alloc-init pattern, you could do this:

```
NSString* destString = [[NSString alloc] initWithUTF8String:srcString];
```

But I prefer doing this:

```
NSString* destString = [NSString stringWithUTF8String:srcString];
```

Not only is this more terse, it also adds autorelease semantics to the object, so there's no need to call `release` on it when you're done.

Next, continue filling in the initialization code with some OpenGL setup. Replace the `OpenGL Initialization` comment with Example 1-3.

Example 1-3. OpenGL initialization in GLView.mm

```
GLuint framebuffer, renderbuffer;
glGenFramebuffersOES(1, &framebuffer);
glGenRenderbuffersOES(1, &renderbuffer);

glBindFramebufferOES(GL_FRAMEBUFFER_OES, framebuffer);
glBindRenderbufferOES(GL_RENDERBUFFER_OES, renderbuffer);

[m_context
    renderbufferStorage:GL_RENDERBUFFER_OES
    fromDrawable: eaglLayer];

glFramebufferRenderbufferOES(
    GL_FRAMEBUFFER_OES, GL_COLOR_ATTACHMENT0_OES,
    GL_RENDERBUFFER_OES, renderbuffer);

glViewport(0, 0, CGRectGetWidth(frame), CGRectGetHeight(frame));

[self drawView];
```

Example 1-3 starts off by generating two OpenGL identifiers, one for a *renderbuffer* and one for a *framebuffer*. Briefly, a renderbuffer is a 2D surface filled with some type of data (in this case, color), and a framebuffer is a bundle of renderbuffers. You'll learn more about framebuffer objects (FBOs) in later chapters.

The use of FBOs is an advanced feature that is not part of the core OpenGL ES 1.1 API, but it is specified in an OpenGL extension that all iPhones support. In OpenGL ES 2.0, FBOs are included in the core API. It may seem odd to use this advanced feature in the simple HelloArrow program, but all OpenGL iPhone applications need to leverage FBOs to draw anything to the screen.

The renderbuffer and framebuffer are both of type GLuint, which is the type that OpenGL uses to represent various objects that it manages. You could just as easily use unsigned int in lieu of GLuint, but I recommend using the GL-prefixed types for objects that get passed to the API. If nothing else, the GL-prefixed types make it easier for humans to identify which pieces of your code interact with OpenGL.

After generating identifiers for the framebuffer and renderbuffer, Example 1-3 then *binds* these objects to the pipeline. When an object is bound, it can be modified or consumed by subsequent OpenGL operations. After binding the renderbuffer, storage is allocated by sending the renderbufferStorage message to the EAGLContext object.

For an off-screen surface, you would use the OpenGL command glRenderbufferStorage to perform allocation, but in this case you're associating the renderbuffer with an EAGL layer. You'll learn more about off-screen surfaces later in this book.

Next, the glFramebufferRenderbufferOES command is used to attach the renderbuffer object to the framebuffer object.

After this, the glViewport command is issued. You can think of this as setting up a coordinate system. In Chapter 2 you'll learn more precisely what's going on here.

The final call in Example 1-3 is to the drawView method. Go ahead and create the drawView implementation:

```
- (void) drawView
{
    glClearColor(0.5f, 0.5f, 0.5f, 1);
    glClear(GL_COLOR_BUFFER_BIT);

    [m_context presentRenderbuffer:GL_RENDERBUFFER_OES];
}
```

This uses OpenGL's "clear" mechanism to fill the buffer with a solid color. First the color is set to gray using four values (red, green, blue, alpha). Then, the clear operation is issued. Finally, the EAGLContext object is told to present the renderbuffer to the screen. Rather than drawing directly to the screen, most OpenGL programs render to a buffer that is then presented to the screen in an atomic operation, just like we're doing here.

You can remove the `drawRect` stub that Xcode provided for you. The `drawRect` method is typically used for a "paint refresh" in more traditional UIKit-based applications; in 3D applications, you'll want finer control over when rendering occurs.

At this point, you almost have a fully functioning OpenGL ES program, but there's one more loose end to tie up. You need to clean up when the `GLView` object is destroyed. Replace the definition of `dealloc` with the following:

```
- (void) dealloc
{
    if ([EAGLContext currentContext] == m_context)
        [EAGLContext setCurrentContext:nil];

    [m_context release];
    [super dealloc];
}
```

You can now build and run the program, but you won't even see the gray background color just yet. This brings us to the next step: hooking up the application delegate.

Hooking Up the Application Delegate

The application delegate template (*HelloArrowAppDelegate.h*) that Xcode provided contains nothing more than an instance of `UIWindow`. Let's add a pointer to an instance of the `GLView` class along with a couple method declarations (new/changed lines are shown in bold):

```
#import <UIKit/UIKit.h>
#import "GLView.h"

@interface HelloArrowAppDelegate : NSObject <UIApplicationDelegate> {
    UIWindow* m_window;
    GLView* m_view;
}

@property (nonatomic, retain) IBOutlet UIWindow *m_window;

@end
```

If you performed the instructions in "Optional: Creating a Clean Slate" on page 12, you won't see the `@property` line, which is fine. Interface Builder leverages Objective-C's property mechanism to establish connections between objects, but we're not using Interface Builder or properties in this book. In brief, the `@property` keyword declares a property; the `@synthesize` keyword defines accessor methods.

Note that the Xcode template already had a `window` member, but I renamed it to `m_window`. This is in keeping with the coding conventions that we use throughout this book.

I recommend using Xcode's *Refactor* feature to rename this variable because it will also rename the corresponding property (if it exists). Simply right-click the window variable and choose *Refactor*. If you did not make the changes shown in "Optional: Creating a Clean Slate" on page 12, you must use *Refactor* so that the *xib* file knows the window is now represented by m_window.

Now open the corresponding *HelloArrowAppDelegate.m* file. Xcode already provided skeleton implementations for applicationDidFinishLaunching and dealloc as part of the *Window-Based Application* template that we selected to create our project.

Since you need this file to handle both Objective-C and C++, you must rename the extension to *.mm*. Right-click the file to bring up the action menu, and then select *Rename*.

Flesh out the file as shown in Example 1-4.

Example 1-4. HelloArrowAppDelegate.mm

```
#import "HelloArrowAppDelegate.h"
#import <UIKit/UIKit.h>
#import "GLView.h"

@implementation HelloArrowAppDelegate

- (BOOL) application: (UIApplication*) application
        didFinishLaunchingWithOptions: (NSDictionary*) launchOptions
{
    CGRect screenBounds = [[UIScreen mainScreen] bounds];

    m_window = [[UIWindow alloc] initWithFrame: screenBounds];
    m_view = [[GLView alloc] initWithFrame: screenBounds];

    [m_window addSubview: m_view];
    [m_window makeKeyAndVisible];
    return YES;
}

- (void) dealloc
{
    [m_view release];
    [m_window release];
    [super dealloc];
}

@end
```

Example 1-4 uses the alloc-init pattern to construct the window and view objects, passing in the bounding rectangle for the entire screen.

If you haven't removed the Interface Builder bits as described in "Optional: Creating a Clean Slate" on page 12, you'll need to make a couple changes to the previous code listing:

- Add a new line after @implementation:

    ```
    @synthesize m_window;
    ```

    As mentioned previously, the @synthesize keyword defines a set of property accessors, and Interface Builder uses properties to hook things up.

- Remove the line that constructs m_window. Interface Builder has a special way of constructing the window behind the scenes. (Leave in the calls to makeKeyAndVisible and release.)

Compile and build, and you should now see a solid gray screen. Hooray!

Setting Up the Icons and Launch Image

To set a custom launch icon for your application, create a 57×57 PNG file (72×72 for the iPad), and add it to your Xcode project in the *Resources* folder. If you refer to a PNG file that is not in the same location as your project folder, Xcode will copy it for you; be sure to check the box labeled "Copy items into destination group's folder (if needed)" before you click Add. Then, open the *HelloArrow-Info.plist* file (also in the *Resources* folder), find the *Icon file* property, and enter the name of your PNG file.

The iPhone will automatically give your icon rounded corners and a shiny overlay. If you want to turn this feature off, find the *HelloArrow-Info.plist* file in your Xcode project, select the last row, click the + button, and choose *Icon already includes gloss and bevel effects* from the menu. Don't do this unless you're really sure of yourself; Apple wants users to have a consistent look in SpringBoard (the built-in program used to launch apps).

In addition to the 57×57 launch icon, Apple recommends that you also provide a 29×29 miniature icon for the Spotlight search and Settings screen. The procedure is similar except that the filename must be *Icon-Small.png*, and there's no need to modify the *.plist* file.

For the splash screen, the procedure is similar to the small icon, except that the filename must be *Default.png* and there's no need to modify the *.plist* file. The iPhone fills the entire screen with your image, so the ideal size is 320×480, unless you want to see an ugly stretchy effect. Apple's guidelines say that this image isn't a splash screen at all but a "launch image" whose purpose is to create a swift and seamless startup experience. Rather than showing a creative logo, Apple wants your launch image to mimic the starting screen of your running application. Of course, many applications ignore this rule!

Dealing with the Status Bar

Even though your application fills the renderbuffer with gray, the iPhone's status bar still appears at the top of the screen. One way of dealing with this would be adding the following line to `didFinishLaunchingWithOptions`:

```
[application setStatusBarHidden: YES withAnimation: UIStatusBarAnimationNone];
```

The problem with this approach is that the status bar does not hide until after the splash screen animation. For HelloArrow, let's remove the pesky status bar from the very beginning. Find the *HelloArrowInfo.plist* file in your Xcode project, and add a new property by selecting the last row, clicking the + button, choosing "Status bar is initially hidden" from the menu, and checking the box.

Of course, for some applications, you'll want to keep the status bar visible—after all, the user might want to keep an eye on battery life and connectivity status! If your application has a black background, you can add a *Status bar style* property and select the black style. For nonblack backgrounds, the semitransparent style often works well.

Defining and Consuming the Rendering Engine Interface

At this point, you have a walking skeleton for HelloArrow, but you still don't have the rendering layer depicted in Figure 1-7. Add a file to your Xcode project to define the C++ interface. Right-click the *Classes* folder, and choose Add→New file, select *C and C++*, and choose Header File. Call it *IRenderingEngine.hpp*. The *.hpp* extension signals that this is a pure C++ file; no Objective-C syntax is allowed.† Replace the contents of this file with Example 1-5.

Coding Convention

Example 1-5 defines an interface in C++ using some component-oriented conventions that we'll follow throughout this book:

- All interface methods are pure virtual.
- Interfaces are of type **struct** because interface methods are always public. (Recall in C++, struct members default to public, and class members default to private.)
- Names of interfaces are prefixed with a capital I.
- Interfaces consist of methods only; no fields are permitted.
- The construction of implementation classes is achieved via factory methods. In this case, the factory method is `CreateRenderer1`.
- All interfaces should have a virtual destructor to enable proper cleanup.

---

† Xcode doesn't care whether you use *hpp* or *h* for headers; we use this convention purely for the benefit of human readers.

Example 1-5. IRenderingEngine.hpp

```
// Physical orientation of a handheld device, equivalent to UIDeviceOrientation.
enum DeviceOrientation {
    DeviceOrientationUnknown,
    DeviceOrientationPortrait,
    DeviceOrientationPortraitUpsideDown,
    DeviceOrientationLandscapeLeft,
    DeviceOrientationLandscapeRight,
    DeviceOrientationFaceUp,
    DeviceOrientationFaceDown,
};

// Creates an instance of the renderer and sets up various OpenGL state.
struct IRenderingEngine* CreateRenderer1();

// Interface to the OpenGL ES renderer; consumed by GLView.
struct IRenderingEngine {
    virtual void Initialize(int width, int height) = 0;
    virtual void Render() const = 0;
    virtual void UpdateAnimation(float timeStep) = 0;
    virtual void OnRotate(DeviceOrientation newOrientation) = 0;
    virtual ~IRenderingEngine() {}
};
```

It seems redundant to include an enumeration for device orientation when one already exists in an iPhone header (namely, UIDevice.h), but this makes the IRenderingEngine interface portable to other environments.

Since the view class consumes the rendering engine interface, you need to add an IRenderingEngine pointer to the GLView class declaration, along with some fields and methods to help with rotation and animation. Example 1-6 shows the complete class declaration. New fields and methods are shown in bold. Note that we removed the two OpenGL ES 1.1 #imports; these OpenGL calls are moving to the RenderingEngine1 class. The EAGL header is not part of the OpenGL standard, but it's required to create the OpenGL ES context.

Example 1-6. GLView.h

```
#import "IRenderingEngine.hpp"
#import <OpenGLES/EAGL.h>
#import <QuartzCore/QuartzCore.h>

@interface GLView : UIView {
@private
    EAGLContext* m_context;
    IRenderingEngine* m_renderingEngine;
    float m_timestamp;
}

- (void) drawView: (CADisplayLink*) displayLink;
- (void) didRotate: (NSNotification*) notification;

@end
```

Example 1-7 is the full listing for the class implementation. Calls to the rendering engine are highlighted in bold. Note that GLView no longer contains any OpenGL calls; we're delegating all OpenGL work to the rendering engine.

Example 1-7. GLView.mm

```
#import <OpenGLES/EAGLDrawable.h>
#import "GLView.h"
#import "mach/mach_time.h"
#import <OpenGLES/ES2/gl.h> // <-- for GL_RENDERBUFFER only

@implementation GLView

+ (Class) layerClass
{
    return [CAEAGLLayer class];
}

- (id) initWithFrame: (CGRect) frame
{
    if (self = [super initWithFrame:frame]) {
        CAEAGLLayer* eaglLayer = (CAEAGLLayer*) super.layer;
        eaglLayer.opaque = YES;

        m_context = [[EAGLContext alloc] initWithAPI:kEAGLRenderingAPIOpenGLES1];

        if (!m_context || ![EAGLContext setCurrentContext:m_context]) {
            [self release];
            return nil;
        }

        m_renderingEngine = CreateRenderer1();

        [m_context
            renderbufferStorage:GL_RENDERBUFFER
            fromDrawable: eaglLayer];

        m_renderingEngine->Initialize(CGRectGetWidth(frame), CGRectGetHeight(frame));

        [self drawView: nil];
        m_timestamp = CACurrentMediaTime();

        CADisplayLink* displayLink;
        displayLink = [CADisplayLink displayLinkWithTarget:self
                                      selector:@selector(drawView:)];

        [displayLink addToRunLoop:[NSRunLoop currentRunLoop]
                    forMode:NSDefaultRunLoopMode];

        [[UIDevice currentDevice] beginGeneratingDeviceOrientationNotifications];

        [[NSNotificationCenter defaultCenter]
            addObserver:self
            selector:@selector(didRotate:)
            name:UIDeviceOrientationDidChangeNotification
```

```
            object:nil];
    }
    return self;
}

- (void) didRotate: (NSNotification*) notification
{
    UIDeviceOrientation orientation = [[UIDevice currentDevice] orientation];
    m_renderingEngine->OnRotate((DeviceOrientation) orientation);
    [self drawView: nil];
}

- (void) drawView: (CADisplayLink*) displayLink
{
    if (displayLink != nil) {
        float elapsedSeconds = displayLink.timestamp - m_timestamp;
        m_timestamp = displayLink.timestamp;
        m_renderingEngine->UpdateAnimation(elapsedSeconds);
    }

    m_renderingEngine->Render();
    [m_context presentRenderbuffer:GL_RENDERBUFFER];
}

@end
```

This completes the Objective-C portion of the project, but it won't build yet because you still need to implement the rendering engine. There's no need to dissect all the code in Example 1-7, but a brief summary follows:

- The initWithFrame method calls the factory method to instantiate the C++ renderer. It also sets up two event handlers. One is for the "display link," which fires every time the screen refreshes. The other event handler responds to orientation changes.

- The didRotate event handler casts the iPhone-specific UIDeviceOrientation to our portable DeviceOrientation type and then passes it on to the rendering engine.

- The drawView method, called in response to a display link event, computes the elapsed time since it was last called and passes that value into the renderer's UpdateAnimation method. This allows the renderer to update any animations or physics that it might be controlling.

- The drawView method also issues the Render command and presents the renderbuffer to the screen.

 At the time of writing, Apple recommends CADisplayLink for triggering OpenGL rendering. An alternative strategy is leveraging the NSTimer class. CADisplayLink became available with iPhone OS 3.1, so if you need to support older versions of the iPhone OS, take a look at NSTimer in the documentation.

Implementing the Rendering Engine

In this section, you'll create an implementation class for the IRenderingEngine interface. Right-click the *Classes* folder, choose Add→New file, click the *C and C++* category, and select the C++ File template. Call it *RenderingEngine1.cpp*, and deselect the "Also create RenderingEngine1.h" option, since you'll declare the class directly within the *.cpp* file. Enter the class declaration and factory method shown in Example 1-8.

Example 1-8. RenderingEngine1 class and factory method

```
#include <OpenGLES/ES1/gl.h>
#include <OpenGLES/ES1/glext.h>
#include "IRenderingEngine.hpp"

class RenderingEngine1 : public IRenderingEngine {
public:
    RenderingEngine1();
    void Initialize(int width, int height);
    void Render() const;
    void UpdateAnimation(float timeStep) {}
    void OnRotate(DeviceOrientation newOrientation) {}
private:
    GLuint m_framebuffer;
    GLuint m_renderbuffer;
};

IRenderingEngine* CreateRenderer1()
{
    return new RenderingEngine1();
}
```

For now, UpdateAnimation and OnRotate are implemented with stubs; you'll add support for the rotation feature after we get up and running.

Example 1-9 shows more of the code from *RenderingEngine1.cpp* with the OpenGL initialization code.

Example 1-9. Vertex data and RenderingEngine construction

```
struct Vertex {
    float Position[2];
    float Color[4];
};

// Define the positions and colors of two triangles.
const Vertex Vertices[] = {
    {{-0.5, -0.866}, {1, 1, 0.5f, 1}},
    {{0.5, -0.866}, {1, 1, 0.5f, 1}},
    {{0, 1},        {1, 1, 0.5f, 1}},
    {{-0.5, -0.866}, {0.5f, 0.5f, 0.5f}},
    {{0.5, -0.866}, {0.5f, 0.5f, 0.5f}},
    {{0, -0.4f},    {0.5f, 0.5f, 0.5f}},
};
```

```
RenderingEngine1::RenderingEngine1()
{
    glGenRenderbuffersOES(1, &m_renderbuffer);
    glBindRenderbufferOES(GL_RENDERBUFFER_OES, m_renderbuffer);
}

void RenderingEngine1::Initialize(int width, int height)
{
    // Create the framebuffer object and attach the color buffer.
    glGenFramebuffersOES(1, &m_framebuffer);
    glBindFramebufferOES(GL_FRAMEBUFFER_OES, m_framebuffer);
    glFramebufferRenderbufferOES(GL_FRAMEBUFFER_OES,
                                 GL_COLOR_ATTACHMENT0_OES,
                                 GL_RENDERBUFFER_OES,
                                 m_renderbuffer);

    glViewport(0, 0, width, height);

    glMatrixMode(GL_PROJECTION);

    // Initialize the projection matrix.
    const float maxX = 2;
    const float maxY = 3;
    glOrthof(-maxX, +maxX, -maxY, +maxY, -1, 1);

    glMatrixMode(GL_MODELVIEW);
}
```

Example 1-9 first defines a POD type (plain old data) that represents the structure of each vertex that makes up the triangles. As you'll learn in the chapters to come, a vertex in OpenGL can be associated with a variety of attributes. HelloArrow requires only two attributes: a 2D position and an RGBA color.

In more complex OpenGL applications, the vertex data is usually read from an external file or generated on the fly. In this case, the geometry is so simple that the vertex data is defined within the code itself. Two triangles are specified using six vertices. The first triangle is yellow, the second gray (see Figure 1-4, shown earlier).

Next, Example 1-9 divides up some framebuffer initialization work between the constructor and the Initialize method. Between instancing the rendering engine and calling Initialize, the caller (GLView) is responsible for allocating the renderbuffer's storage. Allocation of the renderbuffer isn't done with the rendering engine because it requires Objective-C.

Last but not least, Initialize sets up the viewport transform and *projection matrix*. The projection matrix defines the 3D volume that contains the visible portion of the scene. This will be explained in detail in the next chapter.

To recap, here's the startup sequence:

1. Generate an identifier for the renderbuffer, and bind it to the pipeline.
2. Allocate the renderbuffer's storage by associating it with an EAGL layer. This has to be done in the Objective-C layer.
3. Create a framebuffer object, and attach the renderbuffer to it.
4. Set up the vertex transformation state with `glViewport` and `glOrthof`.

Example 1-10 contains the implementation of the `Render` method.

Example 1-10. Initial Render implementation

```
void RenderingEngine1::Render() const
{
    glClearColor(0.5f, 0.5f, 0.5f, 1);
    glClear(GL_COLOR_BUFFER_BIT);❶

    glEnableClientState(GL_VERTEX_ARRAY);❷
    glEnableClientState(GL_COLOR_ARRAY);

    glVertexPointer(2, GL_FLOAT, sizeof(Vertex), &Vertices[0].Position[0]);❸
    glColorPointer(4, GL_FLOAT, sizeof(Vertex), &Vertices[0].Color[0]);

    GLsizei vertexCount = sizeof(Vertices) / sizeof(Vertex);
    glDrawArrays(GL_TRIANGLES, 0, vertexCount);❹

    glDisableClientState(GL_VERTEX_ARRAY);❺
    glDisableClientState(GL_COLOR_ARRAY);
}
```

We'll examine much of this in the next chapter, but briefly here's what's going on:

❶ Clear the renderbuffer to gray.

❷ Enable two vertex attributes (position and color).

❸ Tell OpenGL how to fetch the data for the position and color attributes. We'll examine these in detail later in the book; for now, see Figure 1-8.

❹ Execute the draw command with `glDrawArrays`, specifying `GL_TRIANGLES` for the topology, 0 for the starting vertex, and `vertexCount` for the number of vertices. This function call marks the exact time that OpenGL fetches the data from the pointers specified in the preceding `gl*Pointer` calls; this is also when the triangles are actually rendered to the target surface.

❺ Disable the two vertex attributes; they need to be enabled only during the preceding draw command. It's bad form to leave attributes enabled because subsequent draw commands might want to use a completely different set of vertex attributes. In this case, we could get by without disabling them because the program is so simple, but it's a good habit to follow.

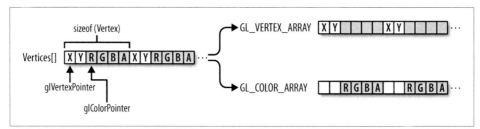

Figure 1-8. Interleaved arrays

Congratulations, you created a complete OpenGL program from scratch! Figure 1-9 shows the result.

Figure 1-9. HelloArrow!

Handling Device Orientation

Earlier in the chapter, I promised you would learn how to rotate the arrow in response to an orientation change. Since you already created the listener in the UIView class in Example 1-7, all that remains is handling it in the rendering engine.

First add a new floating-point field to the RenderingEngine class called m_currentAngle. This represents an angle in degrees, not radians. Note the changes to UpdateAnimation and OnRotate (they are no longer stubs and will be defined shortly).

```
class RenderingEngine1 : public IRenderingEngine {
public:
    RenderingEngine1();
    void Initialize(int width, int height);
```

```
        void Render() const;
        void UpdateAnimation(float timeStep);
        void OnRotate(DeviceOrientation newOrientation);
    private:
        float m_currentAngle;
        GLuint m_framebuffer;
        GLuint m_renderbuffer;
    };
```

Now let's implement the OnRotate method as follows:

```
void RenderingEngine1::OnRotate(DeviceOrientation orientation)
{
    float angle = 0;

    switch (orientation) {
        case DeviceOrientationLandscapeLeft:
            angle = 270;
            break;

        case DeviceOrientationPortraitUpsideDown:
            angle = 180;
            break;

        case DeviceOrientationLandscapeRight:
            angle = 90;
            break;
    }

    m_currentAngle = angle;
}
```

Note that orientations such as Unknown, Portrait, FaceUp, and FaceDown are not included in the switch statement, so the angle defaults to zero in those cases.

Now you can rotate the arrow using a call to glRotatef in the Render method, as shown in Example 1-11. New code lines are shown in bold. This also adds some calls to glPushMatrix and glPopMatrix to prevent rotations from accumulating. You'll learn more about these commands (including glRotatef) in the next chapter.

Example 1-11. Final Render implementation

```
void RenderingEngine1::Render() const
{
    glClearColor(0.5f, 0.5f, 0.5f, 1);
    glClear(GL_COLOR_BUFFER_BIT);

    glPushMatrix();
    glRotatef(m_currentAngle, 0, 0, 1);

    glEnableClientState(GL_VERTEX_ARRAY);
    glEnableClientState(GL_COLOR_ARRAY);

    glVertexPointer(2, GL_FLOAT, sizeof(Vertex), &Vertices[0].Position[0]);
    glColorPointer(4, GL_FLOAT, sizeof(Vertex), &Vertices[0].Color[0]);
```

```
GLsizei vertexCount = sizeof(Vertices) / sizeof(Vertex);
glDrawArrays(GL_TRIANGLES, 0, vertexCount);

glDisableClientState(GL_VERTEX_ARRAY);
glDisableClientState(GL_COLOR_ARRAY);

glPopMatrix();
}
```

Animating the Rotation

You now have a HelloArrow program that rotates in response to an orientation change, but it's lacking a bit of grace—most iPhone applications smoothly rotate the image, rather than suddenly jolting it by 90°.

It turns out that Apple provides infrastructure for smooth rotation via the UIViewController class, but this is not the recommended approach for OpenGL ES applications. There are several reasons for this:

- For best performance, Apple recommends avoiding interaction between Core Animation and OpenGL ES.
- Ideally, the renderbuffer stays the same size and aspect ratio for the lifetime of the application. This helps performance and simplifies code.
- In graphically intense applications, developers need to have complete control over animations and rendering.

To achieve the animation effect, Example 1-12 adds a new floating-point field to the RenderingEngine class called m_desiredAngle. This represents the destination value of the current animation; if no animation is occurring, then m_currentAngle and m_desiredAngle are equal.

Example 1-12 also introduces a floating-point constant called RevolutionsPerSecond to represent angular velocity, and the private method RotationDirection, which I'll explain later.

Example 1-12. Final RenderingEngine class declaration and constructor

```
#include <OpenGLES/ES1/gl.h>
#include <OpenGLES/ES1/glext.h>
#include "IRenderingEngine.hpp"

static const float RevolutionsPerSecond = 1;

class RenderingEngine1 : public IRenderingEngine {
public:
    RenderingEngine1();
    void Initialize(int width, int height);
    void Render() const;
    void UpdateAnimation(float timeStep);
    void OnRotate(DeviceOrientation newOrientation);
```

```
private:
    float RotationDirection() const;
    float m_desiredAngle;
    float m_currentAngle;
    GLuint m_framebuffer;
    GLuint m_renderbuffer;
};

...

void RenderingEngine1::Initialize(int width, int height)
{
    // Create the framebuffer object and attach the color buffer.
    glGenFramebuffersOES(1, &m_framebuffer);
    glBindFramebufferOES(GL_FRAMEBUFFER_OES, m_framebuffer);
    glFramebufferRenderbufferOES(GL_FRAMEBUFFER_OES,
                                 GL_COLOR_ATTACHMENT0_OES,
                                 GL_RENDERBUFFER_OES,
                                 m_renderbuffer);

    glViewport(0, 0, width, height);

    glMatrixMode(GL_PROJECTION);

    // Initialize the projection matrix.
    const float maxX = 2;
    const float maxY = 3;
    glOrthof(-maxX, +maxX, -maxY, +maxY, -1, 1);

    glMatrixMode(GL_MODELVIEW);

    // Initialize the rotation animation state.
    OnRotate(DeviceOrientationPortrait);
    m_currentAngle = m_desiredAngle;
}
```

Now you can modify OnRotate so that it changes the desired angle rather than the current angle:

```
void RenderingEngine1::OnRotate(DeviceOrientation orientation)
{
    float angle = 0;

    switch (orientation) {
        ...
    }

    m_desiredAngle = angle;
}
```

Before implementing UpdateAnimation, think about how the application decides whether to rotate the arrow clockwise or counterclockwise. Simply checking whether the desired angle is greater than the current angle is incorrect; if the user changes his device from a 270° orientation to a 0° orientation, the angle should *increase* up to 360°.

This is where the `RotationDirection` method comes in. It returns −1, 0, or +1, depending on which direction the arrow needs to spin. Assume that `m_currentAngle` and `m_desiredAngle` are both normalized to values between 0 (inclusive) and 360 (exclusive).

```
float RenderingEngine1::RotationDirection() const
{
    float delta = m_desiredAngle - m_currentAngle;
    if (delta == 0)
        return 0;

    bool counterclockwise = ((delta > 0 && delta <= 180) || (delta < -180));
    return counterclockwise ? +1 : -1;
}
```

Now you're ready to write the `UpdateAnimation` method, which takes a time step in seconds:

```
void RenderingEngine1::UpdateAnimation(float timeStep)
{
    float direction = RotationDirection();
    if (direction == 0)
        return;

    float degrees = timeStep * 360 * RevolutionsPerSecond;
    m_currentAngle += degrees * direction;

    // Ensure that the angle stays within [0, 360).
    if (m_currentAngle >= 360)
        m_currentAngle -= 360;
    else if (m_currentAngle < 0)
        m_currentAngle += 360;

    // If the rotation direction changed, then we overshot the desired angle.
    if (RotationDirection() != direction)
        m_currentAngle = m_desiredAngle;
}
```

This is fairly straightforward, but that last conditional might look curious. Since this method incrementally adjusts the angle with floating-point numbers, it could easily overshoot the destination, especially for large time steps. Those last two lines correct this by simply snapping the angle to the desired position. You're not trying to emulate a shaky compass here, even though doing so might be a compelling iPhone application!

You now have a fully functional HelloArrow application. As with the other examples, you can find the complete code on this book's website (see the preface for more information on code samples).

HelloArrow with Shaders

In this section you'll create a new rendering engine that uses ES 2.0. This will show you the immense difference between ES 1.1 and 2.0. Personally I like the fact that Khronos decided against making ES 2.0 backward compatible with ES 1.1; the API is leaner and more elegant as a result.

Thanks to the layered architecture of HelloArrow, it's easy to add ES 2.0 support while retaining 1.1 functionality for older devices. You'll be making these four changes:

1. Add some new source files to the project for the vertex shader and fragment shader.
2. Update frameworks references if needed.
3. Change the logic in GLView so that it attempts initWithAPI with ES 2.0.
4. Create the new RenderingEngine2 class by modifying a copy of RenderingEngine1.

These changes are described in detail in the following sections. Note that step 4 is somewhat artificial; in the real world, you'll probably want to write your ES 2.0 backend from the ground up.

Shaders

By far the most significant new feature in ES 2.0 is the shading language. *Shaders* are relatively small pieces of code that run on the graphics processor, and they are divided into two categories: vertex shaders and fragment shaders. Vertex shaders are used to transform the vertices that you submit with glDrawArrays, while fragment shaders compute the colors for every pixel in every triangle. Because of the highly parallel nature of graphics processors, thousands of shader instances execute simultaneously.

Shaders are written in a C-like language called OpenGL Shading Language (GLSL), but unlike C, you do not compile GLSL programs within Xcode. Shaders are compiled at runtime, on the iPhone itself. Your application submits shader source to the OpenGL API in the form of a C-style string, which OpenGL then compiles to machine code.

 Some implementations of OpenGL ES do allow you to compile your shaders offline; on these platforms your application submits binaries rather than strings at runtime. Currently, the iPhone supports shader compilation only at runtime. Its ARM processor compiles the shaders and sends the resulting machine code over to the graphics processor for execution. That little ARM does some heavy lifting!

The first step to upgrading HelloArrow is creating a new project folder for the shaders. Right-click the HelloArrow root node in the Groups & Files pane, and choose Add→New Group. Call the new group *Shaders*.

Next, right-click the *Shaders* folder, and choose Add→New file. Select the Empty File template in the Other category. Name it *Simple.vert*, and add */Shaders* after *HelloArrow* in the location field. You can deselect the checkbox under Add To Targets, because there's no need to deploy the file to the device. In the next dialog, allow it to create a new directory. Now repeat the procedure with a new file called *Simple.frag*.

Before showing you the code for these two files, let me explain a little trick. Rather than reading in the shaders with file I/O, you can simply embed them within your C/C++ code through the use of `#include`. Multiline strings are usually cumbersome in C/C++, but they can be tamed with a sneaky little macro:

```
#define STRINGIFY(A)  #A
```

Later in this section, we'll place this macro definition at the top of the rendering engine source code, right before `#include`ing the shaders. The entire shader gets wrapped into a single string—without the use of quotation marks on every line!

Multiline Strings

While the `STRINGIFY` macro is convenient for simple shaders, I don't recommend it for production code. For one thing, the line numbers reported by Apple's shader compiler may be incorrect. The gcc preprocessor can also get confused if your shader string defines functions. A common practice is to read a shader from a file into a monolithic string, which can easily be done from the Objective-C side using the `stringWithContentsOfFile` method.

Examples 1-13 and 1-14 show the contents of the vertex shader and fragment shader. For brevity's sake, we'll leave out the `STRINGIFY` accouterments in future shader listings, but we're including them here for clarity.

Example 1-13. Simple.vert

```
const char* SimpleVertexShader = STRINGIFY(

attribute vec4 Position;
attribute vec4 SourceColor;
varying vec4 DestinationColor;
uniform mat4 Projection;
uniform mat4 Modelview;

void main(void)
{
    DestinationColor = SourceColor;
    gl_Position = Projection * Modelview * Position;
}
);
```

First the vertex shader declares a set of attributes, varyings, and uniforms. For now you can think of these as connection points between the vertex shader and the outside world. The vertex shader itself simply passes through a color and performs a standard transformation on the position. You'll learn more about transformations in the next chapter. The fragment shader (Example 1-14) is even more trivial.

Example 1-14. Simple.frag

```
const char* SimpleFragmentShader = STRINGIFY(

varying lowp vec4 DestinationColor;

void main(void)
{
    gl_FragColor = DestinationColor;
}
);
```

Again, the varying parameter is a connection point. The fragment shader itself does nothing but pass on the color that it's given.

Frameworks

Next, make sure all the frameworks in HelloArrow are referencing a 3.1 (or greater) version of the SDK. To find out which version a particular framework is using, right-click it in Xcode's Groups & Files pane, and select Get Info to look at the full path.

 There's a trick to quickly change all your SDK references by manually modifying the project file. First you need to quit Xcode. Next, open Finder, right-click *HelloArrow.xcodeproj*, and select *Show package contents*. Inside, you'll find a file called *project.pbxproj*, which you can then open with TextEdit. Find the two places that define SDKROOT, and change them appropriately.

GLView

You might recall passing in a version constant when constructing the OpenGL context; this is another place that obviously needs to be changed. In the *Classes* folder, open *GLView.mm*, and change this snippet:

```
    m_context = [[EAGLContext alloc] initWithAPI:kEAGLRenderingAPIOpenGLES1];

    if (!m_context || ![EAGLContext setCurrentContext:m_context]) {
        [self release];
        return nil;
    }

    m_renderingEngine = CreateRenderer1();
```

to this:

```
    EAGLRenderingAPI api = kEAGLRenderingAPIOpenGLES2;
    m_context = [[EAGLContext alloc] initWithAPI:api];
```

```
if (!m_context || ForceES1) {
    api = kEAGLRenderingAPIOpenGLES1;
    m_context = [[EAGLContext alloc] initWithAPI:api];
}

if (!m_context || ![EAGLContext setCurrentContext:m_context]) {
    [self release];
    return nil;
}

if (api == kEAGLRenderingAPIOpenGLES1) {
    m_renderingEngine = CreateRenderer1();
} else {
    m_renderingEngine = CreateRenderer2();
}
```

The previous code snippet creates a fallback path to allow the application to work on older devices while leveraging ES 2.0 on newer devices. For convenience, the ES 1.1 path is used even on newer devices if the ForceES1 constant is enabled. Add this to the top of *GLView.mm*:

```
const bool ForceES1 = false;
```

There's no need to make any changes to the IRenderingEngine interface, but you do need to add a declaration for the new CreateRenderer2 factory method in *IRenderingEngine.hpp*:

```
...

// Create an instance of the renderer and set up various OpenGL state.
struct IRenderingEngine* CreateRenderer1();
struct IRenderingEngine* CreateRenderer2();

// Interface to the OpenGL ES renderer; consumed by GLView.
struct IRenderingEngine {
    virtual void Initialize(int width, int height) = 0;
    virtual void Render() const = 0;
    virtual void UpdateAnimation(float timeStep) = 0;
    virtual void OnRotate(DeviceOrientation newOrientation) = 0;
    virtual ~IRenderingEngine() {}
};
```

RenderingEngine Implementation

You're done with the requisite changes to the glue code; now it's time for the meat. Use Finder to create a copy of *RenderingEngine1.cpp* (right-click or Control-click *RenderingEngine1.cpp* and choose *Reveal in Finder*), and name the new file *RenderingEngine2.cpp*. Add it to your Xcode project by right-clicking the *Classes* group and choosing Add→Existing Files. Next, revamp the top part of the file as shown in Example 1-15. New or modified lines are shown in bold.

Example 1-15. RenderingEngine2 declaration

```
#include <OpenGLES/ES2/gl.h>
#include <OpenGLES/ES2/glext.h>
#include <cmath>
#include <iostream>
#include "IRenderingEngine.hpp"

#define STRINGIFY(A)  #A
#include "../Shaders/Simple.vert"
#include "../Shaders/Simple.frag"

static const float RevolutionsPerSecond = 1;

class RenderingEngine2 : public IRenderingEngine {
public:
    RenderingEngine2();
    void Initialize(int width, int height);
    void Render() const;
    void UpdateAnimation(float timeStep);
    void OnRotate(DeviceOrientation newOrientation);
private:
    float RotationDirection() const;
    GLuint BuildShader(const char* source, GLenum shaderType) const;
    GLuint BuildProgram(const char* vShader, const char* fShader) const;
    void ApplyOrtho(float maxX, float maxY) const;
    void ApplyRotation(float degrees) const;
    float m_desiredAngle;
    float m_currentAngle;
    GLuint m_simpleProgram;
    GLuint m_framebuffer;
    GLuint m_renderbuffer;
};
```

As you might expect, the implementation of **Render** needs to be replaced. Flip back to Example 1-11 to compare it with Example 1-16.

Example 1-16. Render with OpenGL ES 2.0

```
void RenderingEngine2::Render() const
{
    glClearColor(0.5f, 0.5f, 0.5f, 1);
    glClear(GL_COLOR_BUFFER_BIT);

    ApplyRotation(m_currentAngle);

    GLuint positionSlot = glGetAttribLocation(m_simpleProgram, "Position");
    GLuint colorSlot = glGetAttribLocation(m_simpleProgram, "SourceColor");

    glEnableVertexAttribArray(positionSlot);
    glEnableVertexAttribArray(colorSlot);

    GLsizei stride = sizeof(Vertex);
    const GLvoid* pCoords = &Vertices[0].Position[0];
    const GLvoid* pColors = &Vertices[0].Color[0];
```

```
glVertexAttribPointer(positionSlot, 2, GL_FLOAT, GL_FALSE, stride, pCoords);
glVertexAttribPointer(colorSlot, 4, GL_FLOAT, GL_FALSE, stride, pColors);

GLsizei vertexCount = sizeof(Vertices) / sizeof(Vertex);
glDrawArrays(GL_TRIANGLES, 0, vertexCount);

glDisableVertexAttribArray(positionSlot);
glDisableVertexAttribArray(colorSlot);
}
```

As you can see, the 1.1 and 2.0 versions of Render are quite different, but at a high level they basically follow the same sequence of actions.

Framebuffer objects have been promoted from a mere OpenGL extension to the core API. Luckily OpenGL has a very strict and consistent naming convention, so this change is fairly mechanical. Simply remove the *OES* suffix everywhere it appears. For function calls, the suffix is *OES*; for constants the suffix is *_OES*. The constructor is very easy to update:

```
RenderingEngine2::RenderingEngine2()
{
    glGenRenderbuffers(1, &m_renderbuffer);
    glBindRenderbuffer(GL_RENDERBUFFER, m_renderbuffer);
}
```

The only remaining public method that needs to be updated is Initialize, shown in Example 1-17.

Example 1-17. RenderingEngine2 initialization

```
void RenderingEngine2::Initialize(int width, int height)
{
    // Create the framebuffer object and attach the color buffer.
    glGenFramebuffers(1, &m_framebuffer);
    glBindFramebuffer(GL_FRAMEBUFFER, m_framebuffer);
    glFramebufferRenderbuffer(GL_FRAMEBUFFER,
                              GL_COLOR_ATTACHMENT0,
                              GL_RENDERBUFFER,
                              m_renderbuffer);

    glViewport(0, 0, width, height);

    m_simpleProgram = BuildProgram(SimpleVertexShader, SimpleFragmentShader);

    glUseProgram(m_simpleProgram);

    // Initialize the projection matrix.
    ApplyOrtho(2, 3);

    // Initialize rotation animation state.
    OnRotate(DeviceOrientationPortrait);
    m_currentAngle = m_desiredAngle;
}
```

This calls the private method BuildProgram, which in turn makes two calls on the private method BuildShader. In OpenGL terminology, a *program* is a module composed of several shaders that get linked together. Example 1-18 shows the implementation of these two methods.

Example 1-18. BuildProgram and BuildShader

```
GLuint RenderingEngine2::BuildProgram(const char* vertexShaderSource,
                                      const char* fragmentShaderSource) const
{
    GLuint vertexShader = BuildShader(vertexShaderSource, GL_VERTEX_SHADER);
    GLuint fragmentShader = BuildShader(fragmentShaderSource, GL_FRAGMENT_SHADER);

    GLuint programHandle = glCreateProgram();
    glAttachShader(programHandle, vertexShader);
    glAttachShader(programHandle, fragmentShader);
    glLinkProgram(programHandle);

    GLint linkSuccess;
    glGetProgramiv(programHandle, GL_LINK_STATUS, &linkSuccess);
    if (linkSuccess == GL_FALSE) {
        GLchar messages[256];
        glGetProgramInfoLog(programHandle, sizeof(messages), 0, &messages[0]);
        std::cout << messages;
        exit(1);
    }

    return programHandle;
}

GLuint RenderingEngine2::BuildShader(const char* source, GLenum shaderType) const
{
    GLuint shaderHandle = glCreateShader(shaderType);
    glShaderSource(shaderHandle, 1, &source, 0);
    glCompileShader(shaderHandle);

    GLint compileSuccess;
    glGetShaderiv(shaderHandle, GL_COMPILE_STATUS, &compileSuccess);

    if (compileSuccess == GL_FALSE) {
        GLchar messages[256];
        glGetShaderInfoLog(shaderHandle, sizeof(messages), 0, &messages[0]);
        std::cout << messages;
        exit(1);
    }

    return shaderHandle;
}
```

You might be surprised to see some console I/O in Example 1-18. This dumps out the shader compiler output if an error occurs. Trust me, you'll always want to gracefully handle these kind of errors, no matter how simple you think your shaders are. The console output doesn't show up on the iPhone screen, but it can be seen in Xcode's

Debugger Console window, which is shown via the Run→Console menu. See Figure 1-10 for an example of how a shader compilation error shows up in the console window.

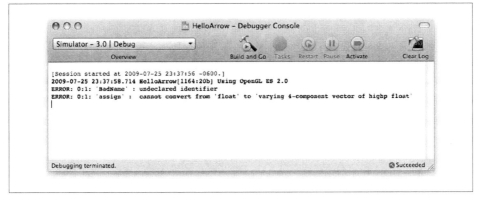

Figure 1-10. Debugger console

Note that the log in Figure 1-10 shows the version of OpenGL ES being used. To include this information, go back to the GLView class, and add the lines in bold:

```
if (api == kEAGLRenderingAPIOpenGLES1) {
    NSLog(@"Using OpenGL ES 1.1");
    m_renderingEngine = CreateRenderer1();
} else {
    NSLog(@"Using OpenGL ES 2.0");
    m_renderingEngine = CreateRenderer2();
}
```

The preferred method of outputting diagnostic information in Objective-C is NSLog, which automatically prefixes your string with a timestamp and follows it with a carriage return. (Recall that Objective-C string objects are distinguished from C-style strings using the @ symbol.)

Return to *RenderingEngine2.cpp*. Two methods remain: ApplyOrtho and ApplyRotation. Since ES 2.0 does not provide glOrthof or glRotatef, you need to implement them manually, as seen in Example 1-19. (In the next chapter, we'll create a simple math library to simplify code like this.) The calls to glUniformMatrix4fv provide values for the uniform variables that were declared in the shader source.

Example 1-19. ApplyOrtho and ApplyRotation

```
void RenderingEngine2::ApplyOrtho(float maxX, float maxY) const
{
    float a = 1.0f / maxX;
    float b = 1.0f / maxY;
    float ortho[16] = {
        a, 0,  0, 0,
        0, b,  0, 0,
```

```
            0, 0, -1, 0,
            0, 0,  0, 1
    };

    GLint projectionUniform = glGetUniformLocation(m_simpleProgram, "Projection");
    glUniformMatrix4fv(projectionUniform, 1, 0, &ortho[0]);
}

void RenderingEngine2::ApplyRotation(float degrees) const
{
    float radians = degrees * 3.14159f / 180.0f;
    float s = std::sin(radians);
    float c = std::cos(radians);
    float zRotation[16] = {
        c, s, 0, 0,
       -s, c, 0, 0,
        0, 0, 1, 0,
        0, 0, 0, 1
    };

    GLint modelviewUniform = glGetUniformLocation(m_simpleProgram, "Modelview");
    glUniformMatrix4fv(modelviewUniform, 1, 0, &zRotation[0]);
}
```

Again, don't be intimidated by the matrix math; I'll explain it all in the next chapter.

Next, go through the file, and change any remaining occurrences of `RenderingEngine1` to `RenderingEngine2`, including the factory method (and be sure to change the name of that method to `CreateRenderer2`). This completes all the modifications required to run against ES 2.0. Phew! It's obvious by now that ES 2.0 is "closer to the metal" than ES 1.1.

Wrapping Up

This chapter has been a headfirst dive into the world of OpenGL ES development for the iPhone. We established some patterns and practices that we'll use throughout this book, and we constructed our first application from the ground up — using *both* versions of OpenGL ES!

In the next chapter, we'll go over some graphics fundamentals and explain the various concepts used in HelloArrow. If you're already a computer graphics ninja, you'll be able to skim through quickly.

## CHAPTER 2

Math and Metaphors

*There's a pizza place near where I live that sells only
slices. In the back you can see a guy tossing
a triangle in the air.*

—Stephen Wright, comedian

Computer graphics requires more mathematics than many other fields in computer science. But if you're a pragmatic OpenGL programmer, all you really need is a basic grasp of linear algebra and an understanding of a few metaphors.

In this chapter, I explain these metaphors and review the relevant linear algebra concepts. Along the way I'll tick off various OpenGL functions that relate to these concepts. Several of such functions were used in the HelloArrow sample, so code that may have seemed mysterious should now become clear.

Near the end of the chapter, we'll leverage these math concepts to push the HelloArrow sample into the third dimension, transforming it into HelloCone.

The Assembly Line Metaphor

You can think of any graphics API, including OpenGL ES, as an assembly line that takes an assortment of raw materials such as textures and vertices for input and eventually produces a neatly packaged grid of colors.

The inputs to the assembly line are the natural starting points for learning OpenGL, and in this chapter we'll focus on vertices. Figure 2-1 depicts the gradual metamorphosis of vertices into pixels. First, a series of transformations is performed on the vertices; next the vertices are assembled into primitives; and finally, primitives are rasterized into pixels.

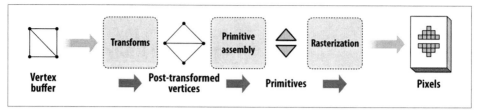

Figure 2-1. The OpenGL ES assembly line

> At a high level, Figure 2-1 applies to both OpenGL ES 1.1 and 2.0, but it's important to note that in 2.0, the Transforms block contains a vertex shader, and the Rasterization block hands his output over to a fragment shader.

In this chapter we'll mostly focus on the transformations that occur early on in the assembly line, but first we'll give a brief overview of the primitive assembly step, since it's fairly easy to digest.

Assembling Primitives from Vertices

The 3D shape of an object is known as its *geometry*. In OpenGL, the geometry of an object constitutes a set of *primitives* that are either triangles, points, or lines. These primitives are defined using an array of vertices, and the vertices are connected according to the primitive's *topology*. OpenGL ES supports seven topologies, as depicted in Figure 2-2.

Recall the one line of code in HelloArrow from Chapter 1 that tells OpenGL to render the triangles to the backbuffer:

```
glDrawArrays(GL_TRIANGLES, 0, vertexCount);
```

The first argument to this function specifies the *primitive topology*: GL_TRIANGLES tells OpenGL to interpret the vertex buffer such that the first three vertices compose the first triangle, the second three vertices compose the second triangle, and so on.

In many situations you need to specify a sequence of adjoining triangles, in which case several vertices would be duplicated in the vertex array. That's when GL_TRIANGLE_STRIP comes in. It allows a much smaller set of vertices to expand to the same number of triangles, as shown in Table 2-1. In the table, *v* is the number of vertices, and *p* is the number of primitives. For example, to draw three triangles using GL_TRIANGLES, you'd need nine vertices (3p). To draw them using GL_TRIANGLE_STRIP, you'd need only five (p + 2).

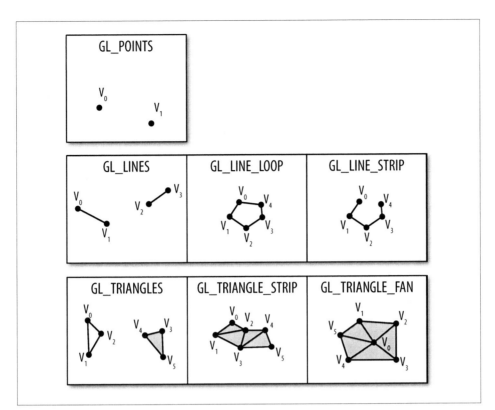

Figure 2-2. Primitive topologies

Table 2-1. Primitive counts

Topology	Number of primitives	Number of vertices
GL_POINTS	v	p
GL_LINES	v / 2	2p
GL_LINE_LOOP	v	p
GL_LINE_STRIP	v - 1	p + 1
GL_TRIANGLES	v / 3	3p
GL_TRIANGLE_STRIP	n - 2	p + 2
GL_TRIANGLE_FAN	n - 1	p + 1

Another way of specifying triangles is GL_TRIANGLE_FAN, which is useful for drawing a polygon, a circle, or the top of a 3D dome. The first vertex specifies the apex while the remaining vertices form the rim. For many of these shapes, it's possible to use GL_TRIANGLE_STRIP, but doing so would result in degenerate triangles (triangles with zero area).

For example, suppose you wanted to draw a square shape using two triangles, as shown in Figure 2-3. (Incidentally, full-blown OpenGL has a GL_QUADS primitive that would come in handy for this, but quads are not supported in OpenGL ES.) The following code snippet draws the same square three times, using a different primitive topology each time:

```
const int stride = 2 * sizeof(float);

float triangles[][2] = { {0, 0}, {0, 1}, {1, 1}, {1, 1}, {1, 0}, {0, 0} };
glVertexPointer(2, GL_FLOAT, stride, triangles);
glDrawArrays(GL_TRIANGLES, 0, sizeof(triangles) / stride);

float triangleStrip[][2] = { {0, 1}, {0, 0}, {1, 1}, {1, 0} };
glVertexPointer(2, GL_FLOAT, stride, triangleStrip);
glDrawArrays(GL_TRIANGLE_STRIP, 0, sizeof(triangleStrip) / stride);

float triangleFan[][2] = { {0, 0}, {0, 1}, {1, 1}, {1, 0} };
glVertexPointer(2, GL_FLOAT, stride, triangleFan);
glDrawArrays(GL_TRIANGLE_FAN, 0, sizeof(triangleFan) / stride);
```

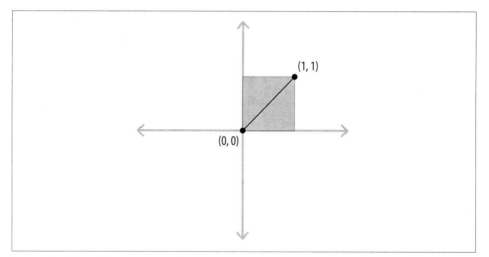

Figure 2-3. Square from two triangles

Triangles aren't the only primitive type supported in OpenGL ES. Individual points can be rendered using GL_POINTS. The size of each point can be specified individually, and large points are rendered as squares. Optionally, a small bitmap can be applied to each point; these are called *point sprites*, and we'll learn more about them in Chapter 7.

OpenGL supports line primitives using three different topologies: separate lines, strips, and loops. With strips and loops, the endpoint of each line serves as the starting point for the following line. With loops, the starting point of the first line also serves as the endpoint of the last line. Suppose you wanted to draw the border of the square shown in Figure 2-3; here's how you could do so using the three different line topologies:

```
const int stride = 2 * sizeof(float);

float lines[][2] = { {0, 0}, {0, 1},
                     {0, 1}, {1, 1},
                     {1, 1}, {1, 0},
                     {1, 0}, {0, 0} };
glVertexPointer(2, GL_FLOAT, stride, lines);
glDrawArrays(GL_LINES, 0, sizeof(lines) / stride);

float lineStrip[][2] = { {0, 0}, {0, 1}, {1, 1}, {1, 0}, {0, 0} };
glVertexPointer(2, GL_FLOAT, stride, lineStrip);
glDrawArrays(GL_LINE_STRIP, 0, sizeof(lineStrip) / stride);

float lineLoop[][2] = { {0, 0}, {0, 1}, {1, 1}, {1, 0} };
glVertexPointer(2, GL_FLOAT, stride, lineLoop);
glDrawArrays(GL_LINE_LOOP, 0, sizeof(lineLoop) / stride);
```

Associating Properties with Vertices

Let's go back to the assembly line and take a closer look at the inputs. Every vertex that you hand over to OpenGL has one or more attributes, the most crucial being its position. Vertex attributes in OpenGL ES 1.1 can have any of the forms listed in Table 2-2.

Table 2-2. Vertex attributes in OpenGL ES

Attribute	OpenGL enumerant	OpenGL function call	Dimensionality	Types
Position	GL_VERTEX_ARRAY	glVertexPointer	2, 3, 4	byte, short, fixed, float
Normal	GL_NORMAL_ARRAY	glNormalPointer	3	byte, short, fixed, float
Color	GL_COLOR_ARRAY	glColorPointer	4	ubyte, fixed, float
Point Size	GL_POINT_SIZE_ARRAY_OES	glPointSizePointerOES	1	fixed, float
Texture Coordinate	GL_TEXTURE_COORD_ARRAY	glTexCoordPointer	2, 3, 4	byte, short, fixed, float
Generic Attribute (ES 2.0)	N/A	glVertexAttribPointer	1, 2, 3, 4	byte, ubyte, short, ushort, fixed, float

With OpenGL ES 2.0, only the last row in Table 2-2 applies; it needs you to define your own custom attributes however you see fit. For example, recall that both rendering engines in HelloArrow enabled two attributes:

```
// OpenGL ES 1.1
glEnableClientState(GL_VERTEX_ARRAY);
glEnableClientState(GL_COLOR_ARRAY);

// OpenGL ES 2.0
glEnableVertexAttribArray(positionSlot);
glEnableVertexAttribArray(colorSlot);
```

The ES 1.1 backend enabled attributes using constants provided by OpenGL, while the ES 2.0 backend used constants that were extracted from the shader program (position Slot and colorSlot). Both backends specified the dimensionality and types of the vertex attributes that they enabled:

```
// OpenGL ES 1.1
glVertexPointer(2, GL_FLOAT, ... );
glColorPointer(4, GL_FLOAT, ... );

// OpenGL ES 2.0
glVertexAttribPointer(positionSlot, 2, GL_FLOAT, ...);
glVertexAttribPointer(colorSlot, 4, GL_FLOAT, ...);
```

The data type of each vertex attribute can be one of the forms in Table 2-3. With ES 2.0, all of these types may be used; with ES 1.1, only a subset is permitted, depending on which attribute you are specifying (see the far right column in Table 2-2).

Table 2-3. Vertex attribute data types

OpenGL type	OpenGL enumerant	Typedef of	Length in bits
GLbyte	GL_BYTE	signed char	8
GLubyte	GL_UNSIGNED_BYTE	unsigned char	8
GLshort	GL_SHORT	short	16
GLushort	GL_UNSIGNED_SHORT	unsigned short	16
GLfixed	GL_FIXED	int	32
GLfloat	GL_FLOAT	float	32

The position attribute in OpenGL ES 1.1 is a bit of a special case because it's the only required attribute. It can be specified as a 2D, 3D, or 4D coordinate. Internally, the OpenGL implementation always converts it into a 4D floating-point number.

Four dimensional? This might conjure images of Dr. Who, but it actually has nothing to do with time or anything else in physics; it's an artificial construction that allows all transformations to be represented with matrix multiplication. These 4D coordinates are known as *homogeneous coordinates*. When converting a 3D coordinate into a homogeneous coordinate, the fourth component (also known as w) usually defaults to one. A w of zero is rarely found but can be taken to mean "point at infinity." (One of the few places in OpenGL that uses $w = 0$ is light source positioning, as we'll see in Chapter 4.) Specifying a vertex with a negative w is almost never useful.

Homogeneous Coordinates

Homogeneous coordinates came into existence in 1827 when August Ferdinand Möbius published *Der barycentrische Calcül*. This is the same Möbius of Möbius strip fame. Just for fun, we'll discuss how to render a Möbius strip later in this book. Incidentally, Möbius also invented the concept of *barycentric* coordinates, which is leveraged by the graphics chip in your iPhone when computing the interior colors of triangles. This term stems from the word *barycentre*, the archaic word for center of mass. If you place three weights at the corners of a triangle, you can compute the balance point using barycentric coordinates. Their derivation is beyond the scope of this book but an interesting aside nonetheless!

So, shortly after entering the assembly line, all vertex positions become 4D; don't they need to become 2D at some point? The answer is yes, at least until Apple releases an iPhone with a holographic screen. We'll learn more about the life of a vertex and how it gets reduced to two dimensions in the next section, but for now let me mention that one of the last transformations is the removal of *w*, which is achieved as shown in Equation 2-1.

Equation 2-1. Perspective transform

$$(x, y, z, w) \longrightarrow \left(\frac{x}{w}, \frac{y}{w}, \frac{z}{w}\right)$$

This divide-by-w computation is known as the *perspective transform*. Note that we didn't discard z; it'll come in handy later, as you'll see in Chapter 4.

The Life of a Vertex

Figure 2-4 and Figure 2-5 depict the process of how a vertex goes from being 4D to being 2D. This portion of the assembly line is commonly known as *transform and lighting*, or T&L. We'll discuss lighting in Chapter 4; for now let's focus on the transforms.

After each transform, the vertex is said to be in a new "space." The original input vertices are in *object space* and are called *object coordinates*. In object space, the origin typically lies at the center of the object. This is also sometimes known as *model space*.

When object coordinates are transformed by the model-view matrix, they enter *eye space*. In eye space, the origin is the camera position.

Next, the vertex position is transformed by the projection matrix to enter *clip space*. It's called clip space because it's where OpenGL typically discards vertices that lie outside the viewing frustum. This is one of the places where the elusive W component comes into play; if the X or Y components are greater than +W or less than -W, then the vertex is clipped.

With ES 1.1, the steps in Figure 2-4 are fixed; every vertex must go through this process. With ES 2.0, it's up to you to do whatever transforms you'd like before clip space. Typically you'll actually want to perform these same transforms anyway.

After clipping comes the perspective transform mentioned earlier in the chapter. This normalizes the coordinates to [-1, +1], so they're known as *normalized device coordinates* at this point. Figure 2-5 depicts the transforms that take place after clip space. Unlike the steps in Figure 2-4, these transforms are integral to both ES 1.1 and ES 2.0.

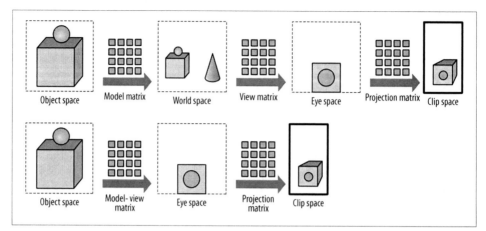

Figure 2-4. Early life of a vertex. Top row is conceptual; bottom row is OpenGL's view

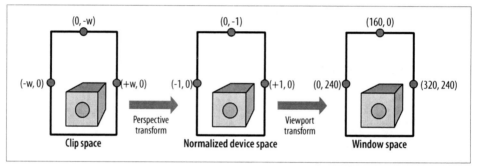

Figure 2-5. Last three stages of a vertex before rasterization

The last transform before rasterization is the viewport transform, which depends on some values supplied from the application. You might recognize this line from *GLView.mm* in HelloArrow:

```
glViewport(0, 0, CGRectGetWidth(frame), CGRectGetHeight(frame));
```

The arguments to `glViewport` are *left*, *bottom*, *width*, and *height*. On the iPhone you'll probably want width and height to be 320 and 480, but to ensure compatibility with future Apple devices (and other platforms), try to avoid hardcoding these values by obtaining the width and height at runtime, just like we did in HelloArrow.

The `glViewport` function controls how X and Y transform to *window space* (somewhat inaptly named for mobile devices; you'll rarely have a nonfullscreen window!). The transform that takes Z into window space is controlled with a different function:

```
glDepthRangef(near, far);
```

In practice, this function is rarely used; its defaults are quite reasonable: `near` and `far` default to zero and one, respectively.

So, you now have a basic idea of what happens to vertex position, but we haven't yet discussed color. When lighting is disabled (as it is by default), colors are passed straight through untouched. When lighting is enabled, these transforms become germane again. We'll discuss lighting in detail in Chapter 4.

The Photography Metaphor

The assembly line metaphor illustrates how OpenGL works behind the scenes, but a photography metaphor is more useful when thinking about a 3D application's workflow. When my wife makes an especially elaborate Indian dinner, she often asks me to take a photo of the feast for her personal blog. I usually perform the following actions to achieve this:

1. Arrange the various dishes on the table.
2. Arrange one or more light sources.
3. Position the camera.
4. Aim the camera toward the food.
5. Adjust the zoom lens.
6. Snap the picture.

It turns out that each of these actions have analogues in OpenGL, although they typically occur in a different order. Setting aside the issue of lighting (which we'll address in a future chapter), an OpenGL program performs the following actions:

1. Adjust the camera's field-of-view angle; this is the *projection matrix*.
2. Position the camera and aim it in the appropriate direction; this is the *view matrix*.
3. For each object:
    a. Scale, rotate, and translate the object; this is the *model matrix*.
    b. Render the object.

The product of the model and view matrices is known as the *model-view matrix*. When rendering an object, OpenGL ES 1.1 transforms every vertex first by the model-view matrix and then by the projection matrix. With OpenGL ES 2.0, you can perform any transforms you want, but it's often useful to follow the same model-view/projection convention, at least in simple scenarios.

Later we'll go over each of the three transforms (projection, view, model) in detail, but first we need to get some preliminaries out of the way. OpenGL has a unified way of dealing with all transforms, regardless of how they're used. With ES 1.1, the current transformation state can be configured by loading matrices explicitly, like this:

```
float projection[16] = { ... };
float modelview[16] = { ... };

glMatrixMode(GL_PROJECTION);
glLoadMatrixf(projection);

glMatrixMode(GL_MODELVIEW);
glLoadMatrixf(modelview);
```

With ES 2.0, there is no inherent concept of model-view and projection; in fact, `glMatrixMode` and `glLoadMatrixf` do not exist in 2.0. Rather, matrices are loaded into *uniform variables* that are then consumed by shaders. Uniforms are a type of shader connection that we'll learn about later, but you can think of them as constants that shaders can't modify. They're loaded like this:

```
float projection[16] = { ... };
float modelview[16] = { ... };

GLint projectionUniform = glGetUniformLocation(program, "Projection");
glUniformMatrix4fv(projectionUniform, 1, 0, projection);

GLint modelviewUniform = glGetUniformLocation(program, "Modelview");
glUniformMatrix4fv(modelviewUniform, 1, 0, modelview);
```

OpenGL Function Suffixes

By now you might be wondering why so many OpenGL functions end in **f** or **fv**. Many functions (including **glUniform***) can take floating-point arguments, integer arguments, or other types. OpenGL is a C API, and C does not support function overloading; the names of each function variant must be distinct. The suffix of the function call denotes the type shown in Table 2-4. Additionally, if the suffix is followed by **v**, then it's a pointer type.

Table 2-4. OpenGL ES function endings

Suffix	Type
i	32-bit integer
x	16-bit fixed-point
f	32-bit floating-point
ub	8-bit unsigned byte
ui	32-bit unsigned integer

ES 1.1 provides additional ways of manipulating matrices that do not exist in 2.0. For example, the following 1.1 snippet loads an identity matrix and multiplies it by two other matrices:

```
float view[16] = { ... };
float model[16] = { ... };

glMatrixMode(GL_MODELVIEW);
glLoadIdentity();
glMultMatrixf(view);
glMultMatrixf(model);
```

The default model-view and projection matrices are identity matrices. The identity transform is effectively a no-op, as shown in Equation 2-2.

Equation 2-2. Identity transform

$$\mathbf{vI} = (v_x \ v_y \ v_z \ 1) * \begin{pmatrix} 1 & 0 & 0 & 0 \\ 0 & 1 & 0 & 0 \\ 0 & 0 & 1 & 0 \\ 0 & 0 & 0 & 1 \end{pmatrix} = (v_x * 1 \ v_y * 1 \ v_z * 1 \ 1) = \mathbf{v}$$

 For details on how to multiply a vector with a matrix, or a matrix with another matrix, check out the code in the appendix.

It's important to note that this book uses row vector notation rather than column vector notation. In Equation 2-2, both the left side of $(v_x \ v_y \ v_z \ 1)$ and right side of $(v_x * 1 \ v_y * 1 \ v_z * 1 \ 1)$ are 4D row vectors. That equation could, however, be expressed in column vector notation like so:

$$\mathbf{Iv} = \begin{pmatrix} 1 & 0 & 0 & 0 \\ 0 & 1 & 0 & 0 \\ 0 & 0 & 1 & 0 \\ 0 & 0 & 0 & 1 \end{pmatrix} * \begin{pmatrix} v_x \\ v_y \\ v_z \\ 1 \end{pmatrix} = \begin{pmatrix} v_x * 1 \\ v_y * 1 \\ v_z * 1 \\ 1 \end{pmatrix} = \mathbf{v}$$

Sometimes it helps to think of a 4D row vector as being a 1×4 matrix, and a 4D column vector as being a 4×1 matrix. (*nxm* denotes the dimensions of a matrix where *n* is the number of rows and *m* is the number of columns.)

Figure 2-6 shows a trick for figuring out whether it's legal to multiply two quantities in a certain order: the inner numbers should match. The outer numbers tell you the dimensions of the result. Applying this rule, we can see that it's legal to multiply the two matrices shown in Equation 2-2: the 4D row vector (effectively a 1×4 matrix) on the left of the * and the 4×4 matrix on the right are multiplied to produce a 1×4 matrix (which also happens to be a 4D row vector).

From a coding perspective, I find that row vectors are more natural than column vectors because they look like tiny C-style arrays. It's valid to think of them as column vectors if you'd like, but if you do so, be aware that the ordering of your transforms will flip around. Ordering is crucial because matrix multiplication is not commutative.

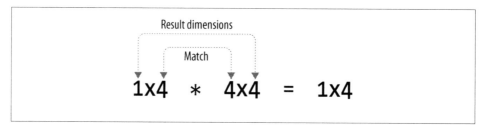

Figure 2-6. Matrix multiplication dimensionality

Consider this snippet of ES 1.1 code:

```
glLoadIdentity();
glMultMatrix(A);
glMultMatrix(B);
glMultMatrix(C);
glDrawArrays(...);
```

With row vectors, you can think of each successive transform as being *pre*multiplied with the current transform, so the previous snippet is equivalent to the following:

$$(v_x \ v_y \ v_z \ 1) * \mathbf{C}*\mathbf{B}*\mathbf{A} = \mathbf{vCBA} = \mathbf{v'}$$

With column vectors, each successive transform is *post*multiplied, so the code snippet is actually equivalent to the following:

$$\mathbf{A}*\mathbf{B}*\mathbf{C}* \begin{pmatrix} v_x \\ v_y \\ v_z \\ 1 \end{pmatrix} = \mathbf{ABCv} = \mathbf{v'}$$

Regardless of whether you prefer row or column vectors, you should always think of the last transformation in your code as being the first one to be applied to the vertex. To make this apparent with column vectors, use parentheses to show the order of operations:

$$\mathbf{ABCv} = (\mathbf{A}(\mathbf{B}(\mathbf{Cv}))) = \mathbf{v'}$$

This illustrates another reason why I like row vectors; they make OpenGL's reverse-ordering characteristic a little more obvious.

Enough of this mathematical diversion; let's get back to the photography metaphor and see how it translates into OpenGL. OpenGL ES 1.1 provides a set of helper functions that can generate a matrix and multiply the current transformation by the result, all in one step. We'll go over each of these helper functions in the coming sections. Since ES 2.0 does not provide helper functions, we'll also show what they do behind the scenes so that you can implement them yourself.

Recall that there are three matrices involved in OpenGL's setup:

1. Adjust the camera's field-of-view angle; this is the *projection matrix.*
2. Position the camera and aim it in the appropriate direction; this is the *view matrix.*
3. Scale, rotate, and translate each object; this is the *model matrix.*

We'll go over each of these three transforms in reverse so that we can present the simplest transformations first.

Setting the Model Matrix

The three most common operations when positioning an object in a scene are scale, translation, and rotation.

Scale

The most trivial helper function is glScalef:

```
float scale[16] = { sx, 0,  0,  0,
                    0,  sy, 0,  0,
                    0,  0,  sz, 0
                    0,  0,  0,  1 };

// The following two statements are equivalent.
glMultMatrixf(scale);
glScalef(sx, sy, sz);
```

The matrix for scale and its derivation are shown in Equation 2-3.

Equation 2-3. Scale transform

$$\mathbf{vS} = (v_x\ v_y\ v_z\ 1) * \begin{pmatrix} s_x & 0 & 0 & 0 \\ 0 & s_y & 0 & 0 \\ 0 & 0 & s_z & 0 \\ 0 & 0 & 0 & 1 \end{pmatrix} = (v_x * s_x\ \ v_y * s_y\ \ v_z * s_z\ 1) = \mathbf{v'}$$

Figure 2-7 depicts a scale transform where $s_x = s_y = 0.5$.

Nonuniform scale is the case where the x, y, and z scale factors are not all equal to the same value. Such a transformation is perfectly valid, but it can hurt performance in some cases. OpenGL has to do more work to perform the correct lighting computations when nonuniform scale is applied.

Translation

Another simple helper transform is glTranslatef, which shifts an object by a fixed amount:

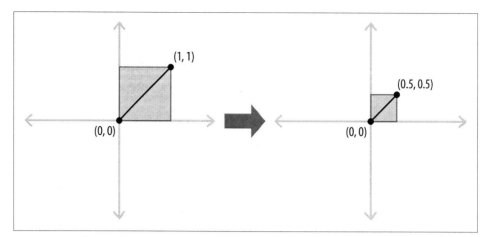

Figure 2-7. Scale transform

```
float translation[16] = { 1,  0,  0,  0,
                          0,  1,  0,  0,
                          0,  0,  1,  0,
                          tx, ty, tz, 1 };

// The following two statements are equivalent.
glMultMatrixf(translation);
glTranslatef(tx, ty, tz);
```

Intuitively, translation is achieved with addition, but recall that homogeneous coordinates allow us to express all transformations using multiplication, as shown in Equation 2-4.

Equation 2-4. Translation transform

$$\mathbf{vT} = (v_x\ v_y\ v_z\ 1) * \begin{pmatrix} 1 & 0 & 0 & 0 \\ 0 & 1 & 0 & 0 \\ 0 & 0 & 1 & 0 \\ t_x & t_y & t_z & 1 \end{pmatrix} = (v_x + t_x\ \ v_y + t_y\ \ v_z + t_z\ 1) = \mathbf{v'}$$

Figure 2-8 depicts a translation transform where $t_x = 0.25$ and $t_y = 0.5$.

Rotation

You might recall this transform from the fixed-function variant (ES 1.1) of the HelloArrow sample:

```
glRotatef(m_currentAngle, 0, 0, 1);
```

This applies a counterclockwise rotation about the z-axis. The first argument is an angle in degrees; the latter three arguments define the axis of rotation. The ES 2.0 renderer in HelloArrow was a bit tedious because it computed the matrix manually:

```
#include <cmath>
...
```

```
float radians = m_currentAngle * Pi / 180.0f;
float s = std::sin(radians);
float c = std::cos(radians);
float zRotation[16] = { c, s, 0, 0,
                       -s, c, 0, 0,
                        0, 0, 1, 0,
                        0, 0, 0, 1 };

GLint modelviewUniform = glGetUniformLocation(m_simpleProgram, "Modelview");
glUniformMatrix4fv(modelviewUniform, 1, 0, &zRotation[0]);
```

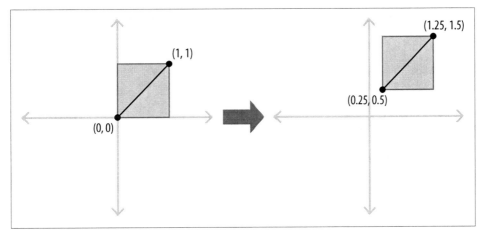

Figure 2-8. Translation transform

Figure 2-9 depicts a rotation transform where the angle is 45°.

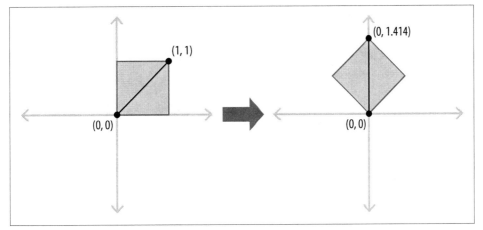

Figure 2-9. Rotation transform

Rotation about the z-axis is relatively simple, but rotation around an arbitrary axis requires a more complex matrix. For ES 1.1, glRotatef generates the matrix for you, so there's no need to get too concerned with its contents. For ES 2.0, check out the appendix to see how to implement this.

By itself, glRotatef rotates only around the origin, so what if you want to rotate around an arbitrary point **p**? To accomplish this, use a three-step process:

1. Translate by **-p**.
2. Perform the rotation.
3. Translate by **+p**.

For example, to change HelloArrow to rotate around (0, 1) rather than the center, you could do this:

```
glTranslatef(0, +1, 0);
glRotatef(m_currentAngle, 0, 0, 1);
glTranslatef(0, -1, 0);
glDrawArrays(...);
```

Remember, the last transform in your code is actually the first one that gets applied!

Setting the View Transform

The simplest way to create a view matrix is with the popular LookAt function. It's not built into OpenGL ES, but it's easy enough to implement it from scratch. LookAt takes three parameters: a camera position, a target location, and an "up" vector to define the camera's orientation (see Figure 2-10).

Using the three input vectors, LookAt produces a transformation matrix that would otherwise be cumbersome to derive using the fundamental transforms (scale, translation, rotation). Example 2-1 is one possible implementation of LookAt.

Example 2-1. LookAt

```
mat4 LookAt(const vec3& eye, const vec3& target, const vec3& up)
{
    vec3 z = (eye - target).Normalized();
    vec3 x = up.Cross(z).Normalized();
    vec3 y = z.Cross(x).Normalized();

    mat4 m;
    m.x = vec4(x, 0);
    m.y = vec4(y, 0);
    m.z = vec4(z, 0);
    m.w = vec4(0, 0, 0, 1);

    vec4 eyePrime = m * -eye;
    m = m.Transposed();
    m.w = eyePrime;

    return m;
}
```

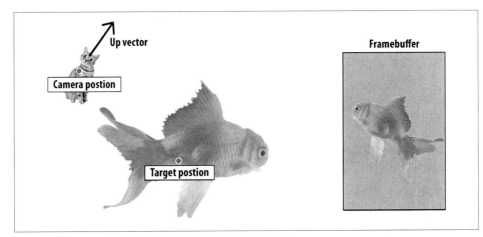

Figure 2-10. The LookAt transform

Note that Example 2-1 uses custom types like vec3, vec4, and mat4. This isn't pseudo-code; it's actual code from the C++ vector library in the appendix. We'll discuss the library later in the chapter.

Setting the Projection Transform

Until this point, we've been dealing with transformations that are typically used to modify the model-view rather than the projection. ES 1.1 operations such as glRotatef and glTranslatef always affect the current matrix, which can be changed at any time using glMatrixMode. Initially the matrix mode is GL_MODELVIEW.

What's the distinction between projection and model-view? Novice OpenGL programmers sometimes think of the projection as being the "camera matrix," but this is an oversimplification, if not completely wrong; the position and orientation of the camera should actually be specified in the model-view. I prefer to think of the projection as being the camera's "zoom lens" because it affects the field of view.

 Camera position and orientation should always go in the model-view, not the projection. OpenGL ES 1.1 depends on this to perform correct lighting calculations.

Two types of projections commonly appear in computer graphics: perspective and orthographic. Perspective projections cause distant objects to appear smaller, just as they do in real life. You can see the difference in Figure 2-11.

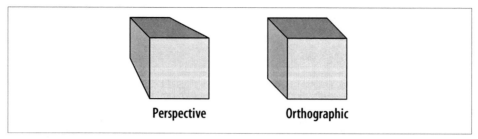

Figure 2-11. Types of projections

An orthographic projection is usually appropriate only for 2D graphics, so that's what we used in HelloArrow:

```
const float maxX = 2;
const float maxY = 3;
glOrthof(-maxX, +maxX, -maxY, +maxY, -1, 1);
```

The arguments for `glOrthof` specify the distance of the six bounding planes from the origin: left, right, bottom, top, near, and far. Note that our example arguments create an aspect ratio of 2:3; this is appropriate since the iPhone's screen is 320×480. The ES 2.0 renderer in HelloArrow reveals how the orthographic projection is computed:

```
float a = 1.0f / maxX;
float b = 1.0f / maxY;
float ortho[16] = {
    a, 0,  0, 0,
    0, b,  0, 0,
    0, 0, -1, 0,
    0, 0,  0, 1
};
```

When an orthographic projection is centered around the origin, it's really just a special case of the scale matrix that we already presented in "Scale" on page 55:

```
sx = 1.0f / maxX
sy = 1.0f / maxY
sz = -1

float scale[16] = { sx, 0,  0,  0,
                    0,  sy, 0,  0,
                    0,  0,  sz, 0
                    0,  0,  0,  1 };
```

Since HelloCone (the example you'll see later in this chapter) will have true 3D rendering, we'll give it a perspective matrix using the `glFrustumf` command, like this:

```
glFrustumf(-1.6f, 1.6, -2.4, 2.4, 5, 10);
```

The arguments to `glFrustumf` are the same as `glOrthof`. Since `glFrustum` does not exist in ES 2.0, HelloCone's 2.0 renderer will compute the matrix manually, like this:

```
void ApplyFrustum(float left, float right, float bottom,
                  float top, float near, float far)
```

```
{
    float a = 2 * near / (right - left);
    float b = 2 * near / (top - bottom);
    float c = (right + left) / (right - left);
    float d = (top + bottom) / (top - bottom);
    float e = - (far + near) / (far - near);
    float f = -2 * far * near / (far - near);

    mat4 m;
    m.x.x = a; m.x.y = 0; m.x.z = 0; m.x.w = 0;
    m.y.x = 0; m.y.y = b; m.y.z = 0; m.y.w = 0;
    m.z.x = c; m.z.y = d; m.z.z = e; m.z.w = -1;
    m.w.x = 0; m.w.y = 0; m.w.z = f; m.w.w = 1;

    glUniformMatrix4fv(projectionUniform, 1, 0, m.Pointer());
}
```

When a perspective projection is applied, the field of view is in the shape of a frustum. The viewing frustum is just a chopped-off pyramid with the eye at the apex of the pyramid (see Figure 2-12).

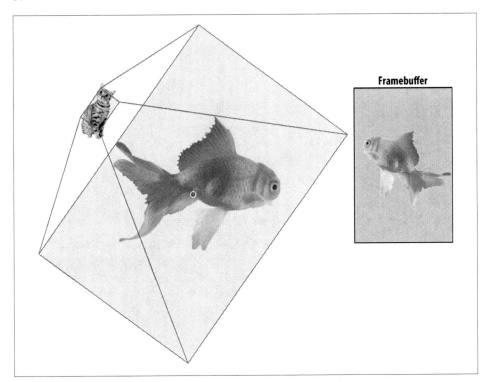

Figure 2-12. Viewing frustum

A viewing frustum can also be computed based on the angle of the pyramid's apex (known as *field of view*); some developers find these to be more intuitive than specifying all six planes. The function in Example 2-2 takes four arguments: the field-of-view angle, the aspect ratio of the pyramid's base, and the near and far planes.

Example 2-2. VerticalFieldOfView

```
void VerticalFieldOfView(float degrees, float aspectRatio,
                         float near, float far)
{
    float top = near * std::tan(degrees * Pi / 360.0f);
    float bottom = -top;
    float left = bottom * aspectRatio;
    float right = top * aspectRatio;

    glFrustum(left, right, bottom, top, near, far);
}
```

 For perspective projection, avoid setting your near or far plane to zero or a negative number. Mathematically this just doesn't work out.

Saving and Restoring Transforms with Matrix Stacks

Recall that the ES 1.1 renderer in HelloArrow used glPushMatrix and glPopMatrix to save and restore the transformation state:

```
void RenderingEngine::Render()
{
    glPushMatrix();
    ...
    glDrawArrays(GL_TRIANGLES, 0, vertexCount);
    ...
    glPopMatrix();
}
```

It's fairly standard practice to wrap the Render method in a push/pop block like this, because it prevents transformations from accumulating from one frame to the next.

In the previous example, the matrix stack is never more than two entries deep, but the iPhone allows up to 16 stack entries. This facilitates complex sequences of transforms, such as those required to render the articulated arm in Figure 2-13, or any other hierarchical model. When writing code with frequent pushes and pops, it helps to add extra indentation, as in Example 2-3.

Example 2-3. Hierarchical transforms

```
void DrawRobotArm()
{
    glPushMatrix();
        glRotatef(shoulderAngle, 0, 0, 1);
        glDrawArrays( ... ); // Upper arm
        glTranslatef(upperArmLength, 0, 0);
        glRotatef(elbowAngle, 0, 0, 1);
```

```
        glDrawArrays( ... ); // Forearm
        glTranslatef(forearmLength, 0, 0);
        glPushMatrix();
            glRotatef(finger0Angle, 0, 0, 1);
            glDrawArrays( ... ); // Finger 0
        glPopMatrix();
        glPushMatrix();
            glRotatef(-finger1Angle, 0, 0, 1);
            glDrawArrays( ... ); // Finger 1
        glPopMatrix();
    glPopMatrix();
}
```

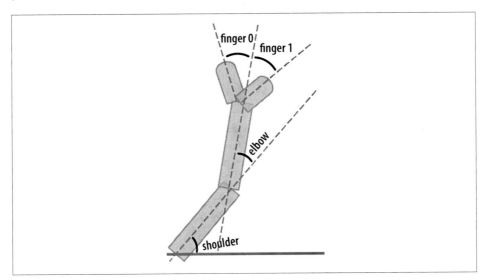

Figure 2-13. Robot arm

Each matrix mode has its own stack, as depicted in Figure 2-14; typically GL_MODELVIEW gets the heaviest use. Don't worry about the GL_TEXTURE stacks; we'll cover them in another chapter. Earlier we mentioned that OpenGL transforms every vertex position by the "current" model-view and projection matrices, by which we meant the topmost element in their respective stacks. To switch from one stack to another, use glMatrixMode.

Matrix stacks do not exist in ES 2.0; if you need them, you'll need to create them in your application code or in your own math library. Again, this may seem cruel, but always keep in mind that ES 2.0 is a "closer to the metal" API and that it actually gives you much more power and control through the use of shaders.

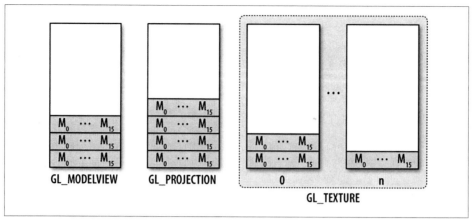

Figure 2-14. Matrix stacks

Animation

As we've seen so far, OpenGL performs quite a bit of math behind the scenes. But ultimately OpenGL is just a low-level graphics API and not an animation API. Luckily, the math required for animation is quite simple.

To sum it up in five words, *animation is all about interpolation*. An application's animation system will often take a set of *keyframes* from an artist, user, or algorithm. At runtime, it computes values between those keyframes. The type of data associated with keyframes can be anything, but typical examples are color, position, and rotation.

Interpolation Techniques

The process of computing an intermediate frame from two keyframes is called *tweening*. If you divide elapsed time by desired duration, you get a *blend weight* between zero and one. There are three easing equations discussed here, depicted in Figure 2-15. The tweened value for blending weight *t* can be computed as follows:

```
float LinearTween(float t, float start, float end)
{
    return t * start + (1 - t) * end;
}
```

Certain types of animation should not use linear tweening; a more natural look can often be achieved with one of Robert Penner's *easing equations*. Penner's quadratic ease-in is fairly straightforward:

```
float QuadraticEaseIn(float t, float start, float end)
{
    return LinearTween(t * t, start, end);
}
```

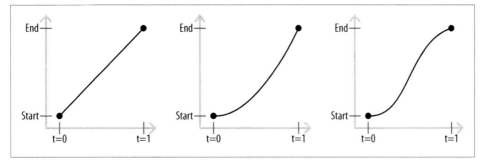

Figure 2-15. Easing equations: linear, quadratic ease-in, and quadratic ease-in-out

Penner's "quadratic ease-in-out" equation is a bit more complex but relatively easy to follow when splitting it into multiple steps, as in Example 2-4.

Example 2-4. Quadratic ease-in-out

```
float QuadraticEaseInOut(float t, float start, float end)
{
    float middle = (start + end) / 2;
    t = 2 * t;
    if (t <= 1)
        return LinearTween(t * t, start, middle);
    t -= 1;
    return LinearTween(t * t, middle, end);
}
```

Animating Rotation with Quaternions

For position and color keyframes, it's easy to perform interpolation: simply call one the aforementioned tweening functions on each of the XYZ or RGB components. At first, rotation seems simple, too; it's just a matter of tweening the angle. But what if you're interpolating between two orientations that don't have the same axis of rotation?

Picture the robot arm example in Figure 2-13. This example was restricted to the plane, but consider what you'd need if each joint were a ball joint. Storing an angle for each joint would be insufficient—you'd also need the axis of rotation. This is known as *axis-angle* notation and requires a total of four floating-point values for each joint.

It turns out there's an artful way to represent an arbitrary rotation using the same number of floats as axis-angle, but in a way that often better lends itself to interpolation. This type of 4D vector is called a *quaternion*, and it was conceived in 1843. Quaternions were somewhat marginalized when modern vector algebra came about, but they experienced a revival in the computer graphics era. Ken Shoemake is one of the people who popularized them in the late 1980s with his famous *slerp* equation for interpolating between two quaternions.

Shoemake's method is actually only one of several methods of quaternion interpolation, but it's the most popular, and it's the one we use in our vector library. Other methods, such as normalized quaternion lerp and log-quaternion lerp, are sometimes more desirable in terms of performance.

Having said all this, be aware that quaternions aren't always the best way to handle an animation problem. Sometimes it suffices to simply compute the angle between two vectors, find an axis of rotation, and interpolate the angle. However, quaternions solve a slightly more complex problem. They don't merely interpolate between two vectors; they interpolate between two *orientations*. This may seem pedantic, but it's an important distinction. Hold your arm straight out in front of you, palm up. Now, bend your arm at the elbow while simultaneously rotating your hand. What you've just done is interpolate between two orientations.

It turns out that quaternions are particularly well suited to the type of "trackball" rotation that we'll be using in much of our sample code. I won't bore you with a bunch of equations here, but you can check out the appendix to see how to implement quaternions. We'll leverage this in the HelloCone sample and in the wireframe viewer presented in the next chapter.

Vector Beautification with C++

Recall the vertex structure in HelloArrow:

```
struct Vertex {
    float Position[2];
    float Color[4];
};
```

If we kept using vanilla C arrays like this throughout this book, life would become very tedious! What we really want is something like this:

```
struct Vertex {
    vec2 Position;
    vec4 Color;
};
```

This is where the power of C++ operator overloading and class templates really shines. It makes it possible (in fact, it makes it *easy*) to write a small class library that makes much of your application code look like it's written in a vector-based language. In fact, that's what we've done for the samples in this book. Our entire library consists of only three header files and no *.cpp* files:

Vector.hpp

Defines a suite of 2D, 3D, and 4D vector types that can be either float-based or integer-based. Has no dependencies on any other header.

Matrix.hpp

Defines classes for 2×2, 3×3, and 4×4 matrices. Depends only on *Vector.hpp*.

Quaternion.hpp

Defines a class for quaternions and provides several methods for interpolation and construction. Depends on *Matrix.hpp*.

These files are listed in their entirety in the appendix, but to give you a taste of how the library is structured, Example 2-5 shows portions of *Vector.hpp*.

Example 2-5. Vector.hpp

```cpp
#pragma once
#include <cmath>

template <typename T>
struct Vector2 {
    Vector2() {}
    Vector2(T x, T y) : x(x), y(y) {}
    T x;
    T y;
    ...
};

template <typename T>
struct Vector3 {
    Vector3() {}
    Vector3(T x, T y, T z) : x(x), y(y), z(z) {}
    void Normalize()
    {
        float length = std::sqrt(x * x + y * y + z * z);
        x /= length;
        y /= length;
        z /= length;
    }
    Vector3 Normalized() const
    {
        Vector3 v = *this;
        v.Normalize();
        return v;
    }
    Vector3 Cross(const Vector3& v) const
    {
        return Vector3(y * v.z - z * v.y,
                       z * v.x - x * v.z,
                       x * v.y - y * v.x);
    }
    T Dot(const Vector3& v) const
    {
        return x * v.x + y * v.y + z * v.z;
    }
    Vector3 operator-() const
    {
        return Vector3(-x, -y, -z);
    }
```

```
        bool operator==(const Vector3& v) const
        {
            return x == v.x && y == v.y && z == v.z;
        }
        T x;
        T y;
        T z;
    };

    template <typename T>
    struct Vector4 {
        ...
    };

    typedef Vector2<int> ivec2;
    typedef Vector3<int> ivec3;
    typedef Vector4<int> ivec4;

    typedef Vector2<float> vec2;
    typedef Vector3<float> vec3;
    typedef Vector4<float> vec4;
```

Note how we parameterized each vector type using C++ templates. This allows the same logic to be used for both float-based vectors and integer-based vectors.

Even though a 2D vector has much in common with a 3D vector, we chose not to share logic between them. This could've been achieved by adding a second template argument for dimensionality, as in the following:

```
    template <typename T, int Dimension>
    struct Vector {
        ...
        T components[Dimension];
    };
```

When designing a vector library, it's important to strike the right balance between generality and readability. Since there's relatively little logic in each vector class and since we rarely need to iterate over vector components, defining separate classes seems like a reasonable way to go. It's also easier for readers to understand the meaning of, say, Position.y than Position[1].

Since a good bit of application code will be making frequent use of these types, the bottom of Example 2-5 defines some abbreviated names using typedefs. Lowercase names such as vec2 and ivec4 break the naming convention we've established for types, but they adopt a look and feel similar to native types in the language itself.

The vec2/ivec2 style names in our C++ vector library are directly pilfered from keywords in GLSL. Take care not to confuse this book's C++ listings with shader listings.

 In GLSL shaders, types such as vec2 and mat4 are built into the language itself. Our C++ vector library merely mimics them.

HelloCone with Fixed Function

We're finally ready to upgrade the HelloArrow program into HelloCone. We'll not go only from rendering in 2D to rendering in 3D; we'll also support two new orientations for when the device is held face up or face down.

Even though the visual changes are significant, they'll all occur within *RenderingEngine1.cpp* and *RenderingEngine2.cpp*. That's the beauty of the layered, interface-based approach presented in the previous chapter. First we'll deal exclusively with the ES 1.1 renderer, *RenderingEngine1.cpp*.

RenderingEngine Declaration

The implementations of HelloArrow and HelloCone diverge in several ways, as shown in Table 2-5.

Table 2-5. Differences between HelloArrow and HelloCone

HelloArrow	HelloCone
Rotation state is an angle on the z-axis.	Rotation state is a quaternion.
One draw call.	Two draw calls: one for the disk, one for the cone.
Vectors are represented with small C arrays.	Vectors are represented with objects like vec3.
Triangle data is small enough to be hardcoded within the program.	Triangle data is generated at runtime.
Triangle data is stored in a C array.	Triangle data is stored in an STL vector.

STL: To Use or Not to Use?

I decided to use the C++ Standard Template Library (STL) in much of this book's sample code. The STL simplifies many tasks by providing classes for commonly used data structures, such as resizeable arrays (std::vector) and doubly linked lists (std::list). Many developers would argue against using STL on a mobile platform like the iPhone when writing performance-critical code. It's true that sloppy usage of STL can cause your application's memory footprint to get out of hand, but nowadays, C++ compilers do a great job at optimizing STL code. Keep in mind that the iPhone SDK provides a rich set of Objective-C classes (e.g., NSDictionary) that are analogous to many of the STL classes, and they have similar costs in terms of memory footprint and performance.

With Table 2-5 in mind, take a look at the top of *RenderingEngine1.cpp*, shown in Example 2-6 (note that this moves the definition of struct Vertex higher up in the file than it was before, so you'll need to remove the old version of this struct from this file).

If you'd like to follow along in code as you read, make a copy of the *HelloArrow* project folder in Finder, and save it as *HelloCone*. Open the project in Xcode, and then select *Rename* from the *Project* menu. Change the project name to *HelloCone*, and click *Rename*. Next, visit the appendix, and add *Vector.hpp*, *Matrix.hpp*, and *Quaternion.hpp* to the project. *RenderingEngine1.cpp* will be almost completely different, so open it and remove all its content. Now you're ready to make the changes shown in this section as you read along.

Example 2-6. RenderingEngine1 class declaration

```
#include <OpenGLES/ES1/gl.h>
#include <OpenGLES/ES1/glext.h>
#include "IRenderingEngine.hpp"
#include "Quaternion.hpp"
#include <vector>

static const float AnimationDuration = 0.25f;

using namespace std;

struct Vertex {
    vec3 Position;
    vec4 Color;
};

struct Animation {❶
    Quaternion Start;
    Quaternion End;
    Quaternion Current;
    float Elapsed;
    float Duration;
};

class RenderingEngine1 : public IRenderingEngine {
public:
    RenderingEngine1();
    void Initialize(int width, int height);
    void Render() const;
    void UpdateAnimation(float timeStep);
    void OnRotate(DeviceOrientation newOrientation);
private:
    vector<Vertex> m_cone;❷
    vector<Vertex> m_disk;
    Animation m_animation;
    GLuint m_framebuffer;
    GLuint m_colorRenderbuffer;
    GLuint m_depthRenderbuffer;❸
};
```

❶ The Animation structure enables smooth 3D transitions. It includes quaternions for three orientations: the starting orientation, the current interpolated orientation, and the ending orientation. It also includes two time spans: Elapsed and Duration, both of which are in seconds. They'll be used to compute a slerp fraction between 0 and 1.

❷ The triangle data lives in two STL containers, m_cone and m_disk. The vector container is ideal because we know how big it needs to be ahead of time, and it guarantees contiguous storage. Contiguous storage of vertices is an absolute requirement for OpenGL.

❸ Unlike HelloArrow, there are *two* renderbuffers here. HelloArrow was 2D and therefore only required a color renderbuffer. HelloCone requires an additional renderbuff for depth. We'll learn more about the depth buffer in a future chapter; briefly, it's a special image plane that stores a single Z value at each pixel.

OpenGL Initialization and Cone Tessellation

The construction methods are very similar to what we had in HelloArrow:

```
IRenderingEngine* CreateRenderer1()
{
    return new RenderingEngine1();
}

RenderingEngine1::RenderingEngine1()
{
    // Create & bind the color buffer so that the caller can allocate its space.
    glGenRenderbuffersOES(1, &m_colorRenderbuffer);
    glBindRenderbufferOES(GL_RENDERBUFFER_OES, m_colorRenderbuffer);
}
```

The Initialize method, shown in Example 2-7, is responsible for generating the vertex data and setting up the framebuffer. It starts off by defining some values for the cone's radius, height, and geometric level of detail. The level of detail is represented by the number of vertical "slices" that constitute the cone. After generating all the vertices, it initializes OpenGL's framebuffer object and transform state. It also enables depth testing since this a true 3D app. We'll learn more about depth testing in Chapter 4.

Example 2-7. RenderingEngine initialization

```
void RenderingEngine1::Initialize(int width, int height)
{
    const float coneRadius = 0.5f;❶
    const float coneHeight = 1.866f;
    const int coneSlices = 40;

    {
      // Generate vertices for the disk.
      ...
    }

    {
      // Generate vertices for the body of the cone.
```

```
    ...
}

// Create the depth buffer.
glGenRenderbuffersOES(1, &m_depthRenderbuffer);❷
glBindRenderbufferOES(GL_RENDERBUFFER_OES, m_depthRenderbuffer);
glRenderbufferStorageOES(GL_RENDERBUFFER_OES,
                         GL_DEPTH_COMPONENT16_OES,
                         width,
                         height);

// Create the framebuffer object; attach the depth and color buffers.
glGenFramebuffersOES(1, &m_framebuffer);❸
glBindFramebufferOES(GL_FRAMEBUFFER_OES, m_framebuffer);
glFramebufferRenderbufferOES(GL_FRAMEBUFFER_OES,
                             GL_COLOR_ATTACHMENT0_OES,
                             GL_RENDERBUFFER_OES,
                             m_colorRenderbuffer);
glFramebufferRenderbufferOES(GL_FRAMEBUFFER_OES,
                             GL_DEPTH_ATTACHMENT_OES,
                             GL_RENDERBUFFER_OES,
                             m_depthRenderbuffer);

// Bind the color buffer for rendering.
glBindRenderbufferOES(GL_RENDERBUFFER_OES, m_colorRenderbuffer);❹

glViewport(0, 0, width, height);❺
glEnable(GL_DEPTH_TEST);❻

glMatrixMode(GL_PROJECTION);❼
glFrustumf(-1.6f, 1.6, -2.4, 2.4, 5, 10);

glMatrixMode(GL_MODELVIEW);
glTranslatef(0, 0, -7);
}
```

Much of Example 2-7 is standard procedure when setting up an OpenGL context, and much of it will become clearer in future chapters. For now, here's a brief summary:

❶ Define some constants to use when generating the vertices for the disk and cone.

❷ Generate an ID for the depth renderbuffer, bind it, and allocate storage for it. We'll learn more about depth buffers later.

❸ Generate an ID for the framebuffer object, bind it, and attach depth and color to it using glFramebufferRenderbufferOES.

❹ Bind the color renderbuffer so that future rendering operations will affect it.

❺ Set up the left, bottom, width, and height properties of the viewport.

❻ Turn on depth testing since this is a 3D scene.

❼ Set up the projection and model-view transforms.

Example 2-7 replaces the two pieces of vertex generation code with ellipses because they deserve an in-depth explanation. The problem of decomposing an object into triangles is called *triangulation*, but more commonly you'll see the term *tessellation*, which actually refers to the broader problem of filling a surface with polygons. Tessellation can be a fun puzzle, as any M.C. Escher fan knows; we'll learn more about it in later chapters.

For now let's form the body of the cone with a triangle strip and the bottom cap with a triangle fan, as shown in Figure 2-16.

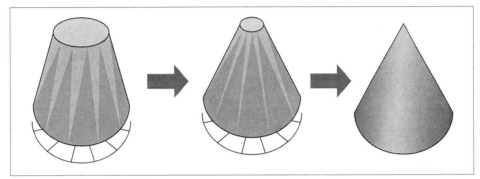

Figure 2-16. Tessellation in HelloCone

To form the shape of the cone's body, we could use a fan rather than a strip, but this would look strange because the color at the fan's center would be indeterminate. Even if we pick an arbitrary color for the center, an incorrect vertical gradient would result, as shown on the left in Figure 2-17.

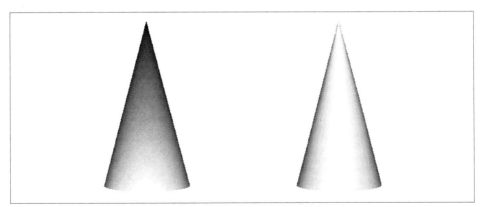

Figure 2-17. Left: Cone with triangle fan. Right: Cone with triangle strip

Using a strip for the cone isn't perfect either because every other triangle is degenerate (shown in gray in Figure 2-16). The only way to fix this would be resorting to

GL_TRIANGLES, which requires twice as many elements in the vertex array. It turns out that OpenGL provides an indexing mechanism to help with situations like this, which we'll learn about in the next chapter. For now we'll use GL_TRIANGLE_STRIP and live with the degenerate triangles. The code for generating the cone vertices is shown in Example 2-8 and depicted visually in Figure 2-18 (this code goes after the comment `// Generate vertices for the body of the cone` in `RenderingEngine1::Initialize`). Two vertices are required for each slice (one for the apex, one for the rim), and an extra slice is required to close the loop (Figure 2-18). The total number of vertices is therefore *(n+1)*2* where *n* is the number of slices. Computing the points along the rim is the classic graphics algorithm for drawing a circle and may look familiar if you remember your trigonometry.

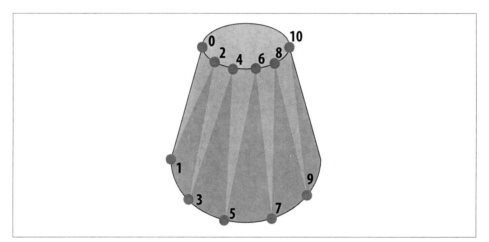

Figure 2-18. Vertex order in HelloCone

Example 2-8. Generation of cone vertices

```
m_cone.resize((coneSlices + 1) * 2);

// Initialize the vertices of the triangle strip.
vector<Vertex>::iterator vertex = m_cone.begin();
const float dtheta = TwoPi / coneSlices;
for (float theta = 0; vertex != m_cone.end(); theta += dtheta) {

    // Grayscale gradient
    float brightness = abs(sin(theta));
    vec4 color(brightness, brightness, brightness, 1);

    // Apex vertex
    vertex->Position = vec3(0, 1, 0);
    vertex->Color = color;
    vertex++;

    // Rim vertex
    vertex->Position.x = coneRadius * cos(theta);
```

```
    vertex->Position.y = 1 - coneHeight;
    vertex->Position.z = coneRadius * sin(theta);
    vertex->Color = color;
    vertex++;
}
```

Note that we're creating a grayscale gradient as a cheap way to simulate lighting:

```
float brightness = abs(sin(theta));
vec4 color(brightness, brightness, brightness, 1);
```

This is a bit of a hack because the color is fixed and does not change as you reorient the object, but it's good enough for our purposes. This technique is sometimes called *baked lighting*, and we'll learn more about it in Chapter 9. We'll also learn how to achieve more realistic lighting in Chapter 4.

Example 2-9 generates vertex data for the disk (this code goes after the comment `// Generate vertices for the disk` in `RenderingEngine1::Initialize`). Since it uses a triangle fan, the total number of vertices is $n+2$: one extra vertex for the center, another for closing the loop.

Example 2-9. Generation of disk vertices

```
// Allocate space for the disk vertices.
m_disk.resize(coneSlices + 2);

// Initialize the center vertex of the triangle fan.
vector<Vertex>::iterator vertex = m_disk.begin();
vertex->Color = vec4(0.75, 0.75, 0.75, 1);
vertex->Position.x = 0;
vertex->Position.y = 1 - coneHeight;
vertex->Position.z = 0;
vertex++;

// Initialize the rim vertices of the triangle fan.
const float dtheta = TwoPi / coneSlices;
for (float theta = 0; vertex != m_disk.end(); theta += dtheta) {
    vertex->Color = vec4(0.75, 0.75, 0.75, 1);
    vertex->Position.x = coneRadius * cos(theta);
    vertex->Position.y = 1 - coneHeight;
    vertex->Position.z = coneRadius * sin(theta);
    vertex++;
}
```

Smooth Rotation in Three Dimensions

To achieve smooth animation, `UpdateAnimation` calls `Slerp` on the rotation quaternion. When a device orientation change occurs, the `OnRotate` method starts a new animation sequence. Example 2-10 shows these methods.

Example 2-10. UpdateAnimation and OnRotate

```
void RenderingEngine1::UpdateAnimation(float timeStep)
{
    if (m_animation.Current == m_animation.End)
        return;

    m_animation.Elapsed += timeStep;
    if (m_animation.Elapsed >= AnimationDuration) {
        m_animation.Current = m_animation.End;
    } else {
        float mu = m_animation.Elapsed / AnimationDuration;
        m_animation.Current = m_animation.Start.Slerp(mu, m_animation.End);
    }
}

void RenderingEngine1::OnRotate(DeviceOrientation orientation)
{
    vec3 direction;

    switch (orientation) {
        case DeviceOrientationUnknown:
        case DeviceOrientationPortrait:
            direction = vec3(0, 1, 0);
            break;

        case DeviceOrientationPortraitUpsideDown:
            direction = vec3(0, -1, 0);
            break;

        case DeviceOrientationFaceDown:
            direction = vec3(0, 0, -1);
            break;

        case DeviceOrientationFaceUp:
            direction = vec3(0, 0, 1);
            break;

        case DeviceOrientationLandscapeLeft:
            direction = vec3(+1, 0, 0);
            break;

        case DeviceOrientationLandscapeRight:
            direction = vec3(-1, 0, 0);
            break;
    }


    m_animation.Elapsed = 0;
    m_animation.Start = m_animation.Current = m_animation.End;
    m_animation.End = Quaternion::CreateFromVectors(vec3(0, 1, 0), direction);
}
```

Render Method

Last but not least, HelloCone needs a Render method, as shown in Example 2-11. It's similar to the Render method in HelloArrow except it makes two draw calls, and the glClear command now has an extra flag for the depth buffer.

Example 2-11. RenderingEngine1::Render

```
void RenderingEngine1::Render() const
{
    glClearColor(0.5f, 0.5f, 0.5f, 1);
    glClear(GL_COLOR_BUFFER_BIT | GL_DEPTH_BUFFER_BIT);
    glPushMatrix();

    glEnableClientState(GL_VERTEX_ARRAY);
    glEnableClientState(GL_COLOR_ARRAY);

    mat4 rotation(m_animation.Current.ToMatrix());
    glMultMatrixf(rotation.Pointer());

    // Draw the cone.
    glVertexPointer(3, GL_FLOAT, sizeof(Vertex), &m_cone[0].Position.x);
    glColorPointer(4, GL_FLOAT, sizeof(Vertex),  &m_cone[0].Color.x);
    glDrawArrays(GL_TRIANGLE_STRIP, 0, m_cone.size());

    // Draw the disk that caps off the base of the cone.
    glVertexPointer(3, GL_FLOAT, sizeof(Vertex), &m_disk[0].Position.x);
    glColorPointer(4, GL_FLOAT, sizeof(Vertex),  &m_disk[0].Color.x);
    glDrawArrays(GL_TRIANGLE_FAN, 0, m_disk.size());

    glDisableClientState(GL_VERTEX_ARRAY);
    glDisableClientState(GL_COLOR_ARRAY);

    glPopMatrix();
}
```

Note the call to rotation.Pointer(). In our C++ vector library, vectors and matrices have a method called Pointer(), which exposes a pointer to the first innermost element. This is useful when passing them to OpenGL.

> We could've made much of our OpenGL code more succinct by changing the vector library such that it provides implicit conversion operators in lieu of Pointer() methods. Personally, I think this would be error prone and would hide too much from the code reader. For similar reasons, STL's string class requires you to call its c_str() when you want to get a char*.

Because you've implemented only the 1.1 renderer so far, you'll also need to enable the ForceES1 switch at the top of *GLView.mm*. At this point, you can build and run your first truly 3D iPhone application! To see the two new orientations, try holding the iPhone over your head and at your waist. See Figure 2-19 for screenshots of all six device orientations.

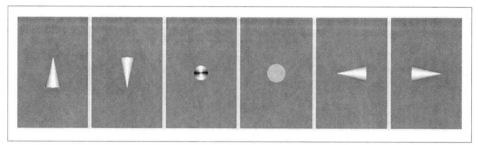

Figure 2-19. Left to right: Portrait, UpsideDown, FaceUp, FaceDown, LandscapeRight, and LandscapeLeft

HelloCone with Shaders

Rather than modify the version of *RenderingEngine2.cpp* from HelloArrow, it will be more instructive if we can start our ES 2.0 backend by copying the contents of *RenderingEngine1.cpp* over whatever is already in *RenderingEngine2.cpp*, with two exceptions: you'll need to save the `BuildShader` and `BuildProgram` methods from the existing *RenderingEngine2.cpp* from HelloArrow, so copy them somewhere safe for the moment. If you're following along, do that now, and then you'll be ready to make some changes to the file. Example 2-12 shows the top part of *RenderingEngine2.cpp*. New and changed lines are shown in bold. Some sections of unchanged code are shown as `...`, so don't copy this over the existing code in its entirety (just make the changes and additions shown in bold).

Example 2-12. RenderingEngine2 class declaration

```
#include <OpenGLES/ES2/gl.h>
#include <OpenGLES/ES2/glext.h>
#include "IRenderingEngine.hpp"
#include "Quaternion.hpp"
#include <vector>
#include <iostream>

#define STRINGIFY(A)  #A
#include "../Shaders/Simple.vert"
#include "../Shaders/Simple.frag"

static const float AnimationDuration = 0.25f;

...

class RenderingEngine2 : public IRenderingEngine {
public:
    RenderingEngine2();
```

```
    void Initialize(int width, int height);
    void Render() const;
    void UpdateAnimation(float timeStep);
    void OnRotate(DeviceOrientation newOrientation);
private:
    GLuint BuildShader(const char* source, GLenum shaderType) const;
    GLuint BuildProgram(const char* vShader, const char* fShader) const;
    vector<Vertex> m_cone;
    vector<Vertex> m_disk;
    Animation m_animation;
    GLuint m_simpleProgram;
    GLuint m_framebuffer;
    GLuint m_colorRenderbuffer;
    GLuint m_depthRenderbuffer;
};
```

The `Initialize` method almost stays as is, but this bit is no longer valid:

```
glMatrixMode(GL_PROJECTION);
glFrustumf(-1.6f, 1.6, -2.4, 2.4, 5, 10);

glMatrixMode(GL_MODELVIEW);
glTranslatef(0, 0, -7);
```

For ES 2.0, this changes to the following:

```
m_simpleProgram = BuildProgram(SimpleVertexShader,
                               SimpleFragmentShader);
glUseProgram(m_simpleProgram);

// Set the projection matrix.
GLint projectionUniform = glGetUniformLocation(m_simpleProgram,
                                               "Projection");
mat4 projectionMatrix = mat4::Frustum(-1.6f, 1.6, -2.4, 2.4, 5, 10);
glUniformMatrix4fv(projectionUniform, 1, 0,
                   projectionMatrix.Pointer());
```

The `BuildShader` and `BuildProgram` methods are the same as they were for the ES 2.0 version of HelloArrow; no need to list them here. The shaders themselves are also the same as HelloArrow's shaders; remember, the lighting is "baked," so simply passing through the colors is sufficient.

We set up the model-view within the `Render` method, as shown in Example 2-13. Remember, `glUniformMatrix4fv` plays a role similar to the `glLoadMatrix` function in ES 1.1.

Example 2-13. RenderingEngine2::Render

```
void RenderingEngine2::Render() const
{
    GLuint positionSlot = glGetAttribLocation(m_simpleProgram,
                                              "Position");
    GLuint colorSlot = glGetAttribLocation(m_simpleProgram,
                                           "SourceColor");

    glClearColor(0.5f, 0.5f, 0.5f, 1);
    glClear(GL_COLOR_BUFFER_BIT | GL_DEPTH_BUFFER_BIT);
```

```
glEnableVertexAttribArray(positionSlot);
glEnableVertexAttribArray(colorSlot);

mat4 rotation(m_animation.Current.ToMatrix());
mat4 translation = mat4::Translate(0, 0, -7);

// Set the model-view matrix.
GLint modelviewUniform = glGetUniformLocation(m_simpleProgram,
                                              "Modelview");
mat4 modelviewMatrix = rotation * translation;
glUniformMatrix4fv(modelviewUniform, 1, 0, modelviewMatrix.Pointer());

// Draw the cone.
{
  GLsizei stride = sizeof(Vertex);
  const GLvoid* pCoords = &m_cone[0].Position.x;
  const GLvoid* pColors = &m_cone[0].Color.x;
  glVertexAttribPointer(positionSlot, 3, GL_FLOAT,
                        GL_FALSE, stride, pCoords);
  glVertexAttribPointer(colorSlot, 4, GL_FLOAT,
                        GL_FALSE, stride, pColors);
  glDrawArrays(GL_TRIANGLE_STRIP, 0, m_cone.size());
}

// Draw the disk that caps off the base of the cone.
{
  GLsizei stride = sizeof(Vertex);
  const GLvoid* pCoords = &m_disk[0].Position.x;
  const GLvoid* pColors = &m_disk[0].Color.x;
  glVertexAttribPointer(positionSlot, 3, GL_FLOAT,
                        GL_FALSE, stride, pCoords);
  glVertexAttribPointer(colorSlot, 4, GL_FLOAT,
                        GL_FALSE, stride, pColors);
  glDrawArrays(GL_TRIANGLE_FAN, 0, m_disk.size());
}

glDisableVertexAttribArray(positionSlot);
glDisableVertexAttribArray(colorSlot);
}
```

The sequence of events in Example 2-13 is actually quite similar to the sequence in Example 2-11; only the details have changed.

Next, go through the file, and change any remaining occurrences of RenderingEngine1 to RenderingEngine2, including the factory method (and be sure to change the name of that method to CreateRenderer2). You also need to remove any occurrences of _OES and OES. Now, turn off the ForceES1 switch in *GLView.mm*; this completes the changes required for the shader-based version of HelloCone. It may seem silly to have added an ES 2.0 renderer without having added any cool shader effects, but it illustrates the differences between the two APIs.

Wrapping Up

This chapter was perhaps the most academic part of this book, but we disseminated some fundamental graphics concepts and cleared up some of the sample code that was glossed over in the first chapter.

Understanding transforms is perhaps the most difficult but also the most crucial hurdle to overcome for OpenGL newbies. I encourage you to experiment with HelloCone to get a better feel for how transformations work. For example, try adding some hard-coded rotations and translations to the Render method, and observe how their ordering affects the final rendering.

In the next chapter, you'll learn more about submitting geometry to OpenGL, and you'll get a primer on the iPhone's touchscreen.

## CHAPTER 3

Vertices and Touch Points

Second star to the right…and straight on 'til morning.

—*Peter Pan*, J.M. Barrie

The iPhone has several input devices, including the accelerometer, microphone, and touchscreen, but your application will probably make the most use of the touchscreen. Since the screen has multitouch capabilities, your application can obtain a list of several touch points at any time. In a way, your 3D application is a "point processor": it consumes points from the touchscreen and produces points (for example, triangle vertices) for OpenGL. So, I thought I'd use the same chapter to both introduce the touchscreen and cover some new ways of submitting vertices to OpenGL.

This chapter also covers some important best practices for vertex submission, such as the usage of vertex buffer objects. I would never argue with the great man who decreed that premature optimization is the root of all evil, but I want to hammer in good habits early on.

Toward the end of the chapter, you'll learn how to generate some interesting geometry using parametric surfaces. This will form the basis for a fun demo app that you'll gradually enhance over the course of the next several chapters.

Reading the Touchscreen

In this section, I'll introduce the touchscreen API by walking through a modification of HelloCone that makes the cone point toward the user's finger. You'll need to change the name of the app from HelloCone to TouchCone, since the user now touches the cone instead of merely greeting it. To do this, make a copy of the project folder in Finder, and name the new folder *TouchCone*. Next, open the Xcode project (it will still have the old name), and select Project→Rename. Change the name to TouchCone, and click Rename.

Apple's multitouch API is actually much richer than what we need to expose through our IRenderingEngine interface. For example, Apple's API supports the concept of *cancellation*, which is useful to robustly handle situations such as an interruption from a phone call. For our purposes, a simplified interface to the rendering engine is sufficient. In fact, we don't even need to accept multiple touches simultaneously; the touch handler methods can simply take a single coordinate.

For starters, let's add three methods to IRenderingEngine for "finger up" (the end of a touch), "finger down" (the beginning of a touch), and "finger move." Coordinates are passed to these methods using the ivec2 type from the vector library we added in "RenderingEngine Declaration" on page 69. Example 3-1 shows the modifications to IRenderingEngine.hpp (new lines are in bold).

Example 3-1. IRenderingEngine interface for TouchCone

```
#include "Vector.hpp"

...

struct IRenderingEngine {
    virtual void Initialize(int width, int height) = 0;
    virtual void Render() const = 0;
    virtual void UpdateAnimation(float timeStep) = 0;
    virtual void OnRotate(DeviceOrientation newOrientation) = 0;
    virtual void OnFingerUp(ivec2 location) = 0;
    virtual void OnFingerDown(ivec2 location) = 0;
    virtual void OnFingerMove(ivec2 oldLocation, ivec2 newLocation) = 0;
    virtual ~IRenderingEngine() {}
};
```

The iPhone notifies your view of touch events by calling methods on your UIView class, which you can then override. The three methods we're interested in overriding are touchesBegan, touchedEnded, and touchesMoved. Open *GLView.mm*, and implement these methods by simply passing on the coordinates to the rendering engine:

```
- (void) touchesBegan: (NSSet*) touches withEvent: (UIEvent*) event
{
    UITouch* touch = [touches anyObject];
    CGPoint location  = [touch locationInView: self];
    m_renderingEngine->OnFingerDown(ivec2(location.x, location.y));
}

- (void) touchesEnded: (NSSet*) touches withEvent: (UIEvent*) event
{
    UITouch* touch = [touches anyObject];
    CGPoint location  = [touch locationInView: self];
    m_renderingEngine->OnFingerUp(ivec2(location.x, location.y));
}

- (void) touchesMoved: (NSSet*) touches withEvent: (UIEvent*) event
{
    UITouch* touch = [touches anyObject];
    CGPoint previous  = [touch previousLocationInView: self];
```

```
        CGPoint current = [touch locationInView: self];
        m_renderingEngine->OnFingerMove(ivec2(previous.x, previous.y),
                                    ivec2(current.x, current.y));
    }
```

The RenderingEngine1 implementation (Example 3-2) is similar to HelloCone, but the
OnRotate and UpdateAnimation methods become empty. Example 3-2 also notifies the
user that the cone is active by using glScalef to enlarge the geometry while the user is
touching the screen. New and changed lines in the class declaration are shown in bold.
Note that we're removing the Animation structure.

Example 3-2. RenderingEngine1.cpp in TouchCone

```
class RenderingEngine1 : public IRenderingEngine {
public:
    RenderingEngine1();
    void Initialize(int width, int height);
    void Render() const;
    void UpdateAnimation(float timeStep) {}
    void OnRotate(DeviceOrientation newOrientation) {}
    void OnFingerUp(ivec2 location);
    void OnFingerDown(ivec2 location);
    void OnFingerMove(ivec2 oldLocation, ivec2 newLocation);
private:
    vector<Vertex> m_cone;
    vector<Vertex> m_disk;
    GLfloat m_rotationAngle;
    GLfloat m_scale;
    ivec2 m_pivotPoint;
    GLuint m_framebuffer;
    GLuint m_colorRenderbuffer;
    GLuint m_depthRenderbuffer;
};

RenderingEngine1::RenderingEngine1() : m_rotationAngle(0), m_scale(1)
{
    glGenRenderbuffersOES(1, &m_colorRenderbuffer);
    glBindRenderbufferOES(GL_RENDERBUFFER_OES, m_colorRenderbuffer);
}

void RenderingEngine1::Initialize(int width, int height)
{
    m_pivotPoint = ivec2(width / 2, height / 2);

    ...
}

void RenderingEngine1::Render() const
{
    glClearColor(0.5f, 0.5f, 0.5f, 1);
    glClear(GL_COLOR_BUFFER_BIT | GL_DEPTH_BUFFER_BIT);
    glPushMatrix();

    glEnableClientState(GL_VERTEX_ARRAY);
    glEnableClientState(GL_COLOR_ARRAY);
```

```
    glRotatef(m_rotationAngle, 0, 0, 1); // Replaces call to rotation()
    glScalef(m_scale, m_scale, m_scale); // Replaces call to glMultMatrixf()

    // Draw the cone.
    glVertexPointer(3, GL_FLOAT, sizeof(Vertex), &m_cone[0].Position.x);
    glColorPointer(4, GL_FLOAT, sizeof(Vertex), &m_cone[0].Color.x);
    glDrawArrays(GL_TRIANGLE_STRIP, 0, m_cone.size());

    // Draw the disk that caps off the base of the cone.
    glVertexPointer(3, GL_FLOAT, sizeof(Vertex), &m_disk[0].Position.x);
    glColorPointer(4, GL_FLOAT, sizeof(Vertex), &m_disk[0].Color.x);
    glDrawArrays(GL_TRIANGLE_FAN, 0, m_disk.size());

    glDisableClientState(GL_VERTEX_ARRAY);
    glDisableClientState(GL_COLOR_ARRAY);

    glPopMatrix();
}

void RenderingEngine1::OnFingerUp(ivec2 location)
{
    m_scale = 1.0f;
}

void RenderingEngine1::OnFingerDown(ivec2 location)
{
    m_scale = 1.5f;
    OnFingerMove(location, location);
}

void RenderingEngine1::OnFingerMove(ivec2 previous, ivec2 location)
{
    vec2 direction = vec2(location - m_pivotPoint).Normalized();

    // Flip the y-axis because pixel coords increase toward the bottom.
    direction.y = -direction.y;

    m_rotationAngle = std::acos(direction.y) * 180.0f / 3.14159f;
    if (direction.x > 0)
        m_rotationAngle = -m_rotationAngle;
}
```

The only bit of code in Example 3-2 that might need some extra explanation is the OnFingerMove method; it uses some trigonometric trickery to compute the angle of rotation. The best way to explain this is with a diagram, as shown in Figure 3-1. Recall from high-school trig that the cosine is "adjacent over hypotenuse." We normalized the direction vector, so we know the hypotenuse length is exactly one. Since $cos(\theta)=y$, then $acos(y)=\theta$. If the direction vector points toward the right of the screen, then the rotation angle should be reversed, as illustrated on the right. This is because rotation angles are counterclockwise in our coordinate system.

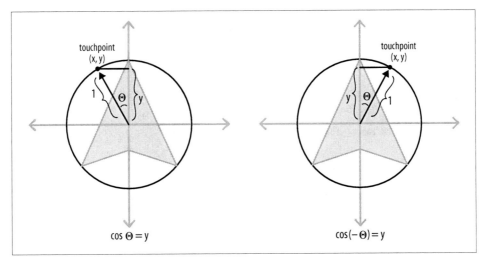

Figure 3-1. Trigonometry in OnFingerMove

Note that `OnFingerMove` flips the y-axis. The pixel-space coordinates that come from `UIView` have the origin at the upper-left corner of the screen, with +Y pointing downward, while OpenGL (and mathematicians) prefer to have the origin at the center, with +Y pointing upward.

That's it! The 1.1 ES version of the Touch Cone app is now functionally complete. If you want to compile and run at this point, don't forget to turn on the `ForceES1` switch at the top of *GLView.mm*.

Let's move on to the ES 2.0 renderer. Open *RenderingEngine2.cpp*, and make the changes shown in bold in Example 3-3. Most of these changes are carried over from our ES 1.1 changes, with some minor differences in the `Render` method.

Example 3-3. RenderingEngine2.cpp in TouchCone

```
class RenderingEngine2 : public IRenderingEngine {
public:
    RenderingEngine2();
    void Initialize(int width, int height);
    void Render() const;
    void UpdateAnimation(float timeStep) {}
    void OnRotate(DeviceOrientation newOrientation) {}
    void OnFingerUp(ivec2 location);
    void OnFingerDown(ivec2 location);
    void OnFingerMove(ivec2 oldLocation, ivec2 newLocation);
private:

    ...

    GLfloat m_rotationAngle;
    GLfloat m_scale;
    ivec2 m_pivotPoint;
};
```

```
RenderingEngine2::RenderingEngine2() : m_rotationAngle(0), m_scale(1)
{
    glGenRenderbuffersOES(1, &m_colorRenderbuffer);
    glBindRenderbufferOES(GL_RENDERBUFFER_OES, m_colorRenderbuffer);
}

void RenderingEngine2::Initialize(int width, int height)
{
    m_pivotPoint = ivec2(width / 2, height / 2);

    ...
}

void RenderingEngine2::Render() const
{
    GLuint positionSlot = glGetAttribLocation(m_simpleProgram,
                                              "Position");
    GLuint colorSlot = glGetAttribLocation(m_simpleProgram,
                                           "SourceColor");

    glClearColor(0.5f, 0.5f, 0.5f, 1);
    glClear(GL_COLOR_BUFFER_BIT | GL_DEPTH_BUFFER_BIT);

    glEnableVertexAttribArray(positionSlot);
    glEnableVertexAttribArray(colorSlot);

    mat4 rotation = mat4::Rotate(m_rotationAngle);
    mat4 scale = mat4::Scale(m_scale);
    mat4 translation = mat4::Translate(0, 0, -7);

    // Set the model-view matrix.
    GLint modelviewUniform = glGetUniformLocation(m_simpleProgram,
                                                  "Modelview");
    mat4 modelviewMatrix = scale * rotation * translation;
    glUniformMatrix4fv(modelviewUniform, 1, 0, modelviewMatrix.Pointer());

    // Draw the cone.
    {
      GLsizei stride = sizeof(Vertex);
      const GLvoid* pCoords = &m_cone[0].Position.x;
      const GLvoid* pColors = &m_cone[0].Color.x;
      glVertexAttribPointer(positionSlot, 3, GL_FLOAT,
                            GL_FALSE, stride, pCoords);
      glVertexAttribPointer(colorSlot, 4, GL_FLOAT,
                            GL_FALSE, stride, pColors);
      glDrawArrays(GL_TRIANGLE_STRIP, 0, m_cone.size());
    }

    // Draw the disk that caps off the base of the cone.
    {
      GLsizei stride = sizeof(Vertex);
      const GLvoid* pCoords = &m_disk[0].Position.x;
      const GLvoid* pColors = &m_disk[0].Color.x;
      glVertexAttribPointer(positionSlot, 3, GL_FLOAT,
```

```
                              GL_FALSE, stride, pCoords);
        glVertexAttribPointer(colorSlot, 4, GL_FLOAT,
                              GL_FALSE, stride, pColors);
        glDrawArrays(GL_TRIANGLE_FAN, 0, m_disk.size());
    }

    glDisableVertexAttribArray(positionSlot);
    glDisableVertexAttribArray(colorSlot);
}

// See Example 3-2 for OnFingerUp, OnFingerDown, and OnFingerMove.
...
```

You can now turn off the ForceES1 switch in *GLView.mm* and build and run TouchCone on any Apple device. In the following sections, we'll continue making improvements to the app, focusing on how to efficiently describe the cone geometry.

Saving Memory with Vertex Indexing

So far we've been using the glDrawArrays function for all our rendering. OpenGL ES offers another way of kicking off a sequence of triangles (or lines or points) through the use of the glDrawElements function. It has much the same effect as glDrawArrays, but instead of simply plowing forward through the vertex list, it first reads a list of indices from an *index buffer* and then uses those indices to choose vertices from the vertex buffer.

To help explain indexing and how it's useful, let's go back to the simple "square from two triangles" example from the previous chapter (Figure 2-3). Here's one way of rendering the square with glDrawArrays:

```
vec2 vertices[6] = { vec2(0, 0), vec2(0, 1), vec2(1, 1),
                     vec2(1, 1), vec2(1, 0), vec2(0, 0) };
glVertexPointer(2, GL_FLOAT, sizeof(vec2), (void*) vertices);
glDrawArrays(GL_TRIANGLES, 0, 6);
```

Note that two vertices—(0, 0) and (1, 1)—appear twice in the vertex list. Vertex indexing can eliminate this redundancy. Here's how:

```
vec2 vertices[4] = { vec2(0, 0), vec2(0, 1), vec2(1, 1), vec2(1, 0) };
GLubyte indices[6] = { 0, 1, 2, 2, 3, 0};
glVertexPointer(2, GL_FLOAT, sizeof(vec2), vertices);
glDrawElements(GL_TRIANGLES, 6, GL_UNSIGNED_BYTE, (void*) indices);
```

So, instead of sending 6 vertices to OpenGL (8 bytes per vertex), we're now sending 4 vertices plus 6 indices (one byte per index). That's a total of 48 bytes with glDrawArrays and 38 bytes with glDrawIndices.

You might be thinking "But I can just use a triangle strip with glDrawArrays and save just as much memory!" That's true in this case. In fact, a triangle strip is the best way to draw our lonely little square:

```
vec2 vertices[6] = { vec2(0, 0), vec2(0, 1), vec2(1, 0), vec2(1, 1) };
glVertexPointer(2, GL_FLOAT, sizeof(vec2), (void*) vertices);
glDrawArrays(GL_TRIANGLE_STRIP, 0, 4);
```

That's only 48 bytes, and adding an index buffer would buy us nothing.

However, more complex geometry (such as our cone model) usually involves even more repetition of vertices, so an index buffer offers much better savings. Moreover, GL_TRIANGLE_STRIP is great in certain cases, but in general it isn't as versatile as GL_TRIANGLES. With GL_TRIANGLES, a single draw call can be used to render multiple disjoint pieces of geometry. To achieve best performance with OpenGL, execute as few draw calls per frame as possible.

Let's walk through the process of updating Touch Cone to use indexing. Take a look at these two lines in the class declaration of RenderingEngine1:

```
vector<Vertex> m_cone;
vector<Vertex> m_disk;
```

Indexing allows you to combine these two arrays, but it also requires a new array for holding the indices. OpenGL ES supports two types of indices: GLushort (16 bit) and GLubyte (8 bit). In this case, there are fewer than 256 vertices, so you can use GLubyte for best efficiency. Replace those two lines with the following:

```
vector<Vertex> m_coneVertices;
vector<GLubyte> m_coneIndices;
GLuint m_bodyIndexCount;
GLuint m_diskIndexCount;
```

Since the index buffer is partitioned into two parts (body and disk), we also added some counts that will get passed to glDrawElements, as you'll see later.

Next you need to update the code that generates the geometry. With indexing, the number of required vertices for our cone shape is $n*2+1$, where n is the number of slices. There are n vertices at the apex, another n vertices at the rim, and one vertex for the center of the base. Example 3-4 shows how to generate the vertices. This code goes inside the Initialize method of the rendering engine class; before you insert it, delete everything between m_pivotPoint = ivec2(width / 2, height / 2); and // Create the depth buffer.

Example 3-4. Vertex generation

```
const float coneRadius = 0.5f;
const float coneHeight = 1.866f;
const int coneSlices = 40;
const float dtheta = TwoPi / coneSlices;
const int vertexCount = coneSlices * 2 + 1;

m_coneVertices.resize(vertexCount);
vector<Vertex>::iterator vertex = m_coneVertices.begin();

// Cone's body
for (float theta = 0; vertex != m_coneVertices.end() - 1; theta += dtheta) {
```

```
// Grayscale gradient
float brightness = abs(sin(theta));
vec4 color(brightness, brightness, brightness, 1);

// Apex vertex
vertex->Position = vec3(0, 1, 0);
vertex->Color = color;
vertex++;

// Rim vertex
vertex->Position.x = coneRadius * cos(theta);
vertex->Position.y = 1 - coneHeight;
vertex->Position.z = coneRadius * sin(theta);
vertex->Color = color;
vertex++;
}

// Disk center
vertex->Position = vec3(0, 1 - coneHeight, 0);
vertex->Color = vec4(1, 1, 1, 1);
```

In addition to the vertices, you need to store indices for *2n* triangles, which requires a total of *6n* indices.

Figure 3-2 uses exploded views to show the tessellation of a cone with *n = 10*. The image on the left depicts the ordering of the vertex buffer; the image on the right depicts the ordering of the index buffer. Note that each vertex at the rim is shared between four different triangles; that's the power of indexing! Remember, the vertices at the apex cannot be shared because each of those vertices requires a unique color attribute, as discussed in the previous chapter (see Figure 2-17).

Example 3-5 shows the code for generating indices (again, this code lives in our `Initialize` method). Note the usage of the modulo operator to wrap the indices back to the start of the array.

Example 3-5. Index generation

```
m_bodyIndexCount = coneSlices * 3;
m_diskIndexCount = coneSlices * 3;

m_coneIndices.resize(m_bodyIndexCount + m_diskIndexCount);
vector<GLubyte>::iterator index = m_coneIndices.begin();

// Body triangles
for (int i = 0; i < coneSlices * 2; i += 2) {
    *index++ = i;
    *index++ = (i + 1) % (2 * coneSlices);
    *index++ = (i + 3) % (2 * coneSlices);
}

// Disk triangles
const int diskCenterIndex = vertexCount - 1;
for (int i = 1; i < coneSlices * 2 + 1; i += 2) {
```

```
        *index++ = diskCenterIndex;
        *index++ = i;
        *index++ = (i + 2) % (2 * coneSlices);
}
```

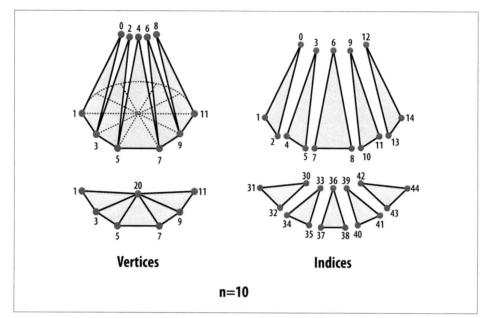

Figure 3-2. Indexed cone tessellation with GL_TRIANGLES

Now it's time to enter the new Render() method, shown in Example 3-6. Take a close look at the core of the rendering calls (in bold). Recall that the body of the cone has a grayscale gradient, but the cap is solid white. The draw call that renders the body should heed the color values specified in the vertex array, but the draw call for the disk should not. So, between the two calls to glDrawElements, the GL_COLOR_ARRAY attribute is turned off with glDisableClientState, and the color is explicitly set with glColor4f. Replace the definition of Render() in its entirety with the code in Example 3-6.

Example 3-6. RenderingEngine1::Render()

```
void RenderingEngine1::Render() const
{
    GLsizei stride = sizeof(Vertex);
    const GLvoid* pCoords = &m_coneVertices[0].Position.x;
    const GLvoid* pColors = &m_coneVertices[0].Color.x;

    glClearColor(0.5f, 0.5f, 0.5f, 1);
    glClear(GL_COLOR_BUFFER_BIT | GL_DEPTH_BUFFER_BIT);
    glPushMatrix();
    glRotatef(m_rotationAngle, 0, 0, 1);
    glScalef(m_scale, m_scale, m_scale);
    glVertexPointer(3, GL_FLOAT, stride, pCoords);
```

```
    glColorPointer(4, GL_FLOAT, stride,  pColors);
    glEnableClientState(GL_VERTEX_ARRAY);

    const GLvoid* bodyIndices = &m_coneIndices[0];
    const GLvoid* diskIndices = &m_coneIndices[m_bodyIndexCount];

    glEnableClientState(GL_COLOR_ARRAY);
    glDrawElements(GL_TRIANGLES, m_bodyIndexCount, GL_UNSIGNED_BYTE, bodyIndices);
    glDisableClientState(GL_COLOR_ARRAY);
    glColor4f(1, 1, 1, 1);
    glDrawElements(GL_TRIANGLES, m_diskIndexCount, GL_UNSIGNED_BYTE, diskIndices);

    glDisableClientState(GL_VERTEX_ARRAY);
    glPopMatrix();
}
```

You should be able to build and run at this point. Next, modify the ES 2.0 backend by making the same changes we just went over. The only tricky part is the Render method, shown in Example 3-7. From a 30,000-foot view, it basically does the same thing as its ES 1.1 counterpart, but with some extra footwork at the beginning for setting up the transformation state.

Example 3-7. RenderingEngine2::Render()

```
void RenderingEngine2::Render() const
{
    GLuint positionSlot = glGetAttribLocation(m_simpleProgram, "Position");
    GLuint colorSlot = glGetAttribLocation(m_simpleProgram, "SourceColor");

    mat4 rotation = mat4::Rotate(m_rotationAngle);
    mat4 scale = mat4::Scale(m_scale);
    mat4 translation = mat4::Translate(0, 0, -7);
    GLint modelviewUniform = glGetUniformLocation(m_simpleProgram, "Modelview");
    mat4 modelviewMatrix = scale * rotation * translation;

    GLsizei stride = sizeof(Vertex);
    const GLvoid* pCoords = &m_coneVertices[0].Position.x;
    const GLvoid* pColors = &m_coneVertices[0].Color.x;

    glClearColor(0.5f, 0.5f, 0.5f, 1);
    glClear(GL_COLOR_BUFFER_BIT | GL_DEPTH_BUFFER_BIT);
    glUniformMatrix4fv(modelviewUniform, 1, 0, modelviewMatrix.Pointer());
    glVertexAttribPointer(positionSlot, 3, GL_FLOAT, GL_FALSE, stride, pCoords);
    glVertexAttribPointer(colorSlot, 4, GL_FLOAT, GL_FALSE, stride, pColors);
    glEnableVertexAttribArray(positionSlot);

    const GLvoid* bodyIndices = &m_coneIndices[0];
    const GLvoid* diskIndices = &m_coneIndices[m_bodyIndexCount];

    glEnableVertexAttribArray(colorSlot);
    glDrawElements(GL_TRIANGLES, m_bodyIndexCount, GL_UNSIGNED_BYTE, bodyIndices);
    glDisableVertexAttribArray(colorSlot);
    glVertexAttrib4f(colorSlot, 1, 1, 1, 1);
    glDrawElements(GL_TRIANGLES, m_diskIndexCount, GL_UNSIGNED_BYTE, diskIndices);
```

```
    glDisableVertexAttribArray(positionSlot);
}
```

That covers the basics of index buffers; we managed to reduce the memory footprint by about 28% over the nonindexed approach. Optimizations like this don't matter much for silly demo apps like this one, but applying them to real-world apps can make a big difference.

Boosting Performance with Vertex Buffer Objects

OpenGL provides a mechanism called *vertex buffer objects* (often known as VBOs) whereby you give it ownership of a set of vertices (and/or indices), allowing you to free up CPU memory and avoid frequent CPU-to-GPU transfers. Using VBOs is such a highly recommended practice that I considered using them even in the HelloArrow sample. Going forward, all sample code in this book will use VBOs.

Let's walk through the steps required to add VBOs to Touch Cone. First, remove these two lines from the RenderingEngine class declaration:

```
    vector<Vertex> m_coneVertices;
    vector<GLubyte> m_coneIndices;
```

They're no longer needed because the vertex data will be stored in OpenGL memory. You do, however, need to store the handles to the vertex buffer objects. Object handles in OpenGL are of type GLuint. So, add these two lines to the class declaration:

```
    GLuint m_vertexBuffer;
    GLuint m_indexBuffer;
```

The vertex generation code in the Initialize method stays the same except that you should use a temporary variable rather than a class member for storing the vertex list. Specifically, replace this snippet:

```
    m_coneVertices.resize(vertexCount);
    vector<Vertex>::iterator vertex = m_coneVertices.begin();

    // Cone's body
    for (float theta = 0; vertex != m_coneVertices.end() - 1; theta += dtheta) {

    ...

    m_coneIndices.resize(m_bodyIndexCount + m_diskIndexCount);
    vector<GLubyte>::iterator index = m_coneIndices.begin();
```

with this:

```
    vector<Vertex> coneVertices(vertexCount);
    vector<Vertex>::iterator vertex = coneVertices.begin();

    // Cone's body
    for (float theta = 0; vertex != coneVertices.end() - 1; theta += dtheta) {
```

...

```
vector<GLubyte> coneIndices(m_bodyIndexCount + m_diskIndexCount);
vector<GLubyte>::iterator index = coneIndices.begin();
```

Next you need to create the vertex buffer objects and populate them. This is done with some OpenGL function calls that follow the same Gen/Bind pattern that you're already using for framebuffer objects. The Gen/Bind calls for VBOs are shown here (don't add these snippets to the class just yet):

```
void glGenBuffers(GLsizei count, GLuint* handles);
void glBindBuffer(GLenum target, GLuint handle);
```

glGenBuffers generates a list of nonzero handles. count specifies the desired number of handles; handles points to a preallocated list. In this book we often generate only one handle at a time, so be aware that the glGen* functions can also be used to efficiently generate several handles at once.

The glBindBuffer function attaches a VBO to one of two binding points specified with the target parameter. The legal values for target are GL_ELEMENT_ARRAY_BUFFER (used for indices) and GL_ARRAY_BUFFER (used for vertices).

Populating a VBO that's already attached to one of the two binding points is accomplished with this function call:

```
void glBufferData(GLenum target, GLsizeiptr size,
                  const GLvoid* data, GLenum usage);
```

target is the same as it is in glBindBuffer, size is the number of bytes in the VBO (GLsizeiptr is a typedef of int), data points to the source memory, and usage gives a hint to OpenGL about how you intend to use the VBO. The possible values for usage are as follows:

GL_STATIC_DRAW
> This is what we'll commonly use in this book; it tells OpenGL that the buffer never changes.

GL_DYNAMIC_DRAW
> This tells OpenGL that the buffer will be periodically updated using glBufferSub Data.

GL_STREAM_DRAW (ES 2.0 only)
> This tells OpenGL that the buffer will be frequently updated (for example, once per frame) with glBufferSubData.

To modify the contents of an existing VBO, you can use glBufferSubData:

```
void glBufferSubData(GLenum target, GLintptr offset,
                     GLsizeiptr size, const GLvoid* data);
```

The only difference between this and glBufferData is the offset parameter, which specifies a number of bytes from the start of the VBO. Note that glBufferSubData should be used only to update a VBO that has previously been initialized with glBufferData.

We won't be using `glBufferSubData` in any of the samples in this book. Frequent updates with `glBufferSubData` should be avoided for best performance, but in many scenarios it can be very useful.

Getting back to Touch Cone, let's add code to create and populate the VBOs near the end of the `Initialize` method:

```
// Create the VBO for the vertices.
glGenBuffers(1, &m_vertexBuffer);
glBindBuffer(GL_ARRAY_BUFFER, m_vertexBuffer);
glBufferData(GL_ARRAY_BUFFER,
             coneVertices.size() * sizeof(coneVertices[0]),
             &coneVertices[0],
             GL_STATIC_DRAW);

// Create the VBO for the indices.
glGenBuffers(1, &m_indexBuffer);
glBindBuffer(GL_ELEMENT_ARRAY_BUFFER, m_indexBuffer);
glBufferData(GL_ELEMENT_ARRAY_BUFFER,
             coneIndices.size() * sizeof(coneIndices[0]),
             &coneIndices[0],
             GL_STATIC_DRAW);
```

Before showing you how to use VBOs for rendering, let me refresh your memory on the gl*Pointer functions that you've been using in the `Render` method:

```
// ES 1.1
glVertexPointer(3, GL_FLOAT, stride, pCoords);
glColorPointer(4, GL_FLOAT, stride,  pColors);

// ES 2.0
glVertexAttribPointer(positionSlot, 3, GL_FLOAT, GL_FALSE, stride, pCoords);
glVertexAttribPointer(colorSlot, 4, GL_FLOAT, GL_FALSE, stride, pColors);
```

The formal declarations for these functions look like this:

```
// From <OpenGLES/ES1/gl.h>
void glVertexPointer(GLint size, GLenum type, GLsizei stride, const GLvoid* pointer);
void glColorPointer(GLint size, GLenum type, GLsizei stride, const GLvoid* pointer);
void glNormalPointer(GLenum type, GLsizei stride, const GLvoid* pointer);
void glTexCoordPointer(GLint size, GLenum type, GLsizei stride, const GLvoid* pointer);
void glPointSizePointerOES(GLenum type, GLsizei stride, const GLvoid* pointer);

// From <OpenGLES/ES2/gl.h>
void glVertexAttribPointer(GLuint attributeIndex, GLint size, GLenum type,
                           GLboolean normalized, GLsizei stride,
                           const GLvoid* pointer);
```

The `size` parameter in all these functions controls the number of vector components per attribute. (The legal combinations of `size` and `type` were covered in the previous chapter in Table 2-1.) The `stride` parameter is the number of bytes between vertices. The `pointer` parameter is the one to watch out for—when no VBOs are bound (that is, the current VBO binding is zero), it's a pointer to CPU memory; when a VBO is bound to `GL_ARRAY_BUFFER`, it changes meaning and becomes a byte offset rather than a pointer.

The gl*Pointer functions are used to set up vertex attributes, but recall that indices are submitted through the last argument of glDrawElements. Here's the formal declaration of glDrawElements:

```
void glDrawElements(GLenum topology, GLsizei count, GLenum type, GLvoid* indices);
```

indices is another "chameleon" parameter. When a nonzero VBO is bound to GL_ELEMENT_ARRAY_BUFFER, it's a byte offset; otherwise, it's a pointer to CPU memory.

 The shape-shifting aspect of gl*Pointer and glDrawElements is an indicator of how OpenGL has grown organically through the years; if the API were designed from scratch, perhaps these functions wouldn't be so overloaded.

To see glDrawElements and gl*Pointer being used with VBOs in Touch Cone, check out the Render method in Example 3-8.

Example 3-8. RenderingEngine1::Render with vertex buffer objects

```
void RenderingEngine1::Render() const
{
    glClear(GL_COLOR_BUFFER_BIT | GL_DEPTH_BUFFER_BIT);
    glPushMatrix();
    glRotatef(m_rotationAngle, 0, 0, 1);
    glScalef(m_scale, m_scale, m_scale);

    const GLvoid* colorOffset = (GLvoid*) sizeof(vec3);

    glBindBuffer(GL_ELEMENT_ARRAY_BUFFER, m_indexBuffer);
    glBindBuffer(GL_ARRAY_BUFFER, m_vertexBuffer);
    glVertexPointer(3, GL_FLOAT, sizeof(Vertex), 0);
    glColorPointer(4, GL_FLOAT, sizeof(Vertex), colorOffset);
    glEnableClientState(GL_VERTEX_ARRAY);

    const GLvoid* bodyOffset = 0;
    const GLvoid* diskOffset = (GLvoid*) m_bodyIndexCount;

    glEnableClientState(GL_COLOR_ARRAY);
    glDrawElements(GL_TRIANGLES, m_bodyIndexCount, GL_UNSIGNED_BYTE, bodyOffset);
    glDisableClientState(GL_COLOR_ARRAY);
    glColor4f(1, 1, 1, 1);
    glDrawElements(GL_TRIANGLES, m_diskIndexCount, GL_UNSIGNED_BYTE, diskOffset);

    glDisableClientState(GL_VERTEX_ARRAY);
    glPopMatrix();
}
```

Example 3-9 shows the ES 2.0 variant. From 30,000 feet, it basically does the same thing, even though many of the actual OpenGL calls are different.

Example 3-9. RenderingEngine2::Render with vertex buffer objects

```
void RenderingEngine2::Render() const
{
    GLuint positionSlot = glGetAttribLocation(m_simpleProgram, "Position");
    GLuint colorSlot = glGetAttribLocation(m_simpleProgram, "SourceColor");

    mat4 rotation = mat4::Rotate(m_rotationAngle);
    mat4 scale = mat4::Scale(m_scale);
    mat4 translation = mat4::Translate(0, 0, -7);
    GLint modelviewUniform = glGetUniformLocation(m_simpleProgram, "Modelview");
    mat4 modelviewMatrix = scale * rotation * translation;

    GLsizei stride = sizeof(Vertex);
    const GLvoid* colorOffset = (GLvoid*) sizeof(vec3);

    glClear(GL_COLOR_BUFFER_BIT | GL_DEPTH_BUFFER_BIT);
    glUniformMatrix4fv(modelviewUniform, 1, 0, modelviewMatrix.Pointer());

    glBindBuffer(GL_ELEMENT_ARRAY_BUFFER, m_indexBuffer);
    glBindBuffer(GL_ARRAY_BUFFER, m_vertexBuffer);
    glVertexAttribPointer(positionSlot, 3, GL_FLOAT, GL_FALSE, stride, 0);
    glVertexAttribPointer(colorSlot, 4, GL_FLOAT, GL_FALSE, stride, colorOffset);
    glEnableVertexAttribArray(positionSlot);

    const GLvoid* bodyOffset = 0;
    const GLvoid* diskOffset = (GLvoid*) m_bodyIndexCount;

    glEnableVertexAttribArray(colorSlot);
    glDrawElements(GL_TRIANGLES, m_bodyIndexCount, GL_UNSIGNED_BYTE, bodyOffset);
    glDisableVertexAttribArray(colorSlot);
    glVertexAttrib4f(colorSlot, 1, 1, 1, 1);
    glDrawElements(GL_TRIANGLES, m_diskIndexCount, GL_UNSIGNED_BYTE, diskOffset);

    glDisableVertexAttribArray(positionSlot);
}
```

That wraps up the tutorial on VBOs; we've taken the Touch Cone sample as far as we can take it!

Creating a Wireframe Viewer

Let's use vertex buffer objects and the touchscreen to create a fun new app. Instead of relying on triangles like we've been doing so far, we'll use GL_LINES topology to create a simple wireframe viewer, as shown in Figure 3-3. The rotation in Touch Cone was restricted to the plane, but this app will let you spin the geometry around to any orientation; behind the scenes, we'll use quaternions to achieve a trackball-like effect. Additionally, we'll include a row of buttons along the bottom of the screen to allow the user to switch between different shapes. They won't be true buttons in the UIKit sense; remember, for best performance, you should let OpenGL do all the rendering.

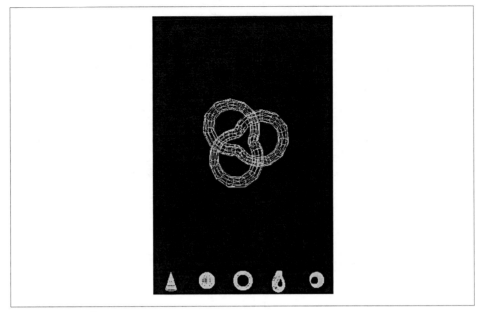

Figure 3-3. Wireframe viewer

This application will provide a good foundation upon which to learn many OpenGL concepts, and we'll continue to evolve it in the coming chapters.

If you're planning on following along with the code, you'll first need to start with the WireframeSkeleton project from this book's example code (available at *http://oreilly .com/catalog/9780596804831*). In the Finder, make a copy of the directory that contains this project, and name the new directory *SimpleWireframe*. Next, open the project (it will still be named WireframeSkeleton), and then choose Project→Rename. Rename it to *SimpleWireframe*.

This skeleton project includes all the building blocks you saw (the vector library from the appendix, the GLView class, and the application delegate). There are a few differences between this and the previous examples, so be sure to look over the classes in the project before you proceed:

1. The application delegate has been renamed to have a very generic name, AppDelegate.
2. The GLView class uses an *application engine* rather than a *rendering engine*. This is because we'll be taking a new approach to how we factor the ES 1.1– and ES 2.0– specific code from the rest of the project; more on this shortly.

Parametric Surfaces for Fun

You might have been put off by all the work required for tessellating the cone shape in the previous samples. It would be painful if you had to figure out a clever tessellation for every shape that pops into your head! Thankfully, most 3D modeling software can export to a format that has post-tessellated content; the popular *.obj* file format is one example of this. Moreover, the cone shape happens to be a mathematically defined shape called a *parametric surface*; all parametric surfaces are relatively easy to tessellate in a generic manner. A parametric surface is defined with a function that takes a 2D vector for input and produces a 3D vector as output. This turns out to be especially convenient because the input vectors can also be used as texture coordinates, as we'll learn in a future chapter.

The input to a parametric function is said to be in its *domain*, while the output is said to be in its *range*. Since all parametric surfaces can be used to generate OpenGL vertices in a consistent manner, it makes sense to create a simple class hierarchy for them. Example 3-10 shows two subclasses: a cone and a sphere. This has been included in the WireframeSkeleton project for your convenience, so there is no need for you to add it here.

Example 3-10. ParametricEquations.hpp

```
#include "ParametricSurface.hpp"

class Cone : public ParametricSurface {
public:
    Cone(float height, float radius) : m_height(height), m_radius(radius)
    {
        ParametricInterval interval = { ivec2(20, 20), vec2(TwoPi, 1) };
        SetInterval(interval);
    }
    vec3 Evaluate(const vec2& domain) const
    {
        float u = domain.x, v = domain.y;
        float x = m_radius * (1 - v) * cos(u);
        float y = m_height * (v - 0.5f);
        float z = m_radius * (1 - v) * -sin(u);
        return vec3(x, y, z);
    }
private:
    float m_height;
    float m_radius;
};

class Sphere : public ParametricSurface {
public:
    Sphere(float radius) : m_radius(radius)
    {
        ParametricInterval interval = { ivec2(20, 20), vec2(Pi, TwoPi) };
        SetInterval(interval);
    }
    vec3 Evaluate(const vec2& domain) const
```

```
    {
        float u = domain.x, v = domain.y;
        float x = m_radius * sin(u) * cos(v);
        float y = m_radius * cos(u);
        float z = m_radius * -sin(u) * sin(v);
        return vec3(x, y, z);
    }
private:
    float m_radius;
};

// ...
```

The classes in Example 3-10 request their desired tessellation granularity and domain bound by calling `SetInterval` from their constructors. More importantly, these classes implement the pure virtual `Evaluate` method, which simply applies Equation 3-1 or 3-2.

Equation 3-1. Cone parameterization

$$x = r(1 - v)\cos u$$
$$y = h(v - \tfrac{1}{2})$$
$$z = r(1 - v) -\sin u$$

$$0 \le u < 2\pi$$
$$0 \le v \le 1$$

Equation 3-2. Sphere parameterization

$$x = r \sin u \cos v$$
$$y = r \cos u$$
$$z = r\text{-}\sin u \cos v$$

$$0 \le u < \pi$$
$$0 \le v \le 2\pi$$

Each of the previous equations is only one of several possible parameterizations for their respective shapes. For example, the z equation for the sphere could be negated, and it would still describe a sphere.

In addition to the cone and sphere, the wireframe viewer allows the user to see four other interesting parametric surfaces: a torus, a knot, a Möbius strip,[*] and a Klein bottle (see Figure 3-4). I've already shown you the classes for the sphere and cone; you can find code for the other shapes at this book's website. They basically do nothing more than evaluate various well-known parametric equations. Perhaps more interesting is their common base class, shown in Example 3-11. To add this file to Xcode, right-click the *Classes* folder, choose Add→New file, select *C and C++*, and choose Header File. Call it *ParametricSurface.hpp*, and replace everything in it with the code shown here.

---

[*] True Möbius strips are one-sided surfaces and can cause complications with the lighting algorithms presented in the next chapter. The wireframe viewer actually renders a somewhat flattened Möbius "tube."

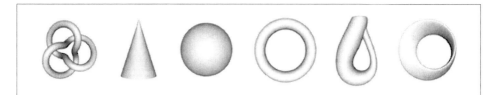

Figure 3-4. Parametric gallery

Example 3-11. ParametricSurface.hpp

```
#include "Interfaces.hpp"

struct ParametricInterval {
    ivec2 Divisions;❶
    vec2 UpperBound;❷
};

class ParametricSurface : public ISurface {
public:
    int GetVertexCount() const;
    int GetLineIndexCount() const;
    void GenerateVertices(vector<float>& vertices) const;
    void GenerateLineIndices(vector<unsigned short>& indices) const;
protected:
    void SetInterval(const ParametricInterval& interval);❸
    virtual vec3 Evaluate(const vec2& domain) const = 0;❹
private:
    vec2 ComputeDomain(float i, float j) const;
    vec2 m_upperBound;
    ivec2 m_slices;
    ivec2 m_divisions;
};
```

I'll explain the ISurface interface later; first let's take a look at various elements that are controlled by subclasses:

❶ The number of divisions that the surface is sliced into. The higher the number, the more lines, and the greater the level of detail. Note that it's an ivec2; in some cases (like the knot shape), it's desirable to have more slices along one axis than the other.

❷ The domain's upper bound. The lower bound is always (0, 0).

❸ Called from the subclass to describe the domain interval.

❹ Abstract method for evaluating the parametric equation.

Example 3-12 shows the implementation of the ParametricSurface class. Add a new C++ file to your Xcode project called *ParametricSurface.cpp* (but deselect the option to create the associated header file). Replace everything in it with the code shown.

Example 3-12. ParametricSurface.cpp

```cpp
#include "ParametricSurface.hpp"

void ParametricSurface::SetInterval(const ParametricInterval& interval)
{
    m_upperBound = interval.UpperBound;
    m_divisions = interval.Divisions;
    m_slices = m_divisions - ivec2(1, 1);
}

int ParametricSurface::GetVertexCount() const
{
    return m_divisions.x * m_divisions.y;
}

int ParametricSurface::GetLineIndexCount() const
{
    return 4 * m_slices.x * m_slices.y;
}

vec2 ParametricSurface::ComputeDomain(float x, float y) const
{
    return vec2(x * m_upperBound.x / m_slices.x,
                y * m_upperBound.y / m_slices.y);
}

void ParametricSurface::GenerateVertices(vector<float>& vertices) const
{
    vertices.resize(GetVertexCount() * 3);
    vec3* position = (vec3*) &vertices[0];
    for (int j = 0; j < m_divisions.y; j++) {
        for (int i = 0; i < m_divisions.x; i++) {
            vec2 domain = ComputeDomain(i, j);
            vec3 range = Evaluate(domain);
            *position++ = range;
        }
    }
}

void ParametricSurface::GenerateLineIndices(vector<unsigned short>& indices) const
{
    indices.resize(GetLineIndexCount());
    vector<unsigned short>::iterator index = indices.begin();
    for (int j = 0, vertex = 0; j < m_slices.y; j++) {
        for (int i = 0; i < m_slices.x; i++) {
            int next = (i + 1) % m_divisions.x;
            *index++ = vertex + i;
            *index++ = vertex + next;
            *index++ = vertex + i;
            *index++ = vertex + i + m_divisions.x;
        }
        vertex += m_divisions.x;
    }
}
```

The GenerateLineIndices method deserves a bit of an explanation. Picture a globe of the earth and how it has lines for latitude and longitude. The first two indices in the loop correspond to a latitudinal line segment; the latter two correspond to a longitudinal line segment (see Figure 3-5). Also note some sneaky usage of the modulo operator for wrapping back to zero when closing a loop.

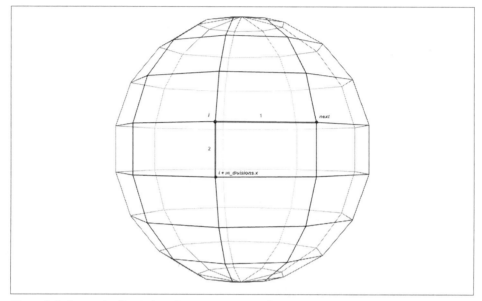

Figure 3-5. Generating line indices for a parametric surface

Designing the Interfaces

In the HelloCone and HelloArrow samples, you might have noticed some duplication of logic between the ES 1.1 and ES 2.0 backends. With the wireframe viewer sample, we're raising the bar on complexity, so we'll avoid duplicated code by introducing a new C++ component called ApplicationEngine (this was mentioned in Chapter 1; see Figure 1-5). The application engine will contain all the logic that isn't coupled to a particular graphics API.

Example 3-13 shows the contents of Interfaces.hpp, which defines three component interfaces and some related types. Add a new C and C++ header file to your Xcode project called *Interfaces.hpp*. Replace everything in it with the code shown.

Example 3-13. Interfaces.hpp

```
#pragma once
#include "Vector.hpp"
#include "Quaternion.hpp"
#include <vector>
```

```
using std::vector;

struct IApplicationEngine {❶
    virtual void Initialize(int width, int height) = 0;
    virtual void Render() const = 0;
    virtual void UpdateAnimation(float timeStep) = 0;
    virtual void OnFingerUp(ivec2 location) = 0;
    virtual void OnFingerDown(ivec2 location) = 0;
    virtual void OnFingerMove(ivec2 oldLocation, ivec2 newLocation) = 0;
    virtual ~IApplicationEngine() {}
};

struct ISurface {❷
    virtual int GetVertexCount() const = 0;
    virtual int GetLineIndexCount() const = 0;
    virtual void GenerateVertices(vector<float>& vertices) const = 0;
    virtual void GenerateLineIndices(vector<unsigned short>& indices) const = 0;
    virtual ~ISurface() {}
};

struct Visual {❸
    vec3 Color;
    ivec2 LowerLeft;
    ivec2 ViewportSize;
    Quaternion Orientation;
};

struct IRenderingEngine {❹
    virtual void Initialize(const vector<ISurface*>& surfaces) = 0;
    virtual void Render(const vector<Visual>& visuals) const = 0;
    virtual ~IRenderingEngine() {}
};

IApplicationEngine* CreateApplicationEngine(IRenderingEngine* renderingEngine);❺
namespace ES1 { IRenderingEngine* CreateRenderingEngine(); }❻
namespace ES2 { IRenderingEngine* CreateRenderingEngine(); }
```

❶ Consumed by GLView; contains logic common to both rendering backends.

❷ Consumed by the rendering engines when they generate VBOs for the parametric surfaces.

❸ Describes the dynamic visual properties of a surface; gets passed from the application engine to the rendering engine at every frame.

❹ Common abstraction of the two OpenGL ES backends.

❺ Factory method for the application engine; the caller determines OpenGL capabilities and passes in the appropriate rendering engine.

❻ Namespace-qualified factory methods for the two rendering engines.

In an effort to move as much logic into the application engine as possible, IRenderingEngine has only two methods: Initialize and Render. We'll describe them in detail later.

Handling Trackball Rotation

To ensure high portability of the application logic, we avoid making any OpenGL calls whatsoever from within the `ApplicationEngine` class. Example 3-14 is the complete listing of its initial implementation. Add a new C++ file to your Xcode project called *ApplicationEngine.cpp* (deselect the option to create the associated *.h* file). Replace everything in it with the code shown.

Example 3-14. ApplicationEngine.cpp

```
#include "Interfaces.hpp"
#include "ParametricEquations.hpp"

using namespace std;

static const int SurfaceCount = 6;

class ApplicationEngine : public IApplicationEngine {
public:
    ApplicationEngine(IRenderingEngine* renderingEngine);
    ~ApplicationEngine();
    void Initialize(int width, int height);
    void OnFingerUp(ivec2 location);
    void OnFingerDown(ivec2 location);
    void OnFingerMove(ivec2 oldLocation, ivec2 newLocation);
    void Render() const;
    void UpdateAnimation(float dt);
private:
    vec3 MapToSphere(ivec2 touchpoint) const;
    float m_trackballRadius;
    ivec2 m_screenSize;
    ivec2 m_centerPoint;
    ivec2 m_fingerStart;
    bool m_spinning;
    Quaternion m_orientation;
    Quaternion m_previousOrientation;
    IRenderingEngine* m_renderingEngine;
};

IApplicationEngine* CreateApplicationEngine(IRenderingEngine* renderingEngine)
{
    return new ApplicationEngine(renderingEngine);
}

ApplicationEngine::ApplicationEngine(IRenderingEngine* renderingEngine) :
    m_spinning(false),
    m_renderingEngine(renderingEngine)
{
}

ApplicationEngine::~ApplicationEngine()
{
    delete m_renderingEngine;
}
```

```
void ApplicationEngine::Initialize(int width, int height)
{
    m_trackballRadius = width / 3;
    m_screenSize = ivec2(width, height);
    m_centerPoint = m_screenSize / 2;

    vector<ISurface*> surfaces(SurfaceCount);
    surfaces[0] = new Cone(3, 1);
    surfaces[1] = new Sphere(1.4f);
    surfaces[2] = new Torus(1.4, 0.3);
    surfaces[3] = new TrefoilKnot(1.8f);
    surfaces[4] = new KleinBottle(0.2f);
    surfaces[5] = new MobiusStrip(1);
    m_renderingEngine->Initialize(surfaces);
    for (int i = 0; i < SurfaceCount; i++)
        delete surfaces[i];
}

void ApplicationEngine::Render() const
{
    Visual visual;
    visual.Color = m_spinning ? vec3(1, 1, 1) : vec3(0, 1, 1);
    visual.LowerLeft = ivec2(0, 48);
    visual.ViewportSize = ivec2(320, 432);
    visual.Orientation = m_orientation;
    m_renderingEngine->Render(&visual);
}

void ApplicationEngine::UpdateAnimation(float dt)
{
}

void ApplicationEngine::OnFingerUp(ivec2 location)
{
    m_spinning = false;
}

void ApplicationEngine::OnFingerDown(ivec2 location)
{
    m_fingerStart = location;
    m_previousOrientation = m_orientation;
    m_spinning = true;
}

void ApplicationEngine::OnFingerMove(ivec2 oldLocation, ivec2 location)
{
    if (m_spinning) {
        vec3 start = MapToSphere(m_fingerStart);
        vec3 end = MapToSphere(location);
        Quaternion delta = Quaternion::CreateFromVectors(start, end);
        m_orientation = delta.Rotated(m_previousOrientation);
    }
}
```

```
vec3 ApplicationEngine::MapToSphere(ivec2 touchpoint) const
{
    vec2 p = touchpoint - m_centerPoint;

    // Flip the y-axis because pixel coords increase toward the bottom.
    p.y = -p.y;

    const float radius = m_trackballRadius;
    const float safeRadius = radius - 1;

    if (p.Length() > safeRadius) {
        float theta = atan2(p.y, p.x);
        p.x = safeRadius * cos(theta);
        p.y = safeRadius * sin(theta);
    }

    float z = sqrt(radius * radius - p.LengthSquared());
    vec3 mapped = vec3(p.x, p.y, z);
    return mapped / radius;
}
```

The bulk of Example 3-14 is dedicated to handling the trackball-like behavior with quaternions. I find the `CreateFromVectors` method to be the most natural way of constructing a quaternion. Recall that it takes two unit vectors at the origin and computes the quaternion that moves the first vector onto the second. To achieve a trackball effect, these two vectors are generated by projecting touch points onto the surface of the virtual trackball (see the `MapToSphere` method). Note that if a touch point is outside the circumference of the trackball (or directly on it), then `MapToSphere` snaps the touch point to just inside the circumference. This allows the user to perform a constrained rotation around the z-axis by sliding his finger horizontally or vertically near the edge of the screen.

Implementing the Rendering Engine

So far we've managed to exhibit most of the wireframe viewer code without any OpenGL whatsoever! It's time to remedy that by showing the ES 1.1 backend class in Example 3-15. Add a new C++ file to your Xcode project called *RenderingEngine.ES1.cpp* (deselect the option to create the associated *.h* file). Replace everything in it with the code shown. You can download the ES 2.0 version from this book's com panion website (and it is included with the skeleton project mentioned early in this section).

Example 3-15. RenderingEngine.ES1.cpp

```
#include <OpenGLES/ES1/gl.h>
#include <OpenGLES/ES1/glext.h>
#include "Interfaces.hpp"
#include "Matrix.hpp"

namespace ES1 {
```

```
struct Drawable {
    GLuint VertexBuffer;
    GLuint IndexBuffer;
    int IndexCount;
};

class RenderingEngine : public IRenderingEngine {
public:
    RenderingEngine();
    void Initialize(const vector<ISurface*>& surfaces);
    void Render(const vector<Visual>& visuals) const;
private:
    vector<Drawable> m_drawables;
    GLuint m_colorRenderbuffer;
    mat4 m_translation;
};

IRenderingEngine* CreateRenderingEngine()
{
    return new RenderingEngine();
}

RenderingEngine::RenderingEngine()
{
    glGenRenderbuffersOES(1, &m_colorRenderbuffer);
    glBindRenderbufferOES(GL_RENDERBUFFER_OES, m_colorRenderbuffer);
}

void RenderingEngine::Initialize(const vector<ISurface*>& surfaces)
{
    vector<ISurface*>::const_iterator surface;
    for (surface = surfaces.begin();
         surface != surfaces.end(); ++surface) {

        // Create the VBO for the vertices.
        vector<float> vertices;
        (*surface)->GenerateVertices(vertices);
        GLuint vertexBuffer;
        glGenBuffers(1, &vertexBuffer);
        glBindBuffer(GL_ARRAY_BUFFER, vertexBuffer);
        glBufferData(GL_ARRAY_BUFFER,
                     vertices.size() * sizeof(vertices[0]),
                     &vertices[0],
                     GL_STATIC_DRAW);

        // Create a new VBO for the indices if needed.
        int indexCount = (*surface)->GetLineIndexCount();
        GLuint indexBuffer;
        if (!m_drawables.empty() &&
            indexCount == m_drawables[0].IndexCount) {
            indexBuffer = m_drawables[0].IndexBuffer;
        } else {
            vector<GLushort> indices(indexCount);
```

```
            (*surface)->GenerateLineIndices(indices);
            glGenBuffers(1, &indexBuffer);
            glBindBuffer(GL_ELEMENT_ARRAY_BUFFER, indexBuffer);
            glBufferData(GL_ELEMENT_ARRAY_BUFFER,
                         indexCount * sizeof(GLushort),
                         &indices[0],
                         GL_STATIC_DRAW);
        }

        Drawable drawable = { vertexBuffer, indexBuffer, indexCount};
        m_drawables.push_back(drawable);
    }

    // Create the framebuffer object.
    GLuint framebuffer;
    glGenFramebuffersOES(1, &framebuffer);
    glBindFramebufferOES(GL_FRAMEBUFFER_OES, framebuffer);
    glFramebufferRenderbufferOES(GL_FRAMEBUFFER_OES,
                                 GL_COLOR_ATTACHMENT0_OES,
                                 GL_RENDERBUFFER_OES,
                                 m_colorRenderbuffer);
    glBindRenderbufferOES(GL_RENDERBUFFER_OES, m_colorRenderbuffer);

    glEnableClientState(GL_VERTEX_ARRAY);
    m_translation = mat4::Translate(0, 0, -7);
}

void RenderingEngine::Render(const vector<Visual>& visuals) const
{
    glClear(GL_COLOR_BUFFER_BIT);

    vector<Visual>::const_iterator visual = visuals.begin();
    for (int visualIndex = 0;
         visual != visuals.end();
         ++visual, ++visualIndex)
    {
        // Set the viewport transform.
        ivec2 size = visual->ViewportSize;
        ivec2 lowerLeft = visual->LowerLeft;
        glViewport(lowerLeft.x, lowerLeft.y, size.x, size.y);

        // Set the model-view transform.
        mat4 rotation = visual->Orientation.ToMatrix();
        mat4 modelview = rotation * m_translation;
        glMatrixMode(GL_MODELVIEW);
        glLoadMatrixf(modelview.Pointer());

        // Set the projection transform.
        float h = 4.0f * size.y / size.x;
        mat4 projection = mat4::Frustum(-2, 2, -h / 2, h / 2, 5, 10);
        glMatrixMode(GL_PROJECTION);
        glLoadMatrixf(projection.Pointer());

        // Set the color.
        vec3 color = visual->Color;
```

```
        glColor4f(color.x, color.y, color.z, 1);

        // Draw the wireframe.
        int stride = sizeof(vec3);
        const Drawable& drawable = m_drawables[visualIndex];
        glBindBuffer(GL_ARRAY_BUFFER, drawable.VertexBuffer);
        glVertexPointer(3, GL_FLOAT, stride, 0);
        glBindBuffer(GL_ELEMENT_ARRAY_BUFFER, drawable.IndexBuffer);
        glDrawElements(GL_LINES, drawable.IndexCount, GL_UNSIGNED_SHORT, 0);
    }
}

}
```

There are no new OpenGL concepts here; you should be able to follow the code in Example 3-15. We now have all the big pieces in place for the wireframe viewer. At this point, it shows only a single wireframe; this is improved in the coming sections.

Poor Man's Tab Bar

Apple provides the UITabBar widget as part of the UIKit framework. This is the familiar list of gray icons that many applications have along the bottom of the screen, as shown in Figure 3-6.

Figure 3-6. UITabBar

Since UIKit widgets are outside the scope of this book, you'll be using OpenGL to create a poor man's tab bar for switching between the various parametric surfaces, as in Figure 3-7.

Figure 3-7. Poor man's tab bar

In many situations like this, a standard UITabBar is preferable since it creates a more consistent look with other iPhone applications. But in our case, we'll create a fun transition effect: pushing a button will cause it to "slide out" of the tab bar and into the main viewport. For this level of control over rendering, UIKit doesn't suffice.

The wireframe viewer has a total of six parametric surfaces, but the button bar has only five. When the user touches a button, we'll swap its contents with the surface being displayed in the main viewport. This allows the application to support six surfaces with only five buttons.

The state for the five buttons and the button-detection code lives in the application engine. New lines in the class declaration from *ApplicationEngine.cpp* are shown in bold in Example 3-16. No modifications to the two rendering engines are required.

Example 3-16. ApplicationEngine declaration with tab bar

```
#include "Interfaces.hpp"
#include "ParametricEquations.hpp"
#include <algorithm>

using namespace std;

static const int SurfaceCount = 6;
static const int ButtonCount = SurfaceCount - 1;

class ApplicationEngine : public IApplicationEngine {
public:
    ApplicationEngine(IRenderingEngine* renderingEngine);
    ~ApplicationEngine();
    void Initialize(int width, int height);
    void OnFingerUp(ivec2 location);
    void OnFingerDown(ivec2 location);
    void OnFingerMove(ivec2 oldLocation, ivec2 newLocation);
    void Render() const;
    void UpdateAnimation(float dt);
private:
    void PopulateVisuals(Visual* visuals) const;
    int MapToButton(ivec2 touchpoint) const;
    vec3 MapToSphere(ivec2 touchpoint) const;
    float m_trackballRadius;
    ivec2 m_screenSize;
    ivec2 m_centerPoint;
    ivec2 m_fingerStart;
    bool m_spinning;
    Quaternion m_orientation;
    Quaternion m_previousOrientation;
    IRenderingEngine* m_renderingEngine;
    int m_currentSurface;
    ivec2 m_buttonSize;
    int m_pressedButton;
    int m_buttonSurfaces[ButtonCount];
};
```

Example 3-17 shows the implementation. Methods left unchanged (such as MapToSphere) are omitted for brevity. You'll be replacing the following methods: ApplicationEngine::ApplicationEngine, Initialize, Render, OnFingerUp, OnFinger Down, and OnFingerMove. There are two new methods you'll be adding: ApplicationEn gine::PopulateVisuals and MapToButton.

Example 3-17. ApplicationEngine implementation with tab bar

```
ApplicationEngine::ApplicationEngine(IRenderingEngine* renderingEngine) :
    m_spinning(false),
    m_renderingEngine(renderingEngine),
    m_pressedButton(-1)
{
    m_buttonSurfaces[0] = 0;
    m_buttonSurfaces[1] = 1;
    m_buttonSurfaces[2] = 2;
    m_buttonSurfaces[3] = 4;
    m_buttonSurfaces[4] = 5;
    m_currentSurface = 3;
}

void ApplicationEngine::Initialize(int width, int height)
{
    m_trackballRadius = width / 3;
    m_buttonSize.y = height / 10;
    m_buttonSize.x = 4 * m_buttonSize.y / 3;
    m_screenSize = ivec2(width, height - m_buttonSize.y);
    m_centerPoint = m_screenSize / 2;

    vector<ISurface*> surfaces(SurfaceCount);
    surfaces[0] = new Cone(3, 1);
    surfaces[1] = new Sphere(1.4f);
    surfaces[2] = new Torus(1.4f, 0.3f);
    surfaces[3] = new TrefoilKnot(1.8f);
    surfaces[4] = new KleinBottle(0.2f);
    surfaces[5] = new MobiusStrip(1);
    m_renderingEngine->Initialize(surfaces);
    for (int i = 0; i < SurfaceCount; i++)
        delete surfaces[i];
}


void ApplicationEngine::PopulateVisuals(Visual* visuals) const
{
    for (int buttonIndex = 0; buttonIndex < ButtonCount; buttonIndex++) {
        int visualIndex = m_buttonSurfaces[buttonIndex];
        visuals[visualIndex].Color = vec3(0.75f, 0.75f, 0.75f);
        if (m_pressedButton == buttonIndex)
            visuals[visualIndex].Color = vec3(1, 1, 1);

        visuals[visualIndex].ViewportSize = m_buttonSize;
        visuals[visualIndex].LowerLeft.x = buttonIndex * m_buttonSize.x;
        visuals[visualIndex].LowerLeft.y = 0;
        visuals[visualIndex].Orientation = Quaternion();
    }

    visuals[m_currentSurface].Color = m_spinning ? vec3(1, 1, 1) : vec3(0, 1, 1);
    visuals[m_currentSurface].LowerLeft = ivec2(0, 48);
    visuals[m_currentSurface].ViewportSize = ivec2(320, 432);
    visuals[m_currentSurface].Orientation = m_orientation;
}
```

```
void ApplicationEngine::Render() const
{
    vector<Visual> visuals(SurfaceCount);
    PopulateVisuals(&visuals[0]);
    m_renderingEngine->Render(visuals);
}

void ApplicationEngine::OnFingerUp(ivec2 location)
{
    m_spinning = false;

    if (m_pressedButton != -1 && m_pressedButton == MapToButton(location))
        swap(m_buttonSurfaces[m_pressedButton], m_currentSurface);

    m_pressedButton = -1;
}

void ApplicationEngine::OnFingerDown(ivec2 location)
{
    m_fingerStart = location;
    m_previousOrientation = m_orientation;
    m_pressedButton = MapToButton(location);
    if (m_pressedButton == -1)
        m_spinning = true;
}

void ApplicationEngine::OnFingerMove(ivec2 oldLocation, ivec2 location)
{
    if (m_spinning) {
        vec3 start = MapToSphere(m_fingerStart);
        vec3 end = MapToSphere(location);
        Quaternion delta = Quaternion::CreateFromVectors(start, end);
        m_orientation = delta.Rotated(m_previousOrientation);
    }

    if (m_pressedButton != -1 && m_pressedButton != MapToButton(location))
        m_pressedButton = -1;
}

int ApplicationEngine::MapToButton(ivec2 touchpoint) const
{
    if (touchpoint.y < m_screenSize.y - m_buttonSize.y)
        return -1;

    int buttonIndex = touchpoint.x / m_buttonSize.x;
    if (buttonIndex >= ButtonCount)
        return -1;

    return buttonIndex;
}
```

Go ahead and try it—at this point, the wireframe viewer is starting to feel like a real application!

Animating the Transition

The button-swapping strategy is clever but possibly jarring to users; after playing with the app for a while, the user might start to notice that his tab bar is slowly being re-arranged. To make the swap effect more obvious and to give the app more of a fun Apple feel, let's create a transition animation that actually shows the button being swapped with the main viewport. Figure 3-8 depicts this animation.

Figure 3-8. Transition animation in wireframe viewer

Again, no changes to the two rendering engines are required, because all the logic can be constrained to `ApplicationEngine`. In addition to animating the viewport, we'll also animate the color (the tab bar wireframes are drab gray) and the orientation (the tab bar wireframes are all in the "home" position). We can reuse the existing `Visual` class for this; we need two sets of `Visual` objects for the start and end of the animation. While the animation is active, we'll tween the values between the starting and ending visuals. Let's also create an `Animation` structure to bundle the visuals with a few other animation parameters, as shown in bold in Example 3-18.

Example 3-18. ApplicationEngine declaration with transition animation

```
struct Animation {
    bool Active;
    float Elapsed;
    float Duration;
    Visual StartingVisuals[SurfaceCount];
    Visual EndingVisuals[SurfaceCount];
};

class ApplicationEngine : public IApplicationEngine {
public:
    // ...
private:
    // ...
    Animation m_animation;
};
```

Example 3-19 shows the new implementation of `ApplicationEngine`. Unchanged methods are omitted for brevity. Remember, animation is all about interpolation! The `Render` method leverages the `Lerp` and `Slerp` methods from our vector class library to achieve the animation in a surprisingly straightforward manner.

Example 3-19. ApplicationEngine implementation with transition animation

```
ApplicationEngine::ApplicationEngine(IRenderingEngine* renderingEngine) :
    m_spinning(false),
    m_renderingEngine(renderingEngine),
    m_pressedButton(-1)
{
    m_animation.Active = false;

    // Same as in Example 3-17
    ....
}

void ApplicationEngine::Render() const
{
    vector<Visual> visuals(SurfaceCount);

    if (!m_animation.Active) {
        PopulateVisuals(&visuals[0]);
    } else {
        float t = m_animation.Elapsed / m_animation.Duration;
        for (int i = 0; i < SurfaceCount; i++) {
            const Visual& start = m_animation.StartingVisuals[i];
            const Visual& end = m_animation.EndingVisuals[i];
            Visual& tweened = visuals[i];

            tweened.Color = start.Color.Lerp(t, end.Color);
            tweened.LowerLeft = start.LowerLeft.Lerp(t, end.LowerLeft);
            tweened.ViewportSize = start.ViewportSize.Lerp(t, end.ViewportSize);
            tweened.Orientation = start.Orientation.Slerp(t, end.Orientation);
        }
    }

    m_renderingEngine->Render(visuals);
}

void ApplicationEngine::UpdateAnimation(float dt)
{
    if (m_animation.Active) {
        m_animation.Elapsed += dt;
        if (m_animation.Elapsed > m_animation.Duration)
            m_animation.Active = false;
    }
}

void ApplicationEngine::OnFingerUp(ivec2 location)
{
    m_spinning = false;

    if (m_pressedButton != -1 && m_pressedButton == MapToButton(location) &&
        !m_animation.Active)
    {
        m_animation.Active = true;
        m_animation.Elapsed = 0;
        m_animation.Duration = 0.25f;
```

```
            PopulateVisuals(&m_animation.StartingVisuals[0]);
            swap(m_buttonSurfaces[m_pressedButton], m_currentSurface);
            PopulateVisuals(&m_animation.EndingVisuals[0]);
    }

    m_pressedButton = -1;
}
```

That completes the wireframe viewer! As you can see, animation isn't difficult, and it can give your application that special Apple touch.

Wrapping Up

This chapter has been a quick exposition of the touchscreen and OpenGL vertex submission. The toy wireframe app is great fun, but it does have a bit of a 1980s feel to it. The next chapter takes iPhone graphics to the next level by explaining the depth buffer, exploring the use of real-time lighting, and showing how to load 3D content from the popular *.obj* file format. While this chapter has been rather heavy on code listings, the next chapter will be more in the style of Chapter 2, mixing in some math review with a lesson in OpenGL.

## CHAPTER 4

Adding Depth and Realism

Lumos!

—*Harry Potter and the Chamber of Secrets,*
J.K. Rowling

When my wife and I go out to see a film packed with special effects, I always insist on sitting through the entire end credits, much to her annoyance. It never ceases to amaze me how many artists work together to produce a Hollywood blockbuster. I'm often impressed with the number of artists whose full-time job concerns lighting. In Pixar's *Up*, at least five people have the title "lighting technical director," four people have the title "key lighting artist," and another four people have the honor of "master lighting artist."

Lighting is obviously a key aspect to understanding realism in computer graphics, and that's much of what this chapter is all about. We'll refurbish the wireframe viewer sample to use lighting and triangles, rechristening it to *Model Viewer*. We'll also throw some light on the subject of shaders, which we've been glossing over until now (in ES 2.0, shaders are critical to lighting). Finally, we'll further enhance the viewer app by giving it the ability to load model files so that we're not stuck with parametric surfaces forever. Mathematical shapes are great for geeking out, but they're pretty lame for impressing your 10-year-old!

Examining the Depth Buffer

Before diving into lighting, let's take a closer look at depth buffers, since we'll need to add one to wireframe viewer. You might recall the funky framebuffer object (FBO) setup code in the HelloCone sample presented in Example 2-7, repeated here in Example 4-1.

Example 4-1. Depth buffer setup

```
// Create the depth buffer.
glGenRenderbuffersOES(1, &m_depthRenderbuffer);❶
glBindRenderbufferOES(GL_RENDERBUFFER_OES, m_depthRenderbuffer);❷
glRenderbufferStorageOES(GL_RENDERBUFFER_OES,❸
                         GL_DEPTH_COMPONENT16_OES,
                         width,
                         height);

// Create the framebuffer object; attach the depth and color buffers.
glGenFramebuffersOES(1, &m_framebuffer);
glBindFramebufferOES(GL_FRAMEBUFFER_OES, m_framebuffer);
glFramebufferRenderbufferOES(GL_FRAMEBUFFER_OES,
                             GL_COLOR_ATTACHMENT0_OES,
                             GL_RENDERBUFFER_OES,
                             m_colorRenderbuffer);
glFramebufferRenderbufferOES(GL_FRAMEBUFFER_OES,❹
                             GL_DEPTH_ATTACHMENT_OES,
                             GL_RENDERBUFFER_OES,
                             m_depthRenderbuffer);

// Bind the color buffer for rendering.
glBindRenderbufferOES(GL_RENDERBUFFER_OES, m_colorRenderbuffer);

glViewport(0, 0, width, height);
glEnable(GL_DEPTH_TEST);❺

...
```

❶ Create a handle to the renderbuffer object that stores depth.

❷ Bind the newly created handle, making it affected by subsequent renderbuffer commands.

❸ Allocate storage for the depth buffer using 16-bit precision.

❹ Attach the depth buffer to the framebuffer object.

❺ Enable depth testing—we'll explain this shortly.

Why does HelloCone need a depth buffer when wireframe viewer does not? When the scene is composed of nothing but monochrome lines, we don't care about *the visibility problem*; this means we don't care which lines are obscured by other lines. HelloCone uses triangles rather than lines, so the visibility problem needs to be addressed. OpenGL uses the depth buffer to handle this problem efficiently.

Figure 4-1 depicts ModelViewer's depth buffer in grayscale: white pixels are far away, black pixels are nearby. Even though users can't see the depth buffer, OpenGL needs it for its rendering algorithm. If it didn't have a depth buffer, you'd be forced to carefully order your draw calls from farthest to nearest. (Incidentally, such an ordering is called the *painter's algorithm*, and there are special cases where you'll need to use it anyway, as you'll see in "Blending Caveats" on page 226.)

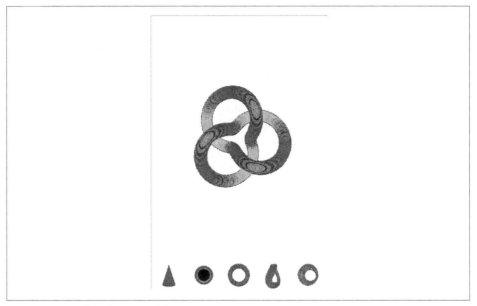

Figure 4-1. Depth buffer in ModelViewer

OpenGL uses a technique called *depth testing* to solve the visibility problem. Suppose you were to render a red triangle directly in front of the camera and then draw a green triangle directly behind the red triangle. Even though the green triangle is drawn last, you'd want to the red triangle to be visible; the green triangle is said to be *occluded*. Here's how it works: every rasterized pixel not only has its RGB values written to the color buffer but also has its Z value written to the depth buffer. OpenGL "rejects" occluded pixels by checking whether their Z value is greater than the Z value that's already in the depth buffer. In pseudocode, the algorithm looks like this:

```
void WritePixel(x, y, z, color)
{
    if (DepthTestDisabled || z < DepthBuffer[x, y]) {
        DepthBuffer[x, y] = z;
        ColorBuffer[x, y] = color;
    }
}
```

Beware the Scourge of Depth Artifacts

Something to watch out for with depth buffers is *Z-fighting*, which is a visual artifact that occurs when overlapping triangles have depths that are too close to each other (see Figure 4-2).

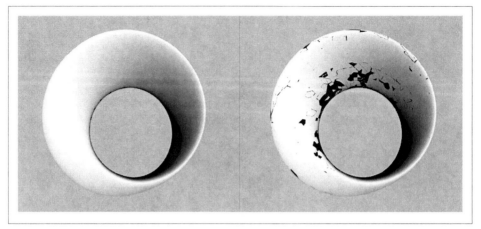

Figure 4-2. Z-fighting in the Möbius strip

Recall that the projection matrix defines a viewing frustum bounded by six planes ("Setting the Projection Transform" on page 59). The two planes that are perpendicular to the viewing direction are called the *near plane* and *far plane*. In ES 1.1, these planes are arguments to the glOrtho or glPerspective functions; in ES 2.0, they're passed to a custom function like the mat4::Frustum method in the C++ vector library from the appendix.

It turns out that if the near plane is too close to the camera or if the far plane is too distant, this can cause precision issues that result in Z-fighting. However this is only one possible cause for Z-fighting; there are many more. Take a look at the following list of suggestions if you ever see artifacts like the ones in Figure 4-2.

Push out your near plane.
> For perspective projections, having the near plane close to zero can be detrimental to precision.

Pull in your far plane.
> Similarly, the far plane should still be pulled in as far as possible without clipping away portions of your scene.

Scale your scene smaller.
> Try to avoid defining an astronomical-scale scene with huge extents.

Increase the bit width of your depth buffer.
> All iPhones and iPod touches (at the time of this writing) support 16-bit and 24-bit depth formats. The bit width is determined according to the argument you pass to glRenderbufferStorageOES when allocating the depth buffer.

Are you accidentally rendering coplanar triangles?
> The fault might not lie with OpenGL but with your application code. Perhaps your generated vertices are lying on the same Z plane because of a rounding error.

Do you really need depth testing in the first place?

In some cases you should probably disable depth testing anyway. For example, you don't need it if you're rendering a 2D heads-up display. Disabling the depth test can also boost performance.

Creating and Using the Depth Buffer

Let's enhance the wireframe viewer by adding in a depth buffer; this paves the way for converting the wireframes into solid triangles. Before making any changes, use Finder to make a copy of the folder that contains the SimpleWireframe project. Rename the folder to *ModelViewer*, and then open the copy of the SimpleWireframe project inside that folder. Select *Project→Rename*, and rename the project to *ModelViewer*.

Open *RenderingEngine.ES1.cpp*, and add GLuint m_depthRenderbuffer; to the pri vate: section of the class declaration. Next, find the Initialize method, and delete everything from the comment // Create the framebuffer object to the glBindRender bufferOES call. Replace the code you deleted with the code in Example 4-2.

Example 4-2. Adding depth to ES1::RenderingEngine::Initialize

```
// Extract width and height from the color buffer.
int width, height;
glGetRenderbufferParameterivOES(GL_RENDERBUFFER_OES,
                                GL_RENDERBUFFER_WIDTH_OES, &width);
glGetRenderbufferParameterivOES(GL_RENDERBUFFER_OES,
                                GL_RENDERBUFFER_HEIGHT_OES, &height);

// Create a depth buffer that has the same size as the color buffer.
glGenRenderbuffersOES(1, &m_depthRenderbuffer);
glBindRenderbufferOES(GL_RENDERBUFFER_OES, m_depthRenderbuffer);
glRenderbufferStorageOES(GL_RENDERBUFFER_OES, GL_DEPTH_COMPONENT16_OES,
                         width, height);

// Create the framebuffer object.
GLuint framebuffer;
glGenFramebuffersOES(1, &framebuffer);
glBindFramebufferOES(GL_FRAMEBUFFER_OES, framebuffer);
glFramebufferRenderbufferOES(GL_FRAMEBUFFER_OES, GL_COLOR_ATTACHMENT0_OES,
                             GL_RENDERBUFFER_OES, m_colorRenderbuffer);
glFramebufferRenderbufferOES(GL_FRAMEBUFFER_OES, GL_DEPTH_ATTACHMENT_OES,
                             GL_RENDERBUFFER_OES, m_depthRenderbuffer);
glBindRenderbufferOES(GL_RENDERBUFFER_OES, m_colorRenderbuffer);

// Enable depth testing.
glEnable(GL_DEPTH_TEST);
```

The ES 2.0 variant of Example 4-2 is almost exactly the same. Repeat the process in that file, but remove all *_OES* and *OES* suffixes.

Next, find the call to glClear (in both rendering engines), and add a flag for depth:

```
glClear(GL_COLOR_BUFFER_BIT | GL_DEPTH_BUFFER_BIT);
```

At this point, you should be able to compile and run, although depth testing doesn't buy you anything yet since the app is still rendering in wireframe.

By default, the depth buffer gets cleared to a value of 1.0; this makes sense since you want all your pixels to initially pass the depth test, and OpenGL clamps the maximum window-space Z coordinate to 1.0. Incidentally, if you want to clear the depth buffer to some other value, you can call glClearDepthf, similar to glClearColor. You can even configure the depth test itself using glDepthFunc. By default, pixels "win" if their Z is *less* than the value in the depth buffer, but you can change the test to any of these conditions:

GL_NEVER
: Pixels never pass the depth test.

GL_ALWAYS
: Pixels always pass the depth test.

GL_LESS
: Pixels pass only if their Z value is less than the Z value in the depth buffer. This is the default.

GL_LEQUAL
: Pixels pass only if their Z value is less than or equal to the Z value in the depth buffer.

GL_EQUAL
: Pixels pass only if their Z value is equal to the Z value in the depth buffer. This could be used to create an infinitely thin slice of the scene.

GL_GREATER
: Pixels pass only if their Z value is greater than the Z value in the depth buffer.

GL_GEQUAL
: Pixels pass only if their Z value is greater than or equal to the Z value in the depth buffer.

GL_NOTEQUAL
: Pixels pass only if their Z value is not equal to the Z value in the depth buffer.

The flexibility of glDepthFunc is a shining example of how OpenGL is often configurable to an extent more than you really need. I personally admire this type of design philosophy in an API; anything that is reasonably easy to implement in hardware is exposed to the developer at a low level. This makes the API forward-looking because it enables developers to dream up unusual effects that the API designers did not necessarily anticipate.

Filling the Wireframe with Triangles

In this section we'll walk through the steps required to render parametric surfaces with triangles rather than lines. First we need to enhance the `ISurface` interface to support the generation of indices for triangles rather than lines. Open *Interfaces.hpp*, and make the changes shown in bold in Example 4-3.

Example 4-3. Enhanced ISurface interface

```
struct ISurface {
    virtual int GetVertexCount() const = 0;
    virtual int GetLineIndexCount() const = 0;
    virtual int GetTriangleIndexCount() const = 0;
    virtual void GenerateVertices(vector<float>& vertices) const = 0;
    virtual void GenerateLineIndices(vector<unsigned short>& indices) const = 0;
    virtual void
      GenerateTriangleIndices(vector<unsigned short>& indices) const = 0;
    virtual ~ISurface() {}
};
```

You'll also need to open `ParametricSurface.hpp` and make the complementary changes to the class declaration of `ParametricSurface` shown in Example 4-4.

Example 4-4. Enhanced ParametricSurface interface

```
class ParametricSurface : public ISurface {
public:
    int GetVertexCount() const;
    int GetLineIndexCount() const;
    int GetTriangleIndexCount() const;
    void GenerateVertices(vector<float>& vertices) const;
    void GenerateLineIndices(vector<unsigned short>& indices) const;
    void GenerateTriangleIndices(vector<unsigned short>& indices) const;
```

Next open *ParametericSurface.cpp*, and add the implementation of `GetTriangleIndex Count` and `GenerateTriangleIndices` per Example 4-5.

Example 4-5. ParametricSurface::GenerateTriangleIndices

```
int ParametricSurface::GetTriangleIndexCount() const
{
    return 6 * m_slices.x * m_slices.y;
}

void
ParametricSurface::GenerateTriangleIndices(vector<unsigned short>& indices) const
{
    indices.resize(GetTriangleIndexCount());
    vector<unsigned short>::iterator index = indices.begin();
    for (int j = 0, vertex = 0; j < m_slices.y; j++) {
        for (int i = 0; i < m_slices.x; i++) {
            int next = (i + 1) % m_divisions.x;
            *index++ = vertex + i;
            *index++ = vertex + next;
```

```
            *index++ = vertex + i + m_divisions.x;
            *index++ = vertex + next;
            *index++ = vertex + next + m_divisions.x;
            *index++ = vertex + i + m_divisions.x;
        }
        vertex += m_divisions.x;
    }
}
```

Example 4-5 is computing indices for two triangles, as shown in Figure 4-3.

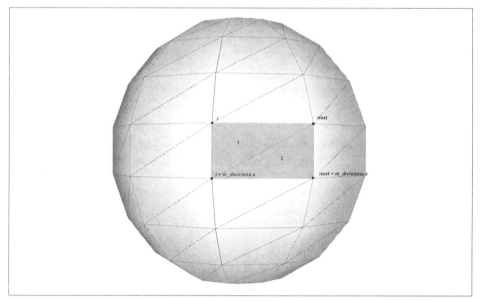

Figure 4-3. Generating triangle indices for a parametric surface

Now we need to modify the rendering engine so that it calls these new methods when generating VBOs, as in Example 4-6. The modified lines are shown in bold. Make these changes to both *RenderingEngine.ES1.cpp* and *RenderingEngine.ES2.cpp*.

Example 4-6. RenderingEngine Modifications for triangles

```
void RenderingEngine::Initialize(const vector<ISurface*>& surfaces)
{
    vector<ISurface*>::const_iterator surface;
    for (surface = surfaces.begin(); surface != surfaces.end(); ++surface) {

        // Create the VBO for the vertices.
        vector<float> vertices;
        (*surface)->GenerateVertices(vertices);
        GLuint vertexBuffer;
        glGenBuffers(1, &vertexBuffer);
        glBindBuffer(GL_ARRAY_BUFFER, vertexBuffer);
        glBufferData(GL_ARRAY_BUFFER,
```

```
                    vertices.size() * sizeof(vertices[0]),
                    &vertices[0],
                    GL_STATIC_DRAW);

        // Create a new VBO for the indices if needed.
        int indexCount = (*surface)->GetTriangleIndexCount();
        GLuint indexBuffer;
        if (!m_drawables.empty() && indexCount == m_drawables[0].IndexCount) {
            indexBuffer = m_drawables[0].IndexBuffer;
        } else {
            vector<GLushort> indices(indexCount);
            (*surface)->GenerateTriangleIndices(indices);
            glGenBuffers(1, &indexBuffer);
            glBindBuffer(GL_ELEMENT_ARRAY_BUFFER, indexBuffer);
            glBufferData(GL_ELEMENT_ARRAY_BUFFER,
                        indexCount * sizeof(GLushort),
                        &indices[0],
                        GL_STATIC_DRAW);
        }

        Drawable drawable = { vertexBuffer, indexBuffer, indexCount};
        m_drawables.push_back(drawable);
    }

    ...

}


void RenderingEngine::Render(const vector<Visual>& visuals) const
{
    glClearColor(0.5, 0.5f, 0.5f, 1);
    glClear(GL_COLOR_BUFFER_BIT | GL_DEPTH_BUFFER_BIT);

    vector<Visual>::const_iterator visual = visuals.begin();
    for (int visualIndex = 0;
        visual != visuals.end();
        ++visual, ++visualIndex)
    {

        //...

        // Draw the surface.
        int stride = sizeof(vec3);
        const Drawable& drawable = m_drawables[visualIndex];
        glBindBuffer(GL_ARRAY_BUFFER, drawable.VertexBuffer);
        glVertexPointer(3, GL_FLOAT, stride, 0);
        glBindBuffer(GL_ELEMENT_ARRAY_BUFFER, drawable.IndexBuffer);
        glDrawElements(GL_TRIANGLES, drawable.IndexCount, GL_UNSIGNED_SHORT, 0);
    }
}
```

Getting back to the sample app, at this point the wireframe viewer has officially become
ModelViewer; feel free to build it and try it. You may be disappointed—the result is
horribly boring, as shown in Figure 4-4. Lighting to the rescue!

Figure 4-4. ModelViewer without lighting

Surface Normals

Before we can enable lighting, there's yet another prerequisite we need to get out of the way. To perform the math for lighting, OpenGL must be provided with a *surface normal* at every vertex. A surface normal (often simply called a *normal*) is simply a vector perpendicular to the surface; it effectively defines the orientation of a small piece of the surface.

Feeding OpenGL with Normals

You might recall that normals are one of the predefined vertex attributes in OpenGL ES 1.1. They can be enabled like this:

```
// OpenGL ES 1.1
glEnableClientState(GL_NORMAL_ARRAY);
glNormalPointer(GL_FLOAT, stride, offset);
glEnable(GL_NORMALIZE);

// OpenGL ES 2.0
glEnableVertexAttribArray(myNormalSlot);
glVertexAttribPointer(myNormalSlot, 3, GL_FLOAT, normalize, stride, offset);
```

I snuck in something new in the previous snippet: the GL_NORMALIZE state in ES 1.1 and the normalize argument in ES 2.0. Both are used to control whether OpenGL processes your normal vectors to make them unit length. If you already know that your normals are unit length, do not turn this feature on; it incurs a performance hit.

 Don't confuse *normalize*, which refers to making any vector into a unit vector, and *normal vector*, which refers to any vector that is perpendicular to a surface. It is not redundant to say "normalized normal."

Even though OpenGL ES 1.1 can perform much of the lighting math on your behalf, it does not compute surface normals for you. At first this may seem rather ungracious on OpenGL's part, but as you'll see later, stipulating the normals yourself give you the power to render interesting effects. While the mathematical notion of a normal is well-defined, the OpenGL notion of a normal is simply another input with discretionary values, much like color and position. Mathematicians live in an ideal world of smooth surfaces, but graphics programmers live in a world of triangles. If you were to make the normals in every triangle point in the exact direction that the triangle is facing, your model would looked faceted and artificial; every triangle would have a uniform color. By supplying normals yourself, you can make your model seem smooth, faceted, or even bumpy, as we'll see later.

The Math Behind Normals

We scoff at mathematicians for living in an artificially ideal world, but we can't dismiss the math behind normals; we need it to come up with sensible values in the first place. Central to the mathematical notion of a normal is the concept of a *tangent plane*, depicted in Figure 4-5.

The diagram in Figure 4-5 is, in itself, perhaps the best definition of the tangent plane that I can give you without going into calculus. It's the plane that "just touches" your surface at a given point **P**. Think like a mathematician: for them, a plane is minimally defined with three points. So, imagine three points at random positions on your surface, and then create a plane that contains them all. Slowly move the three points toward each other; just before the three points converge, the plane they define is the tangent plane.

The tangent plane can also be defined with tangent and binormal vectors (**u** and **v** in Figure 4-5), which are easiest to define within the context of a parametric surface. Each of these correspond to a dimension of the domain; we'll make use of this when we add normals to our `ParametricSurface` class.

Finding two vectors in the tangent plane is usually fairly easy. For example, you can take any two sides of a triangle; the two vectors need not be at right angles to each other. Simply take their cross product and unitize the result. For parametric surfaces, the procedure can be summarized with the following pseudocode:

```
p = Evaluate(s, t)
u = Evaluate(s + ds, t) - p
```

```
v = Evaluate(s, t + dt) - p
N = Normalize(u × v)
```

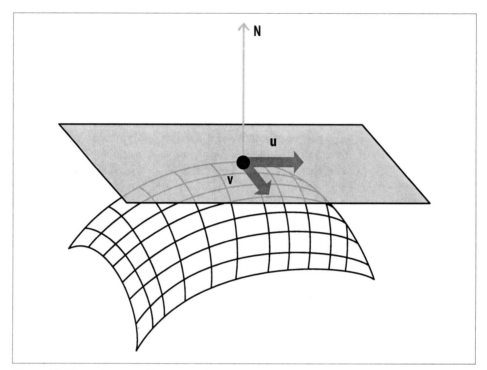

Figure 4-5. Normal vector with tangent plane

Don't be frightened by the cross product; I'll give you a brief refresher. The cross product always generates a vector perpendicular to its two input vectors. You can visualize the cross product of **A** with **B** using your right hand. Point your index finger in the direction of **A**, and then point your middle finger toward **B**; your thumb now points in the direction of **A**×**B** (pronounced "A cross B," not "A times B"). See Figure 4-6.

Here's the relevant snippet from our C++ library (see the appendix for a full listing):

```cpp
template <typename T>
struct Vector3 {
    // ...
    Vector3 Cross(const Vector3& v) const
    {
        return Vector3(y * v.z - z * v.y,
                       z * v.x - x * v.z,
                       x * v.y - y * v.x);
    }
    // ...
    T x, y, z;
};
```

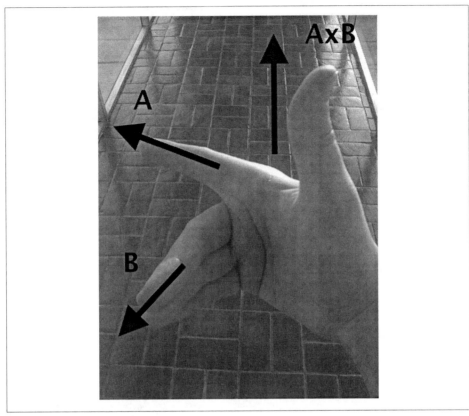

Figure 4-6. Righthand rule

Normal Transforms Aren't Normal

Let's not lose focus of why we're generating normals in the first place: they're required for the lighting algorithms that we cover later in this chapter. Recall from Chapter 2 that vertex position can live in different spaces: object space, world space, and so on. Normal vectors can live in these different spaces too; it turns out that lighting in the vertex shader is often performed in eye space. (There are certain conditions in which it can be done in object space, but that's a discussion for another day.)

So, we need to transform our normals to eye space. Since vertex positions get transformed by the model-view matrix to bring them into eye space, it follows that normal vectors get transformed the same way, right? Wrong! Actually, wrong *sometimes*. This is one of the trickier concepts in graphics to understand, so bear with me.

Look at the heart shape in Figure 4-7, and consider the surface normal at a point in the upper-left quadrant (depicted with an arrow). The figure on the far left is the original shape, and the middle figure shows what happens after we translate, rotate, and uniformly shrink the heart. The transformation for the normal vector is almost the same as the model's transformation; the only difference is that it's a vector and therefore doesn't require translation. Removing translation from a 4×4 transformation matrix is easy. Simply extract the upper-left 3×3 matrix, and you're done.

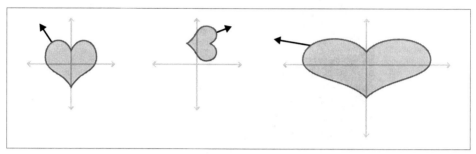

Figure 4-7. Normal transforms

Now take a look at the figure on the far right, which shows what happens when stretching the model along only its x-axis. In this case, if we were to apply the upper 3×3 of the model-view matrix to the normal vector, we'd get an incorrect result; the normal would no longer be perpendicular to the surface. This shows that simply extracting the upper-left 3×3 matrix from the model-view matrix doesn't always suffice. I won't bore you with the math, but it can be shown that the correct transform for normal vectors is actually the *inverse-transpose* of the model-view matrix, which is the result of two operations: first an inverse, then a transpose.

The *inverse* matrix of M is denoted M^{-1}; it's the matrix that results in the identity matrix when multiplied with the original matrix. Inverse matrices are somewhat nontrivial to compute, so again I'll refrain from boring you with the math. The *transpose* matrix, on the other hand, is easy to derive; simply swap the rows and columns of the matrix such that `M[i][j]` becomes `M[j][i]`.

Transposes are denoted M^{T}, so the proper transform for normal vectors looks like this:

$$\mathbf{N}' = \mathbf{N} * (\mathbf{M}^{-1})^{T}$$

Don't forget the middle shape in Figure 4-7; it shows that, at least in some cases, the upper 3×3 of the original model-view matrix *can* be used to transform the normal vector. In this case, the matrix just happens to be equal to its own inverse-transpose; such matrices are called *orthogonal*. Rigid body transformations like rotation and uniform scale always result in orthogonal matrices.

Why did I bore you with all this mumbo jumbo about inverses and normal transforms? Two reasons. First, in ES 1.1, keeping nonuniform scale out of your matrix helps performance because OpenGL can avoid computing the inverse-transpose of the model-view. Second, for ES 2.0, you need to understand nitty-gritty details like this anyway to write sensible lighting shaders!

Generating Normals from Parametric Surfaces

Enough academic babble; let's get back to coding. Since our goal here is to add lighting to ModelViewer, we need to implement the generation of normal vectors. Let's tweak ISurface in *Interfaces.hpp* by adding a flags parameter to GenerateVertices, as shown in Example 4-7. New or modified lines are shown in bold.

Example 4-7. Modifying ISurface with support for normals

```
enum VertexFlags {
    VertexFlagsNormals = 1 << 0,
    VertexFlagsTexCoords = 1 << 1,
};

struct ISurface {
    virtual int GetVertexCount() const = 0;
    virtual int GetLineIndexCount() const = 0;
    virtual int GetTriangleIndexCount() const = 0;
    virtual void GenerateVertices(vector<float>& vertices,
                                  unsigned char flags = 0) const = 0;
    virtual void GenerateLineIndices(vector<unsigned short>& indices) const = 0;
    virtual void
      GenerateTriangleIndices(vector<unsigned short>& indices) const = 0;
    virtual ~ISurface() {}
};
```

The argument we added to GenerateVertices could have been a boolean instead of a bit mask, but we'll eventually want to feed additional vertex attributes to OpenGL, such as texture coordinates. For now, just ignore the VertexFlagsTexCoords flag; it'll come in handy in the next chapter.

Next we need to open ParametricSurface.hpp and make the complementary change to the class declaration of ParametricSurface, as shown in Example 4-8. We'll also add a new protected method called InvertNormal, which derived classes can optionally override.

Example 4-8. ParametricSurface class declaration

```
class ParametricSurface : public ISurface {
public:
    int GetVertexCount() const;
    int GetLineIndexCount() const;
    int GetTriangleIndexCount() const;
    void GenerateVertices(vector<float>& vertices, unsigned char flags) const;
    void GenerateLineIndices(vector<unsigned short>& indices) const;
    void GenerateTriangleIndices(vector<unsigned short>& indices) const;
protected:
    void SetInterval(const ParametricInterval& interval);
    virtual vec3 Evaluate(const vec2& domain) const = 0;
    virtual bool InvertNormal(const vec2& domain) const { return false; }
private:
    vec2 ComputeDomain(float i, float j) const;
    vec2 m_upperBound;
```

```
    ivec2 m_slices;
    ivec2 m_divisions;
};
```

Next let's open *ParametericSurface.cpp* and replace the implementation of `Generate Vertices`, as shown in Example 4-9.

Example 4-9. Adding normals to ParametricSurface::GenerateVertices

```
void ParametricSurface::GenerateVertices(vector<float>& vertices,
                                         unsigned char flags) const
{
    int floatsPerVertex = 3;
    if (flags & VertexFlagsNormals)
        floatsPerVertex += 3;

    vertices.resize(GetVertexCount() * floatsPerVertex);
    float* attribute = (float*) &vertices[0];

    for (int j = 0; j < m_divisions.y; j++) {
        for (int i = 0; i < m_divisions.x; i++) {

            // Compute Position❶
            vec2 domain = ComputeDomain(i, j);
            vec3 range = Evaluate(domain);
            attribute = range.Write(attribute);❷

            // Compute Normal
            if (flags & VertexFlagsNormals) {
                float s = i, t = j;

                // Nudge the point if the normal is indeterminate.❸
                if (i == 0) s += 0.01f;
                if (i == m_divisions.x - 1) s -= 0.01f;
                if (j == 0) t += 0.01f;
                if (j == m_divisions.y - 1) t -= 0.01f;

                // Compute the tangents and their cross product.❹
                vec3 p = Evaluate(ComputeDomain(s, t));
                vec3 u = Evaluate(ComputeDomain(s + 0.01f, t)) - p;
                vec3 v = Evaluate(ComputeDomain(s, t + 0.01f)) - p;
                vec3 normal = u.Cross(v).Normalized();
                if (InvertNormal(domain))❺
                    normal = -normal;
                attribute = normal.Write(attribute);❻
            }
        }
    }
}
```

❶ Compute the position of the vertex by calling `Evaluate`, which has a unique implementation for each subclass.

❷ Copy the `vec3` position into the flat floating-point buffer. The `Write` method returns an updated pointer.

❸ Surfaces might be nonsmooth in some places where the normal is impossible to determine (for example, at the apex of the cone). So, we have a bit of a hack here, which is to nudge the point of interest in the problem areas.

❹ As covered in "Feeding OpenGL with Normals" on page 128, compute the two tangent vectors, and take their cross product.

❺ Subclasses are allowed to invert the normal if they want. (If the normal points away from the light source, then it's considered to be the back of the surface and therefore looks dark.) The only shape that overrides this method is the Klein bottle.

❷ Copy the normal vector into the data buffer using its `Write` method.

This completes the changes to `ParametricSurface`. You should be able to build ModelViewer at this point, but it will look the same since we have yet to put the normal vectors to good use. That comes next.

Lighting Up

Drawing is deception.

—M. C. Escher

The foundations of real-time graphics are rarely based on principles from physics and optics. In a way, the lighting equations we'll cover in this section are cheap hacks, simple models based on rather shallow empirical observations. We'll be demonstrating three different lighting models: *ambient* lighting (subtle, monotone light), *diffuse* lighting (the dull matte component of reflection), and *specular* lighting (the shiny spot on a fresh red apple). Figure 4-8 shows how these three lighting models can be combined to produce a high-quality image.

Figure 4-8. Ambient + diffuse + specular = final

Of course, in the real world, there are no such things as "diffuse photons" and "specular photons." Don't be disheartened by this pack of lies! Computer graphics is always just a great big hack at some level, and knowing this will make you stronger. Even the fact that colors are ultimately represented by a red-green-blue triplet has more to do with human perception than with optics. The reason we use RGB? It happens to match the three types of color-sensing cells in the human retina! A good graphics programmer can think like a politician and use lies to his advantage.

Ho-Hum Ambiance

Realistic ambient lighting, with the soft, muted shadows that it conjures up, can be very complex to render (you can see an example of *ambient occlusion* in "Baked Lighting" on page 373), but ambient lighting in the context of OpenGL usually refers to something far more trivial: a solid, uniform color. Calling this "lighting" is questionable since its intensity is not impacted by the position of the light source or the orientation of the surface, but it is often combined with the other lighting models to produce a brighter surface.

Matte Paint with Diffuse Lighting

The most common form of real-time lighting is *diffuse lighting*, which varies its brightness according to the angle between the surface and the light source. Also known as *lambertian reflection*, this form of lighting is predominant because it's simple to compute, and it adequately conveys depth to the human eye. Figure 4-9 shows how diffuse lighting works. In the diagram, **L** is the unit length vector pointing to the light source, and **N** is the *surface normal*, which is a unit-length vector that's perpendicular to the surface. We'll learn how to compute **N** later in the chapter.

The *diffuse factor* (known as df in Figure 4-9) lies between 0 and 1 and gets multiplied with the light intensity and material color to produce the final diffuse color, as shown in Equation 4-1.

Equation 4-1. Diffuse color

DiffuseColor = LightIntensity * MaterialColor * df

df is computed by taking the dot product of the surface normal with the light direction vector and then clamping the result to a non-negative number, as shown in Equation 4-2.

Equation 4-2. Diffuse coefficient

$$df = \max(0, \mathbf{N} \bullet \mathbf{L})$$

The dot product is another operation that you might need a refresher on. When applied to two unit-length vectors (which is what we're doing for diffuse lighting), you can think of the dot product as a way of measuring the angle between the vectors. If the two vectors are perpendicular to each other, their dot product is zero; if they point away

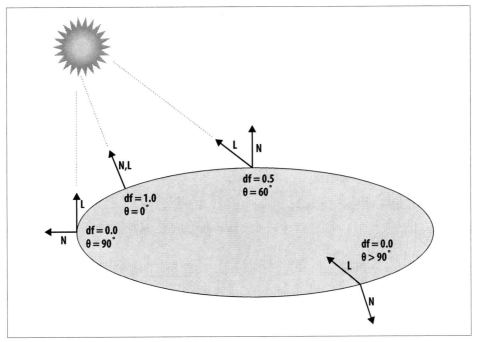

Figure 4-9. Diffuse lighting

from each other, their dot product is negative. Specifically, the dot product of two unit vectors is the cosine of the angle between them. To see how to compute the dot product, here's a snippet from our C++ vector library (see the appendix for a complete listing):

```
template <typename T>
struct Vector3 {
    // ...
    T Dot(const Vector3& v) const
    {
        return x * v.x + y * v.y + z * v.z;
    }
    // ...
    T x, y, z;
};
```

Don't confuse the dot product with the cross product! For one thing, cross products produce vectors, while dot products produce scalars.

With OpenGL ES 1.1, the math required for diffuse lighting is done for you behind the scenes; with 2.0, you have to do the math yourself in a shader. You'll learn both methods later in the chapter.

The **L** vector in Equation 4-2 can be computed like this:

$$\mathbf{L} = \text{normalize (LightPosition} - \text{VertexPosition)}$$

In practice, you can often pretend that the light is so far away that all vertices are at the origin. The previous equation then simplifies to the following:

$$\mathbf{L} = \text{normalize (LightPosition)}$$

When you apply this optimization, you're said to be using an *infinite light source*. Taking each vertex position into account is slower but more accurate; this is a *positional light source*.

Give It a Shine with Specular

> *I guess you could say the Overlook Hotel here has somethin' almost like "shining."*
>
> —Mr. Hallorann to Danny, *The Shining*

Diffuse lighting is not affected by the position of the camera; the diffuse brightness of a fixed point stays the same, no matter which direction you observe it from. This is in contrast to *specular lighting*, which moves the area of brightness according to your eye position, as shown in Figure 4-10. Specular lighting mimics the shiny highlight seen on polished surfaces. Hold a shiny apple in front of you, and shift your head to the left and right; you'll see that the apple's shiny spot moves with you. Specular is more costly to compute than diffuse because it uses exponentiation to compute falloff. You choose the exponent according to how you want the material to look; the higher the exponent, the shinier the model.

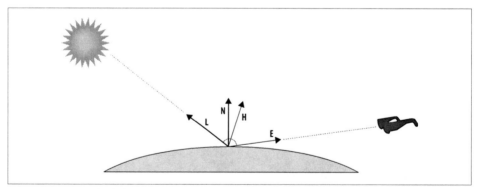

Figure 4-10. Specular lighting

The **H** vector in Figure 4-10 is called the *half-angle* because it divides the angle between the light and the camera in half. Much like diffuse lighting, the goal is to compute an intensity coefficient (in this case, sf) between 0 and 1. Equation 4-3 shows how to compute sf.

Equation 4-3. Specular lighting

$$H = normalize(\mathbf{L} + \mathbf{E})$$

$$sf = [max\,(0,\,\mathbf{N} \bullet \mathbf{H})]^{shininess}$$

In practice, you can often pretend that the viewer is infinitely far from the vertex, in which case the **E** vector is substituted with (0, 0, 1). This technique is called *infinite viewer*. When **E** is used, this is called *local viewer*.

Adding Light to ModelViewer

We'll first add lighting to the OpenGL ES 1.1 backend since it's much less involved than the 2.0 variant. Example 4-10 shows the new `Initialize` method (unchanged portions are replaced with ellipses for brevity).

Example 4-10. ES1::RenderingEngine::Initialize

```
void RenderingEngine::Initialize(const vector<ISurface*>& surfaces)
{
    vector<ISurface*>::const_iterator surface;
    for (surface = surfaces.begin(); surface != surfaces.end(); ++surface) {

        // Create the VBO for the vertices.
        vector<float> vertices;
        (*surface)->GenerateVertices(vertices, VertexFlagsNormals);❶
        GLuint vertexBuffer;
        glGenBuffers(1, &vertexBuffer);
        glBindBuffer(GL_ARRAY_BUFFER, vertexBuffer);
        glBufferData(GL_ARRAY_BUFFER,
                     vertices.size() * sizeof(vertices[0]),
                     &vertices[0],
                     GL_STATIC_DRAW);

        // Create a new VBO for the indices if needed.
        ...
    }

    // Set up various GL state.
    glEnableClientState(GL_VERTEX_ARRAY);❷
    glEnableClientState(GL_NORMAL_ARRAY);
    glEnable(GL_LIGHTING);❸
    glEnable(GL_LIGHT0);
    glEnable(GL_DEPTH_TEST);

    // Set up the material properties.❹
    vec4 specular(0.5f, 0.5f, 0.5f, 1);
    glMaterialfv(GL_FRONT_AND_BACK, GL_SPECULAR, specular.Pointer());
    glMaterialf(GL_FRONT_AND_BACK, GL_SHININESS, 50.0f);

    m_translation = mat4::Translate(0, 0, -7);
}
```

❶ Tell the `ParametricSurface` object that we need normals by passing in the new `VertexFlagsNormals` flag.

❷ Enable two vertex attributes: one for position, the other for surface normal.

❸ Enable lighting, and turn on the first light source (known as `GL_LIGHT0`). The iPhone supports up to eight light sources, but we're using only one.

❹ The default specular color is black, so here we set it to gray and set the specular exponent to 50. We'll set diffuse later.

Example 4-10 uses some new OpenGL functions: `glMaterialf` and `glMaterialfv`. These are useful only when lighting is turned on, and they are unique to ES 1.1—with 2.0 you'd use `glVertexAttrib` instead. The declarations for these functions are the following:

```
void glMaterialf(GLenum face, GLenum pname, GLfloat param);
void glMaterialfv(GLenum face, GLenum pname, const GLfloat *params);
```

The `face` parameter is a bit of a carryover from desktop OpenGL, which allows the back and front sides of a surface to have different material properties. For OpenGL ES, this parameter must always be set to `GL_FRONT_AND_BACK`.

The `pname` parameter can be one of the following:

GL_SHININESS
> This specifies the specular exponent as a float between 0 and 128. This is the only parameter that you set with `glMaterialf`; all other parameters require `glMaterialfv` because they have four floats each.

GL_AMBIENT
> This specifies the ambient color of the surface and requires four floats (red, green, blue, alpha). The alpha value is ignored, but I always set it to one just to be safe.

GL_SPECULAR
> This specifies the specular color of the surface and also requires four floats, although alpha is ignored.

GL_EMISSION
> This specifies the emission color of the surface. We haven't covered emission because it's so rarely used. It's similar to ambient except that it's unaffected by light sources. This can be useful for debugging; if you want to verify that a surface of interest is visible, set its emission color to white. Like ambient and specular, it requires four floats and alpha is ignored.

GL_DIFFUSE
> This specifies the diffuse color of the surface and requires four floats. The final alpha value of the pixel originates from the diffuse color.

GL_AMBIENT_AND_DIFFUSE
> Using only one function call, this allows you to specify the same color for both ambient and diffuse.

When lighting is enabled, the final color of the surface is determined at run time, so OpenGL ignores the color attribute that you set with glColor4f or GL_COLOR_ARRAY (see Table 2-2). Since you'd specify the color attribute only when lighting is turned off, it's often referred to as *nonlit color*.

 As an alternative to calling glMaterialfv, you can embed diffuse and ambient colors into the vertex buffer itself, through a mechanism called *color material*. When enabled, this redirects the nonlit color attribute into the GL_AMBIENT and GL_DIFFUSE material parameters. You can enable it by calling glEnable(GL_COLOR_MATERIAL).

Next we'll flesh out the Render method so that it uses normals, as shown in Example 4-11. New/changed lines are in bold. Note that we moved up the call to glMatrixMode; this is explained further in the callouts that follow the listing.

Example 4-11. ES1::RenderingEngine::Render

```
void RenderingEngine::Render(const vector<Visual>& visuals) const
{
    glClearColor(0.5f, 0.5f, 0.5f, 1);
    glClear(GL_COLOR_BUFFER_BIT | GL_DEPTH_BUFFER_BIT);

    vector<Visual>::const_iterator visual = visuals.begin();
    for (int visualIndex = 0;
         visual != visuals.end();
         ++visual, ++visualIndex)
    {

        // Set the viewport transform.
        ivec2 size = visual->ViewportSize;
        ivec2 lowerLeft = visual->LowerLeft;
        glViewport(lowerLeft.x, lowerLeft.y, size.x, size.y);

        // Set the light position. ❶
        glMatrixMode(GL_MODELVIEW);
        glLoadIdentity();
        vec4 lightPosition(0.25, 0.25, 1, 0);
        glLightfv(GL_LIGHT0, GL_POSITION, lightPosition.Pointer());

        // Set the model-view transform.
        mat4 rotation = visual->Orientation.ToMatrix();
        mat4 modelview = rotation * m_translation;
        glLoadMatrixf(modelview.Pointer());

        // Set the projection transform.
        float h = 4.0f * size.y / size.x;
        mat4 projection = mat4::Frustum(-2, 2, -h / 2, h / 2, 5, 10);
        glMatrixMode(GL_PROJECTION);
        glLoadMatrixf(projection.Pointer());
```

```
        // Set the diffuse color.❷
        vec3 color = visual->Color * 0.75f;
        vec4 diffuse(color.x, color.y, color.z, 1);
        glMaterialfv(GL_FRONT_AND_BACK, GL_DIFFUSE, diffuse.Pointer());

        // Draw the surface.
        int stride = 2 * sizeof(vec3);
        const Drawable& drawable = m_drawables[visualIndex];
        glBindBuffer(GL_ARRAY_BUFFER, drawable.VertexBuffer);
        glVertexPointer(3, GL_FLOAT, stride, 0);
        const GLvoid* normalOffset = (const GLvoid*) sizeof(vec3);❸
        glNormalPointer(GL_FLOAT, stride, normalOffset);
        glBindBuffer(GL_ELEMENT_ARRAY_BUFFER, drawable.IndexBuffer);
        glDrawElements(GL_TRIANGLES, drawable.IndexCount, GL_UNSIGNED_SHORT, 0);
    }
}
```

❶ Set the position of GL_LIGHT0. Be careful about when you make this call, because
OpenGL applies the current model-view matrix to the position, much like it does
to vertices. Since we don't want the light to rotate along with the model, here we've
reset the model-view before setting the light position.

❷ The nonlit version of the app used glColor4f in the section that started with the
comment // Set the color. We're replacing that with glMaterialfv. More on this
later.

❸ Point OpenGL to the right place in the VBO for obtaining normals. Position comes
first, and it's a vec3, so the normal offset is sizeof(vec3).

That's it! Figure 4-11 depicts the app now that lighting has been added. Since we haven't
implemented the ES 2.0 renderer yet, you'll need to enable the ForceES1 constant at the
top of *GLView.mm*.

Using Light Properties

Example 4-11 introduced a new OpenGL function for modifying light parameters,
glLightfv:

```
    void glLightfv(GLenum light, GLenum pname, const GLfloat *params);
```

The light parameter identifies the light source. Although we're using only one light
source in ModelViewer, up to eight are allowed (GL_LIGHT0–GL_LIGHT7).

The pname argument specifies the light property to modify. OpenGL ES 1.1 supports
10 light properties:

GL_AMBIENT, GL_DIFFUSE, GL_SPECULAR
    As you'd expect, each of these takes four floats to specify a color. Note that light
    colors alone do not determine the hue of the surface; they get multiplied with the
    surface colors specified by glMaterialfv.

Figure 4-11. ModelViewer with lighting

GL_POSITION

> The position of the light is specified with four floats. If you don't set the light's position, it defaults to (0, 0, 1, 0). The **W** component should be 0 or 1, where 0 indicates an infinitely distant light. Such light sources are just as bright as normal light sources, but their "rays" are parallel. This is computationally cheaper because OpenGL does not bother recomputing the **L** vector (see Figure 4-9) at every vertex.

GL_SPOT_DIRECTION, GL_SPOT_EXPONENT, GL_SPOT_CUTOFF

> You can restrict a light's area of influence to a cone using these parameters. Don't set these parameters if you don't need them; doing so can degrade performance. I won't go into detail about spotlights since they are somewhat esoteric to ES 1.1, and you can easily write a shader in ES 2.0 to achieve a similar effect. Consult an OpenGL reference to see how to use spotlights (see the section "Further Reading" on page 387).

GL_CONSTANT_ATTENUATION, GL_LINEAR_ATTENUATION, GL_QUAD-RATIC_ATTENUATION

> These parameters allow you to dim the light intensity according to its distance from the object. Much like spotlights, attenuation is surely covered in your favorite OpenGL reference book. Again, be aware that setting these parameters could impact your frame rate.

You may've noticed that the inside of the cone appears especially dark. This is because the normal vector is facing away from the light source. On third-generation iPhones and iPod touches, you can enable a feature called *two-sided lighting*, which inverts the normals on back-facing triangles, allowing them to be lit. It's enabled like this:

```
glLightModelf(GL_LIGHT_MODEL_TWO_SIDE, GL_TRUE);
```

Use this function with caution, because it is not supported on older iPhones. One way to avoid two-sided lighting is to redraw the geometry at a slight offset using flipped normals. This effectively makes your one-sided surface into a two-sided surface. For example, in the case of our cone shape, we could draw another equally sized cone that's just barely "inside" the original cone.

 Just like every other lighting function, `glLightModelf` doesn't exist under ES 2.0. With ES 2.0, you can achieve two-sided lighting by using a special shader variable called `gl_FrontFacing`.

Shaders Demystified

Before we add lighting to the ES 2.0 rendering engine of ModelViewer, let's go over some shader fundamentals. What exactly is a shader? In Chapter 1, we mentioned that shaders are relatively small snippets of code that run on the graphics processor and that thousands of shader instances can execute simultaneously.

Let's dissect the simple vertex shader that we've been using in our sample code so far, repeated here in Example 4-12.

Example 4-12. Simple.vert

```
attribute vec4 Position; ❶
attribute vec4 SourceColor;
varying vec4 DestinationColor; ❷
uniform mat4 Projection; ❸
uniform mat4 Modelview;

void main(void) ❹
{
    DestinationColor = SourceColor; ❺
    gl_Position = Projection * Modelview * Position; ❻
}
```

❶ Declare two 4D floating-point vectors with the **attribute** storage qualifier. Vertex shaders have read-only access to attributes.

❷ Declare a 4D floating-point vector as a varying. The vertex shader must write to all varyings that it declares—if it doesn't, OpenGL's shader compiler will report an error. The initial value is undefined.

❸ Declare two 4×4 matrices as *uniforms*. Much like attributes, the vertex shader has read-only access to uniforms. But unlike vertex attributes, uniforms cannot change from one vertex to the next.

❹ The entry point to the shader. Some shading languages let you define your own entry point, but with GLSL, it's always `main`.

❺ No lighting or fancy math here; just pass the `SourceColor` attribute into the `DestinationColor` varying.

❻ Here we transform the position by the projection and model-view matrices, much like OpenGL ES 1.1 automatically does on our behalf. Note the usage of `gl_Position`, which is a special output variable built into the vertex shading language.

The keywords `attribute`, `uniform`, and `varying` are storage qualifiers in GLSL. Table 4-1 summarizes the five storage qualifiers available in GLSL.

Table 4-1. GLSL storage qualifiers

Qualifier	Maximum permitted[a]	Readable from VS	Writable from VS	Readable from FS	Writable from FS
default	N/A	Yes	Yes	Yes	Yes
const	N/A	Yes	Yes	Yes	Yes
attribute	8 vec4	Yes	No	No	No
uniform	512 scalars (VS), 64 scalars (FS)	Yes	No	Yes	No
varying	8 vec4	No	Yes	Yes	No

[a] Implementation-specific data; pertains only to the iPhone 3GS.

Figure 4-12 shows one way to visualize the flow of shader data. Be aware that this diagram is very simplified; for example, it does not include blocks for texture memory or program storage.

The fragment shader we've been using so far is incredibly boring, as shown in Example 4-13.

Example 4-13. Boring fragment shader

```
varying lowp vec4 DestinationColor;❶

void main(void)❷
{
    gl_FragColor = DestinationColor;❸
}
```

❶ This declares a 4D floating-point varying (read-only) with `lowp` precision. Precision qualifiers are required for floating-point types in fragment shaders.

❷ The entry point to every fragment shader is its `main` function.

❸ `gl_FragColor` is a special built-in `vec4` that indicates the output of the fragment shader.

Perhaps the most interesting new concept here is the precision qualifier. Fragment shaders require a precision qualifier for all floating-point declarations. The valid

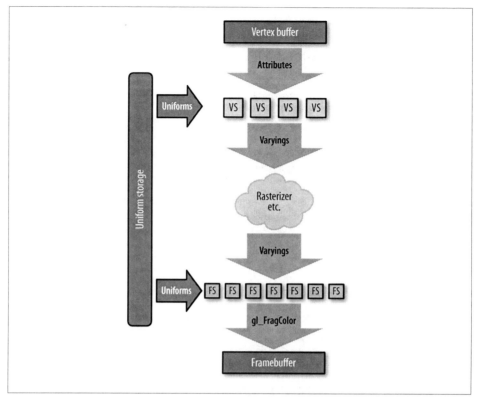

Figure 4-12. Shader-centric view of OpenGL (VS = vertex shader, FS = fragment shader)

qualifiers are lowp, mediump, and highp. The GLSL specification gives implementations some leeway in the underlying binary format that corresponds to each of these qualifiers; Table 4-2 shows specific details for the graphics processor in the iPhone 3GS.

 An alternative to specifying precision in front of every type is to supply a default using the precision keyword. Vertex shaders implicitly have a default floating-point precision of highp. To create a similar default in your fragment shader, add precision highp float; to the top of your shader.

Table 4-2. Floating-point precision in third-generation devices

Qualifier	Underlying type	Range	Typical usage
highp	32-bit floating point	$[-9.999999 \times 10^{96}, +9.999999 \times 10^{96}]$	colors, normals
mediump	16-bit floating point	$[-65520, +65520]$	texture coordinates
lowp	10-bit fixed point	$[-2, +2]$	vertex positions, matrices

Also of interest in Example 4-13 is the gl_FragColor variable, which is a bit of a special case. It's a variable that is built into the language itself and always refers to the color that gets applied to the framebuffer. The fragment shading language also defines the following built-in variables:

gl_FragData[0]
> gl_FragData is an array of output colors that has only one element. This exists in OpenGL ES only for compatibility reasons; use gl_FragColor instead.

gl_FragCoord
> This is an input variable that contains window coordinates for the current fragment, which is useful for image processing.

gl_FrontFacing
> Use this boolean input variable to implement two-sided lighting. Front faces are true; back faces are false.

gl_PointCoord
> This is an input texture coordinate that's used only for point sprite rendering; we'll cover it in the section "Rendering Confetti, Fireworks, and More: Point Sprites" on page 313.

Adding Shaders to ModelViewer

OpenGL ES 2.0 does not automatically perform lighting math behind the scenes; instead, it relies on developers to provide it with shaders that perform whatever type of lighting they desire. Let's come up with a vertex shader that mimics the math done by ES 1.1 when lighting is enabled.

To keep things simple, we'll use the infinite light source model for diffuse ("Feeding OpenGL with Normals" on page 128) combined with the infinite viewer model for specular ("Give It a Shine with Specular" on page 138). We'll also assume that the light is white. Example 4-14 shows the pseudocode.

Example 4-14. Basic lighting pseudocode
```
vec3 ComputeLighting(vec3 normal)
{
    N = NormalMatrix * normal
    L = Normalize(LightPosition)
    E = (0, 0, 1)
    H = Normalize(L + E)
    df = max(0, N · L)
    sf = max(0, N · H)
    sf = sf ^ Shininess
    return AmbientMaterial + DiffuseMaterial * df + SpecularMaterial * sf
}
```

Note the NormalMatrix variable in the pseudocode; it would be silly to recompute the inverse-transpose of the model-view at every vertex, so we'll compute it up front in the application code then pass it in as the `NormalMatrix` uniform. In many cases, it happens to be equivalent to the model-view, but we'll leave it to the application to decide how to compute it.

Let's add a new file to the ModelViewer project called *SimpleLighting.vert* for the lighting algorithm. In Xcode, right-click the *Shaders* folder, and choose Add→New file. Select the *Empty File* template in the *Other* category. Name it *SimpleLighting.vert*, and add */Shaders* after the project folder name in the location field. Deselect the checkbox in the *Targets* list, and click *Finish*.

Example 4-15 translates the pseudocode into GLSL. To make the shader usable in a variety of situations, we use uniforms to store light position, specular, and ambient properties. A vertex attribute is used to store the diffuse color; for many models, the diffuse color may vary on a per-vertex basis (although in our case it does not). This would allow us to use a single draw call to draw a multicolored model.

 Remember, we're leaving out the `STRINGIFY` macros in all shader listings from here on out, so take a look at Example 1-13 to see how to add that macro to this file.

Example 4-15. SimpleLighting.vert

```
attribute vec4 Position;
attribute vec3 Normal;
attribute vec3 DiffuseMaterial;

uniform mat4 Projection;
uniform mat4 Modelview;
uniform mat3 NormalMatrix;
uniform vec3 LightPosition;
uniform vec3 AmbientMaterial;
uniform vec3 SpecularMaterial;
uniform float Shininess;

varying vec4 DestinationColor;

void main(void)
{
    vec3 N = NormalMatrix * Normal;
    vec3 L = normalize(LightPosition);
    vec3 E = vec3(0, 0, 1);
    vec3 H = normalize(L + E);

    float df = max(0.0, dot(N, L));
    float sf = max(0.0, dot(N, H));
    sf = pow(sf, Shininess);

    vec3 color = AmbientMaterial + df * DiffuseMaterial + sf * SpecularMaterial;

    DestinationColor = vec4(color, 1);
    gl_Position = Projection * Modelview * Position;
}
```

Take a look at the pseudocode in Example 4-14; the vertex shader is an implementation of that. The main difference is that GLSL requires you to qualify many of the variables as being attributes, uniforms, or varyings. Also note that in its final code line, Example 4-15 performs the standard transformation of the vertex position, just as it did for the nonlit case.

 GLSL is a bit different from many other languages in that it does not autopromote literals from integers to floats. For example, `max(0, myFloat)` generates a compile error, but `max(0.0, myFloat)` does not. On the other hand, constructors for vector-based types *do* perform conversion implicitly; it's perfectly legal to write either `vec2(0, 0)` or `vec3(0.0, 0.0)`.

New Rendering Engine

To create the ES 2.0 backend to ModelViewer, let's start with the ES 1.1 variant and make the following changes, some of which should be familiar by now:

1. Copy the contents of *RenderingEngine.ES1.cpp* into *RenderingEngine.ES2.cpp*.
2. Remove the *_OES* and *OES* suffixes from the FBO code.
3. Change the namespace from `ES1` to `ES2`.
4. Change the two `#includes` to point to the *ES2* folder rather than the *ES1* folder.
5. Add the `BuildShader` and `BuildProgram` methods (see Example 1-18). You must change all instances of `RenderingEngine2` to `RenderingEngine` because we are using namespaces to distinguish between the 1.1 and 2.0 renderers.
6. Add declarations for `BuildShader` and `BuildProgram` to the class declaration as shown in Example 1-15.
7. Add the `#include` for `iostream` as shown in Example 1-15.

Now that the busywork is out of the way, let's add declarations for the uniform handles and attribute handles that are used to communicate with the vertex shader. Since the vertex shader is now much more complex than the simple pass-through program we've been using, let's group the handles into simple substructures, as shown in Example 4-16. Add this code to `RenderingEngine.ES2.cpp`, within the namespace declaration, not above it. (The bold part of the listing shows the two lines you must add to the class declaration's **private:** section.)

Example 4-16. ES2::RenderingEngine structures

```
#define STRINGIFY(A)  #A
#include "../Shaders/SimpleLighting.vert"
#include "../Shaders/Simple.frag"

struct UniformHandles {
    GLuint Modelview;
    GLuint Projection;
```

```
    GLuint NormalMatrix;
    GLuint LightPosition;
};

struct AttributeHandles {
    GLint Position;
    GLint Normal;
    GLint Ambient;
    GLint Diffuse;
    GLint Specular;
    GLint Shininess;
};

class RenderingEngine : public IRenderingEngine {
    // ...
    UniformHandles m_uniforms;
    AttributeHandles m_attributes;
};
```

Next we need to change the Initialize method so that it compiles the shaders, extracts the handles to all the uniforms and attributes, and sets up some default material colors. Replace everything from the comment // Set up various GL state to the end of the method with the contents of Example 4-17.

Example 4-17. ES2::RenderingEngine::Initialize()

...

```
// Create the GLSL program.
GLuint program = BuildProgram(SimpleVertexShader, SimpleFragmentShader);
glUseProgram(program);

// Extract the handles to attributes and uniforms.
m_attributes.Position = glGetAttribLocation(program, "Position");
m_attributes.Normal = glGetAttribLocation(program, "Normal");
m_attributes.Ambient = glGetAttribLocation(program, "AmbientMaterial");
m_attributes.Diffuse = glGetAttribLocation(program, "DiffuseMaterial");
m_attributes.Specular = glGetAttribLocation(program, "SpecularMaterial");
m_attributes.Shininess = glGetAttribLocation(program, "Shininess");
m_uniforms.Projection = glGetUniformLocation(program, "Projection");
m_uniforms.Modelview = glGetUniformLocation(program, "Modelview");
m_uniforms.NormalMatrix = glGetUniformLocation(program, "NormalMatrix");
m_uniforms.LightPosition = glGetUniformLocation(program, "LightPosition");

// Set up some default material parameters.
glVertexAttrib3f(m_attributes.Ambient, 0.04f, 0.04f, 0.04f);
glVertexAttrib3f(m_attributes.Specular, 0.5, 0.5, 0.5);
glVertexAttrib1f(m_attributes.Shininess, 50);

// Initialize various state.
glEnableVertexAttribArray(m_attributes.Position);
glEnableVertexAttribArray(m_attributes.Normal);
glEnable(GL_DEPTH_TEST);
```

```
// Set up transforms.
m_translation = mat4::Translate(0, 0, -7);
```

Next let's replace the Render() method, shown in Example 4-18.

Example 4-18. ES2::RenderingEngine::Render()

```
void RenderingEngine::Render(const vector<Visual>& visuals) const
{
    glClearColor(0, 0.125f, 0.25f, 1);
    glClear(GL_COLOR_BUFFER_BIT | GL_DEPTH_BUFFER_BIT);

    vector<Visual>::const_iterator visual = visuals.begin();
    for (int visualIndex = 0;
         visual != visuals.end();
         ++visual, ++visualIndex) {

        // Set the viewport transform.
        ivec2 size = visual->ViewportSize;
        ivec2 lowerLeft = visual->LowerLeft;
        glViewport(lowerLeft.x, lowerLeft.y, size.x, size.y);

        // Set the light position.
        vec4 lightPosition(0.25, 0.25, 1, 0);
        glUniform3fv(m_uniforms.LightPosition, 1, lightPosition.Pointer());

        // Set the model-view transform.
        mat4 rotation = visual->Orientation.ToMatrix();
        mat4 modelview = rotation * m_translation;
        glUniformMatrix4fv(m_uniforms.Modelview, 1, 0, modelview.Pointer());

        // Set the normal matrix.
        // It's orthogonal, so its Inverse-Transpose is itself!
        mat3 normalMatrix = modelview.ToMat3();
        glUniformMatrix3fv(m_uniforms.NormalMatrix, 1,
                           0, normalMatrix.Pointer());

        // Set the projection transform.
        float h = 4.0f * size.y / size.x;
        mat4 projectionMatrix = mat4::Frustum(-2, 2, -h / 2, h / 2, 5, 10);
        glUniformMatrix4fv(m_uniforms.Projection, 1,
                           0, projectionMatrix.Pointer());

        // Set the diffuse color.
        vec3 color = visual->Color * 0.75f;
        glVertexAttrib4f(m_attributes.Diffuse, color.x,
                         color.y, color.z, 1);

        // Draw the surface.
        int stride = 2 * sizeof(vec3);
        const GLvoid* offset = (const GLvoid*) sizeof(vec3);
        GLint position = m_attributes.Position;
        GLint normal = m_attributes.Normal;
        const Drawable& drawable = m_drawables[visualIndex];
        glBindBuffer(GL_ARRAY_BUFFER, drawable.VertexBuffer);
```

```
        glVertexAttribPointer(position, 3, GL_FLOAT,
                             GL_FALSE, stride, 0);
        glVertexAttribPointer(normal, 3, GL_FLOAT, GL_FALSE,
                             stride, offset);
        glBindBuffer(GL_ELEMENT_ARRAY_BUFFER, drawable.IndexBuffer);
        glDrawElements(GL_TRIANGLES, drawable.IndexCount,
                      GL_UNSIGNED_SHORT, 0);
    }
}
```

That's it for the ES 2.0 backend! Turn off the ForceES1 switch in *GLView.mm*, and you should see something very similar to the ES 1.1 screenshot shown in Figure 4-11.

Per-Pixel Lighting

When a model has coarse tessellation, performing the lighting calculations at the vertex level can result in the loss of specular highlights and other detail, as shown in Figure 4-13.

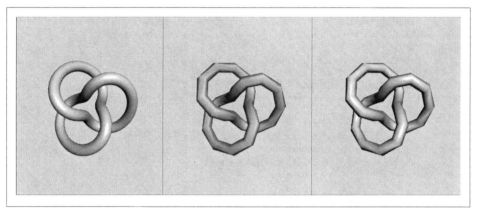

Figure 4-13. Tessellation and lighting (from left to right: infinite tessellation, vertex lighting, and pixel lighting)

One technique to counteract this unattractive effect is *per-pixel lighting*; this is when most (or all) of the lighting algorithm takes place in the fragment shader.

 Shifting work from the vertex shader to the pixel shader can often be detrimental to performance. I encourage you to experiment with performance before you commit to a specific technique.

The vertex shader becomes vastly simplified, as shown in Example 4-19. It simply passes the diffuse color and eye-space normal to the fragment shader.

Example 4-19. PixelLighting.vert

```
attribute vec4 Position;
attribute vec3 Normal;
attribute vec3 DiffuseMaterial;

uniform mat4 Projection;
uniform mat4 Modelview;
uniform mat3 NormalMatrix;

varying vec3 EyespaceNormal;
varying vec3 Diffuse;

void main(void)
{
    EyespaceNormal = NormalMatrix * Normal;
    Diffuse = DiffuseMaterial;
    gl_Position = Projection * Modelview * Position;
}
```

The fragment shader now performs the burden of the lighting math, as shown in Example 4-20. The main distinction it has from its per-vertex counterpart (Example 4-15) is the presence of precision specifiers throughout. We're using lowp for colors, mediump for the varying normal, and highp for the internal math.

Example 4-20. PixelLighting.frag

```
varying mediump vec3 EyespaceNormal;
varying lowp vec3 Diffuse;

uniform highp vec3 LightPosition;
uniform highp vec3 AmbientMaterial;
uniform highp vec3 SpecularMaterial;
uniform highp float Shininess;

void main(void)
{
    highp vec3 N = normalize(EyespaceNormal);
    highp vec3 L = normalize(LightPosition);
    highp vec3 E = vec3(0, 0, 1);
    highp vec3 H = normalize(L + E);

    highp float df = max(0.0, dot(N, L));
    highp float sf = max(0.0, dot(N, H));
    sf = pow(sf, Shininess);

    lowp vec3 color = AmbientMaterial + df * Diffuse + sf * SpecularMaterial;

    gl_FragColor = vec4(color, 1);
}
```

To try these, you can replace the contents of your existing *.vert* and *.frag* files. Just be sure not to delete the first line with STRINGIFY or the last line with the closing parenthesis and semicolon.

Shifting work from the vertex shader to the fragment shader was simple enough, but watch out: we're dealing with the normal vector in a sloppy way. OpenGL performs linear interpolation on each component of each varying. This causes inaccurate results, as you might recall from the coverage of quaternions in Chapter 3. Pragmatically speaking, simply renormalizing the incoming vector is often good enough. We'll cover a more rigorous way of dealing with normals when we present bump mapping in "Bump Mapping and DOT3 Lighting" on page 335.

Toon Shading

Mimicking the built-in lighting functionality in ES 1.1 gave us a fairly painless segue to the world of GLSL. We could continue mimicking more and more ES 1.1 features, but that would get tiresome. After all, we're upgrading to ES 2.0 to enable *new* effects, right? Let's leverage shaders to create a simple effect that would otherwise be difficult (if not impossible) to achieve with ES 1.1.

Toon shading (sometimes *cel shading*) achieves a cartoony effect by limiting gradients to two or three distinct colors, as shown in Figure 4-14.

Figure 4-14. Toon shading

Assuming you're already using per-pixel lighting, achieving this is actually incredibly simple; just add the bold lines in Example 4-21.

Example 4-21. ToonShading.frag

```
varying mediump vec3 EyespaceNormal;
varying lowp vec3 Diffuse;

uniform highp vec3 LightPosition;
uniform highp vec3 AmbientMaterial;
uniform highp vec3 SpecularMaterial;
uniform highp float Shininess;

void main(void)
{
    highp vec3 N = normalize(EyespaceNormal);
    highp vec3 L = normalize(LightPosition);
    highp vec3 E = vec3(0, 0, 1);
    highp vec3 H = normalize(L + E);

    highp float df = max(0.0, dot(N, L));
    highp float sf = max(0.0, dot(N, H));
    sf = pow(sf, Shininess);

    if (df < 0.1) df = 0.0;
    else if (df < 0.3) df = 0.3;
    else if (df < 0.6) df = 0.6;
    else df = 1.0;

    sf = step(0.5, sf);

    lowp vec3 color = AmbientMaterial + df * Diffuse + sf * SpecularMaterial;

    gl_FragColor = vec4(color, 1);
}
```

Better Wireframes Using Polygon Offset

The toon shading example belongs to a class of effects called *nonphotorealistic* effects, often known as *NPR* effects. Having dangled the carrot of shaders in front of you, I'd now like to show that ES 1.1 can also render some cool effects.

For example, you might want to produce a intentionally faceted look to better illustrate the geometry; this is useful in applications such as CAD visualization or technical illustration. Figure 4-15 shows a two-pass technique whereby the model is first rendered with triangles and then with lines. The result is less messy than the wireframe viewer because hidden lines have been eliminated.

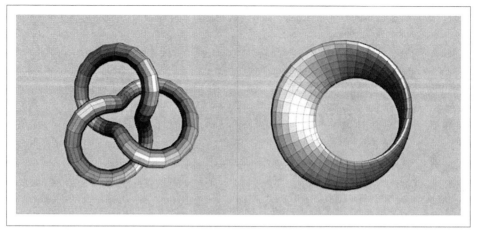

Figure 4-15. Two-pass wireframe with the Trefoil knot and Möbius strip

An issue with this two-pass technique is Z-fighting (see "Beware the Scourge of Depth Artifacts" on page 121). An obvious workaround is translating the first pass backward ever so slightly, or translating the second pass forward. Unfortunately, that approach causes issues because of the nonlinearity of depth precision; some portions of your model would look fine, but other parts may have lines on the opposite side that poke through.

It turns out that both versions of OpenGL ES offer a solution to this specific issue, and it's called *polygon offset*. Polygon offset tweaks the Z value of each pixel according to the depth slope of the triangle that it's in. You can enable and set it up like so:

```
glEnable(GL_POLYGON_OFFSET_FILL);
glPolygonOffset(factor, units);
```

factor scales the depth slope, and units gets added to the result. When polygon offset is enabled, the Z values in each triangle get tweaked as follows:

$$Z' = Z + slope * factor + units$$

You can find the code to implement this effect in ModelViewer in the downloadable examples (see "How to Contact Us" on page xvii). Note that your RenderingEngine class will need to store two VBO handles for index buffers: one for the line indices, the other for the triangle indices. In practice, finding the right values for factor and units almost always requires experimentation.

 Because of a hardware limitation, first- and second-generation iPhones ignore the factor argument in glPolygonOffset.

Loading Geometry from OBJ Files

So far we've been dealing exclusively with a gallery of parametric surfaces. They make a great teaching tool, but parametric surfaces probably aren't what you'll be rendering in your app. More likely, you'll have 3D assets coming from artists who use modeling software such as Maya or Blender.

The first thing to decide on is the file format we'll use for storing geometry. The COLLADA format was devised to solve the problem of interchange between various 3D packages, but COLLADA is quite complex; it's capable of conveying much more than just geometry, including effects, physics, and animation.

A more suitable format for our modest purposes is the simple OBJ format, first developed by Wavefront Technologies in the 1980s and still in use today. We won't go into its full specification here (there are plenty of relevant sources on the Web), but we'll cover how to load a conformant file that uses a subset of OBJ features.

Even though the OBJ format is simple and portable, I don't recommend using it in a production game or application. The parsing overhead can be avoided by inventing your own raw binary format, slurping up the entire file in a single I/O call, and then directly uploading its contents into a vertex buffer. This type of blitz loading can greatly improve the start-up time of your iPhone app.

Another popular geometry file format for the iPhone is PowerVR's POD format. The PowerVR Insider SDK (discussed in Chapter 5) includes tools and code samples for generating and reading POD files.

Without further ado, Example 4-22 shows an example OBJ file.

Example 4-22. Insanely simple OBJ file

```
# This is a comment.

v 0.0 1.0 1.0
v 0.0 -1.0 1.0
v 0.0 -1.0 -1.0
v -1.0 1.0 1.0

f 1 2 3
f 2 3 4
```

Lines that start with a v specify a vertex position using three floats separated by spaces. Lines that start with f specify a "face" with a list of indices into the vertex list. If the OBJ consists of triangles only, then every face has exactly three indices, which makes it a breeze to render with OpenGL. Watch out, though: in OBJ files, indices are one-based, not zero-based as they are in OpenGL.

OBJ also supports vertex normals with lines that start with vn. For a face to refer to a vertex normal, it references it using an index that's separate from the vertex index, as shown in Example 4-23. The slashes are doubled because the format is actually f v/ vt/vn; this example doesn't use texture coordinates (vt), so it's blank.

Example 4-23. An OBJ file with vertex normals

```
v 0.0 1.0 1.0
v 0.0 -1.0 1.0
v 0.0 -1.0 -1.0
vn 1 0 0
f 1//1 2//1 3//1
```

One thing that's a bit awkward about this (from an OpenGL standpoint) is that each face specifies separate position indices and normal indices. In OpenGL ES, you only specify a single list of indices; each index simultaneously refers to both a normal and a position.

Because of this complication, the normals found in OBJ files are often ignored in many tools. It's fairly easy to compute the normals yourself analytically, which we'll demonstrate soon.

3D artist Christopher Desse has graciously donated some models to the public domain, two of which we'll be using in ModelViewer: a character named *MicroNapalm* (the selected model in Figure 4-16) and a ninja character (far left in the tab bar). This greatly enhances the cool factor when you want to show off to your 4-year-old; why have cones and spheres when you can have ninjas?

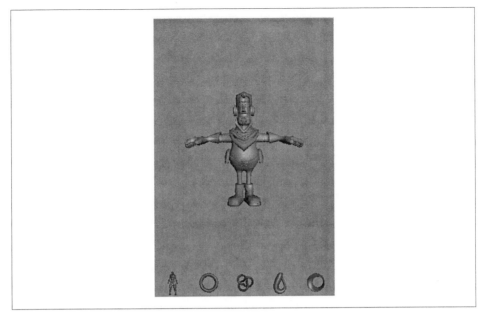

Figure 4-16. ModelViewer with two OBJ models

> I should also mention that I processed Christopher's OBJ files so that they contain only **v** lines and **f** lines with three indices each and that I scaled the models to fit inside a unit cube.

Managing Resource Files

Note that we'll be loading resources from external files for the first time. Adding file resources to a project is easy in Xcode. Download the two files (*micronapalmv2.obj* and *Ninja.obj*) from the examples site, and put them on your desktop or in your *Downloads* folder.

Create a new folder called *Models* by right-clicking the *ModelViewer* root in the *Overview* pane, and choose Add→New Group. Right-click the new folder, and choose Add→Existing Files. Select the two OBJ files (available from this book's website) by holding the Command key, and then click *Add*. In the next dialog box, check the box labeled "Copy items...", accept the defaults, and then click Add. Done!

The iPhone differs from other platforms in how it handles bundled resources, so it makes sense to create a new interface to shield this from the application engine. Let's call it `IResourceManager`, shown in Example 4-24. For now it has a single method that simply returns the absolute path to the folder that has resource files. This may seem too simple to merit its own interface at the moment, but we'll extend it in future chapters to handle more complex tasks, such as loading image files. Add these lines, and make the change shown in bold to *Interface.hpp*.

Example 4-24. Adding IResourceManager to Interface.hpp

```
#include <string>
using std::string;

// ...
struct IResourceManager {
    virtual string GetResourcePath() const = 0;
    virtual ~IResourceManager() {}
};

IResourceManager* CreateResourceManager();

IApplicationEngine* CreateApplicationEngine(IRenderingEngine* renderingEngine,
                                            IResourceManager* resourceManager);

// ...
```

We added a new argument to `CreateApplicationEngine` to allow the platform-specific layer to pass in its implementation class. In our case the implementation class needs to be a mixture of C++ and Objective-C. Add a new C++ file to your Xcode project called *ResourceManager.mm* (don't create the corresponding *.h* file), shown in Example 4-25.

Example 4-25. ResourceManager implementation

```
#import <UIKit/UIKit.h>
#import <QuartzCore/QuartzCore.h>
#import <string>
#import <iostream>
#import "Interfaces.hpp"

using namespace std;

class ResourceManager : public IResourceManager {
public:
    string GetResourcePath() const
    {
        NSString* bundlePath = [[NSBundle mainBundle] resourcePath];❶
        return [bundlePath UTF8String];❷
    }
};

IResourceManager* CreateResourceManager()
{
    return new ResourceManager();
}
```

❶ Retrieve the global `mainBundle` object, and call its `resourcePath` method, which returns something like this when running on a simulator:

```
/Users/username/Library/Application Support/iPhone Simulator
/User/Applications/uuid/ModelViewer.app
```

When running on a physical device, it returns something like this:

```
/var/mobile/Applications/uuid/ModelViewer.app
```

❷ Convert the Objective-C string object into a C++ STL string object using the
UTF8String method.

The resource manager should be instanced within the GLView class and passed to the
application engine. *GLView.h* has a field called m_resourceManager, which gets instanced somewhere in initWithFrame and gets passed to CreateApplicationEngine.
(This is similar to how we're already handling the rendering engine.) So, you'll need to
do the following:

1. In *GLView.h*, add the line IResourceManager* m_resourceManager; to the
   @private section.

2. In *GLView.mm*, add the line m_resourceManager = CreateResourceManager(); to
   initWithFrame (you can add it just above the line if (api == kEAGLRenderingAPIO
   penGLES1). Next, add m_resourceManager as the second argument to CreateAppli
   cationEngine.

Next we need to make a few small changes to the application engine per Example 4-26. The lines in bold show how we're reusing the ISurface interface to avoid
changing any code in the rendering engine. Modified/new lines in *ApplicationEn-
gine.cpp* are shown in bold (make sure you replace the existing assignments to
surfaces[0] and surfaces[0] in Initialize):

Example 4-26. Consuming IResourceManager from ApplicationEngine

```
#include "Interfaces.hpp"
#include "ObjSurface.hpp"

...

class ApplicationEngine : public IApplicationEngine {
public:
    ApplicationEngine(IRenderingEngine* renderingEngine,
                      IResourceManager* resourceManager);
    ...
private:
    ...
    IResourceManager* m_resourceManager;
};

IApplicationEngine* CreateApplicationEngine(IRenderingEngine* renderingEngine,
                                            IResourceManager* resourceManager)
{
    return new ApplicationEngine(renderingEngine, resourceManager);
}
```

```
ApplicationEngine::ApplicationEngine(IRenderingEngine* renderingEngine,
                                     IResourceManager* resourceManager) :
    m_spinning(false),
    m_pressedButton(-1),
    m_renderingEngine(renderingEngine),
    m_resourceManager(resourceManager)
{
...
}

void ApplicationEngine::Initialize(int width, int height)
{
    ...

    string path = m_resourceManager->GetResourcePath();
    surfaces[0] = new ObjSurface(path + "/micronapalmv2.obj");
    surfaces[1] = new ObjSurface(path + "/Ninja.obj");
    surfaces[2] = new Torus(1.4, 0.3);
    surfaces[3] = new TrefoilKnot(1.8f);
    surfaces[4] = new KleinBottle(0.2f);
    surfaces[5] = new MobiusStrip(1);

    ...
}
```

Implementing ISurface

The next step is creating the ObjSurface class, which implements all the ISurface methods and is responsible for parsing the OBJ file. This class will be more than just a dumb
loader; recall that we want to compute surface normals analytically. Doing so allows
us to reduce the size of the app, but at the cost of a slightly longer startup time.

We'll compute the vertex normals by first finding the facet normal of every face and
then averaging together the normals from adjoining faces. The C++ implementation
of this algorithm is fairly rote, and you can get it from the book's companion website
(*http://oreilly.com/catalog/9780596804831*); for brevity's sake, Example 4-27 shows
the pseudocode.

Example 4-27. Pseudocode to compute vertex normals from facets

```
ivec3 faces[faceCount] = read from OBJ
vec3 positions[vertexCount] = read from OBJ
vec3 normals[vertexCount] = { (0,0,0), (0,0,0), ... }

for each face in faces:
    vec3 a = positions[face.Vertex0]
    vec3 b = positions[face.Vertex1]
    vec3 c = positions[face.Vertex2]
    vec3 facetNormal = (a - b) × (c - b)
```

```
        normals[face.Vertex0] += facetNormal
        normals[face.Vertex1] += facetNormal
        normals[face.Vertex2] += facetNormal

for each normal in normals:
    normal = normalize(normal)
```

The mechanics of loading face indices and vertex positions from the OBJ file are somewhat tedious, so you should download *ObjSurface.cpp* and *ObjSurface.hpp* from this book's website (see "How to Contact Us" on page xvii) and add them to your Xcode project. Example 4-28 shows the ObjSurface constructor, which loads the vertex indices using the fstream facility in C++. Note that I subtracted one from all vertex indices; watch out for the one-based pitfall!

Example 4-28. ObjSurface constructor

```
ObjSurface::ObjSurface(const string& name) :
    m_name(name),
    m_faceCount(0),
    m_vertexCount(0)
{
    m_faces.resize(this->GetTriangleIndexCount() / 3);
    ifstream objFile(m_name.c_str());
    vector<ivec3>::iterator face = m_faces.begin();
    while (objFile) {
        char c = objFile.get();
        if (c == 'f') {
            assert(face != m_faces.end() && "parse error");
            objFile >> face->x >> face->y >> face->z;
            *face++ -= ivec3(1, 1, 1);
        }
        objFile.ignore(MaxLineSize, '\n');
    }
    assert(face == m_faces.end() && "parse error");
}
```

Wrapping Up

We covered quite a bit of territory in this chapter: we took a deep dive into GLSL, examined some algorithms for lighting and simple effects, and finally managed to replace some tiresome mathematical shapes with artistic 3D content. Another type of content that artists can offer is actually 2D, and yet it's a vital ingredient to almost all real-time 3D rendering. *Textures* are images that get "wrapped" around the objects in your scene. They sound simple enough, but trust me, they're thorny enough to deserve their own chapter or two. And so we come to the next stop on our graphics trek!

## CHAPTER 5

Textures and Image Capture

Not everybody trusts paintings, but people
believe photographs.

—Ansel Adams

Shading algorithms are required for effects that need to respond to a changing condition in real time, such as the movement of a light source. But procedural methods can go only so far on their own; they can never replace the creativity of a professional artist. That's where *textures* come to the rescue. Texturing allows any predefined image, such as a photograph, to be projected onto a 3D surface.

Simply put, textures are images; yet somehow, an entire vocabulary is built around them. Pixels that make up a texture are known as *texels*. When the hardware reads a texel color, it's said to be *sampling*. When OpenGL scales a texture, it's also *filtering* it. Don't let the vocabulary intimidate you; the concepts are simple. In this chapter, we'll focus on presenting the basics, saving some advanced techniques for later in this book.

We'll begin by modifying ModelViewer to support image loading and simple texturing. Afterward we'll take a closer look at some of the OpenGL features involved, such as mipmapping and filtering. Toward the end of the chapter we'll use texturing to perform a fun trick with the iPhone camera.

Adding Textures to ModelViewer

Our final enhancement to ModelViewer wraps a simple grid texture around each of the surfaces in the parametric gallery, as shown in Figure 5-1. We need to store only one cell of the grid in an image file; OpenGL can repeat the source pattern as many times as desired.

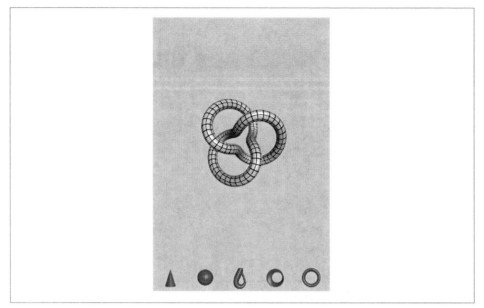

Figure 5-1. Textured ModelViewer

The image file can be in a number of different file formats, but we'll go with PNG for now. It's popular because it supports an optional alpha channel, lossless compression, and variable color precision. (Another common format on the iPhone platform is PVR, which we'll cover later in the chapter.)

You can either download the image file for the grid cell from this book's companion site or create one using your favorite paint or graphics program. I used a tiny 16×16 white square with a 1-pixel black border. Save the file as *Grid16.png*.

Since we'll be loading a resource file from an external file, let's use the *.OBJ*-loading sample from the previous chapter as the starting point. To keep things simple, the first step is rewinding a bit and using parametric surfaces exclusively. Simply revert the `ApplicationEngine::Initialize` method so that it uses the sphere and cone shapes. To do this, find the following code:

```
string path = m_resourceManager->GetResourcePath();
surfaces[0] = new ObjSurface(path + "/micronapalmv2.obj");
surfaces[1] = new ObjSurface(path + "/Ninja.obj");
```

And replace it with the following:

```
surfaces[0] = new Cone(3, 1);
surfaces[1] = new Sphere(1.4f);
```

Keep everything else the same. We'll enhance the `IResourceManager` interface later to support image loading.

Next you need to add the actual image file to your Xcode project. As with the OBJ files in the previous chapter, Xcode automatically deploys these resources to your iPhone. Even though this example has only a single image file, I recommend creating a dedicated group anyway. Right-click the *ModelViewer* root in the *Overview* pane, choose Add→New Group, and call it *Textures*. Right-click the new group, and choose Get Info. To the right of the *Path* label on the General tab, click Choose, and create a new folder called *Textures*. Click Choose, and close the group info window.

Right-click the new group, and choose Add→Existing Files. Select the PNG file, click Add, and in the next dialog box, make sure the "Copy items" checkbox is checked; then click Add.

Enhancing IResourceManager

Unlike OBJ files, it's a bit nontrivial to decode the PNG file format by hand since it uses a lossless compression algorithm. Rather than manually decoding the PNG file in the application code, it makes more sense to leverage the infrastructure that Apple provides for reading image files. Recall that the `ResourceManager` implementation is a mix of Objective-C and C++; so, it's an ideal place for calling Apple-specific APIs. Let's make the resource manager responsible for decoding the PNG file. The first step is to open `Interfaces.hpp` and make the changes shown in Example 5-1. New lines are in bold (the changes to the last two lines, which you'll find at the end of the file, are needed to support a change we'll be making to the rendering engine).

Example 5-1. Enhanced IResourceManager

```
struct IResourceManager {
    virtual string GetResourcePath() const = 0;
    virtual void LoadPngImage(const string& filename) = 0;❶
    virtual void* GetImageData() = 0;❷
    virtual ivec2 GetImageSize() = 0;❸
    virtual void UnloadImage() = 0;❹
    virtual ~IResourceManager() {}
};

// ...
namespace ES1 { IRenderingEngine*
            CreateRenderingEngine(IResourceManager* resourceManager); }
namespace ES2 { IRenderingEngine*
            CreateRenderingEngine(IResourceManager* resourceManager); }
```

❶ Load the given PNG file into the resource manager.

❷ Return a pointer to the decoded color buffer. For now, this is always 8-bit-per-component RGBA data.

❸ Return the width and height of the loaded image using the `ivec2` class from our vector library.

❹ Free memory used to store the decoded data.

Now let's open *ResourceManager.mm* and update the actual implementation class (don't delete the #imports, the using statement, or the CreateResourceManager definition). It needs two additional items to maintain state: the decoded memory buffer (m_imageData) and the size of the image (m_imageSize). Apple provides several ways of loading PNG files; Example 5-2 is the simplest way of doing this.

Example 5-2. ResourceManager with PNG loading

```
class ResourceManager : public IResourceManager {
public:
    string GetResourcePath() const
    {
        NSString* bundlePath =[[NSBundle mainBundle] resourcePath];
        return [bundlePath UTF8String];
    }
    void LoadPngImage(const string& name)
    {
        NSString* basePath = [NSString stringWithUTF8String:name.c_str()];❶
        NSString* resourcePath = [[NSBundle mainBundle] resourcePath];
        NSString* fullPath = [resourcePath stringByAppendingPathComponent:basePath];❷
        UIImage* uiImage = [UIImage imageWithContentsOfFile:fullPath];❸
        CGImageRef cgImage = uiImage.CGImage;❹
        m_imageSize.x = CGImageGetWidth(cgImage);❺
        m_imageSize.y = CGImageGetHeight(cgImage);
        m_imageData = CGDataProviderCopyData(CGImageGetDataProvider(cgImage));❻
    }
    void* GetImageData()
    {
        return (void*) CFDataGetBytePtr(m_imageData);
    }
    ivec2 GetImageSize()
    {
        return m_imageSize;
    }
    void UnloadImage()
    {
        CFRelease(m_imageData);
    }
private:
    CFDataRef m_imageData;
    ivec2 m_imageSize;
};
```

Most of Example 5-2 is straightforward, but LoadPngImage deserves some extra explanation:

❶ Convert the C++ string into an Objective-C string object.

❷ Obtain the fully qualified path the PNG file.

❸ Create an instance of a UIImage object using the imageWithContentsOfFile method, which slurps up the contents of the entire file.

❹ Extract the inner `CGImage` object from `UIImage`. `UIImage` is essentially a convenience wrapper for `CGImage`. Note that `CGImage` is a Core Graphics class, which is shared across the Mac OS X and iPhone OS platforms; `UIImage` comes from UIKit and is therefore iPhone-specific.

❺ Extract the image size from the inner `CGImage` object.

❻ Generate a `CFData` object from the `CGImage` object. `CFData` is a core foundation object that represents a swath of memory.

> The image loader in Example 5-2 is simple but not robust. For production code, I recommend using one of the enhanced methods presented later in the chapter.

Next we need to make sure that the resource manager can be accessed from the right places. It's already instanced in the `GLView` class and passed to the application engine; now we need to pass it to the rendering engine as well. The OpenGL code needs it to retrieve the raw image data.

Go ahead and change `GLView.mm` so that the resource manager gets passed to the rendering engine during construction. Example 5-3 shows the relevant section of code (additions are shown in bold).

Example 5-3. Creation of ResourceManager, RenderingEngine, and ApplicationEngine

```
m_resourceManager = CreateResourceManager();

if (api == kEAGLRenderingAPIOpenGLES1) {
    NSLog(@"Using OpenGL ES 1.1");
    m_renderingEngine = ES1::CreateRenderingEngine(m_resourceManager);
} else {
    NSLog(@"Using OpenGL ES 2.0");
    m_renderingEngine = ES2::CreateRenderingEngine(m_resourceManager);
}

m_applicationEngine = CreateApplicationEngine(m_renderingEngine,
                                              m_resourceManager);
```

Generating Texture Coordinates

To control how the texture gets applied to the models, we need to add a 2D texture coordinate attribute to the vertices. The natural place to generate texture coordinates is in the `ParametricSurface` class. Each subclass should specify how many repetitions of the texture get tiled across each axis of domain. Consider the torus: its outer circumference is much longer than the circumference of its cross section. Since the x-axis in the domain follows the outer circumference and the y-axis circumscribes the cross section, it follows that more copies of the texture need to be tiled across the x-axis than the y-axis. This prevents the grid pattern from being stretched along one axis.

Recall that each parametric surface describes its domain using the `ParametricIn` `terval` structure, so that's a natural place to store the number of repetitions; see Example 5-4. Note that the repetition counts for each axis are stored in a `vec2`.

Example 5-4. Texture support in ParametricSurface.hpp

```
#include "Interfaces.hpp"

struct ParametricInterval {
    ivec2 Divisions;
    vec2 UpperBound;
    vec2 TextureCount;
};

class ParametricSurface : public ISurface {
...
private:
    vec2 ComputeDomain(float i, float j) const;
    ivec2 m_slices;
    ivec2 m_divisions;
    vec2 m_upperBound;
    vec2 m_textureCount;
};
```

The texture counts that I chose for the cone and sphere are shown in bold in Example 5-5. For brevity's sake, I've omitted the other parametric surfaces; as always, you can download the code from this book's website (*http://oreilly.com/catalog/ 9780596804831*).

Example 5-5. Texture support in ParametricEquations.hpp

```
#include "ParametricSurface.hpp"

class Cone : public ParametricSurface {
public:
    Cone(float height, float radius) : m_height(height), m_radius(radius)
    {
        ParametricInterval interval = { ivec2(20, 20), vec2(TwoPi, 1), vec2(30,20) };
        SetInterval(interval);
    }
    ...
};

class Sphere : public ParametricSurface {
public:
    Sphere(float radius) : m_radius(radius)
    {
        ParametricInterval interval = { ivec2(20, 20), vec2(Pi, TwoPi), vec2(20, 35) };
        SetInterval(interval);
    }
    ...
};
```

Next we need to flesh out a couple methods in ParametericSurface (Example 5-6). Recall that we're passing in a set of flags to GenerateVertices to request a set of vertex attributes; until now, we've been ignoring the VertexFlagsTexCoords flag.

Example 5-6. Texture support in ParametricSurface.cpp

```
void ParametricSurface::SetInterval(const ParametricInterval& interval)
{
    m_divisions = interval.Divisions;
    m_slices = m_divisions - ivec2(1, 1);
    m_upperBound = interval.UpperBound;
    m_textureCount = interval.TextureCount;
}

...

void ParametricSurface::GenerateVertices(vector<float>& vertices,
                                         unsigned char flags) const
{
    int floatsPerVertex = 3;
    if (flags & VertexFlagsNormals)
        floatsPerVertex += 3;
    if (flags & VertexFlagsTexCoords)
        floatsPerVertex += 2;

    vertices.resize(GetVertexCount() * floatsPerVertex);
    float* attribute = &vertices[0];

    for (int j = 0; j < m_divisions.y; j++) {
        for (int i = 0; i < m_divisions.x; i++) {

            // Compute Position
            vec2 domain = ComputeDomain(i, j);
            vec3 range = Evaluate(domain);
            attribute = range.Write(attribute);

            // Compute Normal
            if (flags & VertexFlagsNormals) {
                ...
            }

            // Compute Texture Coordinates
            if (flags & VertexFlagsTexCoords) {
                float s = m_textureCount.x * i / m_slices.x;
                float t = m_textureCount.y * j / m_slices.y;
                attribute = vec2(s, t).Write(attribute);
            }
        }
    }
}
```

In OpenGL, texture coordinates are normalized such that (0,0) maps to one corner of the image and (1, 1) maps to the other corner, regardless of its size. The inner loop in Example 5-6 computes the texture coordinates like this:

```
float s = m_textureCount.x * i / m_slices.x;
float t = m_textureCount.y * j / m_slices.y;
```

Since the s coordinate ranges from zero up to m_textureCount.x (inclusive), OpenGL horizontally tiles m_textureCount.x repetitions of the texture across the surface. We'll take a deeper look at how texture coordinates work later in the chapter.

Note that if you were loading the model data from an OBJ file or other 3D format, you'd probably obtain the texture coordinates directly from the model file rather than computing them like we're doing here.

Enabling Textures with ES1::RenderingEngine

As always, let's start with the ES 1.1 rendering engine since the 2.0 variant is more complex. The first step is adding a pointer to the resource manager as shown in Example 5-7. Note we're also adding a GLuint for the grid texture. Much like framebuffer objects and vertex buffer objects, OpenGL textures have integer names.

Example 5-7. RenderingEngine.ES1.cpp

```
class RenderingEngine : public IRenderingEngine {
public:
    RenderingEngine(IResourceManager* resourceManager);
    void Initialize(const vector<ISurface*>& surfaces);
    void Render(const vector<Visual>& visuals) const;
private:
    vector<Drawable> m_drawables;
    GLuint m_colorRenderbuffer;
    GLuint m_depthRenderbuffer;
    mat4 m_translation;
    GLuint m_gridTexture;
    IResourceManager* m_resourceManager;
};

IRenderingEngine* CreateRenderingEngine(IResourceManager* resourceManager)
{
    return new RenderingEngine(resourceManager);
}

RenderingEngine::RenderingEngine(IResourceManager* resourceManager)
{
    m_resourceManager = resourceManager;
    glGenRenderbuffersOES(1, &m_colorRenderbuffer);
    glBindRenderbufferOES(GL_RENDERBUFFER_OES, m_colorRenderbuffer);
}
```

Example 5-8 shows the code for loading the texture, followed by a detailed explanation.

Example 5-8. Creating the OpenGL texture

```
void RenderingEngine::Initialize(const vector<ISurface*>& surfaces)
{
    vector<ISurface*>::const_iterator surface;
```

```
    for (surface = surfaces.begin(); surface != surfaces.end(); ++surface) {

        // Create the VBO for the vertices.
        vector<float> vertices;
        (*surface)->GenerateVertices(vertices, VertexFlagsNormals
                                     |VertexFlagsTexCoords);

    // ...

    // Load the texture.
    glGenTextures(1, &m_gridTexture);❶
    glBindTexture(GL_TEXTURE_2D, m_gridTexture);
    glTexParameteri(GL_TEXTURE_2D, GL_TEXTURE_MIN_FILTER, GL_LINEAR);❷
    glTexParameteri(GL_TEXTURE_2D, GL_TEXTURE_MAG_FILTER, GL_LINEAR);

    m_resourceManager->LoadPngImage("Grid16.png");❸
    void* pixels = m_resourceManager->GetImageData();
    ivec2 size = m_resourceManager->GetImageSize();
    glTexImage2D(GL_TEXTURE_2D, 0, GL_RGBA, size.x,
                 size.y, 0, GL_RGBA, GL_UNSIGNED_BYTE, pixels);❹
    m_resourceManager->UnloadImage();

    // Set up various GL state.
    glEnableClientState(GL_VERTEX_ARRAY);
    glEnableClientState(GL_NORMAL_ARRAY);
    glEnableClientState(GL_TEXTURE_COORD_ARRAY);❺
    glEnable(GL_LIGHTING);
    glEnable(GL_LIGHT0);
    glEnable(GL_DEPTH_TEST);
    glEnable(GL_TEXTURE_2D);❻

    ...
}
```

❶ Generate the integer identifier for the object, and then bind it to the pipeline. This follows the Gen/Bind pattern used by FBOs and VBOs.

❷ Set the *minification filter* and *magnification filter* of the texture object. The texture filter is the algorithm that OpenGL uses to shrink or enlarge a texture; we'll cover filtering in detail later.

❸ Tell the resource manager to load and decode the *Grid16.png* file.

❹ Upload the raw texture data to OpenGL using glTexImage2D; more on this later.

❺ Tell OpenGL to enable the texture coordinate vertex attribute.

❻ Tell OpenGL to enable texturing.

Example 5-8 introduces the glTexImage2D function, which unfortunately has more parameters than it needs because of historical reasons. Don't be intimidated by the eight parameters; it's much easier to use than it appears. Here's the formal declaration:

```
void glTexImage2D(GLenum target, GLint level, GLint internalformat,
                  GLsizei width, GLsizei height, GLint border,
                  GLenum format, GLenum type, const GLvoid* pixels);
```

target

This specifies which binding point to upload the texture to. For ES 1.1, this must be `GL_TEXTURE_2D`.

level

This specifies the mipmap level. We'll learn more about mipmaps soon. For now, use zero for this.

internalFormat

This specifies the format of the texture. We're using `GL_RGBA` for now, and other formats will be covered shortly. It's declared as a `GLint` rather than a `GLenum` for historical reasons.

width, height

This specifies the size of the image being uploaded.

border

Set this to zero; texture borders are not supported in OpenGL ES. Be happy, because that's one less thing you have to remember!

format

In OpenGL ES, this has to match `internalFormat`. The argument may seem redundant, but it's yet another carryover from desktop OpenGL, which supports format conversion. Again, be happy; this is a simpler API.

type

This describes the type of each color component. This is commonly `GL_UNSIGNED_BYTE`, but we'll learn about some other types later.

pixels

This is the pointer to the raw data that gets uploaded.

Next let's go over the `Render` method. The only difference is that the vertex stride is larger, and we need to call `glTexCoordPointer` to give OpenGL the correct offset into the VBO. See Example 5-9.

Example 5-9. ES1::RenderingEngine::Render with texture

```
void RenderingEngine::Render(const vector<Visual>& visuals) const
{
    glClearColor(0.5f, 0.5f, 0.5f, 1);
    glClear(GL_COLOR_BUFFER_BIT | GL_DEPTH_BUFFER_BIT);

    vector<Visual>::const_iterator visual = visuals.begin();
    for (int visualIndex = 0;
         visual != visuals.end();
         ++visual, ++visualIndex)
    {

        // ...
```

```
        // Draw the surface.
        int stride = sizeof(vec3) + sizeof(vec3) + sizeof(vec2);
        const GLvoid* texCoordOffset = (const GLvoid*) (2 * sizeof(vec3));
        const Drawable& drawable = m_drawables[visualIndex];
        glBindBuffer(GL_ARRAY_BUFFER, drawable.VertexBuffer);
        glVertexPointer(3, GL_FLOAT, stride, 0);
        const GLvoid* normalOffset = (const GLvoid*) sizeof(vec3);
        glNormalPointer(GL_FLOAT, stride, normalOffset);
        glTexCoordPointer(2, GL_FLOAT, stride, texCoordOffset);
        glBindBuffer(GL_ELEMENT_ARRAY_BUFFER, drawable.IndexBuffer);
        glDrawElements(GL_TRIANGLES, drawable.IndexCount, GL_UNSIGNED_SHORT, 0);
    }
}
```

That's it for the ES 1.1 backend! Incidentally, in more complex applications you should take care to delete your textures after you're done with them; textures can be one of the biggest resource hogs in OpenGL. Deleting a texture is done like so:

```
glDeleteTextures(1, &m_gridTexture)
```

This function is similar to `glGenTextures` in that it takes a count and a list of names. Incidentally, vertex buffer objects are deleted in a similar manner using `glDeleteBuffers`.

Enabling Textures with ES2::RenderingEngine

The ES 2.0 backend requires some changes to both the vertex shader (to pass along the texture coordinate) and the fragment shader (to apply the texel color). You do not call `glEnable(GL_TEXTURE_2D)` with ES 2.0; it simply depends on what your fragment shader does.

Let's start with the vertex shader, shown in Example 5-10. This is a modification of the simple lighting shader presented in the previous chapter (Example 4-15). Only three new lines are required (shown in bold).

 If you tried some of the other vertex shaders in that chapter, such as the pixel shader or toon shader, the current shader in your project may look different from Example 4-15.

Example 5-10. SimpleLighting.vert with texture

```
attribute vec4 Position;
attribute vec3 Normal;
attribute vec3 DiffuseMaterial;
attribute vec2 TextureCoord;

uniform mat4 Projection;
uniform mat4 Modelview;
uniform mat3 NormalMatrix;
```

```
uniform vec3 LightPosition;
uniform vec3 AmbientMaterial;
uniform vec3 SpecularMaterial;
uniform float Shininess;

varying vec4 DestinationColor;
varying vec2 TextureCoordOut;

void main(void)
{
    vec3 N = NormalMatrix * Normal;
    vec3 L = normalize(LightPosition);
    vec3 E = vec3(0, 0, 1);
    vec3 H = normalize(L + E);

    float df = max(0.0, dot(N, L));
    float sf = max(0.0, dot(N, H));
    sf = pow(sf, Shininess);

    vec3 color = AmbientMaterial + df * DiffuseMaterial + sf * SpecularMaterial;

    DestinationColor = vec4(color, 1);
    gl_Position = Projection * Modelview * Position;
    TextureCoordOut = TextureCoord;
}
```

> To try these, you can replace the contents of your existing *.vert*
> and *.frag* files. Just be sure not to delete the first line with STRINGIFY or
> the last line with the closing parenthesis and semicolon.

Example 5-10 simply passes the texture coordinates through, but you can achieve many interesting effects by manipulating the texture coordinates, or even generating them from scratch. For example, to achieve a "movie projector" effect, simply replace the last line in Example 5-10 with this:

```
TextureCoordOut = gl_Position.xy * 2.0;
```

For now, let's stick with the boring pass-through shader because it better emulates the behavior of ES 1.1. The new fragment shader is a bit more interesting; see Example 5-11.

Example 5-11. Simple.frag with texture

```
varying lowp vec4 DestinationColor;❶
varying mediump vec2 TextureCoordOut;❷

uniform sampler2D Sampler;❸

void main(void)
{
    gl_FragColor = texture2D(Sampler, TextureCoordOut) * DestinationColor;❹
}
```

❶ As before, declare a low-precision varying to receive the color produced by lighting.

❷ Declare a medium-precision varying to receive the texture coordinates.

❸ Declare a uniform *sampler*, which represents the texture stage from which we'll retrieve the texel color.

❹ Use the `texture2D` function to look up a texel color from the sampler, then multiply it by the lighting color to produce the final color. This is component-wise multiplication, not a dot product or a cross product.

When setting a uniform sampler from within your application, a common mistake is to set it to the handle of the texture object you'd like to sample:

```
glBindTexture(GL_TEXTURE_2D, textureHandle);
GLint location = glGetUniformLocation(programHandle, "Sampler");

glUniform1i(location, textureHandle); // Incorrect
glUniform1i(location, 0); // Correct
```

The correct value of the sampler is the stage index that you'd like to sample from, not the handle. Since all uniforms default to zero, it's fine to not bother setting sampler values if you're not using multitexturing (we'll cover multitexturing later in this book).

Uniform samplers should be set to the stage index, not the texture handle.

Newly introduced in Example 5-11 is the `texture2D` function call. For input, it takes a uniform sampler and a `vec2` texture coordinate. Its return value is always a `vec4`, regardless of the texture format.

The OpenGL ES specification stipulates that `texture2D` can be called from vertex shaders as well, but on many platforms, including the iPhone, it's actually limited to fragment shaders only.

Note that Example 5-11 uses multiplication to combine the lighting color and texture color; this often produces good results. Multiplying two colors in this way is called *modulation*, and it's the default method used in ES 1.1.

Now let's make the necessary changes to the C++ code. First we need to add new class members to store the texture ID and resource manager pointer, but that's the same as ES 1.1, so I won't repeat it here. I also won't repeat the texture-loading code because it's the same with both APIs.

One new thing we need for the ES 2.0 backend is an attribute ID for texture coordinates. See Example 5-12. Note the lack of a `glEnable` for texturing; remember, there's no need for it in ES 2.0.

Example 5-12. RenderingEngine.ES2.cpp

```cpp
struct AttributeHandles {
    GLint Position;
    GLint Normal;
    GLint Ambient;
    GLint Diffuse;
    GLint Specular;
    GLint Shininess;
    GLint TextureCoord;
};

...

void RenderingEngine::Initialize(const vector<ISurface*>& surfaces)
{

    vector<ISurface*>::const_iterator surface;
    for (surface = surfaces.begin(); surface != surfaces.end(); ++surface) {

        // Create the VBO for the vertices.
        vector<float> vertices;
        (*surface)->GenerateVertices(vertices, VertexFlagsNormals|VertexFlagsTexCoords);

    // ...

    m_attributes.TextureCoord = glGetAttribLocation(program, "TextureCoord");

    // Load the texture.
    glGenTextures(1, &m_gridTexture);
    glBindTexture(GL_TEXTURE_2D, m_gridTexture);
    glTexParameteri(GL_TEXTURE_2D, GL_TEXTURE_MIN_FILTER, GL_LINEAR);
    glTexParameteri(GL_TEXTURE_2D, GL_TEXTURE_MAG_FILTER, GL_LINEAR);

    m_resourceManager->LoadPngImage("Grid16.png");
    void* pixels = m_resourceManager->GetImageData();
    ivec2 size = m_resourceManager->GetImageSize();
    glTexImage2D(GL_TEXTURE_2D, 0, GL_RGBA, size.x,
                 size.y, 0, GL_RGBA, GL_UNSIGNED_BYTE, pixels);
    m_resourceManager->UnloadImage();

    // Initialize various state.
    glEnableVertexAttribArray(m_attributes.Position);
    glEnableVertexAttribArray(m_attributes.Normal);
    glEnableVertexAttribArray(m_attributes.TextureCoord);
    glEnable(GL_DEPTH_TEST);

    ...
}
```

You may have noticed that the fragment shader declared a sampler uniform, but we're not setting it to anything in our C++ code. There's actually no need to set it; all uniforms default to zero, which is what we want for the sampler's value anyway. You don't need a nonzero sampler unless you're using multitexturing, which is a feature that we'll cover in Chapter 8.

Next up is the Render method, which is pretty straightforward (Example 5-13). The only way it differs from its ES 1.1 counterpart is that it makes three calls to glVertex AttribPointer rather than glVertexPointer, glColorPointer, and glTexCoordPointer. (Replace everything from // Draw the surface to the end of the method with the corresponding code.)

 You must also make the same changes to the ES 2.0 renderer that were shown earlier in Example 5-7.

Example 5-13. ES2::RenderingEngine::Render with texture

```
void RenderingEngine::Render(const vector<Visual>& visuals) const
{
    glClearColor(0.5f, 0.5f, 0.5f, 1);
    glClear(GL_COLOR_BUFFER_BIT | GL_DEPTH_BUFFER_BIT);

    vector<Visual>::const_iterator visual = visuals.begin();
    for (int visualIndex = 0;
         visual != visuals.end();
         ++visual, ++visualIndex)
    {

        // ...

        // Draw the surface.
        int stride = sizeof(vec3) + sizeof(vec3) + sizeof(vec2);
        const GLvoid* normalOffset = (const GLvoid*) sizeof(vec3);
        const GLvoid* texCoordOffset = (const GLvoid*) (2 * sizeof(vec3));
        GLint position = m_attributes.Position;
        GLint normal = m_attributes.Normal;
        GLint texCoord = m_attributes.TextureCoord;
        const Drawable& drawable = m_drawables[visualIndex];
        glBindBuffer(GL_ARRAY_BUFFER, drawable.VertexBuffer);
        glVertexAttribPointer(position, 3, GL_FLOAT, GL_FALSE, stride, 0);
        glVertexAttribPointer(normal, 3, GL_FLOAT, GL_FALSE, stride, normalOffset);
        glVertexAttribPointer(texCoord, 2, GL_FLOAT, GL_FALSE, stride, texCoordOffset);
        glBindBuffer(GL_ELEMENT_ARRAY_BUFFER, drawable.IndexBuffer);
        glDrawElements(GL_TRIANGLES, drawable.IndexCount, GL_UNSIGNED_SHORT, 0);
    }
}
```

That's it! You now have a textured model viewer. Before you build and run it, select Build→Clean All Targets (we've made a lot of changes to various parts of this app, and this will help avoid any surprises by building the app from a clean slate). I'll explain some of the details in the sections to come.

Texture Coordinates Revisited

Recall that texture coordinates are defined such that (0,0) is the lower-left corner and (1,1) is the upper-right corner. So, what happens when a vertex has texture coordinates that lie outside this range? The sample code is actually already sending coordinates outside this range. For example, the TextureCount parameter for the sphere is (20,35).

By default, OpenGL simply repeats the texture at every integer boundary; it lops off the integer portion of the texture coordinate before sampling the texel color. If you want to make this behavior explicit, you can add something like this to the rendering engine code:

```
glBindTexture(GL_TEXTURE_2D, m_gridTexture);
glTexParameteri(GL_TEXTURE_2D, GL_TEXTURE_WRAP_S, GL_REPEAT);
glTexParameteri(GL_TEXTURE_2D, GL_TEXTURE_WRAP_T, GL_REPEAT);
```

The wrap mode passed in to the third argument of glTexParameteri can be one of the following:

GL_REPEAT
: This is the default wrap mode; discard the integer portion of the texture coordinate.

GL_CLAMP_TO_EDGE
: Select the texel that lies at the nearest boundary.

GL_MIRRORED_REPEAT*
: If the integer portion is an even number, this acts exactly like GL_REPEAT. If it's an odd number, the fractional portion is inverted before it's applied.

Figure 5-2 shows the three wrap modes. From left to right they're repeat, clamp-to-edge, and mirrored. The figure on the far right uses GL_REPEAT for the S coordinate and GL_CLAMP_TO_EDGE for the T coordinate.

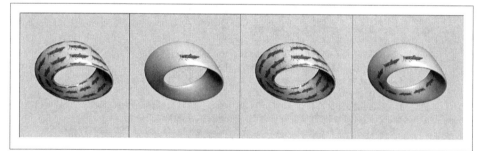

Figure 5-2. Four texture wrap configurations

What would you do if you wanted to animate your texture coordinates? For example, say you want to gradually move the grasshoppers in Figure 5-2 so that they scroll around

---

* Mirrored wrapping is not included in core OpenGL ES 1.1, but the iPhone (all generations) supports it via the GL_OES_texture_mirrored_repeat extension; simply append the _OES suffix to the constant.

the Möbius strip. You certainly wouldn't want to upload a new VBO at every frame with updated texture coordinates; that would detrimental to performance. Instead, you would set up a *texture matrix*. Texture matrices were briefly mentioned in "Saving and Restoring Transforms with Matrix Stacks" on page 62, and they're configured much the same way as the model-view and projection matrices. The only difference is that they're applied to texture coordinates rather than vertex positions. The following snippet shows how you'd set up a texture matrix with ES 1.1 (with ES 2.0, there's no built-in texture matrix, but it's easy to create one with a uniform variable):

```
glMatrixMode(GL_TEXTURE);
glTranslatef(grasshopperOffset, 0, 0);
```

In this book, we use the convention that (0,0) maps to the upper-left of the source image (Figure 5-3) and that the Y coordinate increases downward.

By the Spec

Our texture coordinate convention is not what you'd find in the OpenGL specification from Khronos, which proclaims (0,0) to be the lower-left corner. However, the spec also says that when uploading an image with `glTexImage2D`, it should be arranged in memory such that the first row of data corresponds to the bottom row in the image. In all of the methods we're using to decode the image, the top row of data comes first.

By the way, saying that (1,1) maps to a texel at the far corner of the texture image isn't a very accurate statement; the corner texel's center is actually a fraction, as shown in Figure 5-3. This may seem pedantic, but you'll see how it's relevant when we cover filtering, which comes next.

Fight Aliasing with Filtering

Is a texture a collection of discrete texels, or is it a continuous function across [0, 1]? This is a dangerous question to ask a graphics geek; it's a bit like asking a physicist if a photon is a wave or a particle.

When you upload a texture to OpenGL using `glTexImage2D`, it's a collection of discrete texels. When you sample a texture using normalized texture coordinates, it's a bit more like a continuous function. You might recall these two lines from the rendering engine:

```
glTexParameteri(GL_TEXTURE_2D, GL_TEXTURE_MIN_FILTER, GL_LINEAR);
glTexParameteri(GL_TEXTURE_2D, GL_TEXTURE_MAG_FILTER, GL_LINEAR);
```

What's going on here? The first line sets the *minification filter*; the second line sets the *magnification filter*. Both of these tell OpenGL how to map those discrete texels into a continuous function.

More precisely, the minification filter specifies the scaling algorithm to use when the texture size in screen space is smaller than the original image; the magnification filter

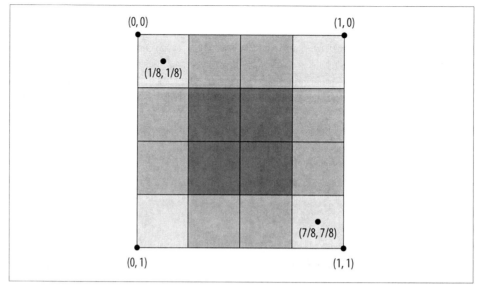

Figure 5-3. Texture coordinates in a 4x4 texture

tells OpenGL what to do when the texture size is screen space is larger than the original image.

The magnification filter can be one of two values:

GL_NEAREST
Simple and crude; use the color of the texel nearest to the texture coordinate.

GL_LINEAR
Indicates bilinear filtering. Samples the local 2×2 square of texels and blends them together using a weighted average. The image on the far right in Figure 5-4 is an example of bilinear magnification applied to a simple 8×8 monochrome texture.

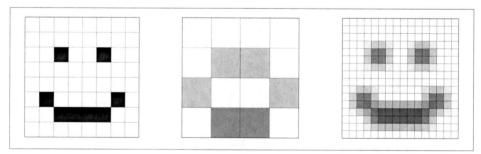

Figure 5-4. Bilinear texture filtering. From left to right: original, minified, magnified

The minification filter supports the same filters as magnification and adds four additional filters that rely on *mipmaps*, which are "preshrunk" images that you need to upload separately from the main image. More on mipmaps soon.

The available minification modes are as follows:

GL_NEAREST
As with magnification, use the color of the nearest texel.

GL_LINEAR
As with magnification, blend together the nearest four texels. The middle image in Figure 5-4 is an example of bilinear minification.

GL_NEAREST_MIPMAP_NEAREST
Find the mipmap that best matches the screen-space size of the texture, and then use `GL_NEAREST` filtering.

GL_LINEAR_MIPMAP_NEAREST
Find the mipmap that best matches the screen-space size of the texture, and then use `GL_LINEAR` filtering.

GL_LINEAR_MIPMAP_LINEAR
Perform `GL_LINEAR` sampling on each of *two* "best fit" mipmaps, and then blend the result. OpenGL takes eight samples for this, so it's the highest-quality filter. This is also known as *trilinear* filtering.

GL_NEAREST_MIPMAP_LINEAR
Take the weighted average of two samples, where one sample is from mipmap A, the other from mipmap B.

Figure 5-5 compares various filtering schemes.

Figure 5-5. Texture filters (from top to bottom: nearest, bilinear, and trilinear)

Deciding on a filter is a bit of a black art; personally I often start with trilinear filtering (GL_LINEAR_MIPMAP_LINEAR), and I try cranking down to a lower-quality filter only when I'm optimizing my frame rate. Note that GL_NEAREST is perfectly acceptable in some scenarios, such as when rendering 2D quads that have the same size as the source texture.

First- and second-generation devices have some restrictions on the filters:

- If magnification is GL_NEAREST, then minification must be one of GL_NEAREST, GL_NEAREST_MIPMAP_NEAREST, or GL_NEAREST_MIPMAP_LINEAR.

- If magnification is GL_LINEAR, then minification must be one of GL_LINEAR, GL_LINEAR_MIPMAP_NEAREST, or GL_LINEAR_MIPMAP_LINEAR.

This isn't a big deal since you'll almost never want a different same-level filter for magnification and minification. Nevertheless, it's important to note that the iPhone Simulator and newer devices do not have these restrictions.

Boosting Quality and Performance with Mipmaps

Mipmaps help with both quality and performance. They can help with performance especially when large textures are viewed from far away. Since the graphics hardware performs sampling on an image potentially much smaller than the original, it's more likely to have the texels available in a nearby memory cache. Mipmaps can improve quality for several reasons; most importantly, they effectively cast a wider net, so the final color is less likely to be missing contributions from important nearby texels.

In OpenGL, mipmap zero is the original image, and every following level is half the size of the preceding level. If a level has an odd size, then the floor function is used, as in Equation 5-1.

Equation 5-1. Mipmap sizes

$$\text{width}_n = \left\lfloor \frac{\text{width}_{n-1}}{2} \right\rfloor$$

$$\text{height}_n = \left\lfloor \frac{\text{height}_{n-1}}{2} \right\rfloor$$

Watch out though, because sometimes you need to ensure that all mipmap levels have an even size. In another words, the original texture must have dimensions that are powers of two. We'll discuss this further later in the chapter. Figure 5-6 depicts a popular way of neatly visualizing mipmaps levels into an area that's 1.5 times the original width.

To upload the mipmaps levels to OpenGL, you need to make a series of separate calls to glTexImage2D, from the original size all the way down to the 1×1 mipmap:

```
glTexImage2D(GL_TEXTURE_2D, 0, GL_RGBA, 16, 16, 0, GL_RGBA, GL_UNSIGNED_BYTE,
    pImageData0);
```

```
glTexImage2D(GL_TEXTURE_2D, 1, GL_RGBA, 8, 8, 0, GL_RGBA,
             GL_UNSIGNED_BYTE, pImageData1);
glTexImage2D(GL_TEXTURE_2D, 2, GL_RGBA, 4, 4, 0, GL_RGBA,
             GL_UNSIGNED_BYTE, pImageData2);
glTexImage2D(GL_TEXTURE_2D, 3, GL_RGBA, 2, 2, 0, GL_RGBA,
             GL_UNSIGNED_BYTE, pImageData3);
glTexImage2D(GL_TEXTURE_2D, 4, GL_RGBA, 1, 1, 0, GL_RGBA,
             GL_UNSIGNED_BYTE, pImageData4);
```

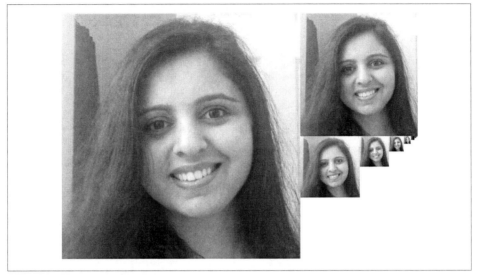

Figure 5-6. Mipmap visualization

Usually code like this occurs in a loop. Many OpenGL developers like to use a right-shift as a sneaky way of halving the size at each iteration. I doubt it really buys you anything, but it's great fun:

```
for (int level = 0;
     level < description.MipCount;
     ++level, width >>= 1, height >>= 1, ppData++)
{
    glTexImage2D(GL_TEXTURE_2D, level, GL_RGBA, width, height,
                 0, GL_RGBA, GL_UNSIGNED_BYTE, *ppData);
}
```

If you'd like to avoid the tedium of creating mipmaps and loading them in individually, OpenGL ES can generate mipmaps on your behalf:

```
// OpenGL ES 1.1
glTexParameteri(GL_TEXTURE_2D, GL_GENERATE_MIPMAP, GL_TRUE);
glTexImage2D(GL_TEXTURE_2D, 0, ...);

// OpenGL ES 2.0
glTexImage2D(GL_TEXTURE_2D, 0, ...);
glGenerateMipmap(GL_TEXTURE_2D);
```

In ES 1.1, mipmap generation is part of the OpenGL state associated with the current texture object, and you should enable it *before* uploading level zero. In ES 2.0, mipmap generation is an action that you take *after* you upload level zero.

You might be wondering why you'd ever want to provide mipmaps explicitly when you can just have OpenGL generate them for you. There are actually a couple reasons for this:

- There's a performance hit for mipmap generation at upload time. This could prolong your application's startup time, which is something all good iPhone developers obsess about.

- When OpenGL performs mipmap generation for you, you're (almost) at the mercy of whatever filtering algorithm it chooses. You can often produce higher-quality results if you provide mipmaps yourself, especially if you have a very high-resolution source image or a vector-based source.

Later we'll learn about a couple free tools that make it easy to supply OpenGL with ready-made, preshrunk mipmaps.

By the way, you do have some control over the mipmap generation scheme that OpenGL uses. The following lines are valid with both ES 1.1 and 2.0:

```
glHint(GL_GENERATE_MIPMAP_HINT, GL_FASTEST);
glHint(GL_GENERATE_MIPMAP_HINT, GL_NICEST);
glHint(GL_GENERATE_MIPMAP_HINT, GL_DONT_CARE); // this is the default
```

Tweaking Which Levels Are Sampled

If you're a control freak and you'd like to tweak the way OpenGL chooses mipmap levels to sample from, you'll be glad to hear the iPhone supports an extension that can shift which mipmap level(s) get sampled. This is useful for intentional blurring or pseudosharpening. For more information, head over to the extension registry on the Khronos site:

http://www.khronos.org/registry/gles/extensions/EXT/texture_lod_bias.txt

This is an ES 1.1 extension only; it's not necessary for ES 2.0 because you can bias the mipmap level from within the fragment shader using an optional third argument to texture2D. The full function signature looks like this:

```
vec4 texture2D(sampler2D sampler, vec2 coord, float bias = 0)
```

Incidentally, don't confuse texture2D, which is a shader function for sampling, and glTexImage2D, which a C function for uploading.

Modifying ModelViewer to Support Mipmaps

It's easy to enable mipmapping in the ModelViewer sample. For the ES 1.1 rendering engine, enable mipmap generation after binding to the texture object, and then replace the minification filter:

```
glGenTextures(1, &m_gridTexture);
glBindTexture(GL_TEXTURE_2D, m_gridTexture);
glTexParameteri(GL_TEXTURE_2D, GL_GENERATE_MIPMAP, GL_TRUE);
glTexParameteri(GL_TEXTURE_2D, GL_TEXTURE_MIN_FILTER, GL_LINEAR_MIPMAP_LINEAR);
glTexParameteri(GL_TEXTURE_2D, GL_TEXTURE_MAG_FILTER, GL_LINEAR);
// ...
glTexImage2D(GL_TEXTURE_2D, 0, GL_RGBA, size.x,
             size.y, 0, GL_RGBA, GL_UNSIGNED_BYTE, pixels);
```

For the ES 2.0 rendering engine, replace the minification filter in the same way, but call
glGenerateMipmap after uploading the texture data:

```
glGenTextures(1, &m_gridTexture);
glBindTexture(GL_TEXTURE_2D, m_gridTexture);
glTexParameteri(GL_TEXTURE_2D, GL_TEXTURE_MIN_FILTER, GL_LINEAR_MIPMAP_LINEAR);
glTexParameteri(GL_TEXTURE_2D, GL_TEXTURE_MAG_FILTER, GL_LINEAR);
// ...
glTexImage2D(GL_TEXTURE_2D, 0, GL_RGBA, size.x,
             size.y, 0, GL_RGBA, GL_UNSIGNED_BYTE, pixels);
glGenerateMipmap(GL_TEXTURE_2D);
```

Texture Formats and Types

Recall that two of the parameters to glTexImage2D stipulate format, and one stipulates
type, highlighted in bold here:

```
glTexImage2D(GL_TEXTURE_2D, 0, GL_RGBA, 16, 16, 0,
             GL_RGBA, GL_UNSIGNED_BYTE, pImageData0);
```

The allowed formats are as follows:

GL_RGB
:   Three-component color.

GL_RGBA
:   Four-component color; includes alpha.

GL_BGRA
:   Same as GL_RGBA but with the blue and red components swapped. This is a non-standard format but available on the iPhone because of the GL_IMG_texture_for mat_BGRA8888 extension.

GL_ALPHA
:   Single component format used as an alpha mask. (We'll learn a lot more about alpha in the next chapter.)

GL_LUMINANCE
:   Single component format used as grayscale.

GL_LUMINANCE_ALPHA
:   Two component format: grayscale + alpha. This is very useful for storing text.

Don't dismiss the non-RGB formats; if you don't need color, you can save significant
memory with the one- or two-component formats.

The type parameter in glTexImage2D can be one of these:

GL_UNSIGNED_BYTE
Each color component is 8 bits wide.

GL_UNSIGNED_SHORT_5_6_5
Each pixel is 16 bits wide; red and blue have five bits each, and green has six. Requires the format to be GL_RGB. The fact that green gets the extra bit isn't random —the human eye is more sensitive to variation in green hues.

GL_UNSIGNED_SHORT_4_4_4_4
Each pixel is 16 bits wide, and each component is 4 bits. This can be used only with GL_RGBA.

GL_UNSIGNED_SHORT_5_5_5_1
This dedicates only one bit to alpha; a pixel can be only fully opaque or fully transparent. Each pixel is 16 bits wide. This requires format to be GL_RGBA.

It's also interesting to note the various formats supported by the PNG file format, even though this has nothing to do with OpenGL:

- Five grayscale formats: each pixel can be 1, 2, 4, 8, or 16 bits wide.
- Two RGB formats: each color component can be 8 or 16 bits.
- Two "gray with alpha" formats: each component can be 8 or 16 bits.
- Two RGBA formats: each component can be 8 or 16 bits.
- Paletted formats—we'll ignore these.

 Just because a PNG file *looks* grayscale doesn't mean that it's using a grayscale-only format! The iPhone SDK includes a command-line tool called pngcrush that can help with this. (Skip ahead to "Texture Compression with PVRTC" on page 191 to see where it's located.) You can also right-click an image file in Mac OS X and use the *Get Info* option to learn about the internal format.

Hands-On: Loading Various Formats

Recall that the LoadPngImage method presented at the beginning of the chapter (Example 5-2) did not return any format information and that the rendering engine assumed the image data to be in RGBA format. Let's try to make this a bit more robust.

We can start by enhancing the IResourceManager interface so that it returns some format information in an API-agnostic way. (Remember, we're avoiding all platform-specific code in our interfaces.) For simplicity's sake, let's support only the subset of formats that are supported by both OpenGL and PNG. Open *Interfaces.hpp*, and make the changes shown in Example 5-14. New and modified lines are shown in bold. Note that the GetImageSize method has been removed because size is part of TextureDescription.

Example 5-14. Adding format support to IResourceManager

```
enum TextureFormat {
    TextureFormatGray,
    TextureFormatGrayAlpha,
    TextureFormatRgb,
    TextureFormatRgba,
};

struct TextureDescription {
    TextureFormat Format;
    int BitsPerComponent;
    ivec2 Size;
};

struct IResourceManager {
    virtual string GetResourcePath() const = 0;
    virtual TextureDescription LoadPngImage(const string& filename) = 0;
    virtual void* GetImageData() = 0;
    virtual void UnloadImage() = 0;
    virtual ~IResourceManager() {}
};
```

Example 5-15 shows the implementation to the new LoadPngImage method. Note the
Core Graphics functions used to extract format and type information, such as CGImage
GetAlphaInfo, CGImageGetColorSpace, and CGColorSpaceGetModel. I won't go into detail
about these functions because they are fairly straightforward; for more information,
look them up on Apple's iPhone Developer site.

Example 5-15. Update to ResourceManager.mm

```
TextureDescription LoadPngImage(const string& file)
{
    NSString* basePath = [NSString stringWithUTF8String:file.c_str()];
    NSString* resourcePath = [[NSBundle mainBundle] resourcePath];
    NSString* fullPath = [resourcePath stringByAppendingPathComponent:basePath];

    NSLog(@"Loading PNG image %s...", fullPath);

    UIImage* uiImage = [UIImage imageWithContentsOfFile:fullPath];
    CGImageRef cgImage = uiImage.CGImage;
    m_imageData = CGDataProviderCopyData(CGImageGetDataProvider(cgImage));

    TextureDescription description;
    description.Size.x = CGImageGetWidth(cgImage);
    description.Size.y = CGImageGetHeight(cgImage);
    bool hasAlpha = CGImageGetAlphaInfo(cgImage) != kCGImageAlphaNone;
    CGColorSpaceRef colorSpace = CGImageGetColorSpace(cgImage);
    switch (CGColorSpaceGetModel(colorSpace)) {
        case kCGColorSpaceModelMonochrome:
            description.Format =
                hasAlpha ? TextureFormatGrayAlpha : TextureFormatGray;
            break;
        case kCGColorSpaceModelRGB:
            description.Format =
```

```
                hasAlpha ? TextureFormatRgba : TextureFormatRgb;
            break;
        default:
            assert(!"Unsupported color space.");
            break;
    }
    description.BitsPerComponent = CGImageGetBitsPerComponent(cgImage);

    return description;
}
```

Next, we need to modify the rendering engines so that they pass in the correct arguments to glTexImage2D after examining the API-agnostic texture description. Example 5-16 shows a private method that can be added to both rendering engines; it works under both ES 1.1 and 2.0, so add it to both renderers (you will also need to add its signature to the private: section of the class declaration).

Example 5-16. RenderingEngine::SetPngTexture()

```
private:
    void SetPngTexture(const string& name) const;
    // ...

void RenderingEngine::SetPngTexture(const string& name) const
{
    TextureDescription description = m_resourceManager->LoadPngImage(name);

    GLenum format;
    switch (description.Format) {
        case TextureFormatGray:      format = GL_LUMINANCE;       break;
        case TextureFormatGrayAlpha: format = GL_LUMINANCE_ALPHA; break;
        case TextureFormatRgb:       format = GL_RGB;             break;
        case TextureFormatRgba:      format = GL_RGBA;            break;
    }

    GLenum type;
    switch (description.BitsPerComponent) {
        case 8: type = GL_UNSIGNED_BYTE; break;
        case 4:
            if (format == GL_RGBA) {
                type = GL_UNSIGNED_SHORT_4_4_4_4;
                break;
            }
            // intentionally fall through
        default:
            assert(!"Unsupported format.");
    }

    void* data = m_resourceManager->GetImageData();
    ivec2 size = description.Size;
    glTexImage2D(GL_TEXTURE_2D, 0, format, size.x, size.y,
                 0, format, type, data);
    m_resourceManager->UnloadImage();
}
```

Now you can remove the following snippet in the Initialize method (both rendering engines, but leave the call to glGenerateMipmap(GL_TEXTURE_2D) in the 2.0 renderer):

```
m_resourceManager->LoadPngImage("Grid16");
void* pixels = m_resourceManager->GetImageData();
ivec2 size = m_resourceManager->GetImageSize();
glTexImage2D(GL_TEXTURE_2D, 0, GL_RGBA, size.x, size.y, 0,
GL_RGBA, GL_UNSIGNED_BYTE, pixels);
m_resourceManager->UnloadImage();
```

Replace it with a call to the new private method:

```
SetPngTexture("Grid16.png");
```

At this point, you should be able to build and run and get the same results as before.

Texture Compression with PVRTC

Textures are often the biggest memory hog in graphically intense applications. *Block compression* is a technique that's quite popular in real-time graphics, even on desktop platforms. Like JPEG compression, it can cause a loss of image quality, but unlike JPEG, its compression ratio is constant and deterministic. If you know the width and height of your original image, then it's simple to compute the number of bytes in the compressed image.

Block compression is particularly good at photographs, and in some cases it's difficult to notice the quality loss. The noise is much more noticeable when applied to images with regions of solid color, such as vector-based graphics and text.

I strongly encourage you to use block compression when it doesn't make a noticeable difference in image quality. Not only does it reduce your memory footprint, but it can boost performance as well, because of increased cache coherency. The iPhone supports a specific type of block compression called PVRTC, named after the PowerVR chip that serves as the iPhone's graphics processor. PVRTC has four variants, as shown in Table 5-1.

Table 5-1. PVRTC formats

GL format	Contains alpha	Compression ratio[a]	Byte count
GL_COMPRESSED_RGBA_PVRTC_4BPPV1_IMG	Yes	8:1	Max(32, Width * Height / 2)
GL_COMPRESSED_RGB_PVRTC_4BPPV1_IMG	No	6:1	Max(32, Width * Height / 2)
GL_COMPRESSED_RGBA_PVRTC_2BPPV1_IMG	Yes	16:1	Max(32, Width * Height / 4)
GL_COMPRESSED_RGB_PVRTC_2BPPV1_IMG	No	12:1	Max(32, Width * Height / 4)

[a] Compared to a format with 8 bits per component.

 Be aware of some important restrictions with PVRTC textures: the image must be square, and its width/height must be a power of two.

The iPhone SDK comes with a command-line program called texturetool that you can use to generate PVRTC data from an uncompressed image, and it's located here:

```
/Developer/Platforms/iPhoneOS.platform/Developer/usr/bin
```

It's possible Apple has modified the path since the time of this writing, so I recommend verifying the location of texturetool using the Spotlight feature in Mac OS X. By the way, there actually several command-line tools at this location (including a rather cool one called pngcrush). They're worth a closer look!

Here's how you could use texturetool to convert *Grid16.png* into a compressed image called *Grid16.pvr*:

```
texturetool -m -e PVRTC -f PVR -p Preview.png -o Grid16.pvr Grid16.png
```

Some of the parameters are explained here.

-m
> Generate mipmaps.

-e PVRTC
> Use PVRTC compression. This can be tweaked with additional parameters, explained here.

-f PVR
> This may seem redundant, but it chooses the file format rather than the encoding. The PVR format includes a simple header before the image data that contains size and format information. I'll explain how to parse the header later.

-p PreviewFile
> This is an optional PNG file that gets generated to allow you to preview the quality loss caused by compression.

-o OutFile
> This is the name of the resulting PVR file.

The encoding argument can be tweaked with optional arguments. Here are some examples:

-e PVRTC --bits-per-pixel-2
> Specifies a 2-bits-per-pixel encoding.

-e PVRTC --bits-per-pixel-4
> Specifies a 4-bits-per-pixel encoding. This is the default, so there's not much reason to include it on the command line.

-e PVRTC --channel-weighting-perceptual -bits-per-pixel-2
> Use perceptual compression and a 2-bits-per-pixel format. Perceptual compression doesn't change the format of the image data; rather, it tweaks the compression algorithm such that the green channel preserves more quality than the red and blue channels. Humans are more sensitive to variations in green.

-e PVRTC --channel-weighting-linear
> Apply compression equally to all color components. This defaults to "on," so there's no need to specify it explicitly.

 At the time of this writing, `texturetool` does not include an argument to control whether the resulting image has an alpha channel. It automatically determines this based on the source format.

Rather than executing `texturetool` from the command line, you can make it an automatic step in Xcode's build process. Go ahead and perform the following steps:

1. Right-click the *Targets* group, and then choose Add→New Build Phase→New Run Script Build Phase.

2. There is lots of stuff in next dialog:

    a. Leave the shell as `/bin/sh`.

    b. Enter this directly into the script box:

    ```
    BIN=${PLATFORM_DIR}/../iPhoneOS.platform/Developer/usr/bin
    INFILE=${SRCROOT}/Textures/Grid16.png
    OUTFILE=${SRCROOT}/Textures/Grid16.pvr
    ${BIN}/texturetool -m -f PVR -e PVRTC $INFILE -o $OUTFILE
    ```

    c. Add this to Input Files:

    ```
    $(SRCROOT)/Textures/Grid16.png
    ```

    Add this to Output Files:

    ```
    $(SRCROOT)/Textures/Grid16.pvr
    ```

    These fields are important to set because they make Xcode smart about rebuilding; in other words, it should run the script only when the input file has been modified.

    d. Close the dialog by clicking the X in the upper-left corner.

3. Open the *Targets* group and its child node. Drag the *Run Script* item so that it appears before the *Copy Bundle Resources* item. You can also rename it if you'd like; simply right-click it and choose *Rename*.

4. Build your project once to run the script. Verify that the resulting PVRTC file exists. Don't try running yet.

5. Add *Grid16.pvr* to your project (right-click the Textures group, select Add→Existing Files and choose *Grid16.pvr*). Since it's a build artifact, I don't recommend checking it into your source code control system. Xcode gracefully handles missing files by highlighting them in red.

6. Make sure that Xcode doesn't needlessly rerun the script when the source file hasn't been modified. If it does, then there could be a typo in script dialog. (Simply double-click the *Run Script* phase to reopen the script dialog.)

Before moving on to the implementation, we need to incorporate a couple source files from Imagination Technology's PowerVR SDK.

1. Go to *http://www.imgtec.com/powervr/insider/powervr-sdk.asp*.
2. Click the link for "Khronos OpenGL ES 2.0 SDKs for PowerVR SGX family."
3. Select the download link under Mac OS / iPhone 3GS.
4. In your Xcode project, create a new group called *PowerVR*. Right-click the new group, and choose Get Info. To the right of the "Path" label on the General tab, click Choose and create a New Folder called PowerVR. Click Choose and close the group info window.
5. After opening up the tarball, look for *PVRTTexture.h* and *PVRTGlobal.h* in the *Tools* folder. Drag these files to the PowerVR group, check the "Copy items" checkbox in the dialog that appears, and then click Add.

Enough Xcode shenanigans, let's get back to writing real code. Before adding PVR support to the `ResourceManager` class, we need to make some enhancements to *Interfaces.hpp*. These changes are highlighted in bold in Example 5-17.

Example 5-17. Adding PVRTC support to Interfaces.hpp

```
enum TextureFormat {
    TextureFormatGray,
    TextureFormatGrayAlpha,
    TextureFormatRgb,
    TextureFormatRgba,
    TextureFormatPvrtcRgb2,
    TextureFormatPvrtcRgba2,
    TextureFormatPvrtcRgb4,
    TextureFormatPvrtcRgba4,
};

struct TextureDescription {
    TextureFormat Format;
    int BitsPerComponent;
    ivec2 Size;
    int MipCount;
};

// ...

struct IResourceManager {
    virtual string GetResourcePath() const = 0;
    virtual TextureDescription LoadPvrImage(const string& filename) = 0;
    virtual TextureDescription LoadPngImage(const string& filename) = 0;
    virtual void* GetImageData() = 0;
    virtual ivec2 GetImageSize() = 0;
    virtual void UnloadImage() = 0;
```

```
    virtual ~IResourceManager() {}
};
```

Example 5-18 shows the implementation of LoadPvrImage (you'll replace everything within the class definition except the GetResourcePath and LoadPngImage methods). It parses the header fields by simply casting the data pointer to a pointer-to-struct. The size of the struct isn't necessarily the size of the header, so the GetImageData method looks at the dwHeaderSize field to determine where the raw data starts.

Example 5-18. Adding PVRTC support to ResourceManager.mm

```
...

#import "../PowerVR/PVRTTexture.h"

class ResourceManager : public IResourceManager {
public:

    // ...

    TextureDescription LoadPvrImage(const string& file)
    {
        NSString* basePath = [NSString stringWithUTF8String:file.c_str()];
        NSString* resourcePath = [[NSBundle mainBundle] resourcePath];
        NSString* fullPath = [resourcePath stringByAppendingPathComponent:basePath];

        m_imageData = [NSData dataWithContentsOfFile:fullPath];
        m_hasPvrHeader = true;
        PVR_Texture_Header* header = (PVR_Texture_Header*) [m_imageData bytes];
        bool hasAlpha = header->dwAlphaBitMask ? true : false;

        TextureDescription description;
        switch (header->dwpfFlags & PVRTEX_PIXELTYPE) {
            case OGL_PVRTC2:
                description.Format = hasAlpha ? TextureFormatPvrtcRgba2 :
                                                TextureFormatPvrtcRgb2;
                break;
            case OGL_PVRTC4:
                description.Format = hasAlpha ? TextureFormatPvrtcRgba4 :
                                                TextureFormatPvrtcRgb4;
                break;
            default:
                assert(!"Unsupported PVR image.");
                break;
        }

        description.Size.x = header->dwWidth;
        description.Size.y = header->dwHeight;
        description.MipCount = header->dwMipMapCount;
        return description;
    }
    void* GetImageData()
    {
```

```
        if (!m_hasPvrHeader)
            return (void*) [m_imageData bytes];

        PVR_Texture_Header* header = (PVR_Texture_Header*) [m_imageData bytes];
        char* data = (char*) [m_imageData bytes];
        unsigned int headerSize = header->dwHeaderSize;
        return data + headerSize;
    }
    void UnloadImage()
    {
        m_imageData = 0;
    }
private:
    NSData* m_imageData;
    bool m_hasPvrHeader;
    ivec2 m_imageSize;
};
```

Note that we changed the type of m_imageData from CFDataRef to NSData*. Since we create the NSData object using autorelease semantics, there's no need to call a release function in the UnloadImage() method.

 CFDataRef and NSData are said to be "toll-free bridged," meaning they are interchangeable in function calls. You can think of CFDataRef as being the vanilla C version and NSData as the Objective-C version. I prefer using NSData (in my Objective-C code) because it can work like a C++ smart pointer.

Because of this change, we'll also need to make one change to LoadPngImage. Find this line:

```
    m_imageData = CGDataProviderCopyData(CGImageGetDataProvider(cgImage));
```

and replace it with the following:

```
    CFDataRef dataRef = CGDataProviderCopyData(CGImageGetDataProvider(cgImage));
    m_imageData = [NSData dataWithData:(NSData*) dataRef];
```

You should now be able to build and run, although your application is still using the PNG file.

Example 5-19 adds a new method to the rendering engine for creating a compressed texture object. This code will work under both ES 1.1 and ES 2.0.

Example 5-19. RenderingEngine::SetPvrTexture()

```
private:
    void SetPvrTexture(const string& name) const;
    // ...


void RenderingEngine::SetPvrTexture(const string& filename) const
{
```

```
TextureDescription description =
  m_resourceManager->LoadPvrImage(filename);
unsigned char* data =
  (unsigned char*) m_resourceManager->GetImageData();
int width = description.Size.x;
int height = description.Size.y;

int bitsPerPixel;
GLenum format;
switch (description.Format) {
    case TextureFormatPvrtcRgba2:
        bitsPerPixel = 2;
        format = GL_COMPRESSED_RGBA_PVRTC_2BPPV1_IMG;
        break;
    case TextureFormatPvrtcRgb2:
        bitsPerPixel = 2;
        format = GL_COMPRESSED_RGB_PVRTC_2BPPV1_IMG;
        break;
    case TextureFormatPvrtcRgba4:
        bitsPerPixel = 4;
        format = GL_COMPRESSED_RGBA_PVRTC_4BPPV1_IMG;
        break;
    case TextureFormatPvrtcRgb4:
        bitsPerPixel = 4;
        format = GL_COMPRESSED_RGB_PVRTC_4BPPV1_IMG;
        break;
}

for (int level = 0; width > 0 && height > 0; ++level) {
    GLsizei size = std::max(32, width * height * bitsPerPixel / 8);
    glCompressedTexImage2D(GL_TEXTURE_2D, level, format, width,
                           height, 0, size, data);
    data += size;
    width >>= 1; height >>= 1;
}

m_resourceManager->UnloadImage();
}
```

You can now replace this:

```
SetPngTexture("Grid16.png");
```

with this:

```
SetPvrTexture("Grid16.pvr");
```

Since the PVR file contains multiple mipmap levels, you'll also need to remove any code you added for mipmap autogeneration (glGenerateMipmap under ES 2.0, glTexParame ter with GL_GENERATE_MIPMAP under ES 1.1).

After rebuilding your project, your app will now be using the compressed texture.

Of particular interest in Example 5-19 is the section that loops over each mipmap level. Rather than calling glTexImage2D, it uses glCompressedTexImage2D to upload the data. Here's its formal declaration:

```
void glCompressedTexImage2D(GLenum target, GLint level, GLenum format,
                            GLsizei width, GLsizei height, GLint border,
                            GLsizei byteCount, const GLvoid* data);
```

target
> Specifies which binding point to upload the texture to. For ES 1.1, this must be `GL_TEXTURE_2D`.

level
> Specifies the mipmap level.

format
> Specifies the compression encoding.

width, height
> Specifies the dimensions of the image being uploaded.

border
> Must be zero. Texture borders are not supported in OpenGL ES.

byteCount
> The size of data being uploaded. Note that `glTexImage2D` doesn't have a parameter like this; for noncompressed data, OpenGL computes the byte count based on the image's dimensions and format.

data
> Pointer to the compressed data.

 In addition to PVRTC formats, the iPhone also supports compressed paletted textures to be conformant to the OpenGL ES 1.1 standard. But, paletted images on the iPhone won't buy you much; internally they get expanded into normal true-color images.

The PowerVR SDK and Low-Precision Textures

The low-precision uncompressed formats (565, 5551, and 4444) are often overlooked. Unlike block compression, they do not cause speckle artifacts in the image. While they work poorly with images that have smooth color gradients, they're quite good at preserving detail in photographs and keeping clean lines in simple vector art.

At the time of this writing, the iPhone SDK does not contain any tools for encoding images to these formats, but the free PowerVR SDK from Imagination Technologies includes a tool called `PVRTexTool` just for this purpose. Download the SDK as directed in "Texture Compression with PVRTC" on page 194. Extract the tarball archive if you haven't already.

After opening up the tarball, execute the application in *Utilities/PVRTexTool/PVRTexToolGUI/MacOS*.

Open your source image in the GUI, and select Edit→Encode. After you choose a format (try RGB 565), you can save the output image to a PVR file. Save it as *Grid16-PVRTool.pvr*, and add it to Xcode as described in Step 5 on page 193. Next, go into both renderers, and find the following:

```
SetPvrTexture("Grid16.pvr");
```

And replace it with the following:

```
SetPvrTexture("Grid16-PVRTool.pvr");
```

You may have noticed that PVRTexTool has many of the same capabilities as the texturetool program presented in the previous section, and much more. It can encode images to a plethora of formats, generate mipmap levels, and even dump out C header files that contain raw image data. This tool also has a command-line variant to allow integration into a script or an Xcode build.

 We'll use the command-line version of PVRTexTool in Chapter 7 for generating a C header file that contains the raw data to an 8-bit alpha texture.

Let's go ahead and flesh out some of the image-loading code to support the uncompressed low-precision formats. New lines in *ResourceManager.mm* are shown in bold in Example 5-20.

Example 5-20. New texture formats in ResourceManager.mm

```
TextureDescription LoadPvrImage(const string& file)
{
    // ...

    TextureDescription description;
    switch (header->dwpfFlags & PVRTEX_PIXELTYPE) {
        case OGL_RGB_565:
            description.Format = TextureFormat565;
            Break;
        case OGL_RGBA_5551:
            description.Format = TextureFormat5551;
            break;
        case OGL_RGBA_4444:
            description.Format = TextureFormatRgba;
            description.BitsPerComponent = 4;
            break;
        case OGL_PVRTC2:
            description.Format = hasAlpha ? TextureFormatPvrtcRgba2 :
                                            TextureFormatPvrtcRgb2;
            break;
        case OGL_PVRTC4:
            description.Format = hasAlpha ? TextureFormatPvrtcRgba4 :
                                            TextureFormatPvrtcRgb4;
            break;
```

```
    }
    // ...
}
```

Next we need to add some new code to the SetPvrTexture method in the rendering engine class, shown in Example 5-21. This code works for both ES 1.1 and 2.0.

Example 5-21. New texture formats in the rendering engines

```
void RenderingEngine::SetPvrTexture(const string& filename) const
{
    // ...

    int bitsPerPixel;
    GLenum format;
    bool compressed = false;
    switch (description.Format) {
        case TextureFormatPvrtcRgba2:
        case TextureFormatPvrtcRgb2:
        case TextureFormatPvrtcRgba4:
        case TextureFormatPvrtcRgb4:
            compressed = true;
            break;
    }

    if (!compressed) {
        GLenum type;
        switch (description.Format) {
            case TextureFormatRgba:
                assert(description.BitsPerComponent == 4);
                format = GL_RGBA;
                type = GL_UNSIGNED_SHORT_4_4_4_4;
                bitsPerPixel = 16;
                break;
            case TextureFormat565:
                format = GL_RGB;
                type = GL_UNSIGNED_SHORT_5_6_5;
                bitsPerPixel = 16;
                break;
            case TextureFormat5551:
                format = GL_RGBA;
                type = GL_UNSIGNED_SHORT_5_5_5_1;
                bitsPerPixel = 16;
                break;
        }
        for (int level = 0; width > 0 && height > 0; ++level) {
            GLsizei size = width * height * bitsPerPixel / 8;
            glTexImage2D(GL_TEXTURE_2D, level, format, width,
                         height, 0, format, type, data);
            data += size;
            width >>= 1; height >>= 1;
        }
```

```
        m_resourceManager->UnloadImage();
        return;
    }
}
```

Next, we need to make a change to *Interfaces.hpp*:

```
enum TextureFormat {
    TextureFormatGray,
    TextureFormatGrayAlpha,
    TextureFormatRgb,
    TextureFormatRgba,
    TextureFormatPvrtcRgb2,
    TextureFormatPvrtcRgba2,
    TextureFormatPvrtcRgb4,
    TextureFormatPvrtcRgba4,
    TextureFormat565,
    TextureFormat5551,
};
```

Generating and Transforming OpenGL Textures with Quartz

You can use Quartz to draw 2D paths into an OpenGL texture, resize the source image, convert from one format to another, and even generate text. We'll cover some of these techniques in Chapter 7; for now let's go over a few simple ways to generate textures.

One way of loading textures into OpenGL is creating a Quartz surface using whatever format you'd like and then drawing the source image to it, as shown in Example 5-22.

Example 5-22. Texture loading with CGContextDrawImage

```
TextureDescription LoadImage(const string& file)
{
    NSString* basePath = [NSString stringWithUTF8String:file.c_str()];
    NSString* resourcePath = [[NSBundle mainBundle] resourcePath];
    NSString* fullPath =
      [resourcePath stringByAppendingPathComponent:basePath];
    UIImage* uiImage = [UIImage imageWithContentsOfFile:fullPath];❶

    TextureDescription description;
    description.Size.x = CGImageGetWidth(uiImage.CGImage);
    description.Size.y = CGImageGetHeight(uiImage.CGImage);
    description.BitsPerComponent = 8;
    description.Format = TextureFormatRgba;
    description.MipCount = 1;
    m_hasPvrHeader = false;

    int bpp = description.BitsPerComponent / 2;❷
    int byteCount = description.Size.x * description.Size.y * bpp;
    unsigned char* data = (unsigned char*) calloc(byteCount, 1);❸

    CGColorSpaceRef colorSpace = CGColorSpaceCreateDeviceRGB();
    CGBitmapInfo bitmapInfo =
      kCGImageAlphaPremultipliedLast | kCGBitmapByteOrder32Big;
```

```
CGContextRef context = CGBitmapContextCreate(data,❹
    description.Size.x,
    description.Size.y,
    description.BitsPerComponent,
    bpp * description.Size.x,
    colorSpace,
    bitmapInfo);
CGColorSpaceRelease(colorSpace);
CGRect rect = CGRectMake(0, 0, description.Size.x, description.Size.y);
CGContextDrawImage(context, rect, uiImage.CGImage);❺
CGContextRelease(context);

m_imageData = [NSData dataWithBytesNoCopy:data
                                  length:byteCount
                            freeWhenDone:YES];❻
return description;
}
```

❶ As before, use the `imageWithContentsOfFile` class method to create and allocate a `UIImage` object that wraps a `CGImage` object.

❷ Since there are four components per pixel (RGBA), the number of bytes per pixel is half the number of bits per component.

❸ Allocate memory for the image surface, and clear it to zeros.

❹ Create a Quartz context with the memory that was just allocated.

❺ Use Quartz to copy the source image onto the destination surface.

❻ Create an `NSData` object that wraps the memory that was allocated.

If you want to try the Quartz-loading code in the sample app, perform the following steps:

1. Add Example 5-22 to `ResourceManager.mm`.

2. Add the following method declaration to `IResourceManager` in *Interfaces.hpp*:

   ```
   virtual TextureDescription LoadImage(const string& file) = 0;
   ```

3. In the `SetPngTexture` method in *RenderingEngine.TexturedES2.cpp*, change the `LoadPngImage` call to `LoadImage`.

4. In your render engine's `Initialize` method, make sure your minification filter is `GL_LINEAR` and that you're calling `SetPngTexture`.

One advantage of loading images with Quartz is that you can have it do some transformations before uploading the image to OpenGL. For example, say you want to flip the image vertically. You could do so by simply adding the following two lines immediately before the line that calls `CGContextDrawImage`:

```
CGContextTranslateCTM(context, 0, description.Size.y);
CGContextScaleCTM(context, 1, -1);
```

Another neat thing you can do with Quartz is generate new images from scratch in real time. This can shrink your application, making it faster to download. This is particularly important if you're trying to trim down to less than 10MB, the maximum size that Apple allows for downloading over the 3G network. Of course, you can do this only for textures that contain simple vector-based images, as opposed to truly artistic content.

For example, you could use Quartz to generate a 256×256 texture that contains a blue filled-in circle, as in Example 5-23. The code for creating the surface should look familiar; lines of interest are shown in bold.

Example 5-23. ResourceManager::GenerateCircle()

```
TextureDescription GenerateCircle()
{
    TextureDescription description;
    description.Size = ivec2(256, 256);
    description.BitsPerComponent = 8;
    description.Format = TextureFormatRgba;

    int bpp = description.BitsPerComponent / 2;
    int byteCount = description.Size.x * description.Size.y * bpp;
    unsigned char* data = (unsigned char*) calloc(byteCount, 1);

    CGColorSpaceRef colorSpace = CGColorSpaceCreateDeviceRGB();
    CGBitmapInfo bitmapInfo = kCGImageAlphaPremultipliedLast | kCGBitmapByteOrder32Big;
    CGContextRef context = CGBitmapContextCreate(data,
                                                 description.Size.x,
                                                 description.Size.y,
                                                 description.BitsPerComponent,
                                                 bpp * description.Size.x,
                                                 colorSpace,
                                                 bitmapInfo);
    CGColorSpaceRelease(colorSpace);

    CGRect rect = CGRectMake(5, 5, 246, 246);
    CGContextSetRGBFillColor(context, 0, 0, 1, 1);
    CGContextFillEllipseInRect(context, rect);

    CGContextRelease(context);

    m_imageData = [NSData dataWithBytesNoCopy:data length:byteCount freeWhenDone:YES];
    return description;
}
```

If you want to try the circle-generation code in the sample app, perform the following steps:

1. Add Example 5-23 to ResourceManager.mm.

2. Add the following method declaration to IResourceManager in *Interfaces.hpp*:

```
virtual TextureDescription GenerateCircle() = 0;
```

3. In the `SetPngTexture` method in *RenderingEngine.TexturedES2.cpp*, change the `LoadImage` call to `GenerateCircle`.

4. In your render engine's `Initialize` method, make sure your minification filter is `GL_LINEAR` and that you're calling `SetPngTexture`.

Quartz is a rich 2D graphics API and could have a book all to itself, so I can't cover it here; check out Apple's online documentation for more information.

Dealing with Size Constraints

Some of the biggest gotchas in texturing are the various constraints imposed on their size. Strictly speaking, OpenGL ES 1.1 stipulates that all textures must have dimensions that are powers of two, and OpenGL ES 2.0 has no such restriction. In the graphics community, textures that have a power-of-two width and height are commonly known as POT textures; non-power-of-two textures are NPOT.

For better or worse, the iPhone platform diverges from the OpenGL core specifications here. The POT constraint in ES 1.1 doesn't always apply, nor does the NPOT feature in ES 2.0.

Newer iPhone models support an extension to ES 1.1 that opens up the POT restriction, but only under a certain set of conditions. It's called `GL_APPLE_texture_2D_limi ted_npot`, and it basically states the following:

> *Nonmipmapped 2D textures that use GL_CLAMP_TO_EDGE wrapping for the S and T coordinates need not have power-of-two dimensions.*

As hairy as this seems, it covers quite a few situations, including the common case of displaying a background texture with the same dimensions as the screen (320×480). Since it requires no minification, it doesn't need mipmapping, so you can create a texture object that fits "just right."

Not all iPhones support the aforementioned extension to ES 1.1; the only surefire way to find out is by programmatically checking for the extension string, which can be done like this:

```
const char* extensions = (char*) glGetString(GL_EXTENSIONS);
bool npot = strstr(extensions, "GL_APPLE_texture_2D_limited_npot") != 0;
```

Readable Extension Strings

The extensions string returned by OpenGL is long and space-delimited, so it's a bit difficult for humans to read. As a useful diagnostic procedure, I often dump a "pretty print" of the extensions list to Xcode's Debugger Console at startup time. This can be done with the following code snippet:

```
void PrettyPrintExtensions()
{
    std::string extensions = (const char*) glGetString(GL_EXTENSIONS);
    char* extensionStart = &extensions[0];
```

```
        char** extension = &extensionStart;
        std::cout << "Supported OpenGL ES Extensions:" << std::endl;
        while (*extension)
            std::cout << '\t' << strsep(extension, " ") << std::endl;
        std::cout << std::endl;
    }
```

If your 320×480 texture needs to be mipmapped (or if you're supporting older iPhones), then you can simply use a 512×512 texture and adjust your texture coordinates to address a 320×480 subregion. One quick way of doing this is with a texture matrix:

```
glMatrixMode(GL_TEXTURE);
glLoadIdentity();
glScalef(320.0f / 512.0f, 480.0f / 512.0f, 1.0f);
```

Unfortunately, the portions of the image that lie outside the 320×480 subregion are wasted. If this causes you to grimace, keep in mind that you can add "mini-textures" to those unused regions. Doing so makes the texture into a *texture atlas*, which we'll discuss further in Chapter 7.

If you don't want to use a 512×512 texture, then it's possible to create five POT textures and carefully puzzle them together to fit the screen, as shown in Figure 5-7. This is a hassle, though, and I don't recommend it unless you have a strong penchant for masochism.

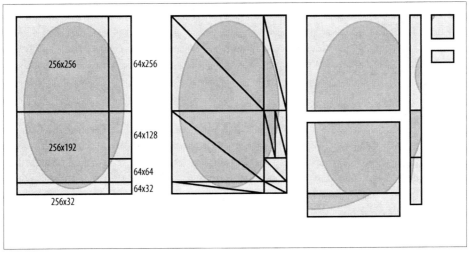

Figure 5-7. Slicing the iPhone screen into POT textures

By the way, according to the official OpenGL ES 2.0 specification, NPOT textures are actually allowed in *any* situation! Apple has made a minor transgression here by imposing the aforementioned limitations.

Keep in mind that even when the POT restriction applies, your texture can still be non-square (for example, 512×256), unless it uses a compressed format.

Think these are a lot of rules to juggle? Well it's not over yet! Textures also have a maximum allowable size. At the time of this writing, the first two iPhone generations have a maximum size of 1024×1024, and third-generation devices have a maximum size of 2048×2048. Again, the only way to be sure is querying its capabilities at runtime, like so:

```
GLint maxSize;
glGetIntegerv(GL_MAX_TEXTURE_SIZE, &maxSize);
```

Don't groan, but there's yet another gotcha I want to mention regarding texture dimensions. By default, OpenGL expects each row of uncompressed texture data to be aligned on a 4-byte boundary. This isn't a concern if your texture is GL_RGBA with UNSIGNED_BYTE; in this case, the data is always properly aligned. However, if your format has a texel size less than 4 bytes, you should take care to ensure each row is padded out to the proper alignment. Alternatively, you can turn off OpenGL's alignment restriction like this:

```
glPixelStorei(GL_UNPACK_ALIGNMENT, 1);
```

Also be aware that the PNG decoder in Quartz may or may not internally align the image data; this can be a concern if you load images using the CGDataProviderCopy Data method presented in Example 5-15. It's more robust (but less performant) to load in images by drawing to a Quartz surface, which we'll go over in the next section.

Before moving on, I'll forewarn you of yet another thing to watch out for: the iPhone Simulator doesn't necessarily impose the same restrictions on texture size that a physical device would. Many developers throw up their hands and simply stick to power-of-two dimensions only; I'll show you how to make this easier in the next section.

Scaling to POT

One way to ensure that your textures are power-of-two is to scale them using Quartz. Normally I'd recommend storing the images in the desired size rather than scaling them at runtime, but there are reasons why you might want to scale at runtime. For example, you might be creating a texture that was generated from the iPhone camera (which we'll demonstrate in the next section).

For the sake of example, let's walk through the process of adding a scale-to-POT feature to your ResourceManager class. First add a new field to the TextureDescription structure called OriginalSize, as shown in bold in Example 5-24.

Example 5-24. Interfaces.hpp

```
struct TextureDescription {
    TextureFormat Format;
    int BitsPerComponent;
    ivec2 Size;
```

```
    int MipCount;
    ivec2 OriginalSize;
};
```

We'll use this to store the image's original size; this is useful, for example, to retrieve the original aspect ratio. Now let's go ahead and create the new ResourceManager::LoadImagePot() method, as shown in Example 5-25.

Example 5-25. ResourceManager::LoadImagePot

```
TextureDescription LoadImagePot(const string& file)
{
    NSString* basePath = [NSString stringWithUTF8String:file.c_str()];
    NSString* resourcePath = [[NSBundle mainBundle] resourcePath];
    NSString* fullPath =
      [resourcePath stringByAppendingPathComponent:basePath];
    UIImage* uiImage = [UIImage imageWithContentsOfFile:fullPath];

    TextureDescription description;
    description.OriginalSize.x = CGImageGetWidth(uiImage.CGImage);
    description.OriginalSize.y = CGImageGetHeight(uiImage.CGImage);
    description.Size.x = NextPot(description.OriginalSize.x);
    description.Size.y = NextPot(description.OriginalSize.y);
    description.BitsPerComponent = 8;
    description.Format = TextureFormatRgba;

    int bpp = description.BitsPerComponent / 2;
    int byteCount = description.Size.x * description.Size.y * bpp;
    unsigned char* data = (unsigned char*) calloc(byteCount, 1);

    CGColorSpaceRef colorSpace = CGColorSpaceCreateDeviceRGB();
    CGBitmapInfo bitmapInfo =
      kCGImageAlphaPremultipliedLast | kCGBitmapByteOrder32Big;
    CGContextRef context = CGBitmapContextCreate(data,
        description.Size.x,
        description.Size.y,
        description.BitsPerComponent,
        bpp * description.Size.x,
        colorSpace,
        bitmapInfo);
    CGColorSpaceRelease(colorSpace);
    CGRect rect = CGRectMake(0, 0, description.Size.x, description.Size.y);
    CGContextDrawImage(context, rect, uiImage.CGImage);
    CGContextRelease(context);

    m_imageData = [NSData dataWithBytesNoCopy:data length:byteCount freeWhenDone:YES];
    return description;
}

unsigned int NextPot(unsigned int n)
{
    n--;
    n |= n >> 1; n |= n >> 2;
    n |= n >> 4; n |= n >> 8;
    n |= n >> 16;
```

```
        n++;
    return n;
}
```

Example 5-25 is fairly straightforward; most of it is the same as the LoadImage method presented in the previous section, with the exception of the NextPot method. It's amazing what can be done with some bit shifting! If the input to the NextPot method is already a power of two, then it returns the same value back to the caller; if not, it returns the *next* power of two. I won't bore you with the derivation of this algorithm, but it's fun to impress your colleagues with this trick.

Creating Textures with the Camera

For the grand finale sample of this chapter, let's create an app called *CameraTexture* that allows the user to snap a photo and wrap it around an ellipsoid (a squashed sphere). The embarrassingly simple user interface consists of a single button for taking a new photo, as shown in Figure 5-8. We'll also add some animation by periodically spinning the ellipsoid along the x-axis.

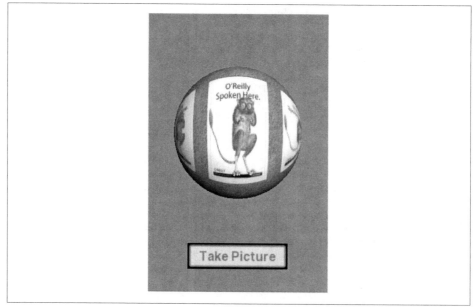

Figure 5-8. CameraTexture sample

Unlike much of the sample code in this book, the interesting parts here will actually be in Objective-C rather than C++. The application logic is simple enough that we can dispense with the IApplicationEngine interface.

Using ModelViewer as the baseline, start by removing all the `ApplicationEngine`-related code as follows:

1. Remove `IApplicationEngine` and `CreateApplicationEngine` from *Interfaces.hpp*.

2. Remove the *ApplicationEngine.ParametricViewer.cpp* file from the Xcode project, and send it to the trash.

3. Remove the `m_applicationEngine` field from *GLView.h*.

4. Remove the call to `CreateApplicationEngine` from *GLView.mm*.

5. Replace the call to `m_applicationEngine->Initialize` with `m_renderingEngine->Initialize()`.

6. Remove `touchesBegan`, `touchesEnded`, and `touchesMoved` from *GLView.mm*.

The code won't build until we fill it out a bit more. Replace the `IRenderingEngine` interface in *Interfaces.hpp* with Example 5-26, and move the `TextureFormat` and `TextureDescription` type definitions to the top of the file.

Example 5-26. CameraTexture's IRenderingEngine interface

```
struct IRenderingEngine {
    virtual void Initialize() = 0;❶
    virtual void Render(float zScale, float theta, bool waiting) const = 0;❷
    virtual void LoadCameraTexture(const TextureDescription&, void* data) = 0;❸
    virtual ~IRenderingEngine() {}
};
```

❶ The `Initialize` method loads the button textures and creates the vertex buffer objects.

❷ The `Render` method takes the following three parameters:

float zScale
> Specifies the multiplication factor for squashing the sphere into an ellipse

float theta
> Specifies the angle (in degrees) for s-axis rotation

bool waiting
> Controls the image on the button, which either says "Take Picture" or "Please Wait"

❸ The `LoadCameraTexture` method tells the rendering engine to load a new texture to wrap around the sphere.

We'll go over the implementation of these methods later. Let's jump back to the Objective-C since that's where the interesting stuff is. For starters, we need to modify the `GLView` class declaration by adopting a couple new protocols and adding a few data fields; see Example 5-27. New code is shown in bold.

Example 5-27. CameraTexture's GLView.h

```
#import <Foundation/Foundation.h>
#import <UIKit/UIKit.h>
#import <OpenGLES/EAGL.h>
#import "Interfaces.hpp"

@interface GLView : UIView <UIImagePickerControllerDelegate,❶
                            UINavigationControllerDelegate> {❷
@private
    IRenderingEngine* m_renderingEngine;
    IResourceManager* m_resourceManager;
    EAGLContext* m_context;
    UIViewController* m_viewController;❸
    bool m_paused;❹
    float m_zScale;❺
    float m_xRotation;❻
}

- (void) drawView: (CADisplayLink*) displayLink;

@end
```

❶ Recall that in Objective-C, the <> notation is used on a class declaration to adopt one or more protocols. (So far, the only other protocol we've come across is UIApplicationDelegate.) In this case, we're adopting UIImagePickerController in order to respond to a couple camera-related events, as you'll see later.

❷ We must also adopt the UINavigationControllerDelegate protocol to handle camera events.

❸ Declare a UIViewController pointer for the camera interface. So far, we have avoided view controllers, instead focusing on pure OpenGL ES, but in this case a view controller is required. This is the only way you can use the camera API on the iPhone.

❹ While the camera interface is visible, we need to stop the recurrent rendering of the OpenGL scene; the m_paused variable is used to indicate this state.

❺ The m_zScale variable indicates the amount of scale to apply on the z-axis to flatten the sphere into an ellipsoid. By varying this, we'll achieve a pulsing effect.

❻ The m_xRotation variable indicates amount of rotation (in degrees) of the ellipsoid along its x-axis.

Next, open *GLView.mm*, and rewrite the drawView method as in Example 5-28. The code that computes the time step is the same as previous examples; perhaps more interesting are the mathematical shenanigans used to oscillate between two types of useless and silly animation: "spinning" and "pulsing."

Example 5-28. CameraTexture's drawView method

```
- (void) drawView: (CADisplayLink*) displayLink
{
    if (m_paused)
```

```
        return;

    if (displayLink != nil) {
        float t = displayLink.timestamp / 3;
        int integer = (int) t;
        float fraction = t - integer;
        if (integer % 2) {
            m_xRotation = 360 * fraction;
            m_zScale = 0.5;
        } else {
            m_xRotation = 0;
            m_zScale = 0.5 + sin(fraction * 6 * M_PI) * 0.3;
        }
    }

    m_renderingEngine->Render(m_zScale, m_xRotation, false);
    [m_context presentRenderbuffer:GL_RENDERBUFFER];
}
```

While we're still in *GLView.mm*, let's go ahead and write the touch handler. Because of the embarrassingly simple UI, we need to handle only a single touch event: touchesEnded, as shown in Example 5-29. Note that the first thing it does is check whether the touch location lies within the bounds of the button's rectangle; if not, it returns early.

Example 5-29. CameraTexture's touchesEnded method

```
- (void) touchesEnded: (NSSet*) touches withEvent: (UIEvent*) event
{
    UITouch* touch = [touches anyObject];
    CGPoint location  = [touch locationInView: self];

    // Return early if touched outside the button's area.
    if (location.y < 395 || location.y > 450 ||
        location.x < 75 || location.x > 245)
        return;

    // Instance the image picker and set up its configuration.
    UIImagePickerController* imagePicker =
      [[UIImagePickerController alloc] init];
    imagePicker.delegate = self;
    imagePicker.navigationBarHidden = YES;
    imagePicker.toolbarHidden = YES;

    // Enable camera mode if supported, otherwise fall back to the default.
    UIImagePickerControllerSourceType source =
      UIImagePickerControllerSourceTypeCamera;
    if ([UIImagePickerController isSourceTypeAvailable:source])
        imagePicker.sourceType = source;

    // Instance the view controller if it doesn't already exist.
    if (m_viewController == 0) {
        m_viewController = [[UIViewController alloc] init];
        m_viewController.view = self;
```

```
    }

    // Turn off the OpenGL rendering cycle and present the image picker.
    m_paused = true;
    [m_viewController presentModalViewController:imagePicker animated:NO];
}
```

 When developing with UIKit, the usual convention is that the view controller owns the view, but in this case, the view owns the view controller. This is acceptable in our situation, since our application is mostly rendered with OpenGL, and we want to achieve the desired functionality in the simplest possible way. I'm hoping that Apple will release a lower-level camera API in future versions of the SDK, so that we don't need to bother with view controllers.

Perhaps the most interesting piece in Example 5-29 is the code that checks whether the camera is supported; if so, it sets the camera as the picker's source type:

```
    UIImagePickerControllerSourceType source =
      UIImagePickerControllerSourceTypeCamera;
    if ([UIImagePickerController isSourceTypeAvailable:source])
        imagePicker.sourceType = source;
```

I recommend following this pattern even if you know a priori that your application will run only on devices with cameras. The fallback path provides a convenient testing platform on the iPhone Simulator; by default, the image picker simply opens a file picker with image thumbnails.

Next we'll add a couple new methods to *GLView.mm* for implementing the UIImage PickerControllerDelegate protocol, as shown in Example 5-30. Depending on the megapixel resolution of your camera, the captured image can be quite large, much larger than what we need for an OpenGL texture. So, the first thing we do is scale the image down to 256×256. Since this destroys the aspect ratio, we'll store the original image's dimensions in the TextureDescription structure just in case. A more detailed explanation of the code follows the listing.

Example 5-30. imagePickerControllerDidCancel and didFinishPickingMediaWithInfo

```
- (void) imagePickerControllerDidCancel:(UIImagePickerController*) picker❶
{
    [m_viewController dismissModalViewControllerAnimated:NO];
    m_paused = false;
    [picker release];
}

- (void) imagePickerController:(UIImagePickerController*) picker ❷
        didFinishPickingMediaWithInfo:(NSDictionary*) info
{
    UIImage* image =
      [info objectForKey:UIImagePickerControllerOriginalImage];

    float theta = 0;
```

```
switch (image.imageOrientation) {❸
    case UIImageOrientationDown: theta =  M_PI; break;
    case UIImageOrientationLeft: theta = M_PI / 2; break;
    case UIImageOrientationRight: theta = -M_PI / 2; break;
}

int bpp = 4;
ivec2 size(256, 256);
int byteCount = size.x * size.y * bpp;
unsigned char* data = (unsigned char*) calloc(byteCount, 1);❹

CGColorSpaceRef colorSpace = CGColorSpaceCreateDeviceRGB();
CGBitmapInfo bitmapInfo =
  kCGImageAlphaPremultipliedLast | kCGBitmapByteOrder32Big;
CGContextRef context = CGBitmapContextCreate(data,
                                             size.x,
                                             size.y,
                                             8,
                                             bpp * size.x,
                                             colorSpace,
                                             bitmapInfo);
CGColorSpaceRelease(colorSpace);
CGRect rect = CGRectMake(0, 0, size.x, size.y);
CGContextTranslateCTM(context, size.x / 2, size.y / 2);❺
CGContextRotateCTM(context, theta);
CGContextTranslateCTM(context, -size.x / 2, -size.y / 2);
CGContextDrawImage(context, rect, image.CGImage);

TextureDescription description;
description.Size = size;
description.OriginalSize.x = CGImageGetWidth(image.CGImage);
description.OriginalSize.y = CGImageGetHeight(image.CGImage);
description.Format = TextureFormatRgba;
description.BitsPerComponent = 8;

m_renderingEngine->LoadCameraTexture(description, data);❻
m_renderingEngine->Render(m_zScale, m_xRotation, true);❼
[m_context presentRenderbuffer:GL_RENDERBUFFER];

CGContextRelease(context);
free(data);

[m_viewController dismissModalViewControllerAnimated:NO];❽
m_paused = false;
[picker release];
}

@end
```

❶ The default camera interface includes a cancel button to allow the user to back out.
When this occurs, we release the image picker and re-enable the OpenGL rendering
loop.

❷ The `imagePickerController:didFinishPickingMediaWithInfo` method gets called
when the user is done picking the image (or, in our case, taking a picture). The

handler receives two parameters: a pointer to the picker control and a dictionary of key-value pairs from which the image can be extracted.

❸ The camera API provides the orientation of the device when the picture was taken; in a subsequent step, we'll use this information to rotate the image to an upright position.

❹ As mentioned earlier, we're scaling the image to 256×256, so here we allocate the destination memory assuming 4 bytes per pixel.

❺ Rotate the image before drawing it to the destination surface. The `CGContextRota teCTM` function assumes that the axis of rotation is at (0,0), so we first shift the image to move its center to (0,0). After the rotation, we translate it back to its original position.

❻ Tell the rendering engine to upload a new texture by passing it a filled-in `TextureDe scription` structure and a pointer to the raw data.

❼ The currently hidden OpenGL surface still shows the ellipsoid with the old texture, so before removing the picker UI, we update the OpenGL surface. This prevents a momentary flicker after closing the image picker.

❽ Much like the `imagePickerControllerDidCancel` method, we now dismiss the view controller and release the picker control.

CameraTexture: Rendering Engine Implementation

Crack your OpenGL ES knuckles; it's time to implement the rendering engine using ES 1.1. Go ahead and remove the contents of `RenderingEngine.ES1.cpp`, and add the new class declaration and `Initialize` method, shown in Example 5-31.

Example 5-31. RenderingEngine class declaration and initialization

```
#include <OpenGLES/ES1/gl.h>
#include <OpenGLES/ES1/glext.h>
#include <iostream>
#include "Interfaces.hpp"
#include "Matrix.hpp"
#include "ParametricEquations.hpp"

using namespace std;

struct Drawable {
    GLuint VertexBuffer;
    GLuint IndexBuffer;
    int IndexCount;
};

namespace ES1 {

class RenderingEngine : public IRenderingEngine {
public:
```

```
        RenderingEngine(IResourceManager* resourceManager);
        void Initialize();
        void Render(float zScale, float theta, bool waiting) const;
        void LoadCameraTexture(const TextureDescription& description,
                               void* data);
    private:
        GLuint CreateTexture(const string& file);
        Drawable CreateDrawable(const ParametricSurface& surface);
        void RenderDrawable(const Drawable& drawable) const;
        void UploadImage(const TextureDescription& description,
                         void* data = 0);
        Drawable m_sphere;
        Drawable m_button;
        GLuint m_colorRenderbuffer;
        GLuint m_depthRenderbuffer;
        GLuint m_cameraTexture;
        GLuint m_waitTexture;
        GLuint m_actionTexture;
        IResourceManager* m_resourceManager;
    };

    IRenderingEngine* CreateRenderingEngine(IResourceManager* resourceManager)
    {
        return new RenderingEngine(resourceManager);
    }

    RenderingEngine::RenderingEngine(IResourceManager* resourceManager)
    {
        m_resourceManager = resourceManager;
        glGenRenderbuffersOES(1, &m_colorRenderbuffer);
        glBindRenderbufferOES(GL_RENDERBUFFER_OES, m_colorRenderbuffer);
    }

    void RenderingEngine::Initialize()
    {
        // Create vertex buffer objects.
        m_sphere = CreateDrawable(Sphere(2.5));
        m_button = CreateDrawable(Quad(4, 1));

        // Load up some textures.
        m_cameraTexture = CreateTexture("Tarsier.png");
        m_waitTexture = CreateTexture("PleaseWait.png");
        m_actionTexture = CreateTexture("TakePicture.png");

        // Extract width and height from the color buffer.
        int width, height;
        glGetRenderbufferParameterivOES(GL_RENDERBUFFER_OES,
                                        GL_RENDERBUFFER_WIDTH_OES, &width);
        glGetRenderbufferParameterivOES(GL_RENDERBUFFER_OES,
                                        GL_RENDERBUFFER_HEIGHT_OES, &height);
        glViewport(0, 0, width, height);

        // Create a depth buffer that has the same size as the color buffer.
        glGenRenderbuffersOES(1, &m_depthRenderbuffer);
        glBindRenderbufferOES(GL_RENDERBUFFER_OES, m_depthRenderbuffer);
```

```
    glRenderbufferStorageOES(GL_RENDERBUFFER_OES,
                             GL_DEPTH_COMPONENT16_OES,
                             width, height);

    // Create the framebuffer object.
    GLuint framebuffer;
    glGenFramebuffersOES(1, &framebuffer);
    glBindFramebufferOES(GL_FRAMEBUFFER_OES, framebuffer);
    glFramebufferRenderbufferOES(GL_FRAMEBUFFER_OES,
                                 GL_COLOR_ATTACHMENT0_OES,
                                 GL_RENDERBUFFER_OES,
                                 m_colorRenderbuffer);
    glFramebufferRenderbufferOES(GL_FRAMEBUFFER_OES,
                                 GL_DEPTH_ATTACHMENT_OES,
                                 GL_RENDERBUFFER_OES,
                                 m_depthRenderbuffer);
    glBindRenderbufferOES(GL_RENDERBUFFER_OES, m_colorRenderbuffer);

    // Set up various GL state.
    glEnableClientState(GL_VERTEX_ARRAY);
    glEnableClientState(GL_NORMAL_ARRAY);
    glEnableClientState(GL_TEXTURE_COORD_ARRAY);
    glEnable(GL_LIGHT0);
    glEnable(GL_TEXTURE_2D);
    glEnable(GL_DEPTH_TEST);

    // Set up the material properties.
    vec4 diffuse(1, 1, 1, 1);
    glMaterialfv(GL_FRONT_AND_BACK, GL_DIFFUSE, diffuse.Pointer());

    // Set the light position.
    glMatrixMode(GL_MODELVIEW);
    glLoadIdentity();
    vec4 lightPosition(0.25, 0.25, 1, 0);
    glLightfv(GL_LIGHT0, GL_POSITION, lightPosition.Pointer());

    // Set the model-view transform.
    mat4 modelview = mat4::Translate(0, 0, -8);
    glLoadMatrixf(modelview.Pointer());

    // Set the projection transform.
    float h = 4.0f * height / width;
    mat4 projection = mat4::Frustum(-2, 2, -h / 2, h / 2, 5, 10);
    glMatrixMode(GL_PROJECTION);
    glLoadMatrixf(projection.Pointer());
    glMatrixMode(GL_MODELVIEW);
}

} // end namespace ES1
```

There are no new concepts in Example 5-31; at a high level, the Initialize method performs the following tasks:

1. Creates two vertex buffers using the parametric surface helper: a quad for the button and a sphere for the ellipsoid.

2. Creates three textures: the initial ellipsoid texture, the "Please Wait" text, and the "Take Picture" button text. (We'll learn better ways of rendering text in future chapters.)

3. Performs some standard initialization work, such as creating the FBO and setting up the transformation matrices.

Next, let's implement the two public methods, Render and LoadCameraTexture, as shown in Example 5-32.

Example 5-32. Render and LoadCameraTexture

```
void RenderingEngine::Render(float zScale, float theta, bool waiting) const
{
    glClearColor(0.5f, 0.5f, 0.5f, 1);
    glClear(GL_COLOR_BUFFER_BIT | GL_DEPTH_BUFFER_BIT);
    glPushMatrix();

    // Draw the button.
    glTranslatef(0, -4, 0);
    glBindTexture(GL_TEXTURE_2D, waiting ? m_waitTexture : m_actionTexture);
    RenderDrawable(m_button);

    // Draw the sphere.
    glBindTexture(GL_TEXTURE_2D, m_cameraTexture);
    glTranslatef(0, 4.75, 0);
    glRotatef(theta, 1, 0, 0);
    glScalef(1, 1, zScale);
    glEnable(GL_LIGHTING);
    RenderDrawable(m_sphere);
    glDisable(GL_LIGHTING);

    glPopMatrix();
}

void RenderingEngine::LoadCameraTexture(const TextureDescription&
                                        desc, void* data)
{
    glBindTexture(GL_TEXTURE_2D, m_cameraTexture);
    UploadImage(desc, data);
}
```

That was simple! Next we'll implement the four private methods (Example 5-33).

Example 5-33. CreateTexture, CreateDrawable, RenderDrawable, UploadImage

```
GLuint RenderingEngine::CreateTexture(const string& file)
{
    GLuint name;
    glGenTextures(1, &name);
    glBindTexture(GL_TEXTURE_2D, name);
    glTexParameteri(GL_TEXTURE_2D,
                    GL_TEXTURE_MIN_FILTER,
                    GL_LINEAR_MIPMAP_LINEAR);
    glTexParameteri(GL_TEXTURE_2D,
```

```
                    GL_TEXTURE_MAG_FILTER,
                    GL_LINEAR);
    glTexParameteri(GL_TEXTURE_2D, GL_GENERATE_MIPMAP, GL_TRUE);
    UploadImage(m_resourceManager->LoadImagePot(file));
    return name;
}

Drawable RenderingEngine::CreateDrawable(const ParametricSurface& surface)
{
    // Create the VBO for the vertices.
    vector<float> vertices;
    unsigned char vertexFlags = VertexFlagsNormals | VertexFlagsTexCoords;
    surface.GenerateVertices(vertices, vertexFlags);
    GLuint vertexBuffer;
    glGenBuffers(1, &vertexBuffer);
    glBindBuffer(GL_ARRAY_BUFFER, vertexBuffer);
    glBufferData(GL_ARRAY_BUFFER,
                 vertices.size() * sizeof(vertices[0]),
                 &vertices[0],
                 GL_STATIC_DRAW);

    // Create a new VBO for the indices if needed.
    int indexCount = surface.GetTriangleIndexCount();
    GLuint indexBuffer;
    vector<GLushort> indices(indexCount);
    surface.GenerateTriangleIndices(indices);
    glGenBuffers(1, &indexBuffer);
    glBindBuffer(GL_ELEMENT_ARRAY_BUFFER, indexBuffer);
    glBufferData(GL_ELEMENT_ARRAY_BUFFER,
                 indexCount * sizeof(GLushort),
                 &indices[0],
                 GL_STATIC_DRAW);

    // Fill in a descriptive struct and return it.
    Drawable drawable;
    drawable.IndexBuffer = indexBuffer;
    drawable.VertexBuffer = vertexBuffer;
    drawable.IndexCount = indexCount;
    return drawable;
}


void RenderingEngine::RenderDrawable(const Drawable& drawable) const
{
    int stride = sizeof(vec3) + sizeof(vec3) + sizeof(vec2);
    const GLvoid* normalOffset = (const GLvoid*) sizeof(vec3);
    const GLvoid* texCoordOffset = (const GLvoid*) (2 * sizeof(vec3));
    glBindBuffer(GL_ARRAY_BUFFER, drawable.VertexBuffer);
    glVertexPointer(3, GL_FLOAT, stride, 0);
    glNormalPointer(GL_FLOAT, stride, normalOffset);
    glTexCoordPointer(2, GL_FLOAT, stride, texCoordOffset);
    glBindBuffer(GL_ELEMENT_ARRAY_BUFFER, drawable.IndexBuffer);
    glDrawElements(GL_TRIANGLES, drawable.IndexCount,
                   GL_UNSIGNED_SHORT, 0);
}
```

```
void RenderingEngine::UploadImage(const TextureDescription& description,
                                  void* data)
{
    GLenum format;
    switch (description.Format) {
        case TextureFormatRgb:  format = GL_RGB;  break;
        case TextureFormatRgba: format = GL_RGBA; break;
    }

    GLenum type = GL_UNSIGNED_BYTE;
    ivec2 size = description.Size;

    if (data == 0) {
        data = m_resourceManager->GetImageData();
        glTexImage2D(GL_TEXTURE_2D, 0, format, size.x, size.y,
                     0, format, type, data);
        m_resourceManager->UnloadImage();
    } else {
        glTexImage2D(GL_TEXTURE_2D, 0, format, size.x, size.y,
                     0, format, type, data);
    }
}
```

Much of Example 5-33 is fairly straightforward. The UploadImage method is used both for camera data (where the raw data is passed in) and for image files (where the raw data is obtained from the resource manager).

We won't bother with an ES 2.0 backend in this case, so you'll want to turn on the ForceES1 flag in *GLView.mm*, comment out the call to ES2::CreateRenderingEngine, and remove *RenderingEngine.ES2.cpp* from the project.

At this point, you're almost ready to run the sample, but you'll need a few image files (*Tarsier.png*, *PleaseWait.png*, and *TakePicture.png*). You can obtain these files from this book's example code (see "How to Contact Us" on page xvii) in the CameraTexture sample. You'll also want to copy over the Quad and Sphere class definitions from *ParametricSurface.hpp*; they've been tweaked to generate good texture coordinates.

This completes the CameraTexture sample, another fun but useless iPhone program!

Wrapping Up

In this chapter, we went over the basics of texturing, and we presented several methods of loading them into an iPhone application:

- Using CGDataProviderCopyData to access the raw data from the standard PNG decoder (Example 5-2).
- Using texturetool ("Texture Compression with PVRTC" on page 191) or PVRTexTool ("The PowerVR SDK and Low-Precision Textures" on page 198) to generate

a PVR file as part of the build process, and then parse its header at runtime (Example 5-18). This is the best method to use in production code.

- Creating a Quartz surface in the desired format, and draw the source image to it using CGContextDrawImage (Example 5-22).
- Creating a Quartz surface in a power-of-two size, and scale the source image (Example 5-25).

We also presented a couple ways of generating new textures at runtime:

- Using Quartz to draw vector art into a surface (Example 5-23).
- Using the UIViewController API to snap a photo, and then shrink it down with Quartz (the CameraTexture sample, starting on "Creating Textures with the Camera" on page 208).

Texturing is a deep subject, and we actually left quite a lot out of this chapter. New techniques relating to texturing will be covered in Chapter 8.

## CHAPTER 6

Blending and Augmented Reality

*All colors are the friends of their neighbors and
the lovers of their opposites.*

—Marc Chagall

If you've ever used Photoshop to place yourself in front of the Taj Mahal in a paroxysm of wishful thinking, you're probably familiar with layers and opacity. Alpha simply represents opacity on a zero-to-one scale: zero is transparent, one is fully opaque. Alpha can be used both with and without textures, and in this chapter we'll pay special attention to textures that contain alpha. *Blending* is the process of compositing a source color with an existing pixel in the framebuffer.

Tangentially related to blending is *anti-aliasing*, or the attempt to mask "jaggies." Antialiased vector art (such as the circle texture we generated in the previous chapter) varies the alpha along the edges of the artwork to allow it to blend into the background. Anti-aliasing is also often used for lines and triangle edges, but unfortunately the iPhone's OpenGL implementation does not support this currently. Fret not, there are ways to get around this limitation, as you'll see in this chapter.

Also associated with blending are heads-up displays and *augmented reality*. Augmented reality is the process of overlaying computer-generated imagery with real-world imagery, and the iPhone is particularly well-suited for this. We'll wrap up the chapter by walking through a sample app that mixes OpenGL content with the iPhone's camera interface, and we'll use the compass and accelerometer APIs to compute the view matrix. Overlaying the environment with fine Mughal architecture will be left as an exercise to the reader.

Blending Recipe

Some of my favorite YouTube videos belong to the *Will It Blend?* series. The episode featuring the pulverization of an iPhone is a perennial favorite, seconded only by the Chuck Norris episode. Alas, this chapter deals with blending of a different sort. OpenGL blending requires five ingredients:

1. Ensure your color contains alpha. If it comes from a texture, make sure the texture format contains alpha; if it comes from a vertex attribute, make sure it has all four color components.
2. Disable depth testing.

   ```
   glDisable(GL_DEPTH_TEST);
   ```
3. Pay attention to the ordering of your draw calls.
4. Enable blending.

   ```
   glEnable(GL_BLENDING);
   ```
5. Set your blending function.

   ```
   glBlendFunc(GL_SRC_ALPHA, GL_ONE_MINUS_SRC_ALPHA);
   ```

For step 5, I'm giving a rather classic blending equation as an example, but that's not always what you'll want! (More on this later.) Specifically, the previous function call sets up the following equation:

$$F = S_\alpha * S + (1 - S_\alpha) * D$$

S is the source color, D is the starting destination color, and F is the final destination color. By default, OpenGL's blending equation is this:

$$F = 1 * S + 0 * D$$

Since the default blending function ignores alpha, blending is effectively turned off even when you've enabled it with `glEnable`. So, always remember to set your blending function—this is a common pitfall in OpenGL programming.

Here's the formal declaration of `glBlendFunc`:

```
void glBlendFunc (GLenum sfactor, GLenum dfactor);
```

The blending equation is always an operation on two scaled operands: the source color and the destination color. The template to the equation is this:

$$F = \text{sfactor} * S + \text{dfactor} * D$$

The sfactor and dfactor arguments can be any of the following:

GL_ZERO
Multiplies the operand with zero.

GL_ONE
Multiplies the operand with one.

GL_SRC_ALPHA
Multiplies the operand by the alpha component of the source color.

GL_ONE_MINUS_SRC_ALPHA
Multiplies the operand by the inverted alpha component of the source color.

GL_DEST_ALPHA
Multiplies the operand by the alpha component of the destination color.

GL_ONE_MINUS_DEST_ALPHA
Multiplies the operand by the inverted alpha component of the destination color.

Additionally, the sfactor parameter supports the following:

GL_DST_COLOR
Component-wise multiplication of the operand with the destination color.

GL_ONE_MINUS_DST_COLOR
Component-wise multiplication of the operand with the inverted destination color.

GL_SRC_ALPHA_SATURATE
Returns the minimum of source alpha and inverted destination alpha. This exists mostly for historical reasons, because it was required for an outmoded anti-aliasing technique.

And the dfactor parameter also supports the following:

GL_SRC_COLOR
Component-wise multiplication of the operand with the source color.

GL_ONE_MINUS_SRC_COLOR
Component-wise multiplication of the operand with the inverted source color.

OpenGL ES 2.0 relaxes the blending constraints by unifying the set of choices for sfactor and dfactor, with the exception of GL_SRC_ALPHA_SATURATE.

 ES 2.0 also adds the concept of "constant color," specified via glBlend Color. For more information, look up glBlendColor and glBlendFunc at the Khronos website:

> *http://www.khronos.org/opengles/sdk/docs/man/*

Wrangle Premultiplied Alpha

One of the biggest gotchas with textures on Apple devices is the issue of *premultiplied alpha*. If the RGB components in an image have already been scaled by their associated alpha value, the image is considered to be premultiplied. Normally, PNG images do not store premultiplied RGB values, but Xcode does some tampering with them when it creates the application bundle.

You might recall that we passed in a flag to the `CGBitmapInfo` mask that's related to this; Example 6-1 shows a snippet of the `ResourceManager` class presented in the previous chapter, with the flag of interest highlighted in bold.

Example 6-1. Using a CGContext

```
CGColorSpaceRef colorSpace = CGColorSpaceCreateDeviceRGB();
CGBitmapInfo bitmapInfo =
  kCGImageAlphaPremultipliedLast | kCGBitmapByteOrder32Big;
CGContextRef context = CGBitmapContextCreate(data,
    description.Size.x,
    description.Size.y,
    description.BitsPerComponent,
    bpp * description.Size.x,
    colorSpace,
    bitmapInfo);
CGColorSpaceRelease(colorSpace);
CGRect rect = CGRectMake(0, 0, description.Size.x, description.Size.y);
CGContextDrawImage(context, rect, uiImage.CGImage);
CGContextRelease(context);
```

For nonpremultiplied alpha, there's a flag called `kCGImageAlphaLast` that you're welcome to try, but at the time of this writing, the Quartz implementation on the iPhone does not support it, and I doubt it ever will, because of the funky preprocessing that Xcode performs on image files.

So, you're stuck with premultiplied alpha. Don't panic! There are two rather elegant ways to deal with it:

- Use PVRTexTool to encode your data into a PVR file. Remember, PVRTexTool can encode your image into *any* OpenGL format; it's not restricted to the compressed formats.

- Or, adjust your blending equation so that it takes premultiplied alpha into account, like so:

  ```
  glBlendFunction(GL_ONE, GL_ONE_MINUS_SRC_ALPHA)
  ```

  By using `GL_ONE` for the `sfactor` argument, you're telling OpenGL there's no need to multiply the RGB components by alpha.

In the previous chapter, we also presented a method of loading PNG files using `CGDataProviderCopyData`, but with that technique, the simulator and the device can differ in how they treat alpha. Again, I recommend using PVR files for fast and reliable results.

In Figure 6-1, the left column contains a normal texture, and the right column contains a texture with premultiplied alpha. In every row, the `dfactor` argument is `GL_ONE_MINUS_SRC_ALPHA`.

The following list summarizes the best results from Figure 6-1:

- For textures with straight alpha, set `sfactor` to `GL_SRC_ALPHA` and `dfactor` to `GL_ONE_MINUS_SRC_ALPHA`.

- For textures with premultiplied alpha, set `sfactor` to `GL_ONE` and `dfactor` to `GL_ONE_MINUS_SRC_ALPHA`.

- To check whether a texture has premultiplied alpha, disable blending, and look at the silhouette.

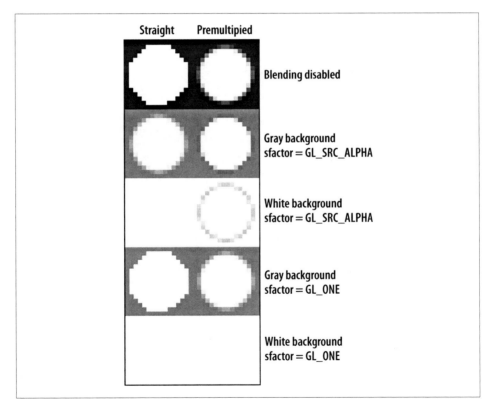

Figure 6-1. Texture alpha

Blending Caveats

It's important to remember to disable depth testing when blending is enabled. If depth testing is turned on, triangles that lie beneath other triangles get completely rejected, so their color can't contribute to the framebuffer.

An equally important caveat is that you should render your triangles in back-to-front order; the standard blending math simply doesn't work if you try to draw the top layer before the layer beneath it. Let's demonstrate why this is so. Suppose you'd like to depict a half-opaque red triangle on top of a half-opaque green triangle. Assuming the clear color is black, the history of a pixel in the framebuffer would look like this if you use back-to-front ordering:

1. Clear to Black. Result: (0, 0, 0).
2. Draw the half-opaque green triangle. Result: (0, 0.5, 0).
3. Draw the half-opaque red triangle. Result: (0.5, 0.25, 0).

So, the resulting pixel is a yellowish red; this is what you'd expect. If you try to draw the red triangle first, the result is different:

1. Clear to Black. Result: (0, 0, 0).
2. Draw the half-opaque red triangle. Result: (0.5, 0, 0).
3. Draw the half-opaque green triangle. Result: (0.25, 0.5, 0).

Now you have yellowish green. Order matters when you're blending! Incidentally, there's a way to adjust the blending equations so that you can draw in front-to-back order instead of back-to-front; we'll show how in the next section.

 When blending is enabled, sort your draw calls from farthest to nearest, and disable depth testing.

Alpha Testing

OpenGL ES supports an alternative to blending called *alpha testing*. Rather than applying an equation at every pixel to determine the final color, alpha testing performs a simple comparison of the source alpha with a presupplied value. If the comparison fails, the framebuffer is left unchanged; otherwise, the source color is written out. Alpha testing is generally used less frequently than blending because it cannot be used for smooth anti-aliasing or fade-out effects. In some ways, alpha testing is similar to blending with one-bit alpha.

With alpha testing, there's no back-to-front ordering requirement like there is with blending. It's simple to enable and configure:

```
glEnable(GL_ALPHA_TEST);
glAlphaFunc(GL_LESS, 1.0f);
```

The first parameter of `glAlphaFunc` is a comparison function, similar to the depth comparison function (see "Creating and Using the Depth Buffer" on page 123). The second parameter is the reference value used for comparison. Use alpha testing with caution: Apple's documentation warns that it can adversely affect performance.

Blending Extensions and Their Uses

Always remember to check for extension support using the method described in "Dealing with Size Constraints" on page 204. At the time of this writing, the iPhone supports the following blending-related extensions in OpenGL ES 1.1:

GL_OES_blend_subtract (all iPhone models)
Allows you to specify a blending operation other than addition, namely, subtraction.

GL_OES_blend_equation_separate (iPhone 3GS and higher)
Allows you to specify two separate blending operations: one for RGB, the other for alpha.

GL_OES_blend_func_separate (iPhone 3GS and higher)
Allows you to specify two separate pairs of blend factors: one pair for RGB, the other for alpha.

With OpenGL ES 2.0, these extensions are part of the core specification. Together they declare the following functions:

```
void glBlendEquation(GLenum operation)
void glBlendFuncSeparate(GLenum sfactorRGB, GLenum dfactorRGB,
                         GLenum sfactorAlpha, GLenum dfactorAlpha);
void glBlendEquationSeparate(GLenum operationRGB, GLenum operationAlpha);
```

For ES 1.1, remember to append *OES* to the end of each function since that's the naming convention for extensions.

The parameters to `glBlendEquation` and `glBlendEquationSeparate` can be one of the following:

GL_FUNC_ADD
Adds the source operand to the source operand; this is the default.

GL_FUNC_SUBTRACT
Subtracts the destination operand from the source operand.

GL_FUNC_REVERSE_SUBTRACT
Subtracts the source operand from the destination operand.

Again, remember to append *_OES* for these constants when working with ES 1.1.

When all these extensions are supported, you effectively have the ability to specify two unique equations: one for alpha, the other for RGB. Each equation conforms to one of the following templates:

```
FinalColor = SrcColor * sfactor + DestColor * dfactor
FinalColor = SrcColor * sfactor - DestColor * dfactor
FinalColor = DestColor * dfactor - SrcColor * sfactor
```

Why Is Blending Configuration Useful?

You might wonder why you'd ever need all the flexibility given by the aforementioned blending extensions. You'll see how various blending configurations come in handy with some samples presented later in the chapter, but I'll briefly go over some common uses here.

One use of GL_FUNC_SUBTRACT is inverting a region of color on the screen to highlight it. Simply draw a solid white rectangle and use GL_ONE for both sfactor and dfactor. You could also use subtraction to perform a comparison, or visual "diff," between two images.

The separate blending equations can be useful too. For example, perhaps you'd like to leave the destination's alpha channel unperturbed because you're storing information there for something other than transparency. In such a case, you could say the following:

```
glBlendFuncSeparate(GL_SRC_ALPHA, GL_ONE_MINUS_SRC_ALPHA, GL_ZERO, GL_ONE);
```

Another time to use separate blending equations is when you need to draw your triangles in front-to-back order rather than the usual back-to-front order. As you'll see later in the chapter, this can be useful for certain effects. To pull this off, take the following steps:

1. Set your clear color to (0, 0, 0, 1).
2. Make sure your source texture (or per-vertex color) has premultiplied alpha.
3. Set your blend equation to the following:

```
glBlendFuncSeparate(GL_DST_ALPHA, GL_ONE, GL_ZERO, GL_ONE_MINUS_SRC_ALPHA);
```

To see why this works, let's go back to the example of a half-opaque red triangle being rendered on top of a half-opaque green triangle:

1. Clear to Black. Result: (0, 0, 0, 1).
2. Draw the half-opaque red triangle. Since it's premultiplied, its source color is (0.5, 0, 0, 0.5). Using the previous blending equation, the result is (0.5, 0, 0, 0.5).
3. Draw the half-opaque green triangle; its source color is (0, 0.5, 0, 0.5). The result after blending is (0.5, 0.25, 0, 0.25).

The resulting pixel is yellowish red, just as you'd expect. Note that the framebuffer's alpha value is always inverted when you're using this trick.

Shifting Texture Color with Per-Vertex Color

Sometimes you'll need to uniformly tweak the alpha values across an entire texture. For example, you may want to create a fade-in effect or make a texture semitransparent for drawing a heads-up display (HUD).

With OpenGL ES 1.1, this can be achieved simply by adjusting the current vertex color:

```
glColor4f(1, 1, 1, alpha);
```

By default, OpenGL multiplies each component of the current vertex color with the color of the texel that it's rendering. This is known as *modulation*, and it's actually only one of many ways that you can combine texture color with per-vertex color (this will be discussed in detail later in this book).

If you're using a texture with premultiplied alpha, then the vertex color should also be premultiplied. The aforementioned function call should be changed to the following:

```
glColor4f(alpha, alpha, alpha, alpha);
```

Sometimes you may want to throttle back only one color channel. For example, say your app needs to render some red and blue buttons and that all the buttons are identical except for their color. Rather than wasting memory with multiple texture objects, you can create a single grayscale texture and modulate its color, like this:

```
// Bind the grayscale button texture.
glBindTexture(GL_TEXTURE_2D, buttonTexture)

// Draw green button.
glColor4f(0, 1, 0, 1);
glDrawElements(...);

// Draw red button.
glColor4f(1, 0, 0, 1);
glDrawElements(...);
```

With ES 2.0, the modulation needs to be performed within the pixel shader itself:

```
varying lowp vec4 Color;
varying mediump vec2 TextureCoord;

uniform sampler2D Sampler;

void main(void)
{
    gl_FragColor = texture2D(Sampler, TextureCoord) * Color;
}
```

The previous code snippet should look familiar. We used the same technique in Chapter 5 when combining lighting color with texture color.

Poor Man's Reflection with the Stencil Buffer

One use for blending in a 3D scene is overlaying a reflection on top of a surface, as shown on the left of Figure 6-2. Remember, computer graphics is often about cheating! To create the reflection, you can redraw the object using an upside-down projection matrix. Note that you need a way to prevent the reflection from "leaking" outside the bounds of the reflective surface, as shown on the right in Figure 6-2. How can this be done?

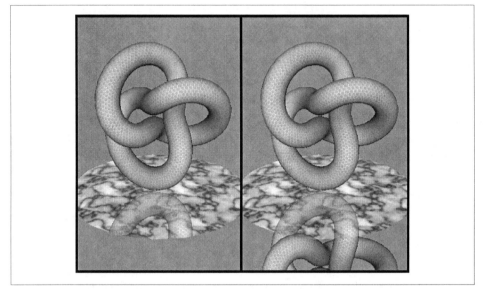

Figure 6-2. Left: reflection with stencil; right: reflection without stencil

It turns out that third-generation iPhones and iPod touches have support for an OpenGL ES feature known as the *stencil buffer*, and it's well-suited to this problem. The stencil buffer is actually just another type of renderbuffer, much like color and depth. But instead of containing RGB or Z values, it holds a small integer value at every pixel that you can use in different ways. There are many applications for the stencil buffer beyond clipping.

 To accommodate older iPhones, we'll cover some alternatives to stenciling later in the chapter.

To check whether stenciling is supported on the iPhone, check for the `GL_OES_sten cil8` extension using the method in "Dealing with Size Constraints" on page 204. At the time of this writing, stenciling is supported on third-generation devices and the simulator, but not on first- and second-generation devices.

The reflection trick can be achieved in four steps (see Figure 6-3):

1. Render the disk to stencil only.
2. Render the reflection of the floating object with the stencil test enabled.
3. Clear the depth buffer, and render the actual floating object.
4. Render the disk using front-to-back blending.

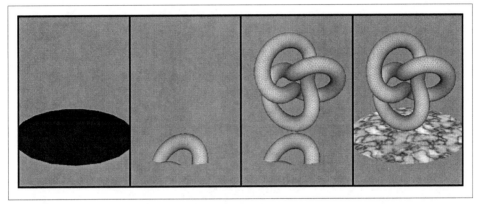

Figure 6-3. Rendering a reflection in four steps

Note that the reflection is drawn *before* the textured podium, which is the reason for the front-to-back blending. We can't render the reflection after the podium because blending and depth-testing cannot both be enabled when drawing complex geometry.

The complete code for this sample is available from this book's website, but we'll go over the key snippets in the following subsections. First let's take a look at the creation of the stencil buffer itself. The first few steps are generating a renderbuffer identifier, binding it, and allocating storage. This may look familiar if you remember how to create the depth buffer:

```
GLuint stencil;
glGenRenderbuffersOES(1, &stencil);
glBindRenderbufferOES(GL_RENDERBUFFER_OES, stencil);
glRenderbufferStorageOES(GL_RENDERBUFFER_OES, GL_STENCIL_INDEX8_OES, width, height);
```

Next, attach the stencil buffer to the framebuffer object, shown in bold here:

```
GLuint framebuffer;
glGenFramebuffersOES(1, &framebuffer);
glBindFramebufferOES(GL_FRAMEBUFFER_OES, framebuffer);
glFramebufferRenderbufferOES(GL_FRAMEBUFFER_OES, GL_COLOR_ATTACHMENT0_OES,
                             GL_RENDERBUFFER_OES, color);
glFramebufferRenderbufferOES(GL_FRAMEBUFFER_OES, GL_DEPTH_ATTACHMENT_OES,
                             GL_RENDERBUFFER_OES, depth);
```

```
glFramebufferRenderbufferOES(GL_FRAMEBUFFER_OES, GL_STENCIL_ATTACHMENT_OES,
                             GL_RENDERBUFFER_OES, stencil);
glBindRenderbufferOES(GL_RENDERBUFFER_OES, color);
```

As always, remember to omit the *OES* endings when working with ES 2.0.

To save memory, sometimes you can interleave the depth buffer and stencil buffer into a single renderbuffer. This is possible only when the OES_packed_depth_stencil extension is supported. At the time of this writing, it's available on third-generation devices, but not on the simulator or older devices. To see how to use this extension, see Example 6-2. Relevant portions are highlighted in bold.

Example 6-2. Using packed depth stencil

```
GLuint depthStencil;
glGenRenderbuffersOES(1, &depthStencil);
glBindRenderbufferOES(GL_RENDERBUFFER_OES, depthStencil);
glRenderbufferStorageOES(GL_RENDERBUFFER_OES, GL_DEPTH24_STENCIL8_OES, width, height);

GLuint framebuffer;
glGenFramebuffersOES(1, &framebuffer);
glBindFramebufferOES(GL_FRAMEBUFFER_OES, framebuffer);
glFramebufferRenderbufferOES(GL_FRAMEBUFFER_OES, GL_COLOR_ATTACHMENT0_OES,
                             GL_RENDERBUFFER_OES, color);
glFramebufferRenderbufferOES(GL_FRAMEBUFFER_OES, GL_DEPTH_ATTACHMENT_OES,
                             GL_RENDERBUFFER_OES, depthStencil);
glFramebufferRenderbufferOES(GL_FRAMEBUFFER_OES, GL_STENCIL_ATTACHMENT_OES,
                             GL_RENDERBUFFER_OES, depthStencil);
glBindRenderbufferOES(GL_RENDERBUFFER_OES, color);
```

Rendering the Disk to Stencil Only

Recall that step 1 in our reflection demo renders the disk to the stencil buffer. Before drawing to the stencil buffer, it needs to be cleared, just like any other renderbuffer:

```
glClearColor(0, 0, 0, 1);
glClear(GL_COLOR_BUFFER_BIT | GL_DEPTH_BUFFER_BIT | GL_STENCIL_BUFFER_BIT);
```

Next you need to tell OpenGL to enable writes to the stencil buffer, and you need to tell it what stencil value you'd like to write. Since you're using an 8-bit buffer in this case, you can set any value between 0x00 and 0xff. Let's go with 0xff and set up the OpenGL state like this:

```
glEnable(GL_STENCIL_TEST);
glStencilOp(GL_REPLACE, GL_REPLACE, GL_REPLACE);
glStencilFunc(GL_ALWAYS, 0xff, 0xff);
```

The first line enables GL_STENCIL_TEST, which is a somewhat misleading name in this case; you're *writing* to the stencil buffer, not *testing* against it. If you don't enable GL_STENCIL_TEST, then OpenGL assumes you're not working with the stencil buffer at all.

The next line, `glStencilOp`, tells OpenGL which stencil operation you'd like to perform at each pixel. Here's the formal declaration:

```
void glStencilOp(GLenum fail, GLenum zfail, GLenum zpass);
```

GLenum fail
> Specifies the operation to perform when the stencil test fails

GLenum zfail
> Specifies the operation to perform when the stencil test passes and the depth test fails

GLenum zpass
> Specifies the operation to perform when the stencil test passes and the depth test passes

Since the disk is the first draw call in the scene, we don't care whether any of these tests fail, so we've set them all to the same value.

Each of the arguments to `glStencilOp` can be one of the following:

GL_REPLACE
> Replace the value that's currently in the stencil buffer with the value specified in `glStencilFunc`.

GL_KEEP
> Don't do anything.

GL_INCR
> Increment the value that's currently in the stencil buffer.

GL_DECR
> Decrement the value that's currently in the stencil buffer.

GL_INVERT
> Perform a bitwise NOT operation with the value that's currently in the stencil buffer.

GL_ZERO
> Clobber the current stencil buffer value with zero.

Again, this may seem like way too much flexibility, more than you'd ever need. Later in this book, you'll see how all this freedom can be used to perform interesting tricks. For now, all we're doing is writing the shape of the disk out to the stencil buffer, so we're using the `GL_REPLACE` operation.

The next function we called to set up our stencil state is `glStencilFunc`. Here's its function declaration:

```
void glStencilFunc(GLenum func, GLint ref, GLuint mask);
```

GLenum func

> This specifies the comparison function to use for the stencil test, much like the depth test "Creating and Using the Depth Buffer" on page 123.

GLint ref

> This "reference value" actually serves two purposes:
>
> - Comparison value to test against if func is something other than GL_ALWAYS or GL_NEVER
> - The value to write if the operation is GL_REPLACE

GLuint mask

> Before performing a comparison, this bitmask gets ANDed with both the reference value and the value that's already in the buffer.

Again, this gives the developer quite a bit of power, but in this case we only need something simple.

Getting back to the task at hand, check out Example 6-3 to see how to render the disk to the stencil buffer only. I adjusted the indentation of the code to show how certain pieces of OpenGL state get modified before the draw call and then restored after the draw call.

Example 6-3. Rendering the disk to stencil only

```
// Prepare the render state for the disk.
glEnable(GL_STENCIL_TEST);
glStencilOp(GL_REPLACE, GL_REPLACE, GL_REPLACE);
glStencilFunc(GL_ALWAYS, 0xff, 0xff);

// Render the disk to the stencil buffer only.
glDisable(GL_TEXTURE_2D);
 glTranslatef(0, DiskY, 0);
  glDepthMask(GL_FALSE);
   glColorMask(GL_FALSE, GL_FALSE, GL_FALSE, GL_FALSE);
   RenderDrawable(m_drawables.Disk); // private method that calls glDrawElements
   glColorMask(GL_TRUE, GL_TRUE, GL_TRUE, GL_TRUE);
  glDepthMask(GL_TRUE);
 glTranslatef(0, -DiskY, 0);
glEnable(GL_TEXTURE_2D);
```

Two new function calls appear in Example 6-3: glDepthMask and glColorMask. Recall that we're interested in affecting values in the stencil buffer only. It's actually perfectly fine to write to all three renderbuffers (color, depth, stencil), but to maximize performance, it's good practice to disable any writes that you don't need.

The four arguments to glColorMask allow you to toggle each of the individual color channels; in this case we don't need any of them. Note that glDepthMask has only one argument, since it's a single-component buffer. Incidentally, OpenGL ES also provides a glStencilMask function, which we're not using here.

Rendering the Reflected Object with Stencil Testing

Step 2 renders the reflection of the object and uses the stencil buffer to clip it to the boundary of the disk. Example 6-4 shows how to do this.

Example 6-4. Rendering the reflection

```
glTranslatef(0, KnotY, 0);
glStencilOp(GL_KEEP, GL_KEEP, GL_KEEP);
glStencilFunc(GL_EQUAL, 0xff, 0xff);
glEnable(GL_LIGHTING);
glBindTexture(GL_TEXTURE_2D, m_textures.Grille);

const float alpha = 0.4f;
vec4 diffuse(alpha, alpha, alpha, 1 - alpha);
glMaterialfv(GL_FRONT_AND_BACK, GL_DIFFUSE, diffuse.Pointer());

glMatrixMode(GL_PROJECTION);
 glLoadMatrixf(m_mirrorProjection.Pointer());
   RenderDrawable(m_drawables.Knot); // private method that calls glDrawElements
 glLoadMatrixf(m_projection.Pointer());
glMatrixMode(GL_MODELVIEW);
```

This time we don't need to change the values in the stencil buffer, so we use GL_KEEP for the argument to glStencilOp. We changed the stencil comparison function to GL_EQUAL so that only the pixels within the correct region will pass.

There are several ways you could go about drawing an object upside down, but I chose to do it with a quick-and-dirty projection matrix. The result isn't a very accurate reflection, but it's good enough to fool the viewer! Example 6-5 shows how I did this using a mat4 method from the C++ vector library in the appendix. (For ES 1.1, you could simply use the provided glFrustum function.)

Example 6-5. Computing two projection matrices

```
const float AspectRatio = (float) height / width;
const float Shift = -1.25;
const float Near = 5;
const float Far = 50;

m_projection = mat4::Frustum(-1, 1,
                             -AspectRatio, AspectRatio,
                             Near, Far);

m_mirrorProjection = mat4::Frustum(-1, 1,
                                    AspectRatio + Shift, -AspectRatio + Shift,
                                    Near, Far);
```

Rendering the "Real" Object

The next step is rather mundane; we simply need to render the actual floating object, without doing anything with the stencil buffer. Before calling `glDrawElements` for the object, we turn off the stencil test and disable the depth buffer:

```
glDisable(GL_STENCIL_TEST);
glClear(GL_DEPTH_BUFFER_BIT);
```

For the first time, we've found a reason to call `glClear` somewhere in the *middle* of the `Render` method! Importantly, we're clearing only the depth buffer, leaving the color buffer intact.

Remember, the reflection is drawn just like any other 3D object, complete with depth testing. Allowing the actual object to be occluded by the reflection would destroy the illusion, so it's a good idea to clear the depth buffer before drawing it. Given the fixed position of the camera in our demo, we could actually get away without performing the clear, but this allows us to tweak the demo without breaking anything.

Rendering the Disk with Front-to-Back Blending

The final step is rendering the marble disk underneath the reflection. Example 6-6 sets this up.

Example 6-6. Render the disk to the color buffer

```
glTranslatef(0, DiskY - KnotY, 0);
glDisable(GL_LIGHTING);
glBindTexture(GL_TEXTURE_2D, m_textures.Marble);
glBlendFuncSeparateOES(GL_DST_ALPHA, GL_ONE,          // RGB factors
                       GL_ZERO, GL_ONE_MINUS_SRC_ALPHA); // Alpha factors
glEnable(GL_BLEND);
```

That's it for the stencil sample! As always, head over to this book's website to download (see "How to Contact Us" on page xvii) the complete code.

Stencil Alternatives for Older iPhones

If your app needs to accommodate first- and second-generation iPhones, in many cases you can use a trick that acts like stenciling without actually requiring a stencil buffer. These various tricks include the following:

- Using the framebuffer's alpha component to store the "stencil" values and setting up a blending equation that tests against those values.

- Turning off color writes and writing to the depth buffer to mask out certain regions. (The easiest way to uniformly offset generated depth values is with the `glDepthRange` function.)

- Cropping simple rectangular regions can be achieved with OpenGL's `glScissor` function.
- Some of the bitwise operations available with stencil buffers are actually possible with colors as well. In fact, there are additional operations possible with colors, such as XOR. To see how to do this, check out the `glLogicOp` function.

Let's demonstrate the first trick in the previous list: using framebuffer alpha as a fake stencil buffer. With this technique, it's possible to achieve the result shown in Figure 6-2 on older iPhones. The sequence of operations becomes the following:

1. Clear the depth buffer.
2. Render the background image with $\alpha = 0$.
3. Render the textured disk normally with $\alpha = 1$.
4. Enable blending, and set the blending equation to $S^*D_\alpha + D^*(1 - D_\alpha)$.
5. Render the reflection of the floating object.
6. Set the blending equation to $S^*S_\alpha + D^*(1 - S_\alpha)$.
7. Turn off depth testing, and render the textured disk again with $\alpha = 0.5$; this fades out the reflection a bit.
8. Clear the depth buffer, and re-enable depth testing.
9. Render the actual floating object.

Example 6-7 shows the rendering code for these nine steps. As always, the entire sample code is available from this book's website.

Example 6-7. Faking the stencil buffer

```
glClear(GL_DEPTH_BUFFER_BIT);

// Set up the transforms for the background.
glMatrixMode(GL_PROJECTION);
glLoadIdentity();
glFrustumf(-0.5, 0.5, -0.5, 0.5, NearPlane, FarPlane);
glMatrixMode(GL_MODELVIEW);
glLoadIdentity();
glTranslatef(0, 0, -NearPlane * 2);

// Render the dark background with alpha = 0.
glDisable(GL_DEPTH_TEST);
glColor4f(0.5, 0.5, 0.5, 0);
glBindTexture(GL_TEXTURE_2D, m_textures.Tiger);
RenderDrawable(m_drawables.Quad);

// Set up the transforms for the 3D scene.
glMatrixMode(GL_PROJECTION);
glLoadMatrixf(m_projection.Pointer());
glMatrixMode(GL_MODELVIEW);
glRotatef(20, 1, 0, 0);
glBindTexture(GL_TEXTURE_2D, m_textures.Marble);
```

```
// Render the disk normally.
glColor4f(1, 1, 1, 1);
glTranslatef(0, DiskY, 0);
RenderDrawable(m_drawables.Disk);
glTranslatef(0, -DiskY, 0);
glEnable(GL_DEPTH_TEST);

// Render the reflection.
glPushMatrix();
glRotatef(theta, 0, 1, 0);
glTranslatef(0, KnotY, 0);
glEnable(GL_LIGHTING);
glBindTexture(GL_TEXTURE_2D, m_textures.Grille);
glBlendFunc(GL_DST_ALPHA, GL_ONE_MINUS_DST_ALPHA);
glEnable(GL_BLEND);
glMatrixMode(GL_PROJECTION);
glLoadMatrixf(m_mirror.Pointer());
RenderDrawable(m_drawables.Knot);
glLoadMatrixf(m_projection.Pointer());
glMatrixMode(GL_MODELVIEW);
glDisable(GL_LIGHTING);
glPopMatrix();

// Render the disk again to make the reflection fade out.
glBlendFunc(GL_SRC_ALPHA, GL_ONE_MINUS_SRC_ALPHA);
glBindTexture(GL_TEXTURE_2D, m_textures.Marble);
glColor4f(1, 1, 1, 0.5);
glDisable(GL_DEPTH_TEST);
glTranslatef(0, DiskY, 0);
RenderDrawable(m_drawables.Disk);
glTranslatef(0, -DiskY, 0);
glEnable(GL_DEPTH_TEST);
glColor4f(1, 1, 1, 1);
glDisable(GL_BLEND);

// Clear the depth buffer.
glClear(GL_DEPTH_BUFFER_BIT);

// Render the floating object.
glEnable(GL_LIGHTING);
glBindTexture(GL_TEXTURE_2D, m_textures.Grille);
glPushMatrix();
glTranslatef(0, KnotY, 0);
glRotatef(theta, 0, 1, 0);
RenderDrawable(m_drawables.Knot);
glPopMatrix();
glDisable(GL_LIGHTING);
```

Anti-Aliasing Tricks with Offscreen FBOs

The iPhone's first-class support for framebuffer objects is perhaps its greatest enabler
of unique effects. In every sample presented so far in this book, we've been using a

single FBO, namely, the FBO that represents the visible Core Graphics layer. It's important to realize that FBOs can also be created as *offscreen surfaces*, meaning they don't show up on the screen unless bound to a texture. In fact, on most platforms, FBOs are *always* offscreen. The iPhone is rather unique in that the visible layer is itself treated as an FBO (albeit a special one).

Binding offscreen FBOs to textures enables a whole slew of interesting effects, including page-curling animations, light blooming, and more. We'll cover some of these techniques later in this book, but recall that one of the topics of this chapter is anti-aliasing. Several sneaky tricks with FBOs can be used to achieve full-scene anti-aliasing, even though the iPhone does not directly support anti-aliasing! We'll cover two of these techniques in the following subsections.

One technique not discussed here is performing a postprocess on the final image to soften it. While this is not true anti-aliasing, it may produce good results in some cases. It's similar to the bloom effect covered in Chapter 8.

A Super Simple Sample App for Supersampling

The easiest and crudest way to achieve full-scene anti-aliasing on the iPhone is to leverage bilinear texture filtering. Simply render to an offscreen FBO that has twice the dimensions of the screen, and then bind it to a texture and scale it down, as shown in Figure 6-4. This technique is known as *supersampling*.

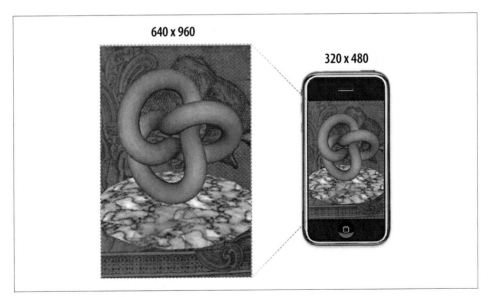

Figure 6-4. Supersampling

To demonstrate how to achieve this effect, we'll walk through the process of extending the stencil sample to use supersampling. As an added bonus, we'll throw in an Apple-esque flipping animation, as shown in Figure 6-5. Since we're creating a secondary FBO anyway, flipping effects like this come virtually for free.

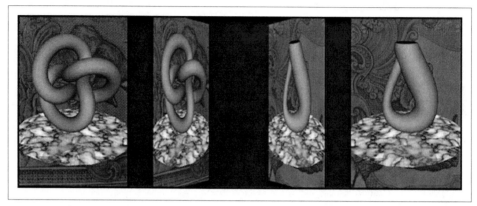

Figure 6-5. Flipping transition with FBO

Example 6-8 shows the RenderingEngine class declaration and related type definitions. Class members that carry over from previous samples are replaced with an ellipses for brevity.

Example 6-8. RenderingEngine declaration for the anti-aliasing sample

```
struct Framebuffers {❶
    GLuint Small;
    GLuint Big;
};

struct Renderbuffers {❷
    GLuint SmallColor;
    GLuint BigColor;
    GLuint BigDepth;
    GLuint BigStencil;
};

struct Textures {
    GLuint Marble;
    GLuint RhinoBackground;
    GLuint TigerBackground;
    GLuint OffscreenSurface;❸
};

class RenderingEngine : public IRenderingEngine {
public:
    RenderingEngine(IResourceManager* resourceManager);
    void Initialize();
    void Render(float objectTheta, float fboTheta) const;❹
private:
```

```
    ivec2 GetFboSize() const; ❺
    Textures m_textures;
    Renderbuffers m_renderbuffers;
    Framebuffers m_framebuffers;
    // ...
};
```

❶ The "small" FBO is attached to the visible EAGL layer (320×480). The "big" FBO is the 640×960 surface that contains the 3D scene.

❷ The small FBO does not need depth or stencil attachments because the only thing it contains is a full-screen quad; the big FBO is where most of the 3D rendering takes place, so it needs depth and stencil.

❸ The 3D scene requires a marble texture for the podium and one background for each side of the animation (Figure 6-5). The fourth texture object, OffscreenSurface, is attached to the big FBO.

❹ The application layer passes in objectTheta to control the rotation of the podium and passes in fboTheta to control the flipping transitions.

❺ GetFboSize is a new private method for conveniently determining the size of the currently bound FBO. This method helps avoid the temptation to hardcode some magic numbers or to duplicate state that OpenGL already maintains.

First let's take a look at the GetFboSize implementation (Example 6-9), which returns a width-height pair for the size. The return type is an instance of ivec2, one of the types defined in the C++ vector library in the appendix.

Example 6-9. GetFboSize() implementation

```
ivec2 RenderingEngine::GetFboSize() const
{
    ivec2 size;
    glGetRenderbufferParameterivOES(GL_RENDERBUFFER_OES,
                                    GL_RENDERBUFFER_WIDTH_OES, &size.x);
    glGetRenderbufferParameterivOES(GL_RENDERBUFFER_OES,
                                    GL_RENDERBUFFER_HEIGHT_OES, &size.y);
    return size;
}
```

Next let's deal with the creation of the two FBOs. Recall the steps for creating the on-screen FBO used in almost every sample so far:

1. In the RenderingEngine constructor, generate an identifier for the color renderbuffer, and then bind it to the pipeline.

2. In the GLView class (Objective-C), allocate storage for the color renderbuffer like so:

   ```
   [m_context renderbufferStorage:GL_RENDERBUFFER fromDrawable:eaglLayer]
   ```

3. In the RenderingEngine::Initialize method, create a framebuffer object, and attach the color renderbuffer to it.

4. If desired, create and allocate renderbuffers for depth and stencil, and then attach them to the FBO.

For the supersampling sample that we're writing, we still need to perform the first three steps in the previous sequence, but then we follow it with the creation of the offscreen FBO. Unlike the on-screen FBO, its color buffer is allocated in much the same manner as depth and stencil:

```
glRenderbufferStorageOES(GL_RENDERBUFFER_OES, GL_RGBA8_OES, width, height);
```

See Example 6-10 for the Initialize method used in the supersampling sample.

Example 6-10. Initialize() for supersampling

```
void RenderingEngine::Initialize()
{
    // Create the on-screen FBO.

    glGenFramebuffersOES(1, &m_framebuffers.Small);
    glBindFramebufferOES(GL_FRAMEBUFFER_OES, m_framebuffers.Small);
    glFramebufferRenderbufferOES(GL_FRAMEBUFFER_OES,
                                 GL_COLOR_ATTACHMENT0_OES,
                                 GL_RENDERBUFFER_OES,
                                 m_renderbuffers.SmallColor);

    // Create the double-size off-screen FBO.

    ivec2 size = GetFboSize() * 2;

    glGenRenderbuffersOES(1, &m_renderbuffers.BigColor);
    glBindRenderbufferOES(GL_RENDERBUFFER_OES, m_renderbuffers.BigColor);
    glRenderbufferStorageOES(GL_RENDERBUFFER_OES, GL_RGBA8_OES,
                             size.x, size.y);

    glGenRenderbuffersOES(1, &m_renderbuffers.BigDepth);
    glBindRenderbufferOES(GL_RENDERBUFFER_OES, m_renderbuffers.BigDepth);
    glRenderbufferStorageOES(GL_RENDERBUFFER_OES, GL_DEPTH_COMPONENT24_OES,
                             size.x, size.y);

    glGenRenderbuffersOES(1, &m_renderbuffers.BigStencil);
    glBindRenderbufferOES(GL_RENDERBUFFER_OES, m_renderbuffers.BigStencil);
    glRenderbufferStorageOES(GL_RENDERBUFFER_OES, GL_STENCIL_INDEX8_OES,
                             size.x, size.y);

    glGenFramebuffersOES(1, &m_framebuffers.Big);
    glBindFramebufferOES(GL_FRAMEBUFFER_OES, m_framebuffers.Big);
    glFramebufferRenderbufferOES(GL_FRAMEBUFFER_OES,
                                 GL_COLOR_ATTACHMENT0_OES,
                                 GL_RENDERBUFFER_OES,
                                 m_renderbuffers.BigColor);
    glFramebufferRenderbufferOES(GL_FRAMEBUFFER_OES,
                                 GL_DEPTH_ATTACHMENT_OES,
                                 GL_RENDERBUFFER_OES,
                                 m_renderbuffers.BigDepth);
    glFramebufferRenderbufferOES(GL_FRAMEBUFFER_OES,
```

```
                    GL_STENCIL_ATTACHMENT_OES,
                    GL_RENDERBUFFER_OES,
                     m_renderbuffers.BigStencil);

    // Create a texture object and associate it with the big FBO.

    glGenTextures(1, &m_textures.OffscreenSurface);
    glBindTexture(GL_TEXTURE_2D, m_textures.OffscreenSurface);
    glTexParameteri(GL_TEXTURE_2D, GL_TEXTURE_MIN_FILTER, GL_LINEAR);
    glTexParameteri(GL_TEXTURE_2D, GL_TEXTURE_MAG_FILTER, GL_LINEAR);
    glTexParameteri(GL_TEXTURE_2D, GL_TEXTURE_WRAP_S, GL_CLAMP_TO_EDGE);
    glTexParameteri(GL_TEXTURE_2D, GL_TEXTURE_WRAP_T, GL_CLAMP_TO_EDGE);
    glTexImage2D(GL_TEXTURE_2D, 0, GL_RGBA, size.x, size.y, 0,
                 GL_RGBA, GL_UNSIGNED_BYTE, 0);
    glFramebufferTexture2DOES(GL_FRAMEBUFFER_OES, GL_COLOR_ATTACHMENT0_OES,
                              GL_TEXTURE_2D, m_textures.OffscreenSurface, 0);

    // Check FBO status.

    GLenum status = glCheckFramebufferStatusOES(GL_FRAMEBUFFER_OES);
    if (status != GL_FRAMEBUFFER_COMPLETE_OES) {
        cout << "Incomplete FBO" << endl;
        exit(1);
    }

    // Load textures, create VBOs, set up various GL state.
    ...
}
```

You may have noticed two new FBO-related function calls in Example 6-10: glFrame
bufferTexture2DOES and glCheckFramebufferStatusOES. The formal function declarations look like this:

```
    void glFramebufferTexture2DOES(GLenum target,
                                   GLenum attachment, GLenum textarget,
                                   GLuint texture, GLint level);

    GLenum glCheckFramebufferStatusOES(GLenum target);
```

(As usual, the *OES* suffix can be removed for ES 2.0.)

The glFramebufferTexture2DOES function allows you to cast a color buffer into a texture object. FBO texture objects get set up just like any other texture object: they have an identifier created with glGenTextures, they have filter and wrap modes, and they have a format that should match the format of the FBO. The main difference with FBO textures is the fact that null gets passed to the last argument of glTexImage2D, since there's no image data to upload.

Note that the texture in Example 6-10 has non-power-of-two dimensions, so it specifies clamp-to-edge wrapping to accommodate third-generation devices. For older iPhones, the sample won't work; you'd have to change it to POT dimensions. Refer to "Dealing with Size Constraints" on page 204 for hints on how to do this. Keep in mind that the values passed to `glViewport` need not match the size of the renderbuffer; this comes in handy when rendering to an NPOT subregion of a POT texture.

The other new function, `glCheckFramebufferStatusOES`, is a useful sanity check to make sure that an FBO has been set up properly. It's easy to bungle the creation of FBOs if the sizes of the attachments don't match up or if their formats are incompatible with each other. `glCheckFramebufferStatusOES` returns one of the following values, which are fairly self-explanatory:

- GL_FRAMEBUFFER_COMPLETE
- GL_FRAMEBUFFER_INCOMPLETE_ATTACHMENT
- GL_FRAMEBUFFER_INCOMPLETE_MISSING_ATTACHMENT
- GL_FRAMEBUFFER_INCOMPLETE_DIMENSIONS
- GL_FRAMEBUFFER_INCOMPLETE_FORMATS
- GL_FRAMEBUFFER_UNSUPPORTED

General OpenGL Errors

OpenGL ES also supports a more generally useful diagnostic function called `glGetError`. Its function declaration is simple:

```
GLenum glGetError();
```

The possible return values are:

- GL_NO_ERROR
- GL_INVALID_ENUM
- GL_INVALID_VALUE
- GL_INVALID_OPERATION
- GL_STACK_OVERFLOW
- GL_STACK_UNDERFLOW
- GL_OUT_OF_MEMORY

Although this book doesn't call `glGetError` in any of the sample code, always keep it in mind as a useful debugging tool. Some developers like to sprinkle it throughout their OpenGL code as a matter of habit, much like an assert.

Aside from building FBO objects, another error-prone activity in OpenGL is building shader objects in ES 2.0. Flip back to Example 1-18 to see how to detect shader errors.

Next let's take a look at the render method of the supersampling sample. Recall from the class declaration that the application layer passes in `objectTheta` to control the rotation of the podium and passes in `fboTheta` to control the flipping transitions. So, the first thing the `Render` method does is look at `fboTheta` to determine which background image should be displayed and which shape should be shown on the podium. See Example 6-11.

Example 6-11. Render() for supersampling

```
void RenderingEngine::Render(float objectTheta, float fboTheta) const
{
    Drawable drawable;
    GLuint background;
    vec3 color;

    // Look at fboTheta to determine which "side" should be rendered:
    //   1) Orange Trefoil knot against a Tiger background
    //   2) Green Klein bottle against a Rhino background

    if (fboTheta > 270 || fboTheta < 90) {
        background = m_textures.TigerBackground;
        drawable = m_drawables.Knot;
        color = vec3(1, 0.5, 0.1);
    } else {
        background = m_textures.RhinoBackground;
        drawable = m_drawables.Bottle;
        color = vec3(0.5, 0.75, 0.1);
    }

    // Bind the double-size FBO.
    glBindFramebufferOES(GL_FRAMEBUFFER_OES, m_framebuffers.Big);
    glBindRenderbufferOES(GL_RENDERBUFFER_OES, m_renderbuffers.BigColor);
    ivec2 bigSize = GetFboSize();
    glViewport(0, 0, bigSize.x, bigSize.y);

    // Draw the 3D scene - download the example to see this code.
    ...

    // Render the background.
    glColor4f(0.7, 0.7, 0.7, 1);
    glBindTexture(GL_TEXTURE_2D, background);
    glMatrixMode(GL_PROJECTION);
    glLoadIdentity();
    glFrustumf(-0.5, 0.5, -0.5, 0.5, NearPlane, FarPlane);
    glMatrixMode(GL_MODELVIEW);
    glLoadIdentity();
    glTranslatef(0, 0, -NearPlane * 2);
    RenderDrawable(m_drawables.Quad);
    glColor4f(1, 1, 1, 1);
    glDisable(GL_BLEND);

    // Switch to the on-screen render target.
    glBindFramebufferOES(GL_FRAMEBUFFER_OES, m_framebuffers.Small);
    glBindRenderbufferOES(GL_RENDERBUFFER_OES, m_renderbuffers.SmallColor);
    ivec2 smallSize = GetFboSize();
    glViewport(0, 0, smallSize.x, smallSize.y);

    // Clear the color buffer only if necessary.
    if ((int) fboTheta % 180 != 0) {
        glClearColor(0, 0, 0, 1);
        glClear(GL_COLOR_BUFFER_BIT);
    }
```

```
// Render the offscreen surface by applying it to a quad.
glDisable(GL_DEPTH_TEST);
glRotatef(fboTheta, 0, 1, 0);
glBindTexture(GL_TEXTURE_2D, m_textures.OffscreenSurface);
RenderDrawable(m_drawables.Quad);
glDisable(GL_TEXTURE_2D);
}
```

Most of Example 6-11 is fairly straightforward. One piece that may have caught your eye is the small optimization made right before blitting the offscreen FBO to the screen:

```
// Clear the color buffer only if necessary.
if ((int) fboTheta % 180 != 0) {
    glClearColor(0, 0, 0, 1);
    glClear(GL_COLOR_BUFFER_BIT);
}
```

This is a sneaky little trick. Since the quad is the exact same size as the screen, there's no need to clear the color buffer; unnecessarily issuing a glClear can hurt performance. However, if a flipping animation is currently underway, the color buffer needs to be cleared to prevent artifacts from appearing in the background; flip back to Figure 6-5 and observe the black areas. If fboTheta is a multiple of 180, then the quad completely fills the screen, so there's no need to issue a clear.

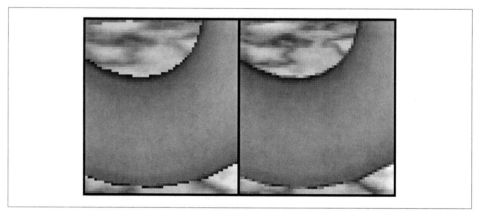

Figure 6-6. Left: normal rendering; right: 2× supersampling

That's it for the supersampling sample. The quality of the anti-aliasing is actually not that great; you can still see some "stair-stepping" along the bottom outline of the shape in Figure 6-6. You might think that creating an even bigger offscreen buffer, say quadruple-size, would provide higher-quality results. Unfortunately, using a quadruple-size buffer would require two passes; directly applying a 1280×1920 texture to a 320×480 quad isn't sufficient because GL_LINEAR filtering only samples from a 2×2 neighborhood of pixels. To achieve the desired result, you'd actually need *three* FBOs as follows:

- 1280×1920 offscreen FBO for the 3D scene
- 640×960 offscreen FBO that contains a quad with the 1280×1920 texture applied to it
- 320×480 on-screen FBO that contains a quad with the 640×960 texture applied to it

Not only is this laborious, but it's a memory hog. Older iPhones don't even support textures this large! It turns out there's another anti-aliasing strategy called *jittering*, and it can produce high-quality results without the memory overhead of supersampling.

Jittering

Jittering is somewhat more complex to implement than supersampling, but it's not rocket science. The idea is to rerender the scene multiple times at slightly different viewpoints, merging the results along the way. You need only two FBOs for this method: the on-screen FBO that accumulates the color and the offscreen FBO that the 3D scene is rendered to. You can create as many jittered samples as you'd like, and you still need only two FBOs. Of course, the more jittered samples you create, the longer it takes to create the final rendering. Example 6-12 shows the pseudocode for the jittering algorithm.

Example 6-12. Jitter pseudocode

```
BindFbo(OnscreenBuffer)
glClear(GL_COLOR_BUFFER_BIT)

for (int sample = 0; sample < SampleCount; sample++) {
   BindFbo(OffscreenBuffer)

   vec2 offset = JitterTable[sample]

   SetFrustum(LeftPlane + offset.x, RightPlane + offset.x,
              TopPlane + offset.y, BottomPlane + offset.y,
              NearPlane, FarPlane)

   Render3DScene()

   f = 1.0 / SampleCount
   glColor4f(f, f, f, 1)
   glEnable(GL_BLEND)
   glBlendFunc(GL_ONE, GL_ONE)

   BindFbo(OnscreenBuffer)
   BindTexture(OffscreenBuffer)
   RenderFullscreenQuad()
}
```

The key part of Example 6-12 is the blending configuration. By using a blend equation of plain old addition (GL_ONE, GL_ONE) and dimming the color according to the number of samples, you're effectively accumulating an average color.

An unfortunate side effect of jittering is reduced color precision; this can cause banding artifacts, as shown in Figure 6-7. On some platforms the banding effect can be neutralized with a high-precision color buffer, but that's not supported on the iPhone. In practice, I find that creating too many samples is detrimental to performance anyway, so the banding effect isn't usually much of a concern.

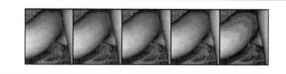

Figure 6-7. 2×, 4×, 8×, 16×, and 32× jittering

Determining the jitter offsets (JitterTable in Example 6-12) is a bit of black art. Totally random values don't work well since they don't guarantee uniform spacing between samples. Interestingly, dividing up each pixel into an equally spaced uniform grid does not work well either! Example 6-13 shows some commonly used jitter offsets.

Example 6-13. Popular jitter offsets

```
const vec2 JitterOffsets2[2] =
{
    vec2(0.25f, 0.75f), vec2(0.75f, 0.25f),
};

const vec2 JitterOffsets4[4] =
{
    vec2(0.375f, 0.25f), vec2(0.125f, 0.75f),
    vec2(0.875f, 0.25f), vec2(0.625f, 0.75f),
};

const vec2 JitterOffsets8[8] =
{
    vec2(0.5625f, 0.4375f), vec2(0.0625f, 0.9375f),
    vec2(0.3125f, 0.6875f), vec2(0.6875f, 0.8125f),

    vec2(0.8125f, 0.1875f), vec2(0.9375f, 0.5625f),
    vec2(0.4375f, 0.0625f), vec2(0.1875f, 0.3125f),
};

const vec2 JitterOffsets16[16] =
{
    vec2(0.375f, 0.4375f), vec2(0.625f, 0.0625f),
    vec2(0.875f, 0.1875f), vec2(0.125f, 0.0625f),

    vec2(0.375f, 0.6875f), vec2(0.875f, 0.4375f),
    vec2(0.625f, 0.5625f), vec2(0.375f, 0.9375f),
```

```
    vec2(0.625f, 0.3125f), vec2(0.125f, 0.5625f),
    vec2(0.125f, 0.8125f), vec2(0.375f, 0.1875f),

    vec2(0.875f, 0.9375f), vec2(0.875f, 0.6875f),
    vec2(0.125f, 0.3125f), vec2(0.625f, 0.8125f),
};
```

Let's walk through the process of creating a simple app with jittering. Much like we did with the supersample example, we'll include a fun transition animation. (You can download the full project from the book's website at *http://oreilly.com/catalog/ 9780596804831.*) This time we'll use the jitter offsets to create a defocusing effect, as shown in Figure 6-8.

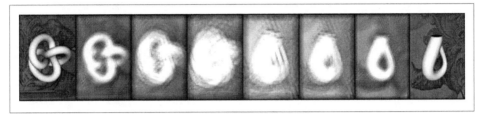

Figure 6-8. Defocus transition with jitter

To start things off, let's take a look at the RenderingEngine class declaration and related types. It's not unlike the class we used for supersampling; the main differences are the labels we give to the FBOs. Accumulated denotes the on-screen buffer, and Scene denotes the offscreen buffer. See Example 6-14.

Example 6-14. RenderingEngine declaration for the jittering sample

```
struct Framebuffers {
    GLuint Accumulated;
    GLuint Scene;
};

struct Renderbuffers {
    GLuint AccumulatedColor;
    GLuint SceneColor;
    GLuint SceneDepth;
    GLuint SceneStencil;
};

struct Textures {
    GLuint Marble;
    GLuint RhinoBackground;
    GLuint TigerBackground;
    GLuint OffscreenSurface;
};
```

```
class RenderingEngine : public IRenderingEngine {
public:
    RenderingEngine(IResourceManager* resourceManager);
    void Initialize();
    void Render(float objectTheta, float fboTheta) const;
private:
    void RenderPass(float objectTheta, float fboTheta, vec2 offset) const;
    Textures m_textures;
    Renderbuffers m_renderbuffers;
    Framebuffers m_framebuffers;
    // ...
};
```

Example 6-14 also adds a new private method called RenderPass; the implementation is shown in Example 6-15. Note that we're keeping the fboTheta argument that we used in the supersample example, but now we're using it to compute a scale factor for the jitter offset rather than a y-axis rotation. If fboTheta is 0 or 180, then the jitter offset is left unscaled, so the scene is in focus.

Example 6-15. RenderPass method for jittering

```
void RenderingEngine::RenderPass(float objectTheta, float fboTheta, vec2 offset) const
{
    // Tweak the jitter offset for the defocus effect:

    offset -= vec2(0.5, 0.5);
    offset *= 1 + 100 * sin(fboTheta * Pi / 180);

    // Set up the frustum planes:

    const float AspectRatio = (float) m_viewport.y / m_viewport.x;
    const float NearPlane = 5;
    const float FarPlane = 50;
    const float LeftPlane = -1;
    const float RightPlane = 1;
    const float TopPlane = -AspectRatio;
    const float BottomPlane = AspectRatio;

    // Transform the jitter offset from window space to eye space:

    offset.x *= (RightPlane - LeftPlane) / m_viewport.x;
    offset.y *= (BottomPlane - TopPlane) / m_viewport.y;

    // Compute the jittered projection matrix:

    mat4 projection = mat4::Frustum(LeftPlane + offset.x,
                                    RightPlane + offset.x,
                                    TopPlane + offset.y,
                                    BottomPlane + offset.y,
                                    NearPlane, FarPlane);

    // Render the 3D scene - download the example to see this code.
```

```
    ...
}
```

Example 6-16 shows the implementation to the main Render method. The call to Ren
derPass is shown in bold.

Example 6-16. Render method for jittering

```
void RenderingEngine::Render(float objectTheta, float fboTheta) const
{
    // This is where you put the jitter offset declarations
    // from Example 6-13.

    const int JitterCount = 8;
    const vec2* JitterOffsets = JitterOffsets8;

    glBindFramebufferOES(GL_FRAMEBUFFER_OES, m_framebuffers.Accumulated);
    glBindRenderbufferOES(GL_RENDERBUFFER_OES,
                          m_renderbuffers.AccumulatedColor);

    glClearColor(0, 0, 0, 1);
    glClear(GL_COLOR_BUFFER_BIT);

    for (int i = 0; i < JitterCount; i++) {

        glBindFramebufferOES(GL_FRAMEBUFFER_OES, m_framebuffers.Scene);
        glBindRenderbufferOES(GL_RENDERBUFFER_OES,
                              m_renderbuffers.SceneColor);

        RenderPass(objectTheta,
                   fboTheta, JitterOffsets[i]);

        glMatrixMode(GL_PROJECTION);
        glLoadIdentity();

        const float NearPlane = 5, FarPlane = 50;
        glFrustumf(-0.5, 0.5, -0.5, 0.5, NearPlane, FarPlane);

        glMatrixMode(GL_MODELVIEW);
        glLoadIdentity();
        glTranslatef(0, 0, -NearPlane * 2);

        float f = 1.0f / JitterCount;
        f *= (1 + abs(sin(fboTheta * Pi / 180)));
        glColor4f(f, f, f, 1);

        glEnable(GL_BLEND);
        glBlendFunc(GL_ONE, GL_ONE);
        glBindFramebufferOES(GL_FRAMEBUFFER_OES,
                             m_framebuffers.Accumulated);
        glBindRenderbufferOES(GL_RENDERBUFFER_OES,
                              m_renderbuffers.AccumulatedColor);
        glDisable(GL_DEPTH_TEST);
        glBindTexture(GL_TEXTURE_2D, m_textures.OffscreenSurface);
```

```
        RenderDrawable(m_drawables.Quad);
        glDisable(GL_TEXTURE_2D);
        glDisable(GL_BLEND);
    }
}
```

Example 6-16 might give you sense of déjà vu; it's basically an implementation of the pseudocode algorithm that we already presented in Example 6-12. One deviation is how we compute the dimming effect:

```
float f = 1.0f / JitterCount;
f *= (1 + abs(sin(fboTheta * Pi / 180)));
glColor4f(f, f, f, 1);
```

The second line in the previous snippet is there only for the special transition effect. In addition to defocusing the scene, it's also brightened to simulate pupil dilation. If fboTheta is 0 or 180, then f is left unscaled, so the scene has its normal brightness.

Other FBO Effects

An interesting variation on jittering is *depth of field*, which blurs out the near and distant portions of the scene. To pull this off, compute the viewing frustum such that a given slice (parallel to the viewing plane) stays the same with each jitter pass; this is the focus plane.

Yet another effect is *motion blur*, which simulates the ghosting effect seen on displays with low response times. With each pass, make incremental adjustments to your animation, and gradually fade in the alpha value using glColor.

Rendering Anti-Aliased Lines with Textures

Sometimes full-screen anti-aliasing is more than you really need and can cause too much of a performance hit. You may find that you need anti-aliasing only on your line primitives rather than the entire scene. Normally this would be achieved in OpenGL ES like so:

```
glEnable(GL_LINE_SMOOTH);
```

Alas, none of the iPhone models supports this at the time of this writing. However, the simulator *does* support line smoothing; watch out for inconsistencies like this!

A clever trick to work around this limitation is filling an alpha texture with a circle and then tessellating the lines into short triangle strips (Figure 6-9). Texture coordinates are chosen such that the circle is stretched in the right places. That has the added benefit of allowing round end-cap styles and wide lines.

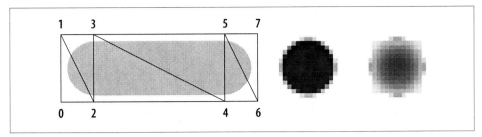

Figure 6-9. Line anti-aliasing with textured triangle strips

Using a 16×16 circle for the texture works well for thick lines (see the left circle in Figure 6-9 and left panel in Figure 6-10). For thinner lines, I find that a highly blurred 16x16 texture produces good results (see the right circle in Figure 6-9 and right panel in Figure 6-10).

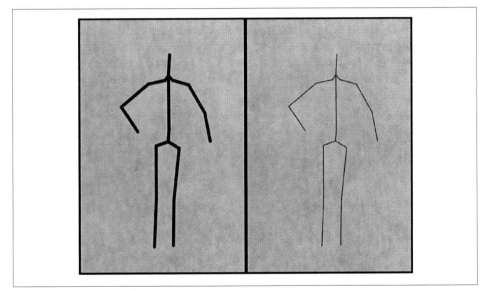

Figure 6-10. Antialiased lines

Let's walk through the process of converting a line list into a textured triangle list. Each source vertex needs to be extruded into four new vertices. It helps to give each extrusion vector a name using cardinal directions, as shown in Figure 6-11.

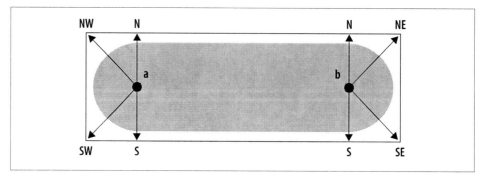

Figure 6-11. Line extrusion

Before going over the extrusion algorithm, let's set up an example scenario. Say we're rendering an animated stick figure similar to Figure 6-10. Note that some vertices are shared by multiple lines, so it makes sense to use an index buffer. Suppose the application can render the stick figure using either line primitives or textured triangles. Let's define a `StickFigure` structure that stores the vertex and index data for either the non-AA variant or the AA variant; see Example 6-17. The non-AA variant doesn't need texture coordinates, but we're including them for simplicity's sake.

Example 6-17. Structures for the extrusion algorithm

```
struct Vertex {
    vec3 Position;
    vec2 TexCoord;
};

typedef std::vector<Vertex> VertexList;
typedef std::vector<GLushort> IndexList;

struct StickFigure {
    IndexList Indices;
    VertexList Vertices;
};
```

The function prototype for the extrusion method needs three arguments: the source `StickFigure` (lines), the destination `StickFigure` (triangles), and the desired line width. See Example 6-18 and refer back to Figure 6-11 to visualize the six extrusion vectors (N, S, NE, NW, SW, SE).

Example 6-18. Line extrusion algorithm

```
void ExtrudeLines(const StickFigure& lines, StickFigure& triangles, float width)
{
    IndexList::iterator sourceIndex = lines.Indices.begin();
    VertexList::iterator destVertex = triangles.Vertices.begin();
    while (sourceIndex != lines.Indices.end()) {
```

```
        vec3 a = lines.Vertices[lines.Indices[*sourceIndex++]].Position;
        vec3 b = lines.Vertices[lines.Indices[*sourceIndex++]].Position;
        vec3 e = (b - a).Normalized() * width;

        vec3 N = vec3(-e.y, e.x, 0);
        vec3 S = -N;
        vec3 NE = N + e;
        vec3 NW = N - e;
        vec3 SW = -NE;
        vec3 SE = -NW;

        destVertex++->Position = a + SW;
        destVertex++->Position = a + NW;
        destVertex++->Position = a + S;
        destVertex++->Position = a + N;
        destVertex++->Position = b + S;
        destVertex++->Position = b + N;
        destVertex++->Position = b + SE;
        destVertex++->Position = b + NE;
    }
}
```

At this point, we've computed the positions of the extruded triangles, but we still haven't provided texture coordinates for the triangles, nor the contents of the index buffer. Note that the animated figure can change its vertex positions at every frame, but the number of lines stays the same. This means we can generate the index list only once; there's no need to recompute it at every frame. The same goes for the texture coordinates. Let's declare a couple functions for these start-of-day tasks:

```
    void GenerateTriangleIndices(size_t lineCount, IndexList& triangles);
    void GenerateTriangleTexCoords(size_t lineCount, VertexList& triangles);
```

Flip back to Figure 6-9, and note the number of triangles and vertices. Every line primitive extrudes into six triangles composed from eight vertices. Since every triangle requires three indices, the number of indices in the new index buffer is lineCount*18. This is different from the number of *vertices*, which is only lineCount*8. See Example 6-19.

Example 6-19. Line extrusion initialization methods

```
void GenerateTriangleIndices(size_t lineCount, IndexList& triangles)
{
    triangles.resize(lineCount * 18);
    IndexList::iterator index = triangles.begin();
    for (GLushort v = 0; index != triangles.end(); v += 8) {
        *index++ = 0 + v; *index++ = 1 + v; *index++ = 2 + v;
        *index++ = 2 + v; *index++ = 1 + v; *index++ = 3 + v;
        *index++ = 2 + v; *index++ = 3 + v; *index++ = 4 + v;
        *index++ = 4 + v; *index++ = 3 + v; *index++ = 5 + v;
        *index++ = 4 + v; *index++ = 5 + v; *index++ = 6 + v;
        *index++ = 6 + v; *index++ = 5 + v; *index++ = 7 + v;
    }
}
```

```
void GenerateTriangleTexCoords(size_t lineCount, VertexList& triangles)
{
    triangles.resize(lineCount * 8);
    VertexList::iterator vertex = triangles.begin();
    while (vertex != triangles.end()) {
        vertex++->TexCoord = vec2(0, 0);
        vertex++->TexCoord = vec2(0, 1);
        vertex++->TexCoord = vec2(0.5, 0);
        vertex++->TexCoord = vec2(0.5, 1);
        vertex++->TexCoord = vec2(0.5, 0);
        vertex++->TexCoord = vec2(0.5, 1);
        vertex++->TexCoord = vec2(1, 0);
        vertex++->TexCoord = vec2(1, 1);
    }
}
```

Et voilà...you now know how to render antialiased lines on a device that doesn't support antialiased lines! To see this in action, check out the AaLines sample from this book's example code.

Holodeck Sample

In this chapter's introduction, we promised to present a poor man's augmented reality app. As a starting point, we'll create a 3D environment that includes the aforementioned geodesic dome with antialiased borders. We'll also render a mossy ground plane and some moving clouds in the background. Later we'll replace the clouds with a live camera image. Another interesting aspect to this sample is that it's designed for landscape mode; see Figure 6-12.

Figure 6-12. The Holodeck sample

For rendering the AA lines in the dome, let's use a different trick than the one presented in the previous section. Rather than a filling a texture with a circle, let's fill it with a triangle, as shown in Figure 6-13. By choosing texture coordinates in the right places (see the hollow circles in the figure), we'll be creating a thick border at every triangle.

Figure 6-13. Antialiased triangle with transparency

For controlling the camera, the app should use the compass and accelerometer APIs to truly qualify as an augmented reality app. However, initially let's just show four buttons in a HUD: touching any button will cause the environment to "scroll." Horizontal buttons control *azimuth* (angle from north); vertical buttons control *altitude* (angle above horizon). These terms may be familiar to you if you're an astronomy buff.

Later we'll replace the azimuth/altitude buttons with the compass and accelerometer APIs. The benefit of this approach is that we can easily provide a fallback option if the app discovers that the compass or accelerometer APIs are not available. This allows us to gracefully handle three scenarios:

iPhone Simulator
    Show buttons for both azimuth and altitude.

First- and second-generation iPhones
    Show buttons for azimuth; use the accelerometer for altitude.

Third-generation iPhones
    Hide all buttons; use the accelerometer for altitude and the compass for azimuth.

In honor of my favorite TV show, the name of this sample is *Holodeck*. Without further ado, let's begin!

Application Skeleton

The basic skeleton for the Holodeck sample is much like every other sample we've presented since Chapter 3. The main difference is that we forgo the creation of an `IApplicationEngine` interface and instead place the application logic directly within the `GLView` class. There's very little logic required for this app anyway; most of the heavy footwork is done in the rendering engine. Skipping the application layer makes life easier when we add support for the accelerometer, compass, and camera APIs.

Another difference lies in how we handle the dome geometry. Rather than loading in the vertices from an OBJ file or generating them at runtime, a Python script generates a C++ header file with the dome data, as shown in Example 6-20; you can download the full listing, along with the Holodeck project, from this book's website (*http://oreilly .com/catalog/9780596804831*). This is perhaps the simplest possible way to load geometry into an OpenGL application, and some modeling tools can actually export their data as a C/C++ header file!

Example 6-20. GeodesicDome.h

```
const int DomeFaceCount = 2782;
const int DomeVertexCount = DomeFaceCount * 3;
const float DomeVertices[DomeVertexCount * 5] = {
    -0.819207, 0.040640, 0.572056,
    0.000000, 1.000000,

    ...

    0.859848, -0.065758, 0.506298,
    1.000000, 1.000000,
};
```

Figure 6-14 shows the overall structure of the Holodeck project.

Note that this app has quite a few textures compared to our previous samples: six PNG files and two compressed PVRTC files. You can also see from the screenshot that we've added a new property to *Info.plist* called UIInterfaceOrientation. Recall that this is a landscape-only app; if you don't set this property, you'll have to manually rotate the virtual iPhone every time you test it in the simulator.

Interfaces.hpp is much the same as in our other sample apps, except that the rendering engine interface is somewhat unique; see Example 6-21.

Example 6-21. Interfaces.hpp for Holodeck

```
...

enum ButtonFlags {
    ButtonFlagsShowHorizontal = 1 << 0,
    ButtonFlagsShowVertical   = 1 << 1,
    ButtonFlagsPressingUp     = 1 << 2,
    ButtonFlagsPressingDown   = 1 << 3,
    ButtonFlagsPressingLeft   = 1 << 4,
    ButtonFlagsPressingRight  = 1 << 5,
};

typedef unsigned char ButtonMask;

struct IRenderingEngine {
    virtual void Initialize() = 0;
    virtual void Render(float theta, float phi,
                        ButtonMask buttons) const = 0;
    virtual ~IRenderingEngine() {}
};

...
```

The new Render method takes three parameters:

float theta
> Azimuth in degrees. This is the horizontal angle off east.

float phi
> Altitude in degrees. This is the vertical angle off the horizon.

ButtonMask buttons
> Bit mask of flags for the HUD.

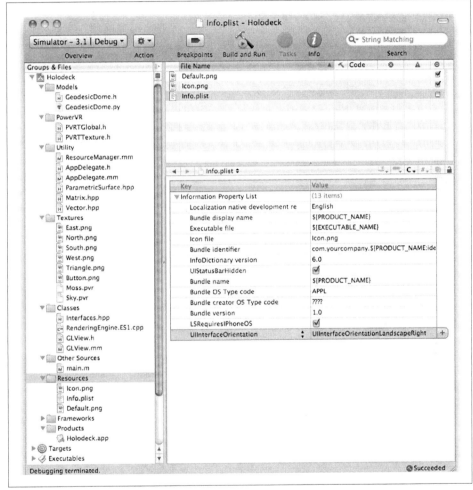

Figure 6-14. Xcode screenshot of the Holodeck project

The idea behind the `buttons` mask is that the Objective-C code (`GLView.mm`) can determine the capabilities of the device and whether a button is being pressed, so it sends this information to the rendering engine as a set of flags.

Rendering the Dome, Clouds, and Text

For now let's ignore the buttons and focus on rendering the basic elements of the 3D scene. See Example 6-22 for the rendering engine declaration and related types. Utility methods that carry over from previous samples, such as `CreateTexture`, are replaced with ellipses for brevity.

Example 6-22. RenderingEngine declaration for Holodeck

```
struct Drawable {
    GLuint VertexBuffer;
    GLuint IndexBuffer;
    int IndexCount;
    int VertexCount;
};

struct Drawables {
    Drawable GeodesicDome;
    Drawable SkySphere;
    Drawable Quad;
};


struct Textures {
    GLuint Sky;
    GLuint Floor;
    GLuint Button;
    GLuint Triangle;
    GLuint North;
    GLuint South;
    GLuint East;
    GLuint West;
};

struct Renderbuffers {
    GLuint Color;
    GLuint Depth;
};

class RenderingEngine : public IRenderingEngine {
public:
    RenderingEngine(IResourceManager* resourceManager);
    void Initialize();
    void Render(float theta, float phi, ButtonMask buttonFlags) const;
private:
    void RenderText(GLuint texture, float theta, float scale) const;
    Drawable CreateDrawable(const float* vertices, int vertexCount);
    // ...
    Drawables m_drawables;
    Textures m_textures;
    Renderbuffers m_renderbuffers;
    IResourceManager* m_resourceManager;
};
```

Note that Example 6-22 declares two new private methods: RenderText for drawing compass direction labels and a new CreateDrawable method for creating the geodesic dome. Even though it declares eight different texture objects (which could be combined into a texture atlas; see Chapter 7), it declares only three VBOs. The Quad VBO is re-used for the buttons, the floor, and the floating text.

Example 6-23 is fairly straightforward. It first creates the VBOs and texture objects and then initializes various OpenGL state.

Example 6-23. RenderingEngine initialization for Holodeck

```
#include "../Models/GeodesicDome.h"

...

void RenderingEngine::Initialize()
{
    // Create vertex buffer objects.
    m_drawables.GeodesicDome =
      CreateDrawable(DomeVertices, DomeVertexCount);
    m_drawables.SkySphere = CreateDrawable(Sphere(1));
    m_drawables.Quad = CreateDrawable(Quad(64));

    // Load up some textures.
    m_textures.Floor = CreateTexture("Moss.pvr");
    m_textures.Sky = CreateTexture("Sky.pvr");
    m_textures.Button = CreateTexture("Button.png");
    m_textures.Triangle = CreateTexture("Triangle.png");
    m_textures.North = CreateTexture("North.png");
    m_textures.South = CreateTexture("South.png");
    m_textures.East = CreateTexture("East.png");
    m_textures.West = CreateTexture("West.png");

    // Extract width and height from the color buffer.
    int width, height;
    glGetRenderbufferParameterivOES(GL_RENDERBUFFER_OES,
                                    GL_RENDERBUFFER_WIDTH_OES, &width);
    glGetRenderbufferParameterivOES(GL_RENDERBUFFER_OES,
                                    GL_RENDERBUFFER_HEIGHT_OES, &height);
    glViewport(0, 0, width, height);

    // Create a depth buffer that has the same size as the color buffer.
    glGenRenderbuffersOES(1, &m_renderbuffers.Depth);
    glBindRenderbufferOES(GL_RENDERBUFFER_OES, m_renderbuffers.Depth);
    glRenderbufferStorageOES(GL_RENDERBUFFER_OES,
                             GL_DEPTH_COMPONENT16_OES, width, height);

    // Create the framebuffer object.
    GLuint framebuffer;
    glGenFramebuffersOES(1, &framebuffer);
    glBindFramebufferOES(GL_FRAMEBUFFER_OES, framebuffer);
    glFramebufferRenderbufferOES(GL_FRAMEBUFFER_OES,
                                 GL_COLOR_ATTACHMENT0_OES,
                                 GL_RENDERBUFFER_OES,
```

```
                                   m_renderbuffers.Color);
    glFramebufferRenderbufferOES(GL_FRAMEBUFFER_OES,
                                GL_DEPTH_ATTACHMENT_OES,
                                GL_RENDERBUFFER_OES,
                                m_renderbuffers.Depth);
    glBindRenderbufferOES(GL_RENDERBUFFER_OES, m_renderbuffers.Color);

    // Set up various GL state.
    glEnableClientState(GL_VERTEX_ARRAY);
    glEnableClientState(GL_TEXTURE_COORD_ARRAY);
    glEnable(GL_TEXTURE_2D);
    glEnable(GL_DEPTH_TEST);
    glBlendFunc(GL_SRC_ALPHA, GL_ONE_MINUS_SRC_ALPHA);

    // Set the model-view transform.
    glMatrixMode(GL_MODELVIEW);
    glRotatef(90, 0, 0, 1);

    // Set the projection transform.
    float h = 4.0f * height / width;
    glMatrixMode(GL_PROJECTION);
    glFrustumf(-2, 2, -h / 2, h / 2, 5, 200);
    glMatrixMode(GL_MODELVIEW);
}

Drawable RenderingEngine::CreateDrawable(const float* vertices,
                                         int vertexCount)
{
    // Each vertex has XYZ and ST, for a total of five floats.
    const int FloatsPerVertex = 5;

    // Create the VBO for the vertices.
    GLuint vertexBuffer;
    glGenBuffers(1, &vertexBuffer);
    glBindBuffer(GL_ARRAY_BUFFER, vertexBuffer);
    glBufferData(GL_ARRAY_BUFFER,
                 vertexCount * FloatsPerVertex * sizeof(float),
                 vertices,
                 GL_STATIC_DRAW);

    // Fill in the description structure and return it.
    Drawable drawable = {0};
    drawable.VertexBuffer = vertexBuffer;
    drawable.VertexCount = vertexCount;
    return drawable;
}
```

Let's finally take a look at the all-important Render method; see Example 6-24.

Example 6-24. Render method for Holodeck

```
void RenderingEngine::Render(float theta, float phi,
                             ButtonMask buttons) const
{
    static float frameCounter = 0;❶
```

```
    frameCounter++;

    glPushMatrix();

    glRotatef(phi, 1, 0, 0);❷
    glRotatef(theta, 0, 1, 0);

    glClear(GL_DEPTH_BUFFER_BIT);❸

    glPushMatrix();
    glScalef(100, 100, 100);
    glRotatef(frameCounter * 2, 0, 1, 0);
    glBindTexture(GL_TEXTURE_2D, m_textures.Sky);
    RenderDrawable(m_drawables.SkySphere);❹
    glPopMatrix();

    glEnable(GL_BLEND);
    glBindTexture(GL_TEXTURE_2D, m_textures.Triangle);
    glPushMatrix();
    glTranslatef(0, 10, 0);
    glScalef(90, 90, 90);
    glColor4f(1, 1, 1, 0.75f);
    RenderDrawable(m_drawables.GeodesicDome);❺
    glColor4f(1, 1, 1, 1);
    glPopMatrix();

    float textScale = 1.0 / 10.0 + sin(frameCounter / 10.0f) / 150.0;❻

    RenderText(m_textures.East, 0, textScale);
    RenderText(m_textures.West, 180, textScale);
    RenderText(m_textures.South, 90, textScale);
    RenderText(m_textures.North, -90, textScale);
    glDisable(GL_BLEND);

    glTranslatef(0, 10, -10);
    glRotatef(90, 1, 0, 0);
    glScalef(4, 4, 4);
    glMatrixMode(GL_TEXTURE);
    glScalef(4, 4, 1);
    glBindTexture(GL_TEXTURE_2D, m_textures.Floor);
    RenderDrawable(m_drawables.Quad);❼
    glLoadIdentity();
    glMatrixMode(GL_MODELVIEW);
    glPopMatrix();

    if (buttons) {❽
        ...
    }
}
```

❶ Use a static variable to keep a frame count for animation. I don't recommend this approach in production code (normally you'd use a delta-time value), but this is fine for an example.

❷ Rotate theta degrees (azimuth) around the y-axis and phi degrees (altitude) around the x-axis.

❸ We're clearing depth only; there's no need to clear color since we're drawing a sky sphere.

❹ Render the sky sphere.

❺ Render the geodesic dome with blending enabled.

❻ Create an animated variable called textScale for the pulse effect, and then pass it in to the RenderText method.

❼ Draw the mossy ground plane.

❽ Render the buttons only if the buttons mask is nonzero. We'll cover button rendering shortly.

The RenderText method is fairly straightforward; see Example 6-25. Some glScalef trickery is used to stretch out the quad and flip it around.

Example 6-25. RenderText method for Holodeck

```
void RenderingEngine::RenderText(GLuint texture, float theta,
                                 float scale) const
{
    glBindTexture(GL_TEXTURE_2D, texture);
    glPushMatrix();
    glRotatef(theta, 0, 1, 0);
    glTranslatef(0, -2, -30);
    glScalef(-2 * scale, -scale, scale);
    RenderDrawable(m_drawables.Quad);
    glPopMatrix();
}
```

Handling the Heads-Up Display

Most applications that need to render a HUD take the following approach when rendering a single frame of animation:

1. Issue a glClear.
2. Set up the model-view and projection matrices for the 3D scene.
3. Render the 3D scene.
4. Disable depth testing, and enable blending.
5. Set up the model-view and projection matrices for 2D rendering.
6. Render the HUD.

Always remember to completely reset your transforms at the beginning of the render routine; otherwise, you'll apply transformations that are left over from the previous frame. For example, calling `glFrustum` alone simply multiplies the current matrix, so you might need to issue a `glLoadIdentity` immediately before calling `glFrustum`.

Let's go ahead and modify the Render method to render buttons; replace the ellipses in Example 6-24 with the code in Example 6-26.

Example 6-26. Adding buttons to Holodeck

```
glEnable(GL_BLEND);
glDisable(GL_DEPTH_TEST);
glBindTexture(GL_TEXTURE_2D, m_textures.Button);
glMatrixMode(GL_PROJECTION);
glPushMatrix();
glLoadIdentity();
glOrthof(-160, 160, -240, 240, 0, 1);

if (buttons & ButtonFlagsShowHorizontal) {
    glMatrixMode(GL_MODELVIEW);
    glTranslatef(200, 0, 0);
    SetButtonAlpha(buttons, ButtonFlagsPressingLeft);
    RenderDrawable(m_drawables.Quad);
    glTranslatef(-400, 0, 0);
    glMatrixMode(GL_TEXTURE);
    glRotatef(180, 0, 0, 1);
    SetButtonAlpha(buttons, ButtonFlagsPressingRight);
    RenderDrawable(m_drawables.Quad);
    glRotatef(-180, 0, 0, 1);
    glMatrixMode(GL_MODELVIEW);
    glTranslatef(200, 0, 0);
}

if (buttons & ButtonFlagsShowVertical) {
    glMatrixMode(GL_MODELVIEW);
    glTranslatef(0, 125, 0);
    glMatrixMode(GL_TEXTURE);
    glRotatef(90, 0, 0, 1);
    SetButtonAlpha(buttons, ButtonFlagsPressingUp);
    RenderDrawable(m_drawables.Quad);
    glMatrixMode(GL_MODELVIEW);
    glTranslatef(0, -250, 0);
    glMatrixMode(GL_TEXTURE);
    glRotatef(180, 0, 0, 1);
    SetButtonAlpha(buttons, ButtonFlagsPressingDown);
    RenderDrawable(m_drawables.Quad);
    glRotatef(90, 0, 0, 1);
    glMatrixMode(GL_MODELVIEW);
    glTranslatef(0, 125, 0);
}
```

```
glColor4f(1, 1, 1, 1);
glMatrixMode(GL_PROJECTION);
glPopMatrix();
glMatrixMode(GL_MODELVIEW);
glEnable(GL_DEPTH_TEST);
glDisable(GL_BLEND);
```

Note that Example 6-26 contains quite a few transform operations; while this is fine for teaching purposes, in a production environment I recommend including all four buttons in a single VBO. You'd still need four separate draw calls, however, since the currently pressed button has a unique alpha value.

In fact, making this optimization would be an interesting project: create a single VBO that contains all four pretransformed buttons, and then render it with four separate draw calls. Don't forget that the second argument to glDrawArrays can be nonzero!

The SetButtonAlpha method sets alpha to one if the button is being pressed; otherwise, it makes the button semitransparent:

```
void RenderingEngine::SetButtonAlpha(ButtonMask buttonFlags,
                                     ButtonFlags flag) const
{
    float alpha = (buttonFlags & flag) ? 1.0 : 0.75;
    glColor4f(1, 1, 1, alpha);
}
```

Next let's go over the code in GLView.mm that detects button presses and maintains the azimuth/altitude angles. See Example 6-27 for the GLView class declaration and Example 6-28 for the interesting potions of the class implementation.

Example 6-27. GLView.h for Holodeck

```
#import "Interfaces.hpp"
#import <UIKit/UIKit.h>
#import <QuartzCore/QuartzCore.h>
#import <CoreLocation/CoreLocation.h>

@interface GLView : UIView {
@private
    IRenderingEngine* m_renderingEngine;
    IResourceManager* m_resourceManager;
    EAGLContext* m_context;
    bool m_paused;
    float m_theta;
    float m_phi;
    vec2 m_velocity;
    ButtonMask m_visibleButtons;
    float m_timestamp;
}

- (void) drawView: (CADisplayLink*) displayLink;

@end
```

Example 6-28. GLView.mm for Holodeck

...

```
- (id) initWithFrame: (CGRect) frame
{
    m_paused = false;
    m_theta = 0;
    m_phi = 0;
    m_velocity = vec2(0, 0);
    m_visibleButtons = ButtonFlagsShowHorizontal | ButtonFlagsShowVertical;  ❶

    if (self = [super initWithFrame:frame]) {
        CAEAGLLayer* eaglLayer = (CAEAGLLayer*) self.layer;
        eaglLayer.opaque = YES;

        EAGLRenderingAPI api = kEAGLRenderingAPIOpenGLES1;
        m_context = [[EAGLContext alloc] initWithAPI:api];

        if (!m_context || ![EAGLContext setCurrentContext:m_context]) {
            [self release];
            return nil;
        }

        m_resourceManager = CreateResourceManager();

        NSLog(@"Using OpenGL ES 1.1");
        m_renderingEngine = CreateRenderingEngine(m_resourceManager);

        [m_context
            renderbufferStorage:GL_RENDERBUFFER
            fromDrawable: eaglLayer];

        m_timestamp = CACurrentMediaTime();

        m_renderingEngine->Initialize();
        [self drawView:nil];

        CADisplayLink* displayLink;
        displayLink = [CADisplayLink displayLinkWithTarget:self
                                    selector:@selector(drawView:)];

        [displayLink addToRunLoop:[NSRunLoop currentRunLoop]
                    forMode:NSDefaultRunLoopMode];
    }
    return self;
}

- (void) drawView: (CADisplayLink*) displayLink
{
    if (m_paused)
        return;

    if (displayLink != nil) {
        const float speed = 30;
```

```
        float elapsedSeconds = displayLink.timestamp - m_timestamp;
        m_timestamp = displayLink.timestamp;
        m_theta -= speed * elapsedSeconds * m_velocity.x;❷
        m_phi += speed * elapsedSeconds * m_velocity.y;
    }

    ButtonMask buttonFlags = m_visibleButtons;❸
    if (m_velocity.x < 0) buttonFlags |= ButtonFlagsPressingLeft;
    if (m_velocity.x > 0) buttonFlags |= ButtonFlagsPressingRight;
    if (m_velocity.y < 0) buttonFlags |= ButtonFlagsPressingUp;
    if (m_velocity.y > 0) buttonFlags |= ButtonFlagsPressingDown;

    m_renderingEngine->Render(m_theta, m_phi, buttonFlags);
    [m_context presentRenderbuffer:GL_RENDERBUFFER];
}

bool buttonHit(CGPoint location, int x, int y)❹
{
    float extent = 32;
    return (location.x > x - extent && location.x < x + extent &&
            location.y > y - extent && location.y < y + extent);
}

- (void) touchesBegan: (NSSet*) touches withEvent: (UIEvent*) event❺
{
    UITouch* touch = [touches anyObject];
    CGPoint location  = [touch locationInView: self];
    float delta = 1;

    if (m_visibleButtons & ButtonFlagsShowVertical) {
        if (buttonHit(location, 35, 240))
            m_velocity.y = -delta;
        else if (buttonHit(location, 285, 240))
            m_velocity.y = delta;
    }

    if (m_visibleButtons & ButtonFlagsShowHorizontal) {
        if (buttonHit(location, 160, 40))
            m_velocity.x = -delta;
        else if (buttonHit(location, 160, 440))
            m_velocity.x = delta;
    }
}

- (void) touchesEnded: (NSSet*) touches withEvent: (UIEvent*) event
{
    m_velocity = vec2(0, 0);
}
```

❶ For now, we're hardcoding both button visibility flags to true. We'll make this dynamic after adding compass and accelerometer support.

❷ The theta and phi angles are updated according to the current velocity vector and delta time.

❸ Right before passing in the button mask to the `Render` method, take a look at the velocity vector to decide which buttons are being pressed.

❹ Simple utility function to detect whether a given point (`location`) is within the bounds of a button centered at (`x`, `y`). Note that we're allowing the intrusion of a vanilla C function into an Objective-C file.

❺ To make things simple, the `velocity` vector is set up in response to a "finger down" event and reset to zero in response to a "finger up" event. Since we don't need the ability for several buttons to be pressed simultaneously, this is good enough.

At this point, you now have a complete app that lets you look around inside a (rather boring) virtual world, but it's still a far cry from augmented reality!

Replacing Buttons with Orientation Sensors

The next step is carefully integrating support for the compass and accelerometer APIs. I say "carefully" because we'd like to provide a graceful runtime fallback if the device (or simulator) does not have a magnetometer or accelerometer.

We'll be using the accelerometer to obtain the gravity vector, which in turn enables us to compute the phi angle (that's "altitude" for you astronomers) but not the theta angle (azimuth). Conversely, the compass API can be used to compute theta but not phi. You'll see how this works in the following sections.

Adding accelerometer support

Using the low-level accelerometer API directly is ill advised; the signal includes quite a bit of noise, and unless your app is somehow related to *The Blair Witch Project*, you probably don't want your camera shaking around like a shivering chihuahua.

Discussing a robust and adaptive low-pass filter implementation is beyond the scope of this book, but thankfully Apple includes some example code for this. Search for the *AccelerometerGraph* sample on the iPhone developer site (*http://developer.apple.com/iphone*) and download it. Look inside for two key files, and copy them to your project folder: *AccelerometerFilter.h* and *AccelerometerFilter.m*.

 You can also refer to "Stabilizing the counter with a low-pass filter" on page 289 for an example implementation of a simple low-pass filter.

After adding the filter code to your Xcode project, open up *GLView.h*, and add the three code snippets that are highlighted in bold in Example 6-29.

Example 6-29. Adding accelerometer support to GLView.h

```
#import "Interfaces.hpp"
#import "AccelerometerFilter.h"
#import <UIKit/UIKit.h>
#import <QuartzCore/QuartzCore.h>

@interface GLView : UIView <UIAccelerometerDelegate> {
@private
    IRenderingEngine* m_renderingEngine;
    IResourceManager* m_resourceManager;
    EAGLContext* m_context;
    AccelerometerFilter* m_filter;
    ...
}

- (void) drawView: (CADisplayLink*) displayLink;

@end
```

Next, open *GLView.mm*, and add the lines shown in bold in Example 6-30. You might grimace at the sight of the #if block, but it's a necessary evil because the iPhone Simulator pretends to support the accelerometer APIs by sending the application fictitious values (without giving the user much control over those values). Since the fake accelerometer won't do us much good, we turn it off when building for the simulator.

 An Egyptian software company called *vimov* produces a compelling tool called iSimulate that can simulate the accelerometer and other device sensors. Check it out at *http://www.vimov.com/isimulate*.

Example 6-30. Adding accelerometer support to initWithFrame

```
- (id) initWithFrame: (CGRect) frame
{
    m_paused = false;
    m_theta = 0;
    m_phi = 0;
    m_velocity = vec2(0, 0);
    m_visibleButtons = 0;

    if (self = [super initWithFrame:frame]) {
        CAEAGLLayer* eaglLayer = (CAEAGLLayer*) self.layer;
        eaglLayer.opaque = YES;

        EAGLRenderingAPI api = kEAGLRenderingAPIOpenGLES1;
        m_context = [[EAGLContext alloc] initWithAPI:api];

        if (!m_context || ![EAGLContext setCurrentContext:m_context]) {
            [self release];
            return nil;
        }
```

```
        m_resourceManager = CreateResourceManager();

        NSLog(@"Using OpenGL ES 1.1");
        m_renderingEngine = CreateRenderingEngine(m_resourceManager);

#if TARGET_IPHONE_SIMULATOR
        BOOL compassSupported = NO;
        BOOL accelSupported = NO;
#else
        BOOL compassSupported = NO; // (We'll add compass support shortly.)
        BOOL accelSupported = YES;
#endif

        if (compassSupported) {
            NSLog(@"Compass is supported.");
        } else {
            NSLog(@"Compass is NOT supported.");
            m_visibleButtons |= ButtonFlagsShowHorizontal;
        }

        if (accelSupported) {
            NSLog(@"Accelerometer is supported.");
            float updateFrequency = 60.0f;
            m_filter =
              [[LowpassFilter alloc] initWithSampleRate:updateFrequency
                                        cutoffFrequency:5.0];
            m_filter.adaptive = YES;

            [[UIAccelerometer sharedAccelerometer]
              setUpdateInterval:1.0 / updateFrequency];
            [[UIAccelerometer sharedAccelerometer] setDelegate:self];
        } else {
            NSLog(@"Accelerometer is NOT supported.");
            m_visibleButtons |= ButtonFlagsShowVertical;
        }

        [m_context
            renderbufferStorage:GL_RENDERBUFFER
            fromDrawable: eaglLayer];

        m_timestamp = CACurrentMediaTime();

        m_renderingEngine->Initialize();
        [self drawView:nil];

        CADisplayLink* displayLink;
        displayLink = [CADisplayLink displayLinkWithTarget:self
                                    selector:@selector(drawView:)];

        [displayLink addToRunLoop:[NSRunLoop currentRunLoop]
                    forMode:NSDefaultRunLoopMode];
    }
    return self;
}
```

Since GLView sets itself as the accelerometer delegate, it needs to implement a response handler. See Example 6-31.

Example 6-31. Accelerometer response handler

```
- (void) accelerometer: (UIAccelerometer*) accelerometer
         didAccelerate: (UIAcceleration*) acceleration
{
    [m_filter addAcceleration:acceleration];
    float x = m_filter.x;
    float z = m_filter.z;
    m_phi = atan2(z, -x) * 180.0f / Pi;
}
```

You might not be familiar with the atan2 function, which takes the arctangent of the its first argument divided by the its second argument (see Equation 6-1). Why not use the plain old single-argument atan function and do the division yourself? You don't because atan2 is smarter; it uses the signs of its arguments to determine which quadrant the angle is in. Plus, it allows the second argument to be zero without throwing a divide-by-zero exception.

 An even more rarely encountered math function is hypot. When used together, atan2 and hypot can convert any 2D Cartesian coordinate into a polar coordinate.

Equation 6-1. Phi as a function of acceleration

$$\varphi = \tan^{-1}\left(\frac{a_z}{-a_x}\right)$$

Equation 6-1 shows how we compute phi from the accelerometer's input values. To understand it, you first need to realize that we're using the accelerometer as a way of measuring the direction of gravity. It's a common misconception that the accelerometer measures speed, but you know better by now! The accelerometer API returns a 3D acceleration vector according to the axes depicted in Figure 6-15.

When you hold the device in landscape mode, there's no gravity along the y-axis (assuming you're not slothfully laying on the sofa and turned to one side). So, the gravity vector is composed of X and Z only—see Figure 6-16.

Adding compass support

The direction of gravity can't tell you which direction you're facing; that's where the compass support in third-generation devices comes in. To begin, open *GLView.h*, and add the bold lines in Example 6-32.

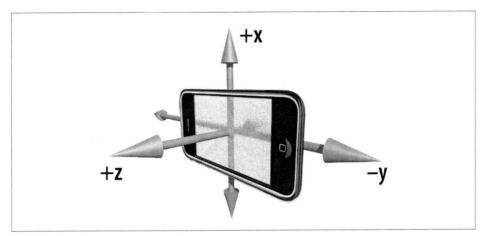

Figure 6-15. Accelerometer axes in landscape mode

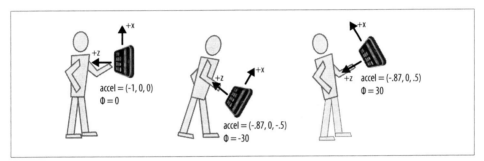

Figure 6-16. Computing phi from acceleration

Example 6-32. Adding compass support to GLView.h

```
#import "Interfaces.hpp"
#import "AccelerometerFilter.h"
#import <UIKit/UIKit.h>
#import <QuartzCore/QuartzCore.h>
#import <CoreLocation/CoreLocation.h>

@interface GLView : UIView <CLLocationManagerDelegate,
                            UIAccelerometerDelegate> {
@private
    IRenderingEngine* m_renderingEngine;
    IResourceManager* m_resourceManager;
    EAGLContext* m_context;
    CLLocationManager* m_locationManager;
    AccelerometerFilter* m_filter;
    ...
}

- (void) drawView: (CADisplayLink*) displayLink;

@end
```

The Core Location API is an umbrella for both GPS and compass functionality, but we'll be using only the compass functionality in our demo. Next we need to create an instance of CLLocationManger somewhere in *GLview.mm*; see Example 6-33.

Example 6-33. Adding compass support to initWithFrame

```
- (id) initWithFrame: (CGRect) frame
{
    ...

    if (self = [super initWithFrame:frame]) {

        ...

        m_locationManager = [[CLLocationManager alloc] init];

#if TARGET_IPHONE_SIMULATOR
        BOOL compassSupported = NO;
        BOOL accelSupported = NO;
#else
        BOOL compassSupported = m_locationManager.headingAvailable;
        BOOL accelSupported = YES;
#endif

        if (compassSupported) {
            NSLog(@"Compass is supported.");
            m_locationManager.headingFilter = kCLHeadingFilterNone;
            m_locationManager.delegate = self;
            [m_locationManager startUpdatingHeading];
        } else {
            NSLog(@"Compass is NOT supported.");
            m_visibleButtons |= ButtonFlagsShowHorizontal;
        }

        ...
    }
    return self;
}
```

Similar to how it handles the accelerometer feedback, GLView sets itself as the compass delegate, so it needs to implement a response handler. See Example 6-31. Unlike the accelerometer, any noise in the compass reading is already eliminated, so there's no need for handling the low-pass filter yourself. The compass API is embarrassingly simple; it simply returns an angle in degrees, where 0 is north, 90 is east, and so on. See Example 6-34 for the compass response handler.

Example 6-34. Compass response handler

```
- (void) locationManager: (CLLocationManager*) manager
        didUpdateHeading: (CLHeading*) heading
{
    // Use magneticHeading rather than trueHeading to avoid usage of GPS:
    CLLocationDirection degrees = heading.magneticHeading;
```

```
        m_theta = (float) -degrees;
}
```

The only decision you have to make when writing a compass handler is whether to use `magneticHeading` or `trueHeading`. The former returns magnetic north, which isn't quite the same as geographic north. To determine the true direction of the geographic north pole, the device needs to know where it's located on the planet, which requires usage of the GPS. Since our app is looking around a virtual world, it doesn't matter which heading to use. I chose to use `magneticHeading` because it allows us to avoid enabling GPS updates in the location manager object. This simplifies the code and may even improve power consumption.

Overlaying with a Live Camera Image

To make this a true augmented reality app, we need to bring the camera into play. If a camera isn't available (as in the simulator), then the app can simply fall back to the "scrolling clouds" background.

The first step is adding another protocol to the `GLView` class—actually we need *two* new protocols! Add the bold lines in Example 6-35, noting the new data fields as well (`m_viewController` and `m_cameraSupported`).

Example 6-35. Adding camera support to GLView.h

```
#import "Interfaces.hpp"
#import "AccelerometerFilter.h"
#import <UIKit/UIKit.h>
#import <QuartzCore/QuartzCore.h>
#import <CoreLocation/CoreLocation.h>

@interface GLView : UIView <UIImagePickerControllerDelegate,
                            UINavigationControllerDelegate,
                            CLLocationManagerDelegate,
                            UIAccelerometerDelegate> {
@private
    IRenderingEngine* m_renderingEngine;
    IResourceManager* m_resourceManager;
    EAGLContext* m_context;
    CLLocationManager* m_locationManager;
    AccelerometerFilter* m_filter;
    UIViewController* m_viewController;
    bool m_cameraSupported;
    ...
}

- (void) drawView: (CADisplayLink*) displayLink;

@end
```

Next we need to enhance the `initWithFrame` and `drawView` methods. See Example 6-36. Until now, every sample in this book has set the **opaque** property in the EAGL layer to YES. In this sample, we decide its value at runtime; if a camera is available, don't make the surface opaque to allow the image "underlay" to show through.

Example 6-36. Adding camera support to GLView.mm

```
- (id) initWithFrame: (CGRect) frame
{
    ...

    if (self = [super initWithFrame:frame]) {

        m_cameraSupported = [UIImagePickerController isSourceTypeAvailable:
                                UIImagePickerControllerSourceTypeCamera];

        CAEAGLLayer* eaglLayer = (CAEAGLLayer*) self.layer;
        eaglLayer.opaque = !m_cameraSupported;
        if (m_cameraSupported)
            NSLog(@"Camera is supported.");
        else
            NSLog(@"Camera is NOT supported.");

        ...

#if TARGET_IPHONE_SIMULATOR
        BOOL compassSupported = NO;
        BOOL accelSupported = NO;
#else
        BOOL compassSupported = m_locationManager.headingAvailable;
        BOOL accelSupported = YES;
#endif

        m_viewController = 0;

        ...

        m_timestamp = CACurrentMediaTime();

        bool opaqueBackground = !m_cameraSupported;
        m_renderingEngine->Initialize(opaqueBackground);

        // Delete the line [self drawView:nil];

        CADisplayLink* displayLink;
        displayLink = [CADisplayLink displayLinkWithTarget:self
                                        selector:@selector(drawView:)];

        ...
    }
    return self;
}

- (void) drawView: (CADisplayLink*) displayLink
{
    if (m_cameraSupported && m_viewController == 0)
        [self createCameraController];
```

```
    if (m_paused)
        return;

    ...

    m_renderingEngine->Render(m_theta, m_phi, buttonFlags);
    [m_context presentRenderbuffer:GL_RENDERBUFFER];
}
```

Next we need to implement the createCameraController method that was called from drawView. This is an example of *lazy instantiation*; we don't create the camera controller until we actually need it. Example 6-37 shows the method, and a detailed explanation follows the listing. (The createCameraController method needs to be defined before the drawView method to avoid a compiler warning.)

Example 6-37. Creating the camera view controller

```
- (void) createCameraController
{
    UIImagePickerController* imagePicker =
        [[UIImagePickerController alloc] init];
    imagePicker.delegate = self;❶
    imagePicker.navigationBarHidden = YES;❷
    imagePicker.toolbarHidden = YES;❸
    imagePicker.sourceType = UIImagePickerControllerSourceTypeCamera;❹
    imagePicker.showsCameraControls = NO;❺
    imagePicker.cameraOverlayView = self;❻

    // The 54 pixel wide empty spot is filled in by scaling the image.
    // The camera view's height gets stretched from 426 pixels to 480.

    float bandWidth = 54;
    float screenHeight = 480;
    float zoomFactor = screenHeight / (screenHeight - bandWidth);

    CGAffineTransform pickerTransform =
        CGAffineTransformMakeScale(zoomFactor, zoomFactor);
    imagePicker.cameraViewTransform = pickerTransform;❼

    m_viewController = [[UIViewController alloc] init];
    m_viewController.view = self;
    [m_viewController presentModalViewController:imagePicker animated:NO];❽
}
```

❶ Set the image picker's delegate to the GLView class. Since we aren't using the camera to capture still images, this isn't strictly necessary, but it's still a good practice.

❷ Hide the navigation bar. Again, we aren't using the camera for image capture, so there's no need for this UI getting in the way.

❸ Ditto with the toolbar.

❹ Set the source type of the image picker to the camera. You might recall this step from the camera texture sample in the previous chapter.

❺ Hide the camera control UI. Again, we're using the camera only as a backdrop, so any UI would just get in the way.

❻ Set the camera overlay view to the GLView class to allow the OpenGL content to be rendered.

❼ The UI that we're hiding would normally leave an annoying gap on the bottom of the screen. By applying a scale transform, we can fill in the gap. Maintaining the correct aspect ratio causes a portion of the image to be cropped, but it's not noticeable in the final app.

❽ Finally, present the view controller to make the camera image show up.

Since we're using the camera API in a way that's quite different from how Apple intended, we had to jump through a few hoops: hiding the UI, stretching the image, and implementing a protocol that never really gets used. This may seem a bit hacky, but ideally Apple will improve the camera API in the future to simplify the development of augmented reality applications.

You may've noticed in Example 6-36 that the view class is now passing in a boolean to the rendering engine's Initialize method; this tells it whether the background should contain clouds as before or whether it should be cleared to allow the camera underlay to show through. You must modify the declaration of Initialize in *Interfaces.cpp* accordingly. Next, the only remaining changes are shown in Example 6-38.

Example 6-38. RenderingEngine modifications to support the camera "underlay"

```
...

class RenderingEngine : public IRenderingEngine {
public:
    RenderingEngine(IResourceManager* resourceManager);
    void Initialize(bool opaqueBackground);
    void Render(float theta, float phi, ButtonMask buttons) const;
private:
    ...
    bool m_opaqueBackground;
};

void RenderingEngine::Initialize(bool opaqueBackground)
{
    m_opaqueBackground = opaqueBackground;

    ...
}

void RenderingEngine::Render(float theta, float phi, ButtonMask buttons) const
{
    static float frameCounter = 0;
    frameCounter++;
```

```
    glPushMatrix();

    glRotatef(phi, 1, 0, 0);
    glRotatef(theta, 0, 1, 0);

    if (m_opaqueBackground) {
        glClear(GL_DEPTH_BUFFER_BIT);

        glPushMatrix();
        glScalef(100, 100, 100);
        glRotatef(frameCounter * 2, 0, 1, 0);
        glBindTexture(GL_TEXTURE_2D, m_textures.Sky);
        RenderDrawable(m_drawables.SkySphere);
        glPopMatrix();
    } else {
        glClearColor(0, 0, 0, 0);
        glClear(GL_COLOR_BUFFER_BIT | GL_DEPTH_BUFFER_BIT);
    }

    ...
}
```

Note that the alpha value of the clear color is zero; this allows the underlay to show through. Also note that the color buffer is cleared only if there's no sky sphere. Experienced OpenGL programmers make little optimizations like this as a matter of habit.

That's it for the Holodeck sample! See Figure 6-17 for a depiction of the app as it now stands.

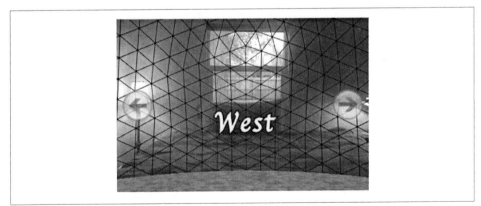

Figure 6-17. Holodeck with camera underlay

Wrapping Up

In this chapter we learned how to put FBOs to good use for the first time. We learned how to achieve anti-aliasing in sneaky ways, how to layer a scene by mixing 2D content with 3D content, and how to use the iPhone's orientation sensors in tandem with OpenGL.

We explored the concept of a 2D HUD in the Holodeck sample, but we largely glossed over the subject of text. Supplying ready-made textures of complete words (as we did for Holodeck) can be a bit cumbersome; often an application needs to render large amounts of dynamic text together with a 3D scene. Since text is something that OpenGL can't really handle on its own (and justifiably so), it deserves more attention. This brings us to the next chapter.

## CHAPTER 7

Sprites and Text

My god, it's full of stars.

—Dave Bowman, *2001: A Space Odyssey*

Even though OpenGL ES is designed for 3D graphics, you'll often find the need to render visual elements that are 2D. OpenGL is actually quite well-suited to rendering a flat world; several popular 2D libraries, such as *cocos2d*, use OpenGL as their rendering engines.

The most common type of 2D rendering is text rendering. The OpenGL API lives too close to the metal to treat text as a first-class citizen, but it's easy to render a pregenerated *glyph* (a character's shape in a given font) using a textured quad, and that's the approach we'll take in this chapter.

 Computing the points along the outline of a glyph can be surprisingly complex. For example, the TrueType file format specifies a unique programming language—complete with loops and `if` statements—solely for the purpose of tweaking the curves in a glyph.

In this chapter, we won't attempt to go over kerning algorithms, ligatures, or line wrapping; simple text layout is good enough for our purposes. (Check out the popular *pango* library if you need a full-featured layout engine.)

Another common 2D concept is the *sprite*, which is a rather generic term for any bitmap that gets composited into a scene. Sprites often contain transparent regions, so their texture format contains alpha. Sprites are often animated in some way. There are two ways of animating a sprite: its screen position can change (imagine a bouncing ball), or its source image can change (imagine a ball that's spinning in place).

The iPhone supports two extensions to OpenGL ES 1.1 that make it easy to render sprites: `GL_OES_draw_texture` and `GL_OES_point_sprite`. We'll make good use of both these extensions throughout the chapter, and we'll wrap up the chapter with a fun sample application that renders a spring system with sprites.

Text Rendering 101: Drawing an FPS Counter

Rather than demonstrating text rendering with yet another goofy toy application, let's do something useful for a change. Overlaying a frames-per-second counter in one corner of the iPhone screen provides a quick and easy way of evaluating graphics performance; see Figure 7-1.

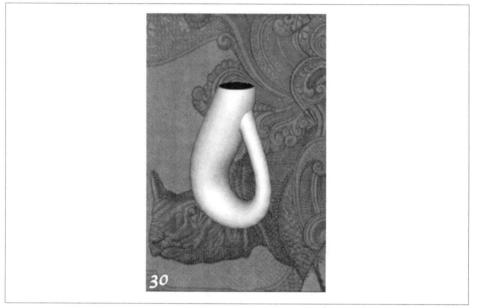

Figure 7-1. FPS counter

 For more sophisticated runtime analysis of graphics performance, Apple provides an excellent free tool called *Instruments*, which we'll cover in a subsequent chapter.

Before writing any application code, you'd need to generate an image that contains bitmaps for the numbers zero through nine, as depicted in Figure 7-2. (Don't bother trying to create this yet; you'll see a way to automate this shortly.)

0123456789

Figure 7-2. Numerals in a 128x32 luminance texture

You probably already guessed that you need to store off the bounding box of each glyph in order to compute the appropriate texture coordinates. Thinking about this a bit more, you'll realize a mere bounding box is not enough. When you're writing a sentence on ruled paper, some parts of letters extend below the baseline, like the descender of the lowercase *p*. And, in the case of the rather artsy font shown in Figure 7-3, the type designer wants the *9* numeral to be vertically offset from the other letters. Further complicating matters is the fact that the bounding boxes of glyphs can overlap in the destination image. In Figure 7-3, observe how the descender of the letter *p* extends right below the letter *i*.

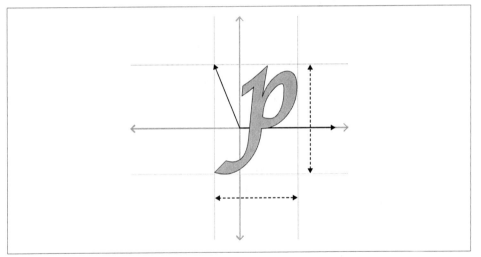

Figure 7-3. Simple text layout with baseline

It turns out that associating a specific set of *glyph metrics* with each character supplies enough information to achieve the simple text layout shown in Figure 7-3. A popular naming convention for these metrics is described in Figure 7-4; in this diagram, the origin represents the current pen position.

Figure 7-4. Glyph metrics: bearing and advance vectors; width and height lengths

To summarize, the four glyph metrics are as follows:

Bearing vector
    2D vector describing the offset from the pen position.

Advance vector
    2D vector describing how to advance the pen to the next position after rendering the current glyph. The y component is always zero for Latin-based alphabets.

Width

The horizontal length of the glyph.

Height

The vertical length of the glyph.

Using these metrics, Example 7-1 the pseudocode for a simple text layout algorithm.

Example 7-1. Simple text layout algorithm

```
void RenderText(string s, vec2 p)
{
    for each character c in s
    {
        metrics m = GlyphTable[c].Metrics
        vec2 topLeft = GlyphTable[c].Position
        box source = box(topLeft, m.Width, m.Height)
        box dest = box(p + m.BearingVector, m.Width, m.Height)
        Blit(source, dest)
        p += m.AdvanceVector
    }
}
```

Generating a Glyphs Texture with Python

Before writing any application code, we need to choose a way of generating a glyphs texture and a set of metrics for each glyph.

Leveraging Quartz is perhaps the most obvious way of generating a glyphs texture (see "Generating and Transforming OpenGL Textures with Quartz" on page 201). This can be done at runtime when your application first starts up. This might slow down your startup time by a tiny amount, but it has the benefit of shrinking the size of the application bundle.

My preference is to generate the glyphs texture as a build step, mostly because it simplifies my application code. Build steps take place in Xcode rather than the iPhone execution environment, which brings a much richer tool set to the table. This is a perfect use case for a scripting language, and Python comes to mind first.

 There are *many* ways of generating a glyphs texture; here I'm giving an overview of my favorite. Take it only as a high-level example.

Given that we're using Python in a build step, we need to find some useful Python modules for image manipulation and image generation. At the time of this writing, the *Python Imaging Library* (PIL) is the most popular imaging manipulation module, and it provides excellent support for manipulating PNG images at a low level. However, it's not quite enough on its own because it doesn't provide direct access to the glyph metrics that we need. Another popular library is *Cairo*, which has a well-maintained Python binding called *pycairo*. Cairo is robust and fast, and it's used as the rendering backend in Firefox, Mono, and GTK. So, let's go with PIL (*http://www.pythonware .com/products/pil/*) and pycairo (*http://www.cairographics.org/pycairo/*).

Installing Python Modules

The copy of Python that's installed on Mac OS X won't have these modules installed by default, so you'll have to do a little bit of prep to install them.

First, install the Python Imaging Library. Go here to download the source: *http://www .pythonware.com/products/pil/*. At the time of this writing, the 1.1.7 version of PIL was the most recent and worked well. Make sure you download the version for Python 2.6 to ensure that the script will work. Extract the tarball (you can double-click it to extract it), open the Terminal, and `cd` to the top-level directory of the source code distribution. Next, execute the following command:

```
sudo python setup.py install
```

Next, install pycairo. Download the source from here: *http://www.cairographics.org/* (the script was tested with version 1.8.8). Extract the tarball, open the Terminal, and `cd` to the top-level directory of the source code distribution. Next, execute the following commands:

```
./configure \
    --prefix=/System/Library/Frameworks/Python.framework/Versions/2.6
make
sudo make install
```

You'll also need to install Cairo itself since pycairo is only a thin wrapper; build instructions and downloads are available from *http://www.cairographics.org/download/*.

Rather than packaging the glyphs texture as a PNG or PVR file, let's serialize the data to a C header file. Since it's a single-channel texture, the amount of data is relatively small. The header file will also provide a convenient place to store the glyph metrics. We'll simply have our Python script spawn `PVRTexTool` (see the section entitled "The PowerVR SDK and Low-Precision Textures" on page 198) for generating the header file from the image. We'll still generate a PNG file for preview purposes, but we won't include it in the application bundle. See Example 7-2 for the complete Python script that generates Figure 7-2.

Example 7-2. CreateNumerals.py

```
import cairo
import os
from PIL import Image

# Create a Cairo image surface:
imagesize = (256,32)
surface = cairo.ImageSurface(cairo.FORMAT_ARGB32, *imagesize) ❶
```

```
cr = cairo.Context(surface)
padding = 3

# Choose a font (look in /Library/Fonts) and set up the transforms.
cr.select_font_face("Apple Chancery",
                    cairo.FONT_SLANT_NORMAL,
                    cairo.FONT_WEIGHT_BOLD) ❷
cr.set_font_size(32)
cr.set_source_rgb(1,1,1)❸

# Create a string for appending the glyph metrics to the texture file:
glyphs = '''❹
struct GlyphPosition {
    int X;
    int Y;
};\n
struct GlyphMetrics {
    int XBearing;
    int YBearing;
    int Width;
    int Height;
    int XAdvance;
    int YAdvance;
};\n
struct Glyph {
    GlyphPosition Position;
    GlyphMetrics Metrics;
};\n
static const Glyph NumeralGlyphs[] = {\n'''

# Render glyphs '0' through '9' and write out their extents:
x, y = 0, 0 ❺
for character in '0123456789': ❻
    extents = cr.text_extents(character) ❼
    x_bearing, y_bearing, width, height, x_advance, y_advance = extents
    glyphs += '    {{ %d, %d }, ' % (x, y) ❽
    glyphs += '{ %d, %d, %d, %d, %d, %d }},\n' % extents ❾
    cr.save()
    cr.translate(x, -y_bearing)
    cr.text_path(character)
    cr.fill() ❿
    cr.restore()
    x += width + padding ⓫
glyphs += '};\n'

# Extract the alpha channel and open it up for a quick preview:
surface.write_to_png("NumeralsTexture.png") ⓬
image = Image.open("NumeralsTexture.png") ⓭
image.load()
image.split()[3].save("NumeralsTexture.png") ⓮
os.system("open NumeralsTexture.png")

# Serialize the image data to a C header file:
os.system('PVRTexTool -h -yflip1 -fOGL8 -iNumeralsTexture.png') ⓯
```

```
# Write to the header file:
headerFile = open('NumeralsTexture.h', 'a') 🔟
headerFile.write(glyphs)
headerFile.close()
```

 For this to work, you must either put the location of PVRTexTool ("The PowerVR SDK and Low-Precision Textures" on page 198) into your shell's PATH environment variable or copy PVRTexTool into one of your PATH entries, such as */usr/local/bin*. If you've extracted the Khronos SDK into your current directory, you could copy the file and mark it executable with these commands:

```
cd SDKPackage/Utilities/PVRTexTool/PVRTexToolCL/MacOS
sudo cp PVRTexTool /usr/local/bin
sudo chmod +x /usr/local/bin/PVRTexTool
cd -
```

Cairo is a fairly extensive library and is beyond the scope of this book, but here's a brief explanation of Example 7-2:

❶ Create a 256×32 image surface with Cairo, and then create a context associated with the surface.

❷ Select a TrueType font file, and then choose its size. In this case, I'm selecting the *Apple Chancery* font found in */Library/Fonts*.

❸ Set Cairo's current draw color to white.

❹ Initialize a string that we'll later append to the header file. For starters, define some structs for the glyphs table.

❺ Initialize the pen position to (0, 0).

❻ Iterate over glyphs 0 through 9.

❼ Obtain the metrics for the glyph.

❽ Populate the `GlyphPosition` structure that we're defining in the generated header file.

❾ Populate the `GlyphMetrics` structure that we're defining in the generated header file.

❿ Tell Cairo to fill in the glyph shape.

⓫ Advance the pen position with some padding.

⓬ Save the Cairo surface to a PNG file.

⓭ Load the PNG image into PIL.

⓮ Use PIL to extract only the alpha channel, and then overwrite the PNG file.

⓯ Use `PVRTexTool` to serialize the image data to a C header file. (At this point, the PNG is no longer needed.)

⓰ Append the metrics data to the same header file that defines the image data.

If you'd like, you can add the number-generation script to your Xcode project and make it into a build step, similar to what we did for texture compression ("Texture Compression with PVRTC" on page 191). For simplicity's sake, I chose not to do this in the sample project that you can download from this book's website.

Rendering the FPS Text

Now that we're past the grunt work of generating the glyphs texture, we can move on to the actual rendering code. A frames-per-second counter is much more useful than our other toy demos, so this time let's strive to make the rendering code very self-contained and easy to integrate into any project. We can do this by creating a C++ class wholly implemented within a single header file. Example 7-3 shows the basic outline for this class.

Example 7-3. FpsRenderer.h skeleton

```
#include <OpenGLES/ES1/gl.h>
#include <OpenGLES/ES1/glext.h>
#include <mach/mach.h>
#include <mach/mach_time.h>
#include "../Textures/NumeralsTexture.h"

typedef unsigned int PVRTuint32;

struct PVR_Texture_Header {
    // ...see PVRTTexture.h in the PowerVR SDK...
};

class FpsRenderer {
public:
    FpsRenderer(vec2 windowSize)
    {
        ...
    }
    void RenderFps()
    {
        ...
    }

private:

    static const int MaxNumDigits = 3;
    static const int VertsPerDigit = 6;
    static const int FloatsPerVert = 4;
    static const int FloatsPerDigit = VertsPerDigit * FloatsPerVert;
    static const int TexCoordOffset = sizeof(float) * 2;
    static const int BytesPerVert = sizeof(float) * FloatsPerVert;
    static const int BytesPerDigit = sizeof(float) * FloatsPerDigit;

    uint64_t GetElapsedNanoseconds()
    {
        uint64_t current = mach_absolute_time();
```

```
        uint64_t duration = current - m_previousTime;
        m_previousTime = current;
        mach_timebase_info_data_t info;
        mach_timebase_info(&info);
        duration *= info.numer;
        duration /= info.denom;
        return duration;
    }

    float* WriteGlyphVertex(const Glyph& glyph, vec2 pos, int corner, float* vertex)❶
    {
        ...
    }

    double m_filterConstant;❷
    double m_fps;❸
    uint64_t m_previousTime;❹
    vec2 m_windowSize;❺
    vec2 m_textureSize;❻
    GLuint m_textureHandle;❼
    GLuint m_vbo;❽
};
```

❶ Private method that generates the vertex and texture coordinates for one of the corners in a glyph rectangle.

❷ Smoothing factor for the low-pass filter; this is explained further in the next section.

❸ Exponentially weighted moving average of the frame rate (again, this is explained in the next section).

❹ Timestamp in nanoseconds of the most recent call to RenderFps().

❺ Width and height of the viewport (usually 320×480).

❻ Width and height of the glyphs texture.

❼ The OpenGL ID of the glyphs texture object.

❽ The OpenGL ID of the vertex buffer object used for rendering the glyphs.

Stabilizing the counter with a low-pass filter

To prevent the FPS counter from fluctuating wildly, we'll using a low-pass filter similar to the one we used for the accelerometer (see "Adding accelerometer support" on page 269). The application can compute a constant called the *smoothing factor*, which is always between zero and one. Here's one way of doing so:

```
double ComputeSmoothingFactor(double sampleRate, double cutoffFrequency)
{
    double dt = 1.0 / sampleRate;
    double RC = 1.0 / cutoffFrequency;
    return dt / (dt + RC);
}
```

In the previous listing, `cutoffFrequency` and `sampleRate` help define what constitutes "noise" in the signal. However, for our purposes, computing a smoothing factor like this is a bit pedantic; pragmatically speaking, it's perfectly fine to come up with a reasonable number through experimentation. I find that a value of 0.1 works well for a frame rate counter. A higher smoothing factor would result in a more spastic counter.

Fleshing out the FpsRenderer class

Let's go ahead and implement the constructor of the `FpsRenderer` class; see Example 7-4. It's responsible for loading up the glyphs texture and creating the empty VBO for rendering up to three digits.

Example 7-4. FpsRenderer constructor

```
FpsRenderer(vec2 windowSize)
{
    m_filterConstant = 0.1;
    m_fps = 0;
    m_windowSize = windowSize;
    m_previousTime = mach_absolute_time();

    glGenTextures(1, &m_textureHandle);
    glBindTexture(GL_TEXTURE_2D, m_textureHandle);
    glTexParameteri(GL_TEXTURE_2D, GL_TEXTURE_MIN_FILTER, GL_NEAREST);
    glTexParameteri(GL_TEXTURE_2D, GL_TEXTURE_MAG_FILTER, GL_NEAREST);
    PVR_Texture_Header* header = (PVR_Texture_Header*) NumeralsTexture;
    const unsigned char* bytes = (unsigned char*) NumeralsTexture;
    const unsigned char* imageData = bytes + header->dwHeaderSize;
    GLenum type = GL_UNSIGNED_BYTE;
    GLenum format = GL_ALPHA;
    int w = header->dwWidth;
    int h = header->dwHeight;
    m_textureSize = vec2(w, h);
    glTexImage2D(GL_TEXTURE_2D, 0, format, w, h,
                 0, format, type, imageData);

    glGenBuffers(1, &m_vbo);
    glBindBuffer(GL_ARRAY_BUFFER, m_vbo);
    int totalSize = BytesPerDigit * MaxNumDigits;
    glBufferData(GL_ARRAY_BUFFER, totalSize, 0, GL_DYNAMIC_DRAW);
}
```

The `FpsRenderer` class has only one public method; see Example 7-5. This method is responsible for updating the moving average and rendering the digits. Note that updating the VBO is quite a hassle; we'll demonstrate a much simpler way of rendering textured rectangles in the next section.

Example 7-5. RenderFps() method

```
void RenderFps()
{
    uint64_t deltaTime = GetElapsedNanoseconds();
    double fps = 1000000000.0 / deltaTime;
    double alpha = m_filterConstant;
    m_fps = fps * alpha + m_fps * (1.0 - alpha);
    fps = round(m_fps);

    char digits[MaxNumDigits + 1] = {0};
    sprintf(digits, "%d", (int) fps);
    int numDigits = strlen(digits);
    vec2 pos(5, 10);

    vector<float> vbo(numDigits * FloatsPerDigit);
    float* vertex = &vbo[0];
    for (char* digit = &digits[0]; *digit; ++digit) {
        int glyphIndex = *digit - '0';
        const Glyph& glyph = NumeralGlyphs[glyphIndex];
        vertex = WriteGlyphVertex(glyph, pos, 0, vertex);
        vertex = WriteGlyphVertex(glyph, pos, 1, vertex);
        vertex = WriteGlyphVertex(glyph, pos, 2, vertex);
        vertex = WriteGlyphVertex(glyph, pos, 2, vertex);
        vertex = WriteGlyphVertex(glyph, pos, 3, vertex);
        vertex = WriteGlyphVertex(glyph, pos, 1, vertex);
        pos.x += glyph.Metrics.XAdvance;
    }

    glBindBuffer(GL_ARRAY_BUFFER, m_vbo);
    glBufferSubData(GL_ARRAY_BUFFER, 0,
                    BytesPerDigit * numDigits, &vbo[0]);
    glBindTexture(GL_TEXTURE_2D, m_textureHandle);
    glVertexPointer(2, GL_FLOAT, BytesPerVert, 0);
    glTexCoordPointer(2, GL_FLOAT, BytesPerVert,
                    (GLvoid*) TexCoordOffset);
    glEnable(GL_BLEND);
    glBlendFunc(GL_SRC_ALPHA, GL_ONE_MINUS_SRC_ALPHA);
    glDisable(GL_DEPTH_TEST);
    glEnable(GL_TEXTURE_2D);
    glMatrixMode(GL_PROJECTION);
    glLoadIdentity();
    glOrthof(0, m_windowSize.x, 0, m_windowSize.y, 0, 1);
    glMatrixMode(GL_MODELVIEW);
    glLoadIdentity();
    glColor4f(1, 1, 1, 1);
    glDisableClientState(GL_NORMAL_ARRAY);
    glDrawArrays(GL_TRIANGLES, 0, numDigits * VertsPerDigit);
    glEnableClientState(GL_NORMAL_ARRAY);
    glDisable(GL_BLEND);
}
```

Next we need to implement the private `WriteGlyphVertex` method, which generates the VBO data for a given corner of a glyph rectangle. It takes a pointer-to-float for input, advances it after writing out each value, and then returns it to the caller (see Example 7-6).

Example 7-6. WriteGlyphVertex() method

```
float* WriteGlyphVertex(const Glyph& glyph, vec2 position,
                        int corner, float* vertex)
{
    vec2 texcoord;
    texcoord.x = glyph.Position.X;
    texcoord.y = glyph.Position.Y + glyph.Metrics.Height;

    position.y -= glyph.Metrics.Height + glyph.Metrics.YBearing;

    if (corner % 2) {
        position.x += glyph.Metrics.Width;
        texcoord.x += glyph.Metrics.Width;
    }

    if (corner / 2) {
        position.y += glyph.Metrics.Height;
        texcoord.y -= glyph.Metrics.Height;
    }

    *vertex++ = position.x;
    *vertex++ = position.y;
    *vertex++ = (1 + texcoord.x) / m_textureSize.x;
    *vertex++ = 1 - (1 + texcoord.y) / m_textureSize.y;

    return vertex;
}
```

That's it for the frame rate counter! It's pretty easy to use the class from within the rendering engine class; see Example 7-7.

Example 7-7. Using the FpsRenderer class

```
...
#include "FpsRenderer.h"

class RenderingEngine : public IRenderingEngine {
public:
    RenderingEngine(IResourceManager* resourceManager);
    void Initialize();
    void Render(float objectTheta, float fboTheta) const;
private:
    ...
    FpsRenderer* m_fpsRenderer;
};

void RenderingEngine::Initialize()
{
```

```
    ...
    m_fpsRenderer = new FpsRenderer(m_screenSize);
}

void RenderingEngine::Render(float objectTheta, float fboTheta) const
{
    ...
    m_fpsRenderer->RenderFps();
}
```

...

Simplify with glDrawTexOES

Recall that updating the VBO at every frame and computing texture coordinates was a bit of a pain; it turns out the iPhone supports an easier way to render pixel rectangles when you're using OpenGL ES 1.1.

 This extension is not supported under OpenGL ES 2.0.

The GL_OES_draw_texture extension (supported on all iPhone models at the time of this writing) adds two new functions to OpenGL's repertoire:

```
void glDrawTexfOES(GLfloat x, GLfloat y, GLfloat z,
                   GLfloat width, GLfloat height);
void glDrawTexfvOES(const GLfloat *destRectangle);
```

These two functions are basically equivalent; either can be used to render a rectangle. The second function takes a pointer to the same five floats described in the first function.

 The GL_OES_draw_texture extension actually introduces eight functions in all because of the variants for GLshort, GLint, and GLfixed. I tend to use the GLfloat variants.

This extension also introduces a new texture parameter called GL_TEX TURE_CROP_RECT_OES, which can be used liked this:

```
int sourceRectangle[] = { x, y, width, height };
glTexParameteriv(GL_TEXTURE_2D, GL_TEXTURE_CROP_RECT_OES, sourceRectangle);
```

When used together, the new glDrawTex* functions and the new texture parameter make it easy to draw rectangles of pixels; there's no need to mess with cumbersome VBOs and triangles.

To summarize, use glDrawTex* to set the destination rectangle on the screen; use the new crop rectangle parameter to set up the rectangle in the source texture.

Let's walk through the process of converting the FpsRenderer sample to use the draw_texture extension. First we can remove several fields from the class, including m_vbo, m_windowSize, and all constants except MaxNumDigits.

We can also replace the cumbersome WriteGlyphVertex method with a new streamlined method called RenderGlyph. See Example 7-8. For brevity, sections of code that remain unchanged are replaced with ellipses.

Example 7-8. Simplified FpsRenderer skeleton

```
...

class FpsRenderer {
public:
    FpsRenderer(vec2 windowSize)
    {
        ...
    }
    void RenderFps()
    {
        uint64_t deltaTime = GetElapsedNanoseconds();
        double fps = 1000000000.0 / deltaTime;
        double alpha = m_filterConstant;
        m_fps = fps * alpha + m_fps * (1.0 - alpha);
        fps = round(m_fps);

        glBindTexture(GL_TEXTURE_2D, m_textureHandle);
        glEnable(GL_BLEND);
        glBlendFunc(GL_SRC_ALPHA, GL_ONE_MINUS_SRC_ALPHA);
        glDisable(GL_DEPTH_TEST);
        glEnable(GL_TEXTURE_2D);
        glColor4f(1, 1, 1, 1);

        char digits[MaxNumDigits + 1] = {0};
        sprintf(digits, "%d", (int) fps);
        vec2 pos(5, 10);

        for (char* digit = &digits[0]; *digit; ++digit) {
            int glyphIndex = *digit - '0';
            const Glyph& glyph = NumeralGlyphs[glyphIndex];
            RenderGlyph(glyph, pos);
            pos.x += glyph.Metrics.XAdvance;
        }

        glDisable(GL_BLEND);
    }

private:

    static const int MaxNumDigits = 3;
```

```
uint64_t GetElapsedNanoseconds()
{
    ...
}

void RenderGlyph(const Glyph& glyph, vec2 position)
{
    position.y -= glyph.Metrics.Height + glyph.Metrics.YBearing;

    int box[] = { glyph.Position.X,
                  m_textureSize.y - 1
                    + glyph.Position.Y - glyph.Metrics.Height,
                  glyph.Metrics.Width + 1,
                  glyph.Metrics.Height + 1 };

    glTexParameteriv(GL_TEXTURE_2D, GL_TEXTURE_CROP_RECT_OES, box);
    glDrawTexfOES(position.x, position.y, 0,
                  glyph.Metrics.Width + 1, glyph.Metrics.Height + 1);
}

double m_filterConstant;
double m_fps;
uint64_t m_previousTime;
vec2 m_textureSize;
GLuint m_textureHandle;
};
```

Crisper Text with Distance Fields

Chris Green of Valve Software wrote a very cool graphics paper in 2007 that I think deserves more attention.* The paper describes a simple way to preserve high-quality edges in vector art (typically text) when storing the art in a relatively low-resolution texture. If you'd like to minimize distraction while coming up to speed with OpenGL, go ahead and skip this section; distance fields are a somewhat advanced concept, and they are not required in simple applications. However, I find them fascinating!

Let's review the standard way of rendering text in OpenGL. Normally you'd store the glyphs in a texture whose format is GL_ALPHA, and you'd set up a fairly standard blending configuration, which would probably look like this:

```
glEnable(GL_BLEND);
glBlendFunc(GL_SRC_ALPHA, GL_ONE_MINUS_SRC_ALPHA);
```

If you're using ES 1.1, you can then set the color of the text using glColor4f. With ES 2.0, you can store the color in a uniform variable and apply it in your fragment shader.

That's a perfectly reasonable approach, but if you zoom in far enough on your texture, you'll see some fuzzy stair-stepping as shown in the leftmost panel in Figure 7-5. The

---

* *http://www.valvesoftware.com/publications/2007/SIGGRAPH2007_AlphaTestedMagnification.pdf*

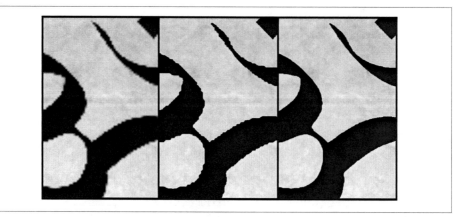

Figure 7-5. Left to right: alpha blending, alpha testing, and alpha testing with distance field

fuzziness can be alleviated by replacing blending with alpha testing ("Alpha Testing" on page 226), but the stair-stepping remains; see the middle panel.

You'll almost always see stair-stepping when zooming in with bilinear filtering. Third-order texture filtering (also known as *cubic filtering*) would mitigate this, but it's not easy to implement with OpenGL ES.

It turns out there's a way to use bilinear filtering and achieve higher-quality results. The trick is to generate a *signed distance field* for your glyphs. A distance field is a grid of values, where each value represents the shortest distance from that grid cell to the glyph boundary. Cells that lie inside the glyph have negative values; cells that lie outside have positive values. If a grid cell lies exactly on the boundary of the glyph, it has a distance value of zero.

To represent a distance field in an OpenGL texture, we need a way to map from the signed distance values to grayscale. One approach is to represent a distance of zero as half-black (0.5) and then to choose maximum and minimum distances, which get mapped to 1.0 and 0. (This effectively clamps large distances, which is fine.) Figure 7-6 shows a distance field for the mystical Aum symbol. Figure 7-7 zooms in on a portion of the Aum distance field with the original glyph boundary represented as a black line.

The concept of a distance field may seem obscure, but it's useful in many surprising ways. Not only does it provide a way to preserve quality of edges (with both ES 1.1 and ES 2.0), but it also makes it easy to apply a bevy of text effects, such as shadows and outlines (these are ES 2.0 only).

Generating Distance Fields with Python

Before diving in to the application of distance fields, let's take a look at how to generate them. The most popular way of doing this is actually quite simple to implement, despite

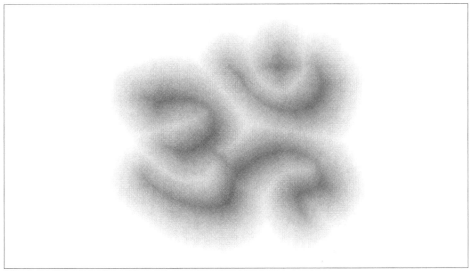

Figure 7-6. Signed distance field for the Aum symbol

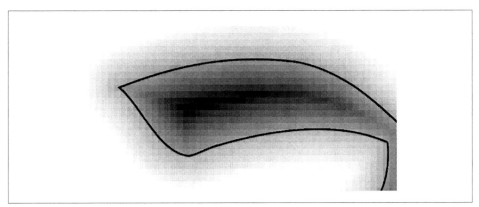

Figure 7-7. Zoomed distance field

having a ridiculously complex name: "the eight-points signed sequential Euclidean distance transform algorithm," or 8SSEDT for short. The basic idea is to store a pair of integers at each grid cell (dx and dy), which represents the number of cells between it and the nearest cell on the opposite side of the vector boundary. Each cell is initialized to either (0, 0) or (+∞, +∞), depending on whether the cell is inside the vector. The algorithm itself consists of "propagating" the distances by having each cell compare its dx:dy pair to its neighbor and then adding it to the current cell if it's closer. To achieve a signed distance, the algorithm is run on two separate grids and then merges the results.

Let's momentarily go back to using Python and the PIL library since they provide a convenient environment for implementing the algorithm; see Example 7-9.

Example 7-9. Distance field generation with Python

```python
import os
import math
from PIL import Image

inside, outside = (0,0), (9999, 9999)

def invert(c):
    return 255 - c

def initCell(pixel):
    if pixel == 0: return inside
    return outside

def distSq(cell):
    return cell[0] * cell[0] + cell[1] * cell[1]

def getCell(grid, x, y):
    if y < 0 or y >= len(grid): return outside
    if x < 0 or x >= len(grid[y]): return outside
    return grid[y][x]

def compare(grid, cell, x, y, ox, oy):
    other = getCell(grid, x + ox, y + oy)
    other = (other[0] + ox, other[1] + oy)
    if distSq(other) < distSq(cell): return other
    return cell

def propagate(grid):
    height = len(grid)
    width = len(grid[0])
    for y in xrange(0, height):
        for x in xrange(0, width):
            cell = grid[y][x]
            cell = compare(grid, cell, x, y, -1,  0)
            cell = compare(grid, cell, x, y,  0, -1)
            cell = compare(grid, cell, x, y, -1, -1)
            cell = compare(grid, cell, x, y, +1, -1)
            grid[y][x] = cell
        for x in xrange(width - 1, -1, -1):
            cell = grid[y][x]
            cell = compare(grid, cell, x, y, 1, 0)
            grid[y][x] = cell
    for y in xrange(height - 1, -1, -1):
        for x in xrange(width - 1, -1, -1):
            cell = grid[y][x]
            cell = compare(grid, cell, x, y, +1,  0)
            cell = compare(grid, cell, x, y,  0, +1)
            cell = compare(grid, cell, x, y, -1, +1)
            cell = compare(grid, cell, x, y, +1, +1)
            grid[y][x] = cell
        for x in xrange(0, width):
            cell = grid[y][x]
            cell = compare(grid, cell, x, y, -1,  0)
            grid[y][x] = cell
```

```
def GenerateDistanceField(inFile, outFile, spread):

    print "Allocating the destination image..."
    image = Image.open(inFile)
    image.load()
    channels = image.split()
    if len(channels) == 4: alphaChannel = channels[3]
    else: alphaChannel = channels[0]
    w = alphaChannel.size[0] + spread * 2
    h = alphaChannel.size[1] + spread * 2
    img = Image.new("L", (w, h), 0)
    img.paste(alphaChannel, (spread, spread))
    width, height = img.size

    print "Creating the two grids..."
    pixels = img.load()
    grid0 = [[initCell(pixels[x, y]) \
             for x in xrange(width)] \
             for y in xrange(height)]
    grid1 = [[initCell(invert(pixels[x, y])) \
             for x in xrange(width)] \
             for y in xrange(height)]

    print "Propagating grids..."
    propagate(grid0)
    propagate(grid1)

    print "Subtracting grids..."
    signedDistance = [[0 for x in xrange(width)] for y in xrange(height)]
    for y in xrange(height):
        for x in xrange(width):
            dist1 = math.sqrt(distSq(grid0[y][x]))
            dist0 = math.sqrt(distSq(grid1[y][x]))
            signedDistance[y][x] = dist0 - dist1

    print "Normalizing..."
    maxDist, minDist = spread, -spread
    for y in xrange(height):
        for x in xrange(width):
            dist = signedDistance[y][x]
            if dist < 0: dist = -128 * (dist - minDist) / minDist
            else: dist = 128 + 128 * dist / maxDist
            if dist < 0: dist = 0
            elif dist > 255: dist = 255
            signedDistance[y][x] = int(dist)
            pixels[x, y] = signedDistance[y][x]

    print "Saving %s..." % outFile
    img.save(outFile)

if __name__ == "__main__":
    inFile, outFile = 'Aum.png', 'DistanceFieldAum.png'
    GenerateDistanceField(inFile, outFile, spread = 15)
```

Don't let Example 7-9 scare you! You're in good shape if you simply grok the concept of a distance field. The formal proof of the generation algorithm is beyond the scope of this book, but you can always flip back to "Generating Distance Fields with Python" on page 296 to review it at a high level.

Use Distance Fields Under ES 1.1 with Alpha Testing

To make use of a distance field with iPhone models that support only OpenGL ES 1.1, simply bind the distance field texture and enable alpha testing with a threshold value of 0.5:

```
glDisable(GL_BLEND);
glEnable(GL_ALPHA_TEST);
glAlphaFunc(GL_LESS, 0.5);
```

Remember, blending applies an equation at every pixel to determine the final color, while alpha testing compares the source alpha with a given value and leaves the framebuffer unchanged if the comparison fails.

Adding Text Effects with Fragment Shaders

One of the reasons I love distance fields is that they enable more than quality enhancements. On iPhone models that support OpenGL ES 2.0, distance fields can be used in conjunction with a fragment shader to achieve a variety of special effects, all using the same source bitmap. See Figure 7-8.

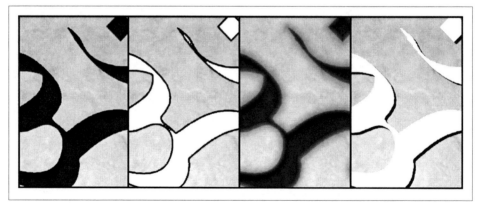

Figure 7-8. Left to right: smooth, outline, glow, shadow

Smoothing and Derivatives

The first distance field effect that I want to cover is smoothing, as shown in the leftmost panel in Figure 7-8.

Go back and take another look at the big stair steps in the left-most panel in Figure 7-5; they correspond to the texels in the source image. Alpha testing with a distance field fixed this up (rightmost panel), but it still exhibits pixel-level aliasing. This is because the rasterized pixels are always either fully lit or discarded; there are no shades of gray. We can fix this up with a fragment shader.

Before diving into the shader code, let's take a look at GLSL's `smoothstep` function. Here's the declaration:

```
float smoothstep(float edge0, float edge1, float x)
```

`smoothstep` returns 0.0 if x is less than or equal to `edge0` and returns 1.0 if x is greater than or equal to `edge1`. If x is between these two values, then it interpolates between 0 and 1. Calling `smoothstep` is equivalent to the following:

```
float t = clamp ((x - edge0) / (edge1 - edge0), 0.0, 1.0);
return t * t * (3.0 - 2.0 * t);
```

To see how `smoothstep` comes in handy for smoothing, visualize two new boundary lines in the distance field: one at `edge0` (a deflated version of the glyph), the other at `edge1` (an inflated version of the glyph). See Figure 7-9; the middle line is the region where distance = 0.

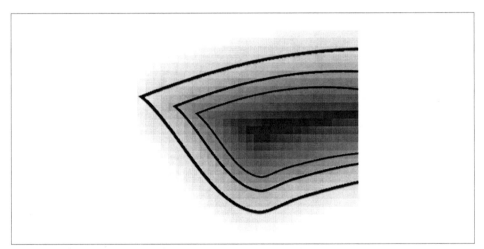

Figure 7-9. Distance field with edge0 (inner line) and edge1 (outer line)

Alpha should be opaque at edge0 and transparent at edge1. To achieve smoothing, the fragment shader needs to create an alpha ramp between these two boundaries. Example 7-10 shows an implementation.

Example 7-10. Naive fragment shader for distance field smoothing

```
varying mediump vec2 TextureCoord;

uniform sampler2D DistanceField;
uniform mediump vec3 GlyphColor;

const mediump float SmoothCenter = 0.5;
const mediump float SmoothWidth = 0.04;

void main(void)
{
    mediump vec4 color = texture2D(DistanceField, TextureCoord);
    mediump float distance = color.a;
    mediump float alpha = smoothstep(SmoothCenter - SmoothWidth,
                                     SmoothCenter + SmoothWidth,
                                     distance);
    gl_FragColor = vec4(GlyphColor, alpha);
}
```

The fragment shader in Example 7-10 is fairly easy to understand, but unfortunately it suffers from a fundamental flaw. The value of SmoothWidth is always the same, regardless of how much the glyph is magnified. As a result, anti-aliasing is too blurry when the camera is near the texture (Figure 7-10), and it's ineffective when the camera is very far away.

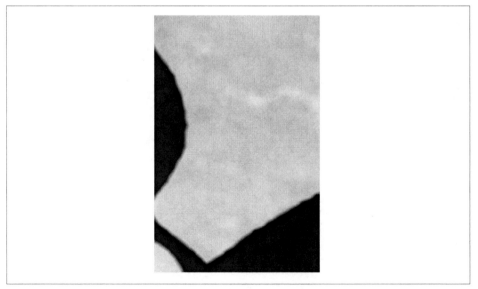

Figure 7-10. Naive smoothing with large magnification

Fortunately, the iPhone supports a fragment shader extension to help out with this. Unfortunately, it's not supported in the simulator at the time of this writing.

 It's easy to deal with this disparity. At runtime, check for extension support using the method described in "Dealing with Size Constraints" on page 204. Compile fragment shader A if it's supported; otherwise, compile fragment shader B.

The name of this extension is OES_standard_derivatives. That's right, "derivatives." Don't run in fear if this conjures up images of a brutal calculus professor! It's not as bad as it sounds. The extension simply adds three new functions to GLSL:

```
float dFdx(float f);
float dFdy(float f);
float fwidth(float f)
```

These functions are available only to the fragment shader. They return a value proportional to the rate of change of the argument when compared to neighboring pixels. The dFdx function returns a rate of change along the x-axis; the dFdy function returns a rate of change along the y-axis. The fwidth function provides a convenient way of combining the two values:

```
fwidth(f) = abs(dFdx(f)) + abs(dFdy(f))
```

In our case, when the camera is far away, the rate of change in the on-screen distance field is greater than when the camera is close-up. To achieve consistent anti-aliasing, we'll simply use a larger filter width when the camera is far away. See Example 7-11 for a new version of the fragment shader that uses derivatives.

Example 7-11. Corrected fragment shader for distance field smoothing

```
#extension GL_OES_standard_derivatives : enable

varying mediump vec2 TextureCoord;

uniform sampler2D DistanceField;
uniform mediump vec3 GlyphColor;

const mediump float SmoothCenter = 0.5;

void main(void)
{
    mediump vec4 color = texture2D(DistanceField, TextureCoord);
    mediump float distance = color.a;
    mediump float smoothWidth = fwidth(distance);
    mediump float alpha = smoothstep(SmoothCenter - smoothWidth,
                                     SmoothCenter + smoothWidth, distance);
    gl_FragColor = vec4(GlyphColor, alpha);
}
```

Implementing Outline, Glow, and Shadow Effects

Using shaders with distance fields can also achieve a variety of special effects, as shown in Figure 7-8. In the interest of brevity, I won't go into too much detail here; much like the smoothing example from the previous section, all these effects rely on using smooth step and various offsets from the *distance=0* boundary. They also make use of a GLSL function called mix; here's its declaration:

```
float mix(float x, float y, float a)
```

You probably already guessed that this function performs linear interpolation between its first two arguments:

```
mix(x, y, a) = x * (1 - a) + y * a
```

See Example 7-12 for an "übershader" that can produce any of the aforementioned distance field effects, depending on how the application sets up the uniforms. If you're trying to run this shader on the simulator, you'll need to remove the top line and replace the fwidth function with a constant.

 As always, you can obtain the complete source for an app that demonstrates this technique from this book's website. The sample in this case is simply called "DistanceField," and it uses #ifdef to automatically avoid derivatives when running in the simulator.

Example 7-12. Distance field übershader

```
#extension GL_OES_standard_derivatives : enable

varying mediump vec2 TextureCoord;

uniform sampler2D DistanceField;
uniform mediump vec3 OutlineColor;
uniform mediump vec3 GlyphColor;
uniform mediump vec3 GlowColor;

uniform bool Outline;❶
uniform bool Glow;
uniform bool Shadow;

const mediump vec2 ShadowOffset = vec2(0.005, 0.01);❷
const mediump vec3 ShadowColor = vec3(0.0, 0.0, 0.125);❸
const mediump float SmoothCenter = 0.5;❹
const mediump float OutlineCenter = 0.4;❺
const mediump float GlowBoundary = 1.0;❻

void main(void)
{
    mediump vec4 color = texture2D(DistanceField, TextureCoord);
    mediump float distance = color.a;
    mediump float smoothWidth = fwidth(distance);
    mediump float alpha;
```

```
    mediump vec3 rgb;

    if (Outline) {
        mediump float mu = smoothstep(OutlineCenter - smoothWidth,
                                      OutlineCenter + smoothWidth,
                                      distance);
        alpha = smoothstep(SmoothCenter - smoothWidth,
                           SmoothCenter + smoothWidth, distance)
        rgb = mix(GlyphColor, OutlineColor, mu);
    }

    if (Glow) {
        mediump float mu = smoothstep(SmoothCenter - smoothWidth,
                                      SmoothCenter + smoothWidth,
                                      distance);
        rgb = mix(GlyphColor, GlowColor, mu);
        alpha = smoothstep(SmoothCenter, GlowBoundary, sqrt(distance));
    }

    if (Shadow) {
        mediump float distance2 = texture2D(DistanceField,
                                            TextureCoord + ShadowOffset).a;
        mediump float s = smoothstep(SmoothCenter - smoothWidth,
                                     SmoothCenter + smoothWidth,
                                     distance2);
        mediump float v = smoothstep(SmoothCenter - smoothWidth,
                                     SmoothCenter + smoothWidth,
                                     distance);

        // If s is 0, then we're inside the shadow;
        // if it's 1, then we're outside the shadow.
        //
        // If v is 0, then we're inside the vector;
        // if it's 1, then we're outside the vector.

        // Totally inside the vector (i.e., inside the glyph):
        if (v == 0.0) {
            rgb = GlyphColor;
            alpha = 0.0;
        }

        // On a nonshadowed vector edge:
        else if (s == 1.0 && v != 1.0) {
            rgb = GlyphColor;
            alpha = v;
        }

        // Totally inside the shadow:
        else if (s == 0.0 && v == 1.0) {
            rgb = ShadowColor;
            alpha = 0.0;
        }

        // On a shadowed vector edge:
        else if (s == 0.0) {
```

```
        rgb = mix(GlyphColor, ShadowColor, v);
        alpha = 0.0;
    }

    // On the shadow's outside edge:
    else {
        rgb = mix(GlyphColor, ShadowColor, v);
        alpha = s;
    }
}

gl_FragColor = vec4(rgb, alpha);
}
```

❶ The Outline, Glow, and Shadow booleans are set from the application to choose which effect to apply. (An alternative strategy would be splitting this into three separate shaders.)

❷ This is the offset of the shadow from the glyph. In this case, the aspect ratio of the texture is 2:1, so the X offset is half the size the Y offset. Note that you may need to negate the X or Y value, depending on how your distance field is oriented.

❸ These are the R G B values of the shadow color.

❹ SmoothCenter is the alpha value that represents the *distance* = 0 boundary.

❺ OutlineCenter tells the shader how far from the glyph edge to render the outline. For an outline that is just inside the glyph, this value should be less than 0.5.

❻ GlowBoundary tells the shader how far out to extend the glow. To create a pulsing glow, change this into a uniform, and cycle its value from within the application code.

The shadow effect in Example 7-12 deserves further explanation. It applies anti-aliasing to the transition not only between the vector and the background but also between the shadow and the background and between the vector and the shadow. The shader pulls this off by deciding which of the following five regions the pixel falls into (see Figure 7-11):

1. Completely within the vector
2. On a vector edge that's not shadowed
3. Completely within the shadow
4. On a vector edge that's shadowed
5. On the shadow's outside edge

Animation with Sprite Sheets

Let's set aside glyph rendering and visit another topic common to 2D graphics: sprites. The iPhone is an ideal platform for casual gaming, and many popular iPhone games

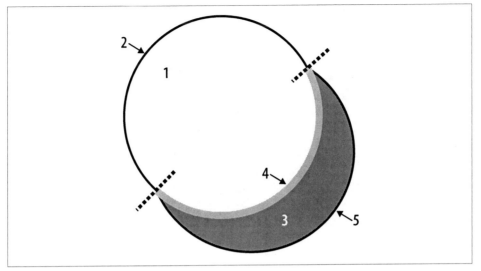

Figure 7-11. Shadow regions

rely heavily on sprites for frame composition. To recap, a sprite is simply a bitmap that gets applied to a rectangular region of the screen. Sprites often use alpha to allow the background (and possibly other sprites) to show through. I like to think of sprite rendering as using an overhead projector, where each sprite is a plastic sheet with a cartoon drawing.

For efficiency, it's common to pack a slew of sprites into a single texture; this is called a *sprite sheet*. In general, a texture that contains multiple disparate images is known as a *texture atlas*. The numerals texture presented in "Text Rendering 101: Drawing an FPS Counter" on page 282 was an example of a texture atlas.

 There are tools out there to help you build sprite sheets. One such tool is a web-based application called *zwopple* by Robert Payne. You can find it at *http://zwoptex.zwopple.com*.

Recall that there are two ways of animating a sprite: the screen position can change (for example, a bouncing ball), or the source image can change (for example, a spinning ball). In the former case, the application code updates the vertex positions at every frame; in the latter case, the application updates the texture coordinates at every frame.

For an example of a sprite with multiple animation frames, see Figure 7-12, a sprite sheet from a game that I created in my college days. (The game's protagonist is named Noop, a blobby fellow who moves horizontally by repeatedly squishing his legs together in wormlike fashion.)

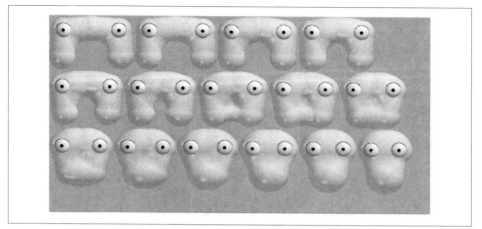

Figure 7-12. Sprite sheet for the Noop character

Image Composition and a Taste of Multitexturing

Sometimes it's desirable to split a sprite sheet into multiple layers, as shown in Figure 7-13. The left sheet has the animation frames for Noop's body; the right sheet has his eyes and shiny highlights. This allows the application to vary the colors of the layers independently. For example, my game can draw Noop using a yellowish hue most of the time but sometimes renders him in orange to convey that he's hurt. In both cases, the eyes and highlights are white.

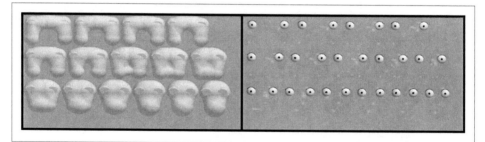

Figure 7-13. Noop layers

We discussed how to shift the apparent color of a texture in "Shifting Texture Color with Per-Vertex Color" on page 229. You can use a luminance or luminance-alpha texture rather than a full-blown RGBA texture and then modulate the texture's color using per-vertex color (for example, by calling glColor4f).

The obvious way of composing Noop's eyes with his body is to render the same quad in two passes with blending enabled. The first pass uses texture coordinates for the body; the second pass uses coordinates for the eyes and highlights. Example 7-13 shows an example of this procedure.

Example 7-13. Rendering Noop in two passes

```
// Enable Blending:
glEnable(GL_BLEND);
glBlendFunc(GL_SRC_ALPHA, GL_ONE_MINUS_SRC_ALPHA);

// Draw Noop's body in a yellowish hue:
glColor4f(1, 0.83f, 0.33f, 1);
glBindTexture(GL_TEXTURE_2D, bodyTexture);
glTexParameteriv(GL_TEXTURE_2D, GL_TEXTURE_CROP_RECT_OES, sourceRectangle);
glDrawTexfOES(x, y, 0, width, height);

// Draw Noop's eyes in white:
glColor4f(1, 1, 1, 1);
glBindTexture(GL_TEXTURE_2D, eyesTexture);
glTexParameteriv(GL_TEXTURE_2D, GL_TEXTURE_CROP_RECT_OES, sourceRectangle);
glDrawTexfOES(x, y, 0, width, height);
```

Note that Example 7-13 is valid only for ES 1.1; under ES 2.0, we need to replace the DrawTex-related lines with calls to `glDrawArrays` or `glDrawElements`, and we need to replace `glColor4f` with `glVertexAttrib4f`. See Example 7-14.

Example 7-14. Two-pass Noop with ES 2.0

```
// Enable Blending:
glEnable(GL_BLEND);
glBlendFunc(GL_SRC_ALPHA, GL_ONE_MINUS_SRC_ALPHA);

// Draw Noop's body in a yellowish hue:
glVertexAttrib4f(MyColorAttribute, 1, 0.83f, 0.33f, 1);
glBindTexture(GL_TEXTURE_2D, bodyTexture);
glDrawArrays(GL_TRIANGLES, 0, 6); // draw a rectangle with two triangles

// Draw Noop's eyes in white:
glVertexAttrib4f(MyColorAttribute, 1, 1, 1, 1);
glBindTexture(GL_TEXTURE_2D, eyesTexture);
glDrawArrays(GL_TRIANGLES, 0, 6); // draw a rectangle with two triangles
```

Both OpenGL ES 1.1 and ES 2.0 provide a way to combine simple two-pass operations like this into a single draw call. It's called *multitexturing*. Multitexturing allows you to set up more than one *texture stage*. Example 7-15 shows the sample code for rendering Noop with multitexturing; note there's only one call to `glDrawTexfOES`.

Example 7-15. One-pass Noop with multitexturing

```
glColor4f(1, 0.83f, 0.33f, 1);
glActiveTexture(GL_TEXTURE0);
glEnable(GL_TEXTURE_2D);
glBindTexture(GL_TEXTURE_2D, bodyTexture);
glTexParameteriv(GL_TEXTURE_2D, GL_TEXTURE_CROP_RECT_OES, sourceRectangle);

glActiveTexture(GL_TEXTURE1);
glEnable(GL_TEXTURE_2D);
glBindTexture(GL_TEXTURE_2D, eyesTexture);
```

```
glTexParameteriv(GL_TEXTURE_2D, GL_TEXTURE_CROP_RECT_OES, sourceRectangle);
glDrawTexfOES(x, y, 0, width, height);
```

The key lines in Example 7-15 are the calls to glActiveTexture, which sets the current texture stage and affects all subsequent texture-related calls, including glEnable(GL_TEXTURE_2D). This allows individual stages to be independently turned on or off.

I should warn you that Example 7-15 alone is not quite enough; you also need to tell OpenGL how to combine the color values from the two texture stages. With ES 1.1, this is quite a hassle; see Example 7-16. This sets up the second texture stage so that it works in a way similar to typical alpha blending. Thankfully, you can often perform this type of configuration only once, when your application first starts up.

Example 7-16. Horrific texture stage configuration with ES 1.1

```
glActiveTexture(GL_TEXTURE1);
glTexEnvi(GL_TEXTURE_ENV, GL_TEXTURE_ENV_MODE, GL_COMBINE);
glTexEnvi(GL_TEXTURE_ENV, GL_COMBINE_RGB, GL_INTERPOLATE);
glTexEnvi(GL_TEXTURE_ENV, GL_SRC0_RGB, GL_TEXTURE);
glTexEnvi(GL_TEXTURE_ENV, GL_OPERAND0_RGB, GL_SRC_COLOR);
glTexEnvi(GL_TEXTURE_ENV, GL_SRC1_RGB, GL_PREVIOUS);
glTexEnvi(GL_TEXTURE_ENV, GL_OPERAND1_RGB, GL_SRC_COLOR);
glTexEnvi(GL_TEXTURE_ENV, GL_SRC2_RGB, GL_TEXTURE);
glTexEnvi(GL_TEXTURE_ENV, GL_OPERAND2_RGB, GL_SRC_ALPHA);
glTexEnvi(GL_TEXTURE_ENV, GL_COMBINE_ALPHA, GL_REPLACE);
glTexEnvi(GL_TEXTURE_ENV, GL_SRC0_ALPHA, GL_PREVIOUS);
glTexEnvi(GL_TEXTURE_ENV, GL_OPERAND0_ALPHA, GL_SRC_ALPHA);
```

OpenGL ES 2.0 simplifies this by allowing you to combine colors from within your fragment shader. We'll discuss this further in the next chapter, and I'll explain glTexEnv in greater detail—I just wanted to whet your appetite!

Mixing OpenGL ES and UIKit

Sprites are often used for rendering interactive widgets in a HUD (see "Handling the Heads-Up Display" on page 264). Handling mouse interaction can be a chore when you don't have a UI framework to stand upon. If you're developing a 3D application and find yourself yearning for UIKit, don't dismiss it right away. It's true that mixing UIKit and OpenGL ES is generally ill-advised for performance reasons, but in many situations, it's the right way to go. This is especially true with 3D applications that aren't as graphically demanding as huge, professionally produced games. Figure 7-14 depicts an application that overlays a UISegmentedControl widget with a 3D scene.

The full source code for the application depicted in Figure 7-14 is available from this book's site (*http://oreilly.com/catalog/9780596804831*) under the name CocoaMix. You might also want to check out the PVRTextureLoader sample from Apple's SDK, which includes a slick sliding animation for a panel of UIKit controls.

Figure 7-14. Mixing UIKit with OpenGL ES

 The performance of "mixed" rendering has been improving as Apple rolls out new devices and new revisions to the iPhone OS. By the time you read this, using nonanimated UIKit controls in conjunction with OpenGL might be a perfectly acceptable practice.

Recall that all OpenGL rendering takes place in a `UIView`-derived class; every sample in this book defines a class called `GLView` for this purpose. Adding a few simple controls to `GLView` is fairly painless, so let's try adding a `UISegmentedControl` that selects a texture minification filter.

First we need to add a field to the `GLView` class declaration for the new control. See the bold line in Example 7-17.

Example 7-17. Adding a UIKit control to GLView.h

```
#import "Interfaces.hpp"
#import <UIKit/UIKit.h>
#import <QuartzCore/QuartzCore.h>

@interface GLView : UIView {
@private
    IRenderingEngine* m_renderingEngine;
    IResourceManager* m_resourceManager;
    EAGLContext* m_context;
    float m_timestamp;
    UISegmentedControl* m_filterChooser;
}
```

```
- (void) drawView: (CADisplayLink*) displayLink;

@end
```

Next, we need to instance the control and create a method for event handling; see Example 7-18.

Example 7-18. Adding a UIKit control to GLView.mm

```
...

- (id) initWithFrame: (CGRect) frame
{
    if (self = [super initWithFrame:frame])
    {
        CAEAGLLayer* eaglLayer = (CAEAGLLayer*) self.layer;
        eaglLayer.opaque = YES;

        EAGLRenderingAPI api = kEAGLRenderingAPIOpenGLES1;
        m_context = [[EAGLContext alloc] initWithAPI:api];

        ...

        // Create and configure the UIKit control:

        NSArray* labels = [NSArray arrayWithObjects:@"Nearest",
                                                    @"Bilinear",
                                                    @"Trilinear", nil];

        m_filterChooser =
          [[[UISegmentedControl alloc] initWithItems:labels] autorelease];
        m_filterChooser.segmentedControlStyle = UISegmentedControlStyleBar;
        m_filterChooser.selectedSegmentIndex = 0;

        [m_filterChooser addTarget:self
                        action:@selector(changeFilter:)
                        forControlEvents:UIControlEventValueChanged];

        // Add the control to GLView's children:

        [self addSubview:m_filterChooser];

        // Position the UIKit control:

        const int ScreenWidth = CGRectGetWidth(frame);
        const int ScreenHeight = CGRectGetHeight(frame);
        const int Margin = 10;

        CGRect controlFrame = m_filterChooser.frame;
        controlFrame.origin.x = ScreenWidth / 2 - controlFrame.size.width / 2;
        controlFrame.origin.y = ScreenHeight - controlFrame.size.height - Margin;
        m_filterChooser.frame = controlFrame;
    }
    return self;
```

```
}

- (void) changeFilter: (id) sender
{
    TextureFilter filter = (TextureFilter) [sender selectedSegmentIndex];
    m_renderingEngine->SetFilter(filter);
}
```

...

Example 7-18 includes some UIKit and Objective-C mechanisms that we haven't seen before (such as `@selector`), but it will be familiar to iPhone developers. Check out Jonathan Zdziarski's *iPhone SDK Application Development* (O'Reilly) to learn more about UIKit.

Note that you can also use UIKit to render "look-alike" controls, rather than using the actual UIKit controls. For example, you can render some buttons into a `CGImage` at launch time and then create an OpenGL texture from that (see "Generating and Transforming OpenGL Textures with Quartz" on page 201). This would give your buttons the look and feel of the iPhone's native UI, plus it wouldn't suffer from the potential performance issues inherent in mixing the actual UIKit control with OpenGL. The downside is that you'd need to implement the interactivity by hand.

Rendering Confetti, Fireworks, and More: Point Sprites

You may find yourself wanting to render a system of particles that need a bit more pizzazz than mere single-pixel points of light. The first thing that might come to mind is rendering a small alpha-blended quad for each particle. This is a perfectly reasonable approach, but it requires you to come up with the coordinates for two textured triangles at each point.

It turns out the iPhone supports an extension to make this much easier by enabling *point sprites*. Point sprites are small screen-aligned quads that get drawn at each vertex in a vertex array or VBO. For simplicity, a point sprite uses an entire texture; there's no need to provide texture coordinates. This makes it a breeze to render particle systems such as the one depicted in Figure 7-15.

For OpenGL ES 1.1, the name of the extension is `GL_OES_point_sprite`, and it allows you to make the following function calls:

```
glEnable(GL_POINT_SPRITE_OES);
glDisable(GL_POINT_SPRITE_OES);
glTexEnvi(GL_POINT_SPRITE_OES, GL_COORD_REPLACE_OES, GL_TRUE);
glTexEnvi(GL_POINT_SPRITE_OES, GL_COORD_REPLACE_OES, GL_FALSE);
```

With OpenGL ES 2.0, point sprites are supported in the core specification rather than an extension. There's no need to call any of these functions because point sprite functionality is implicit. You'll see how to use point sprites in both ES 1.1 and ES 2.0 in the upcoming SpringyStars sample.

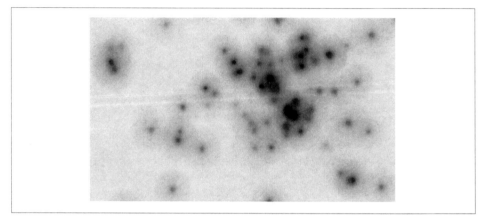

Figure 7-15. Point sprites

Chapter Finale: SpringyStars

To show off point sprites in action, let's wrap up the chapter with a mass-spring simulation that renders a network of little white stars, as shown in Figure 7-16. The "star net" droops down in the direction of gravity according to how you're holding the iPhone. You can find the complete source for this example from this book's web page.

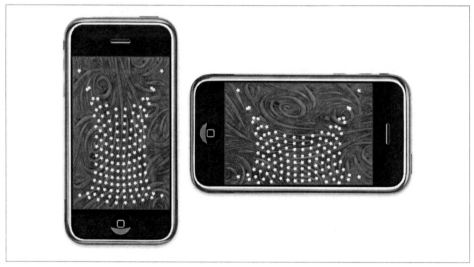

Figure 7-16. The SpringyStars sample app

Physics Diversion: Mass-Spring System

Before we dive into the code, let's take a brief detour from graphics and review some physics. The easiest way to create a simple physics simulation to call an `Update()`

method on every object in the simulation. The update method has an argument for the time step, which represents elapsed time since the previous call. (This isn't much different from the `UpdateAnimation()` method presented way back in Chapter 1.) For our SpringyStars app, the pseudocode for the update method looks like this:

```
void Update(float dt)
{
    Acceleration = TotalForces / Mass;
    Velocity += Acceleration * dt;
    Position += Velocity * dt;
}
```

The previous code snippet should make sense if you remember your high-school physics. Perhaps a bit foggier in your memory is *Hooke's law*, which we'll need for modeling the spring forces between the star sprites; see Equation 7-1.

Equation 7-1. Hooke's law of elasticity

$$\mathbf{F} = -\mathbf{kx}$$

F is the restoring force of the spring, so called because it represents the effort to restore the spring's length to its rest position. You can think of the k constant as being the stiffness of the spring. **x** is the displacement between the current end of the spring and its rest position.

 To learn physics from a much more authoritative source, take a look at *Physics for Game Developers* (O'Reilly) by David Bourg.

Hooke's law deals with only a single spring, but in our case we have a network of springs. Our simulation needs to maintain a list of "nodes" (rigid bodies), each of which is connected to a set of neighboring nodes. Here's a code snippet that applies Hooke's law to a node and its neighbor:

```
vec2 v = neighbor->position - this->position;
float length = v.Length();
vec2 direction = v.Normalized();
vec2 restoringForce = direction * StiffnessContant * (length - RestLength);
```

In the previous snippet, the `restoringForce` vector applies to the `this` node, while an equal and opposite force (that is, `-restoringForce`) applies to the `neighbor` node.

Taken alone, Hooke's law can produce oscillations that last forever. To be more realistic, the simulation needs to include a *damping force* to subdue the spring's effect. The damping force between two nodes is proportional to their relative velocity:

$$F_d = k_d(v_1 - v_2)$$

In this case, k_d is a damping constant. Much like the stiffness constant in Hooke's law, I find that the best way to come up with a reasonable value is through experimentation. (More rigorous mass-spring systems include a global damping force, but this is good enough for our purposes.)

The C++ code snippet for computing damping force looks like this:

```
vec2 relativeVelocity = neighbor->velocity - this->m_velocity;
vec2 dampingForce = relativeVelocity * DampingConstant;
```

At this point, we're ready to design a C++ class to represent a star sprite in a simple mass-spring system. See Example 7-19.

Example 7-19. SpringNode.hpp

```
#include <list>

class SpringNode;

typedef std::list<SpringNode*> NeighborList;

class SpringNode {
public:
    SpringNode()
    {
        m_position = vec2(0, 0);
        m_velocity = vec2(0, 0);
        m_mass = 1;
        m_pinned = false;
    }
    void Pin()
    {
        m_pinned = true;
    }
    void SetPosition(const vec2& p)
    {
        m_position = p;
    }
    vec2 GetPosition() const
    {
        return m_position;
    }
    void AddNeighbor(SpringNode* node)
    {
        m_neighbors.push_back(node);
    }
    void ResetForce(vec2 force)
    {
        m_force = force;
    }
    void ComputeForce()
    {
        const float StiffnessContant = 3.0f;
        const float RestLength = 0.075f;
        const float DampingConstant = 2.0f;
```

```
    NeighborList::const_iterator n = m_neighbors.begin();
    for (; n != m_neighbors.end(); ++n) {

        // Compute the spring force:
        vec2 v = (*n)->m_position - m_position;
        float length = v.Length();
        vec2 direction = v.Normalized();
        vec2 restoringForce = direction * StiffnessContant
          * (length - RestLength);

        // Compute the damping force:
        vec2 relativeVelocity = (*n)->m_velocity - m_velocity;
        vec2 dampingForce = relativeVelocity * DampingConstant;

        // Add the two forces to this node and subtract them
        // from the neighbor:
        vec2 totalForce = restoringForce + dampingForce;
        m_force += totalForce;
        (*n)->m_force -= totalForce;
    }
}
void Update(float dt)
{
    if (m_pinned)
        return;

    vec2 acceleration = m_force / m_mass;
    m_velocity += acceleration * dt;
    m_position += m_velocity * dt;
}
private:
    vec2 m_force;
    vec2 m_position;
    vec2 m_velocity;
    float m_mass;
    bool m_pinned;
    NeighborList m_neighbors;
};
```

Note the boolean field called m_pinned, which causes a node to be impervious to the forces acted upon it. We'll use this to affix the four corners of the net to their starting positions. This prevents the net from falling off the screen.

Speaking of falling off the screen, note that there's nothing obvious in Example 7-19 that takes gravity into account. That's because the application can use the ResetForce() method to initialize the m_force field to the gravity vector and then call ComputeForce() in a separate pass to add in all the relevant spring forces. The simulation will perform three separate passes through the node list; see the pseudocode in Example 7-20. (Don't combine these into a single loop.)

Example 7-20. Simulation pseudocode

```
void UpdateSimulation(float timeStep, vec2 gravityVector)
{
    for each node:
        node->ResetForce(gravityVector)

    for each node:
        node->AddSpringForces()

    for each node:
        node->Update(timeStep)
}
```

C++ Interfaces and GLView

To avoid code duplication between the ES 2.0 and ES 1.1 backends, let's put the physics into the application engine and pass it a normalized 2D vector for the direction of gravity. As a result, the IRenderingEngine interface is very simple; see Example 7-21.

Example 7-21. Interfaces.hpp (SpringyStars)

```
#pragma once
#include "Vector.hpp"
#include <vector>

typedef std::vector<vec2> PositionList;

struct IApplicationEngine {
    virtual void Initialize(int width, int height) = 0;
    virtual void Render() const = 0;
    virtual void UpdateAnimation(float timeStep) = 0;
    virtual void SetGravityDirection(vec2 direction) = 0;
    virtual ~IApplicationEngine() {}
};

struct IRenderingEngine {
    virtual void Initialize() = 0;
    virtual void Render(const PositionList& positions) const = 0;
    virtual ~IRenderingEngine() {}
};

IApplicationEngine* CreateApplicationEngine(IRenderingEngine*);

namespace ES1 { IRenderingEngine* CreateRenderingEngine(); }
namespace ES2 { IRenderingEngine* CreateRenderingEngine(); }
```

The GLView class looks much like all the other samples in this book, except that it needs to pass in a gravity vector. See Example 7-22. For more information about setting up the accelerometer, flip back to the section "Replacing Buttons with Orientation Sensors" on page 269.

Example 7-22. Snippet of GLView.mm (SpringyStars)

```
- (void) accelerometer: (UIAccelerometer*) accelerometer
        didAccelerate: (UIAcceleration*) acceleration
{
    [m_filter addAcceleration:acceleration];

    vec2 direction(m_filter.x, m_filter.y);
    m_applicationEngine->SetGravityDirection(direction);
}
```

ApplicationEngine Implementation

See Example 7-23 for the application engine implementation. Recall that the `GLView` class calls `UpdateAnimation` according to the refresh rate of the display. This provides enough time to perform several simulation iterations, each using a small time step. Performing several small iterations produces more accurate results than a single iteration with a large time step. In fact, an overly large time step can cause the simulation to go ballistic.

> Updating the physics along with the rendering is a bit of a hack but good enough for our purposes. For a production-quality application, you might want to create a timer object in your `GLView` class just for physics.

Example 7-23. ApplicationEngine.cpp (SpringyStars)

```
#include "Interfaces.hpp"
#include "SpringNode.hpp"

using namespace std;

class ApplicationEngine : public IApplicationEngine {
public:
    ApplicationEngine(IRenderingEngine* renderingEngine);
    ~ApplicationEngine();
    void Initialize(int width, int height);
    void SetGravityDirection(vec2 direction);
    void Render() const;
    void UpdateAnimation(float dt);
private:
    vec2 m_gravityDirection;❶
    vector<SpringNode> m_springNodes;❷
    PositionList m_positions;❸
    IRenderingEngine* m_renderingEngine;
};

IApplicationEngine* CreateApplicationEngine
  (IRenderingEngine* renderingEngine)
{
    return new ApplicationEngine(renderingEngine);
}
```

```
ApplicationEngine::~ApplicationEngine()
{
    delete m_renderingEngine;
}

void ApplicationEngine::Initialize(int width, int height)
{
    m_renderingEngine->Initialize();
}

void ApplicationEngine::SetGravityDirection(vec2 direction)
{
    m_gravityDirection = direction;
}

void ApplicationEngine::Render() const
{
    m_renderingEngine->Render(m_positions);
}

ApplicationEngine::ApplicationEngine(IRenderingEngine* renderingEngine) :
    m_renderingEngine(renderingEngine),
    m_gravityDirection(vec2(0, -1))
{
    const int NumColumns = 10;❹
    const int NumRows = 14;
    const float SpreadFactor = 0.125f;

    m_springNodes.resize(NumColumns * NumRows);
    m_positions.resize(m_springNodes.size());

    vector<SpringNode>::iterator node = m_springNodes.begin();
    for (int r = 0; r < NumRows; ++r) {
        for (int c = 0; c < NumColumns; ++c) {

            vec2 position;
            position.x = c - (NumColumns - 1) / 2.0f;❺
            position.y = r - (NumRows - 1) / 2.0f;
            node->SetPosition(position * SpreadFactor);

            if (c > 0)
                node->AddNeighbor(&*node - 1);❻

            if (r > 0)
                node->AddNeighbor(&*node - NumColumns);❼

            ++node;
        }
    }

    m_springNodes[0].Pin();❽
    m_springNodes[NumColumns - 1].Pin();
    m_springNodes[NumColumns * NumRows - 1].Pin();
    m_springNodes[NumColumns * (NumRows - 1)].Pin();
```

```
        UpdateAnimation(0);❾
}

void ApplicationEngine::UpdateAnimation(float dt)
{
    const float GravityStrength = 0.01f;❿
    const int SimulationIterations = 10;⓫

    vector<SpringNode>::iterator node;
    vec2 force = m_gravityDirection * GravityStrength;

    for (int i = 0; i < SimulationIterations; ++i) {⓬
        for (node = m_springNodes.begin();
             node != m_springNodes.end();
             ++node)
            node->ResetForce(force);

        for (node = m_springNodes.begin();
             node != m_springNodes.end();
             ++node)
            node->ComputeForce();

        PositionList::iterator position = m_positions.begin();
        for (node = m_springNodes.begin();
             node != m_springNodes.end();
             ++node)
        {
            node->Update(dt);
            *position++ = node->GetPosition();⓭
        }
    }
}
```

❶ The `m_gravityDirection` field stores the normalized direction provided by the `GLView` layer.

❷ The `m_springNodes` vector stores the rigid bodies in the simulation.

❸ The `m_positions` vector provides a contiguous list of node positions to the rendering engine.

❹ The `NumColumns`, `NumPositions`, and `SpreadFactor` constants determine the initial layout of the star sprites.

❺ Center the grid of stars with respect to (0, 0).

❻ Add a connection to the node to the left. The `&*` prefix converts an STL iterator into a vanilla pointer.

❼ Add a connection to the above node.

❽ Pin the four corners of the net so that they don't move.

❾ Call `UpdateAnimation` once at startup to initialize the position list.

⓾ The gravity direction vector is normalized, so it needs to be scaled by the `Gravity Strength` constant before passing it in as a force vector.

⓫ As mentioned earlier, we make several passes through the simulation loop for increased precision.

⓬ The contents of this loop corresponds to pseudocode in Example 7-20.

⓭ Copy the node position into the vertex array that gets passed to the rendering engine.

OpenGL ES 1.1 Rendering Engine and Additive Blending

One difficulty you might come across with point sprites is the order-dependency problem imposed by some blending equations (flip back to the section "Blending Caveats" on page 226 to review this issue). One way to avoid this is to use additive blending. Here's how to set it up:

```
glBlendFunc(GL_SRC_ALPHA, GL_ONE);
```

This sets up the following equation:

$$\text{Final}_{\text{RGB}} = S_\alpha{}^* S_{\text{RGB}} + D_{\text{RGB}}$$

You can see how this differs from traditional blending because it can only make the framebuffer color brighter and brighter as more sprites are rendered. This produces an effect that may be desirable anyway; for example, if you're rendering fireworks with a dense cloud of point sprites, additive blending helps vary the brightness and make the scene more interesting.

Recall that the `IRenderingEngine` interface has only two methods; Example 7-24 shows the ES 1.1 implementations of these. The remainder of the file is much the same as other samples in this book. For the full source, download the code from this book's website.

Example 7-24. RenderingEngine.ES1.cpp (SpringyStars)

```
void RenderingEngine::Initialize()
{
    // Load up some textures:
    m_textures.Star = CreateTexture(Star);
    m_textures.Background = CreateTexture(_Background_pvrtc);

    // Extract width and height from the color buffer:
    ivec2 screenSize;
    glGetRenderbufferParameterivOES(GL_RENDERBUFFER_OES,
                                    GL_RENDERBUFFER_WIDTH_OES,
                                    &screenSize.x);
    glGetRenderbufferParameterivOES(GL_RENDERBUFFER_OES,
                                    GL_RENDERBUFFER_HEIGHT_OES,
                                    &screenSize.y);
```

```
    // Create the on-screen FBO:
    glGenFramebuffersOES(1, &m_framebuffers.Screen);
    glBindFramebufferOES(GL_FRAMEBUFFER_OES, m_framebuffers.Screen);
    glFramebufferRenderbufferOES(GL_FRAMEBUFFER_OES,
                                 GL_COLOR_ATTACHMENT0_OES,
                                 GL_RENDERBUFFER_OES,
                                 m_renderbuffers.Screen);

    // Set up various OpenGL state:
    glViewport(0, 0, screenSize.x, screenSize.y);
    glEnable(GL_TEXTURE_2D);
    glPointSize(15);
    glBlendFunc(GL_SRC_ALPHA, GL_ONE);

    // Set up the transforms:
    glMatrixMode(GL_PROJECTION);
    glLoadIdentity();

    const float NearPlane = 5, FarPlane = 100;
    const float Scale = 0.0005;
    glFrustumf(-Scale * screenSize.x / 2, Scale * screenSize.x / 2,
               -Scale * screenSize.y / 2, Scale * screenSize.y / 2,
               NearPlane, FarPlane);

    glMatrixMode(GL_MODELVIEW);

    vec3 eye(0, 0, 40);
    vec3 target(0, 0, 0);
    vec3 up(0, 1, 0);
    mat4 modelview = mat4::LookAt(eye, target, up);
    glLoadMatrixf(modelview.Pointer());
}

void RenderingEngine::Render(const PositionList& positions) const
{
    // Render the background:
    int backgroundRectangle[] = { 0, 0, 480, 320 };
    glTexParameteriv(GL_TEXTURE_2D,
                     GL_TEXTURE_CROP_RECT_OES,
                     backgroundRectangle);
    glBindTexture(GL_TEXTURE_2D, m_textures.Background);
    glColor4f(0.75, 0.75, 0.75, 1);
    glDrawTexfOES(0, 0, 0, 320, 480);

    // Set the state for point rendering:
    glEnable(GL_BLEND);
    glEnable(GL_POINT_SPRITE_OES);
    glTexEnvi(GL_POINT_SPRITE_OES, GL_COORD_REPLACE_OES, GL_TRUE);

    // Set up the vertex array:
    glEnableClientState(GL_VERTEX_ARRAY);
    glVertexPointer(2, GL_FLOAT, sizeof(vec2), &positions[0].x);

    // Render the point sprites:
    glBindTexture(GL_TEXTURE_2D, m_textures.Star);
```

```
    glColor4f(1, 1, 1, 1);
    glDrawArrays(GL_POINTS, 0, positions.size());

    // Restore the OpenGL state:
    glDisable(GL_BLEND);
    glDisable(GL_POINT_SPRITE_OES);
    glTexEnvi(GL_POINT_SPRITE_OES, GL_COORD_REPLACE_OES, GL_FALSE);
}
```

The only new OpenGL function in Example 7-24 is glPointSize. This sets the width
(and height) of the point sprites. OpenGL uses the current model-view matrix to determine the distance of each point sprite from the camera and shrinks the size of distant
point sprites. This effect can be abrogated like this:

```
    float params[] = { 1, 0, 0 };
    glPointParameterfv(GL_POINT_DISTANCE_ATTENUATION, params);
```

This seems rather obscure, but it has to do with how OpenGL computes the point size:

```
    actualSize = desiredSize / sqrt(p[0] + p[1] * d + p[2] * d * d)
```

In the previous formula, desiredSize is what you pass to glPointSize, d is the distance
from the camera, and p is the array of values passed to glPointParameterfv. (I've simplified this a bit by leaving out some clamping that can occur.) In my opinion, the API
designers made this a bit too complex!

 You can even vary the size of the point sprites on a per-vertex basis
through the use of the OES_point_size_array extension, which is supported on all iPhone models.

OpenGL ES 2.0 handles point size quite differently from ES 1.1, which brings us to the
next section.

Point Sprites with OpenGL ES 2.0

Before going over the C++ code for the ES 2.0 rendering engine, let's take a look at the
shaders. See Examples 7-25 and 7-26.

Example 7-25. Vertex shader (SpringyStars)

```
attribute vec4 Position;
attribute vec2 TextureCoord;

uniform mat4 Projection;
uniform mat4 Modelview;

varying vec2 TextureCoordOut;

void main(void)
{
```

```
    gl_Position = Projection * Modelview * Position;
    TextureCoordOut = TextureCoord;
    gl_PointSize = 15.0;
}
```

Example 7-26. Fragment shader (SpringyStars)

```
varying mediump vec2 TextureCoordOut;

uniform sampler2D Sampler;
uniform bool IsSprite;

void main(void)
{
    gl_FragColor = texture2D(Sampler,
                             IsSprite ? gl_PointCoord : TextureCoordOut);
}
```

You've probably noticed that all built-in variables can be recognized by their gl_ prefix. There are two new built-in variables introduced in the previous listings: gl_PointSize (written to by the vertex shader) and gl_PointCoord (fed into the fragment shader).

OpenGL ES 2.0 requires you to set up the point size from the vertex shader rather than the application code, which gives you the option to compute it dynamically; if you want, you can evaluate the same distance formula that ES 1.1 does. Or, you can do something much simpler, like what we're doing here.

The gl_PointCoord variable gives you the autocomputed texture coordinate that varies across the point sprite. That's why ES 2.0 doesn't require you to call glTexEnvi with GL_COORD_REPLACE; it's implicit in your fragment shader.

Example 7-27. RenderingEngine.ES2.cpp (SpringyStars)

```
void RenderingEngine::Initialize()
{
    // Load up some textures:
    m_textures.Star = CreateTexture(Star);
    m_textures.Background = CreateTexture(_Background_pvrtc);

    // Extract width and height from the color buffer.
    glGetRenderbufferParameteriv(GL_RENDERBUFFER,
                                 GL_RENDERBUFFER_WIDTH, &m_screenSize.x);
    glGetRenderbufferParameteriv(GL_RENDERBUFFER,
                                 GL_RENDERBUFFER_HEIGHT, &m_screenSize.y);

    // Create the on-screen FBO.
    glGenFramebuffers(1, &m_framebuffers.Screen);
    glBindFramebuffer(GL_FRAMEBUFFER, m_framebuffers.Screen);
    glFramebufferRenderbuffer(GL_FRAMEBUFFER, GL_COLOR_ATTACHMENT0,
                              GL_RENDERBUFFER, m_renderbuffers.Screen);

    // Create the GLSL program.
    GLuint program = BuildProgram(SimpleVertexShader, SimpleFragmentShader);
    glUseProgram(program);
```

```
    // Extract the handles to attributes and uniforms.
    m_attributes.Position = glGetAttribLocation(program, "Position");
    m_attributes.TextureCoord = glGetAttribLocation(program, "TextureCoord");
    m_uniforms.Projection = glGetUniformLocation(program, "Projection");
    m_uniforms.Modelview = glGetUniformLocation(program, "Modelview");
    m_uniforms.Sampler = glGetUniformLocation(program, "Sampler");
    m_uniforms.IsSprite = glGetUniformLocation(program, "IsSprite");

    // Set up various GL state.
    glViewport(0, 0, m_screenSize.x, m_screenSize.y);
    glBlendFunc(GL_SRC_ALPHA, GL_ONE);

    // Set up the transforms.
    const float NearPlane = 5, FarPlane = 100;
    const float Scale = 0.0005;
    const float HalfWidth = Scale * m_screenSize.x / 2;
    const float HalfHeight = Scale * m_screenSize.y / 2;

    mat4 projection = mat4::Frustum(-HalfWidth, HalfWidth,
                                    -HalfHeight, HalfHeight,
                                    NearPlane, FarPlane);
    glUniformMatrix4fv(m_uniforms.Projection, 1, 0, projection.Pointer());

    vec3 eye(0, 0, 40);
    vec3 target(0, 0, 0);
    vec3 up(0, 1, 0);
    mat4 modelview = mat4::LookAt(eye, target, up);
    glUniformMatrix4fv(m_uniforms.Modelview, 1, 0, modelview.Pointer());
}

void RenderingEngine::Render(const PositionList& positions) const
{

    RenderBackground();

    glBindTexture(GL_TEXTURE_2D, m_textures.Star);
    glEnableVertexAttribArray(m_attributes.Position);
    glDisableVertexAttribArray(m_attributes.TextureCoord);
    glUniform1i(m_uniforms.IsSprite, GL_TRUE);

    glVertexAttribPointer(m_attributes.Position,
                          2,
                          GL_FLOAT,
                          GL_FALSE,
                          sizeof(vec2),
                          &positions[0].x);

    glEnable(GL_BLEND);
    glDrawArrays(GL_POINTS, 0, positions.size());
    glDisable(GL_BLEND);
}
```

Wrapping Up

This chapter has shown that OpenGL is quite adept at 2D rendering, even though most developers primarily think of it as a 3D graphics API.

If you've made it this far in this book, you're more than ready to make an entry into the world of 3D iPhone programming; subsequent chapters will cover more advanced material. Recall that we gave a brief taste of multitexturing and the glTexEnv function in this chapter—we'll go over these concepts in further detail in the next chapter, along with a bevy of other advanced effects.

## CHAPTER 8

Advanced Lighting and Texturing

> *There are two kinds of light—the glow that illumines*
> *and the glare that obscures.*
>
> —James Thurber

At this point in this book, you may have written a couple simple OpenGL demos to impress your co-workers and family members. But, your app may need that extra little something to stand out from the crowd. This chapter goes over a small selection of more advanced techniques that can give your app an extra oomph.

The selection of effects dealt with in this chapter is by no means comprehensive. I encourage you to check out other graphics books, blogs, and academic papers to learn additional ways of dazzling your users. For example, this book does not cover rendering shadows; there are too many techniques for rendering shadows (or crude approximations thereof), so I can't cover them while keeping this book concise. But, there's plenty of information out there, and now that you know the fundamentals, it won't be difficult to digest it.

This chapter starts off by detailing some of the more obscure texturing functionality in OpenGL ES 1.1. In a way, some of these features—specifically *texture combiners*, which allow textures to be combined in a variety of ways—are powerful enough to serve as a substitute for very simple fragment shaders.

The chapter goes on to cover normal maps and DOT3 lighting, useful for increasing the amount of perceived detail in your 3D models. (DOT3 simply refers to a three-component dot product; despite appearances, it's not an acronym.) Next we discuss a technique for creating reflective surfaces that employs a special *cube map* texture, supported only in ES 2.0. We'll then briefly cover anisotropic texturing, which improves texturing quality in some cases. Finally, we'll go over an image-processing technique that adds a soft glow to the scene called *bloom*. The bloom effect may remind you of a camera technique used in cheesy 1980s soap operas, and I claim no responsibility if it compels you to marry your nephew in order to secure financial assistance for your father's ex-lover.

Texture Environments under OpenGL ES 1.1

Multitexturing was briefly introduced in the previous chapter ("Image Composition and a Taste of Multitexturing" on page 308), but there's a lot more to explain. See Figure 8-1 for a high-level overview of the iPhone's texturing capabilities.

 This section doesn't have much in the way of example code; if you're not interested in the details of texture combination under OpenGL ES 1.1, skip to the next section ("Bump Mapping and DOT3 Lighting" on page 335).

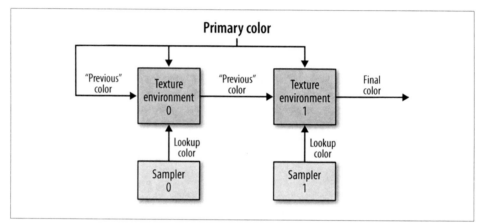

Figure 8-1. Texture pipeline for OpenGL ES 1.1

Here are a few disclaimers regarding Figure 8-1. First, the diagram assumes that both texture stages are enabled; if stage 1 is disabled, the "previous color" gets passed on to become the "final color." Second, the diagram shows only two texture stages. This is accurate for first- and second-generation devices, but newer devices have eight texture units.

In Figure 8-1, the "primary" color comes from the interpolation of per-vertex colors. Per-vertex colors are produced by lighting or set directly from the application using `glColor4f` or `GL_COLOR_ARRAY`.

The two *lookup colors* are the postfiltered texel colors, sampled from a particular texture image.

Each of the two *texture environments* is configured to combine its various inputs and produce an output color. The default configuration is *modulation*, which was briefly mentioned in Chapter 5; this means that the output color results from a per-component multiply of the previous color with the lookup color.

There are a whole slew of ways to configure each texture environment using the glTexEnv function. In my opinion, this is the worst function in OpenGL, and I'm thankful that it doesn't exist in OpenGL ES 2.0. The expressiveness afforded by GLSL makes glTexEnv unnecessary.

glTexEnv has the following prototypes:

```
void glTexEnvi(GLenum target, GLenum pname, GLint param);
void glTexEnviv(GLenum target, GLenum pname, const GLint* params);
void glTexEnvf(GLenum target, GLenum pname, GLfloat param);
void glTexEnvfv(GLenum target, GLenum pname, const GLfloat* params);
```

 There are actually a couple more variants for fixed-point math, but I've omitted them since there's never any reason to use fixed-point math on the iPhone. Because of its chip architecture, fixed-point numbers require more processing than floats.

The first parameter, target, is always set to GL_TEXTURE_ENV, unless you're enabling point sprites as described in "Rendering Confetti, Fireworks, and More: Point Sprites" on page 313. The second parameter, pname, can be any of the following:

GL_TEXTURE_ENV_COLOR
Sets the constant color. As you'll see later, this used only if the mode is GL_BLEND or GL_COMBINE.

GL_COMBINE_RGB
Sets up a configurable equation for the RGB component of color. Legal values of param are discussed later.

GL_COMBINE_ALPHA
Sets up a configurable equation for the alpha component of color. Legal values of param are discussed later.

GL_RGB_SCALE
Sets optional scale on the RGB components that takes place after all other operations. Scale can be 1, 2, or 4.

GL_ALPHA_SCALE
Sets optional scale on the alpha component that takes place after all other operations. Scale can be 1, 2, or 4.

GL_TEXTURE_ENV_MODE
Sets the mode of the current texture environment; the legal values of param are shown next.

If pname is GL_TEXTURE_ENV_MODE, then param can be any of the following:

GL_REPLACE
Set the output color equal to the lookup color:

```
OutputColor = LookupColor
```

GL_MODULATE

This is the default mode; it simply does a per-component multiply of the lookup color with the previous color:

```
OutputColor = LookupColor * PreviousColor
```

GL_DECAL

Use the alpha value of the lookup color to overlay it with the previous color. Specifically:

```
OutputColor = PreviousColor * (1 - LookupAlpha) + LookupColor * LookupAlpha
```

GL_BLEND

Invert the lookup color, then modulate it with the previous color, and then add the result to a scaled lookup color:

```
OutputColor = PreviousColor * (1 - LookupColor) + LookupColor * ConstantColor
```

GL_ADD

Use per-component addition to combine the previous color with the lookup color:

```
OutputColor = PreviousColor + LookupColor
```

GL_COMBINE

Generate the RGB outputs in the manner configured by GL_COMBINE_RGB, and generate the alpha output in the manner configured by GL_COMBINE_ALPHA.

The two texture stages need not have the same mode. For example, the following snippet sets the first texture environment to GL_REPLACE and the second environment to GL_MODULATE:

```
glActiveTexture(GL_TEXTURE0);
glEnable(GL_TEXTURE_2D);
glBindTexture(GL_TEXTURE_2D, myFirstTextureObject);
glTexEnvi(GL_TEXTURE_ENV, GL_TEXTURE_ENV_MODE, GL_REPLACE);

glActiveTexture(GL_TEXTURE1);
glEnable(GL_TEXTURE_2D);
glBindTexture(GL_TEXTURE_2D, mySecondTextureObject);
glTexEnvi(GL_TEXTURE_ENV, GL_TEXTURE_ENV_MODE, GL_MODULATE);
```

Texture Combiners

If the mode is set to GL_COMBINE, you can set up two types of combiners: the *RGB combiner* and the *alpha combiner*. The former sets up the output color's RGB components; the latter configures its alpha value.

Each of the two combiners needs to be set up using at least five additional (!) calls to glTexEnv. One call chooses the arithmetic operation (addition, subtraction, and so on), while the other four calls set up the arguments to the operation. For example, here's how you can set up the RGB combiner of texture stage 0:

```
glActiveTexture(GL_TEXTURE0);
glEnable(GL_TEXTURE_2D);
glBindTexture(GL_TEXTURE_2D, myTextureObject);
glTexEnvi(GL_TEXTURE_ENV, GL_TEXTURE_ENV_MODE, GL_COMBINE);

// Tell OpenGL which arithmetic operation to use:
glTexEnvi(GL_TEXTURE_ENV, GL_COMBINE_RGB, <operation>);

// Set the first argument:
glTexEnvi(GL_TEXTURE_ENV, GL_SRC0_RGB, <source0>);
glTexEnvi(GL_TEXTURE_ENV, GL_OPERAND0_RGB, <operand0>);

// Set the second argument:
glTexEnvi(GL_TEXTURE_ENV, GL_SRC1_RGB, <source1>);
glTexEnvi(GL_TEXTURE_ENV, GL_OPERAND1_RGB, <operand1>);
```

Setting the alpha combiner is done in the same way; just swap the *RGB* suffix with *ALPHA*, like this:

```
// Tell OpenGL which arithmetic operation to use:
glTexEnvi(GL_TEXTURE_ENV, GL_COMBINE_ALPHA, <operation>);

// Set the first argument:
glTexEnvi(GL_TEXTURE_ENV, GL_SRC0_ALPHA, <source0>);
glTexEnvi(GL_TEXTURE_ENV, GL_OPERAND0_ALPHA, <operand0>);

// Set the second argument:
glTexEnvi(GL_TEXTURE_ENV, GL_SRC1_ALPHA, <source1>);
glTexEnvi(GL_TEXTURE_ENV, GL_OPERAND1_ALPHA, <operand1>);
```

The following is the list of arithmetic operations you can use for RGB combiners (in other words, the legal values of *<operation>* when pname is set to GL_COMBINE_RGB):

GL_REPLACE

```
OutputColor = Arg0
```

GL_MODULATE

```
OutputColor = Arg0 * Arg1
```

GL_ADD

```
OutputColor = Arg0 + Arg1
```

GL_ADD_SIGNED

```
OutputColor = Arg0 + Arg1 - 0.5
```

GL_INTERPOLATE

```
OutputColor = Arg0 * Arg2 + Arg1 * (1 - Arg2)
```

GL_SUBTRACT

```
OutputColor = Arg0 - Arg1
```

GL_DOT3_RGB

> OutputColor = 4 * Dot(Arg0 - H, Arg1 - H) where H = (0.5, 0.5, 0.5)

GL_DOT3_RGBA

> OutputColor = 4 * Dot(Arg0 - H, Arg1 - H) where H = (0.5, 0.5, 0.5)

Note that GL_DOT3_RGB and GL_DOT3_RGBA produce a scalar rather than a vector. With GL_DOT3_RGB, that scalar is duplicated into each of the three RGB channels of the output color, leaving alpha untouched. With GL_DOT3_RGBA, the resulting scalar is written out to all four color components. The dot product combiners may seem rather strange, but you'll see how they come in handy in the next section.

GL_INTERPOLATE actually has *three* arguments. As you'd expect, setting up the third argument works the same way as setting up the others; you use GL_SRC2_RGB and GL_OPER AND2_RGB.

For alpha combiners (GL_COMBINE_ALPHA), the list of legal arithmetic operations is the same as RGB combiners, except that the two dot-product operations are not supported.

The *<source>* arguments in the preceding code snippet can be any of the following:

GL_TEXTURE
> Use the lookup color.

GL_CONSTANT
> Use the constant color that's set with GL_TEXTURE_ENV_COLOR.

GL_PRIMARY_COLOR
> Use the primary color (this is the color that comes from lighting or **glColor4f**).

GL_PREVIOUS
> Use the output of the previous texture stage. For stage 0, this is equivalent to GL_PRIMARY_COLOR.

For RGB combiners, the *<operand>* arguments can be any of the following:

GL_SRC_COLOR
> Pull the RGB components from the source color.

GL_ONE_MINUS_SRC_COLOR
> Use the inverted RGB components from the source color.

GL_SRC_ALPHA
> Pull the alpha component from the source color.

GL_ONE_MINUS_SRC_ALPHA
> Use the inverted alpha component from the source color.

For alpha combiners, only the last two of the preceding list can be used.

By now, you can see that combiners effectively allow you to set up a set of equations, which is something that's much easier to express with a shading language!

All the different ways of calling `glTexEnv` are a bit confusing, so I think it's best to go over a specific example in detail; we'll do just that in the next section, with an in-depth explanation of the DOT3 texture combiner and its equivalent in GLSL.

Bump Mapping and DOT3 Lighting

If you'd like to render an object with fine surface detail but you don't want to use an incredibly dense mesh of triangles, there's a technique called *bump mapping* that fits the bill. It's also called *normal mapping*, since it works by varying the surface normals to affect the lighting. You can use this technique to create more than mere bumps; grooves or other patterns can be etched into (or raised from) a surface. Remember, a good graphics programmer thinks like a politician and uses lies to her advantage! Normal mapping doesn't actually affect the geometry at all. This is apparent when you look along the silhouette of a normal-mapped object; it appears flat. See Figure 8-2.

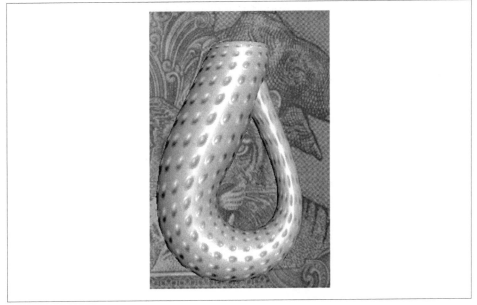

Figure 8-2. Bumpy demo with OpenGL ES 2.0

You can achieve this effect with either OpenGL ES 2.0 or OpenGL ES 1.1, although bump mapping under 1.1 is much more limited.

Either approach requires the use of a *normal map*, which is a texture that contains normal vectors (XYZ components) rather than colors (RGB components). Since color components are, by definition, non-negative, a conversion needs to occur to represent a vector as a color:

```
vec3 TransformedVector = (OriginalVector + vec3(1, 1, 1)) / 2
```

The previous transformation simply changes the range of each component from [−1, +1] to [0, +1].

Representing vectors as colors can sometimes cause problems because of relatively poor precision in the texture format. On some platforms, you can work around this with a high-precision texture format. At the time of this writing, the iPhone does not support high-precision formats, but I find that standard 8-bit precision is good enough in most scenarios.

 Another way to achieve bump mapping with shaders is to cast aside the normal map and opt for a procedural approach. This means doing some fancy math in your shader. While procedural bump mapping is fine for simple patterns, it precludes artist-generated content.

There are a number of ways to generate a normal map. Often an artist will create a *height map*, which is a grayscale image where intensity represents surface displacement. The height map is then fed into a tool that builds a terrain from which the surface normals can be extracted (conceptually speaking).

PVRTexTool (see "The PowerVR SDK and Low-Precision Textures" on page 198) is such a tool. If you invoke it from a terminal window, simply add -b to the command line, and it generates a normal map. Other popular tools include Ryan Clark's crazybump application and NVIDIA's Melody, but neither of these is supported on Mac OS X at the time of this writing. For professional artists, Pixologic's Z-Brush is probably the most sought-after tool for normal map creation (and yes, it's Mac-friendly). For an example of a height map and its resulting normal map, see the left two panels in Figure 8-3.

An important factor to consider with normal maps is the "space" that they live in. Here's a brief recap from Chapter 2 concerning the early life of a vertex:

1. Vertex positions are stored in a VBO (or vertex array) in *object space*.
2. Objects are placed into the scene using a *model matrix*, which takes them into *world space*.
3. The vertices are then transformed by a *view matrix*, which takes them into *eye space*.

For bog standard lighting (not bump mapped), normals are sent to OpenGL in object space. However, the normal maps that get generated by tools like crazybump are defined in *tangent space* (also known as *surface local space*). Tangent space is the 2D universe that textures live in; if you were to somehow "unfold" your object and lay it flat on a table, you'd see what tangent space looks like.

Another tidbit to remember from an earlier chapter is that OpenGL takes object-space normals and transforms them into eye space using the inverse-transpose of the model-view matrix ("Normal Transforms Aren't Normal" on page 131). Here's the kicker:

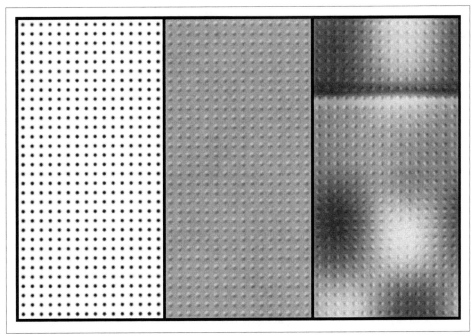

Figure 8-3. Left two panels: height map and tangent-space normals; right panel: object-space normals for the Klein bottle

transformation of the normal vector can actually be skipped in certain circumstances. If your light source is infinitely distant, you can simply perform the lighting in object space! Sure, the lighting is a bit less realistic, but when has that stopped us?

So, normal maps are (normally) defined in tangent space, but lighting is (normally) performed in eye space or object space. How do we handle this discrepancy? With OpenGL ES 2.0, we can revise the lighting shader so that it transforms the normals from tangent space to object space. With OpenGL ES 1.1, we'll need to transform the normal map itself, as depicted in the rightmost panel in Figure 8-3. More on this later; first we'll go over the shader-based approach since it can give you a better understanding of what's going on.

Another Foray into Linear Algebra

Before writing any code, we need to figure out how the shader should go about transforming the normals from tangent space to object space. In general, we've been using matrices to make transformations like this. How can we come up with the right magical matrix?

Any coordinate system can be defined with a set of *basis vectors*. The set is often simply called a *basis*. The formal definition of *basis* involves phrases like "linearly independent spanning set," but I don't want you to run away in abject terror, so I'll just give an example.

For 3D space, we need three basis vectors, one for each axis. The *standard basis* is the space that defines the Cartesian coordinate system that we all know and love:

- Basis Vector A: $(1, 0, 0)$
- Basis Vector B: $(0, 1, 0)$
- Basis Vector C: $(0, 0, 1)$

Any set of unit-length vectors that are all perpendicular to each other is said to be *orthonormal*. Turns out that there's an elegant way to transform a vector from any orthonormal basis to the standard basis. All you need to do is create a matrix by filling in each row with a basis vector:

$$\mathbf{v}' = (v_x \ v_y \ v_z) * \begin{pmatrix} \mathbf{A}_x & \mathbf{A}_y & \mathbf{A}_z \\ \mathbf{B}_x & \mathbf{B}_y & \mathbf{B}_z \\ \mathbf{C}_x & \mathbf{C}_y & \mathbf{C}_z \end{pmatrix}$$

If you prefer column-vector notation, then the basis vectors form columns rather than rows:

$$\mathbf{v}' = \begin{pmatrix} \mathbf{A}_x & \mathbf{B}_x & \mathbf{C}_x \\ \mathbf{A}_y & \mathbf{B}_y & \mathbf{C}_y \\ \mathbf{A}_z & \mathbf{B}_z & \mathbf{C}_z \end{pmatrix} * \begin{pmatrix} v_x \\ v_y \\ v_z \end{pmatrix}$$

In any case, we now have the magic matrix for transforming normals! Incidentally, basis vectors can also be used to derive a matrix for general rotation around an arbitrary axis. Basis vectors are so foundational to linear algebra that mathematicians are undoubtedly scoffing at me for not covering them much earlier. I wanted to wait until a practical application cropped up—which brings us back to bump mapping.

Generating Basis Vectors

So, our bump mapping shader will need three basis vectors to transform the normal map's values from tangent space to object space. Where can we get these three basis vectors? Recall for a moment the ParametricSurface class that was introduced early in this book. In "The Math Behind Normals" on page 129, the following pseudocode was presented:

```
p = Evaluate(s, t)
u = Evaluate(s + ds, t) - p
v = Evaluate(s, t + dt) - p
n = Normalize(u × v)
```

The three vectors **u**, **v**, and **n** are all perpendicular to each other—perfect for forming an orthonormal basis! The `ParametricSurface` class already computes **n** for us, so all we need to do is amend it to write out one of the tangent vectors. Either **u** or **v** will work fine; there's no need to send both because the shader can easily compute the third basis vector using a cross product. Take a look at Example 8-1; for a baseline, this uses the parametric surface code that was first introduced in Chapter 3 and enhanced in subsequent chapters. New lines are highlighted in bold.

Example 8-1. Tangent support in ParametricSurface.hpp

```
void ParametricSurface::GenerateVertices(vector<float>& vertices,
                                         unsigned char flags) const
{
    int floatsPerVertex = 3;
    if (flags & VertexFlagsNormals)
        floatsPerVertex += 3;
    if (flags & VertexFlagsTexCoords)
        floatsPerVertex += 2;
    if (flags & VertexFlagsTangents)
        floatsPerVertex += 3;

    vertices.resize(GetVertexCount() * floatsPerVertex);
    float* attribute = &vertices[0];

    for (int j = 0; j < m_divisions.y; j++) {
        for (int i = 0; i < m_divisions.x; i++) {

            // Compute Position
            vec2 domain = ComputeDomain(i, j);
            vec3 range = Evaluate(domain);
            attribute = range.Write(attribute);

            // Compute Normal
            if (flags & VertexFlagsNormals) {
                ...
            }

            // Compute Texture Coordinates
            if (flags & VertexFlagsTexCoords) {
                ...
            }

            // Compute Tangent
            if (flags & VertexFlagsTangents) {
                float s = i, t = j;
                vec3 p = Evaluate(ComputeDomain(s, t));
                vec3 u = Evaluate(ComputeDomain(s + 0.01f, t)) - p;
                if (InvertNormal(domain))
                    u = -u;
                attribute = u.Write(attribute);
            }
        }
    }
}
```

Normal Mapping with OpenGL ES 2.0

Let's crack some knuckles and write some shaders. A good starting point is the pair of shaders we used for pixel-based lighting in Chapter 4. I've repeated them here (Example 8-2), with uniform declarations omitted for brevity.

Example 8-2. Per-pixel lighting vertex and fragment shaders

```
attribute vec4 Position;
attribute vec3 Normal;

varying mediump vec3 EyespaceNormal;

// Vertex Shader
void main(void)
{
    EyespaceNormal = NormalMatrix * Normal;
    gl_Position = Projection * Modelview * Position;
}

// Fragment Shader
void main(void)
{
    highp vec3 N = normalize(EyespaceNormal);
    highp vec3 L = LightVector;
    highp vec3 E = EyeVector;
    highp vec3 H = normalize(L + E);
    highp float df = max(0.0, dot(N, L));
    highp float sf = max(0.0, dot(N, H));
    sf = pow(sf, Shininess);

    lowp vec3 color = AmbientMaterial + df
      * DiffuseMaterial + sf * SpecularMaterial;
    gl_FragColor = vec4(color, 1);
}
```

To extend this to support bump mapping, we'll need to add new attributes for the tangent vector and texture coordinates. The vertex shader doesn't need to transform them; we can leave that up to the pixel shader. See Example 8-3.

Example 8-3. Vertex shader for the Bumpy sample

```
attribute vec4 Position;
attribute vec3 Normal;
attribute vec3 Tangent;
attribute vec2 TextureCoordIn;

uniform mat4 Projection;
uniform mat4 Modelview;

varying vec2 TextureCoord;
varying vec3 ObjectSpaceNormal;
varying vec3 ObjectSpaceTangent;
```

```
void main(void)
{
    ObjectSpaceNormal = Normal;
    ObjectSpaceTangent = Tangent;
    gl_Position = Projection * Modelview * Position;
    TextureCoord = TextureCoordIn;
}
```

Before diving into the fragment shader, let's review what we'll be doing:

1. Extract a perturbed normal from the normal map, transforming it from [0, +1] to [−1, +1].

2. Create three basis vectors using the normal and tangent vectors that were passed in from the vertex shader.

3. Perform a change of basis on the perturbed normal to bring it to object space.

4. Execute the same lighting algorithm that we've used in the past, but use the perturbed normal.

Now we're ready! See Example 8-4.

 When computing tangentSpaceNormal, you might need to swap the normal map's x and y components, just like we did in Example 8-4. This may or may not be necessary, depending on the coordinate system used by your normal map generation tool.

Example 8-4. Fragment shader for the Bumpy sample

```
varying mediump vec2 TextureCoord;
varying mediump vec3 ObjectSpaceNormal;
varying mediump vec3 ObjectSpaceTangent;

uniform highp vec3 AmbientMaterial;
uniform highp vec3 DiffuseMaterial;
uniform highp vec3 SpecularMaterial;
uniform highp float Shininess;
uniform highp vec3 LightVector;
uniform highp vec3 EyeVector;

uniform sampler2D Sampler;

void main(void)
{
    // Extract the perturbed normal from the texture:
    highp vec3 tangentSpaceNormal =
      texture2D(Sampler, TextureCoord).yxz * 2.0 - 1.0;

    // Create a set of basis vectors:
    highp vec3 n = normalize(ObjectSpaceNormal);
    highp vec3 t = normalize(ObjectSpaceTangent);
    highp vec3 b = normalize(cross(n, t));
```

```
    // Change the perturbed normal from tangent space to object space:
    highp mat3 basis = mat3(n, t, b);
    highp vec3 N = basis * tangentSpaceNormal;

    // Perform standard lighting math:
    highp vec3 L = LightVector;
    highp vec3 E = EyeVector;
    highp vec3 H = normalize(L + E);
    highp float df = max(0.0, dot(N, L));
    highp float sf = max(0.0, dot(N, H));
    sf = pow(sf, Shininess);

    lowp vec3 color = AmbientMaterial + df
      * DiffuseMaterial + sf * SpecularMaterial;
    gl_FragColor = vec4(color, 1);
}
```

We're not done just yet, though—since the lighting math operates on a normal vector that lives in object space, the `LightVector` and `EyeVector` uniforms that we pass in from the application need to be in object space too. To transform them from world space to object space, we can simply multiply them by the model matrix using our C++ vector library. Take care not to confuse the model matrix with the model-view matrix; see Example 8-5.

Example 8-5. Render() method for the Bumpy sample (OpenGL ES 2.0)

```
void RenderingEngine::Render(float theta) const
{
    // Render the background image:
    ...

    const float distance = 10;
    const vec3 target(0, 0, 0);
    const vec3 up(0, 1, 0);
    const vec3 eye = vec3(0, 0, distance);
    const vec3 view = mat4::LookAt(eye, target, up);
    const mat4 model = mat4::RotateY(theta);
    const mat4 modelview = model * view;

    const vec4 lightWorldSpace = vec4(0, 0, 1, 1);
    const vec4 lightObjectSpace = model * lightWorldSpace;

    const vec4 eyeWorldSpace(0, 0, 1, 1);
    const vec4 eyeObjectSpace = model * eyeWorldSpace;

    glUseProgram(m_bump.Program);
    glUniform3fv(m_bump.Uniforms.LightVector, 1,
                 lightObjectSpace.Pointer());
    glUniform3fv(m_bump.Uniforms.EyeVector, 1, eyeObjectSpace.Pointer());
    glUniformMatrix4fv(m_bump.Uniforms.Modelview, 1,
                       0, modelview.Pointer());
    glBindTexture(GL_TEXTURE_2D, m_textures.TangentSpaceNormals);
```

```
// Render the Klein bottle:
...
}
```

Normal Mapping with OpenGL ES 1.1

You might be wondering why we used object-space lighting for shader-based bump mapping, rather than eye-space lighting. After all, eye-space lighting is what was presented way back in Chapter 4 as the "standard" approach. It's actually fine to perform bump map lighting in eye space, but I wanted to segue to the fixed-function approach, which *does* require object space!

 Another potential benefit to lighting in object space is performance. I'll discuss this more in the next chapter.

Earlier in the chapter, I briefly mentioned that OpenGL ES 1.1 requires the normal map itself to be transformed to object space (depicted in the far-right panel in Figure 8-3). If it were transformed it to eye space, then we'd have to create a brand new normal map every time the camera moves. Not exactly practical!

The secret to bump mapping with fixed-function hardware lies in a special texture combiner operation called GL_DOT3_RGB. This technique is often simply known as *DOT3 lighting*. The basic idea is to have the texture combiner generate a gray color whose intensity is determined by the dot product of its two operands. This is sufficient for simple diffuse lighting, although it can't produce specular highlights. See Figure 8-4 for a screenshot of the Bumpy app with OpenGL ES 1.1.

Here's the sequence of glTexEnv calls that sets up the texturing state used to generate Figure 8-4:

```
glTexEnvi(GL_TEXTURE_ENV, GL_TEXTURE_ENV_MODE, GL_COMBINE);
glTexEnvi(GL_TEXTURE_ENV, GL_COMBINE_RGB, GL_DOT3_RGB);
glTexEnvi(GL_TEXTURE_ENV, GL_SRC0_RGB, GL_PRIMARY_COLOR);
glTexEnvi(GL_TEXTURE_ENV, GL_OPERAND0_RGB, GL_SRC_COLOR);
glTexEnvi(GL_TEXTURE_ENV, GL_SRC1_RGB, GL_TEXTURE);
glTexEnvi(GL_TEXTURE_ENV, GL_OPERAND1_RGB, GL_SRC_COLOR);
```

The previous code snippet tells OpenGL to set up an equation like this:

$$L = 4 * (\mathbf{C} - \mathbf{H}) \bullet (\mathbf{T} - \mathbf{H})$$

Where:

- $\mathbf{C}$ is the per-vertex color, set with glColor4f. This represents the light direction.
- $\mathbf{T}$ is the texel color. This represents the perturbed normal.
- L is the luminance value of the final color. This represents the diffuse factor.

- **H** is (½, ½, ½).

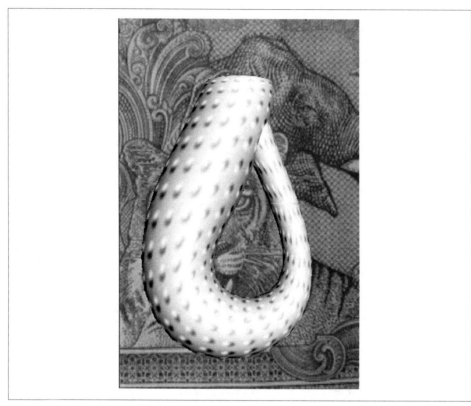

Figure 8-4. Bumpy app with OpenGL ES 1.1

Curious about the **H** offset and the final multiply-by-four? Remember, we had to transform our normal vectors from unit space to color space:

```
vec3 TransformedVector = (OriginalVector + vec3(1, 1, 1)) / 2
```

The **H** offset and multiply-by-four simply puts the final result back into unit space. Since this assumes that *both* vectors have been transformed in the previous manner, take care to transform the light position. Here's the relevant snippet of application code, once again leveraging our C++ vector library:

```
vec4 lightWorldSpace = vec4(0, 0, 1, 0);
vec4 lightObjectSpace = modelMatrix * lightWorldSpace;
lightObjectSpace = (lightObjectSpace + vec4(1, 1, 1, 0)) * 0.5f;

glColor4f(lightObjectSpace.x,
          lightObjectSpace.y,
          lightObjectSpace.z, 1);
```

The result from DOT3 lighting is often modulated with a second texture stage to produce a final color that's nongray. Note that DOT3 lighting is basically performing per-pixel lighting but without the use of shaders!

Generating Object-Space Normal Maps

Perhaps the most awkward aspect of DOT3 lighting is that it requires you to somehow create a normal map in object space. Some generator tools don't know what your actual geometry looks like; these tools take only a simple heightfield for input, so they can generate the normals only in tangent space.

The trick I used for the Klein bottle was to use OpenGL ES 2.0 as part of my "art pipeline," even though the final application used only OpenGL ES 1.1. By running a modified version of the OpenGL ES 2.0 demo and taking a screenshot, I obtained an object-space normal map for the Klein bottle. See Figure 8-5.

Figure 8-5. Object space normals (before cropping)

Examples 8-6 and 8-7 show the shaders for this. Note that the vertex shader ignores the model-view matrix and the incoming vertex position. It instead uses the incoming texture coordinate to determine the final vertex position. This effectively "unfolds" the object. The Distance, Scale, and Offset constants are used to center the image on the screen. (I also had to do some cropping and scaling on the final image to make it have power-of-two dimensions.)

Example 8-6. Vertex shader for the object-space generator

```
attribute vec3 Normal;
attribute vec3 Tangent;
attribute vec2 TextureCoordIn;

uniform mat4 Projection;

varying vec2 TextureCoord;
varying vec3 ObjectSpaceNormal;
varying vec3 ObjectSpaceTangent;

const float Distance = 10.0;
const vec2 Offset = vec2(0.5, 0.5);
const vec2 Scale = vec2(2.0, 4.0);

void main(void)
{
    ObjectSpaceNormal = Normal;
    ObjectSpaceTangent = Tangent;

    vec4 v = vec4(TextureCoordIn - Offset, -Distance, 1);
    gl_Position = Projection * v;
    gl_Position.xy *= Scale;

    TextureCoord = TextureCoordIn;
}
```

The fragment shader is essentially the same as what was presented in "Normal Mapping with OpenGL ES 2.0" on page 340, but without the lighting math.

Example 8-7. Fragment shader for the object-space generator

```
varying mediump vec2 TextureCoord;
varying mediump vec3 ObjectSpaceNormal;
varying mediump vec3 ObjectSpaceTangent;

uniform sampler2D Sampler;

void main(void)
{
    // Extract the perturbed normal from the texture:
    highp vec3 tangentSpaceNormal =
      texture2D(Sampler, TextureCoord).yxz * 2.0 - 1.0;

    // Create a set of basis vectors:
    highp vec3 n = normalize(ObjectSpaceNormal);
    highp vec3 t = normalize(ObjectSpaceTangent);
    highp vec3 b = normalize(cross(n, t));
```

```
    // Change the perturbed normal from tangent space to object space:
    highp mat3 basis = mat3(n, t, b);
    highp vec3 N = basis * tangentSpaceNormal;

    // Transform the normal from unit space to color space:
    gl_FragColor = vec4((N + 1.0) * 0.5, 1);
}
```

Reflections with Cube Maps

You might recall a technique presented in Chapter 6, where we rendered an upside-down object to simulate reflection. This was sufficient for reflecting a limited number of objects onto a flat plane, but if you'd like the surface of a 3D object to reflect a richly detailed environment, as shown in Figure 8-6, a cube map is required. Cube maps are special textures composed from six individual images: one for each of the six axis-aligned directions in 3D space. Cube maps are supported only in OpenGL ES 2.0.

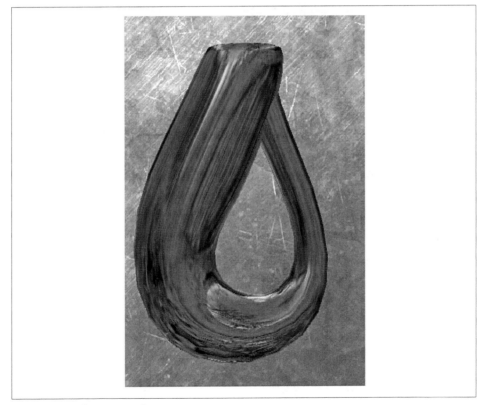

Figure 8-6. Reflection sample

Cube maps are often visualized using a cross shape that looks like an unfolded box, as shown in Figure 8-7.

Figure 8-7. Cube map cross of the Minnehaha Falls (courtesy of Edward Fink)

The cross shape is for the benefit of humans only; OpenGL does expect it when you give it the image data for a cube map. Rather, it requires you to upload each of the six faces individually, like this:

```
glTexImage2D(GL_TEXTURE_CUBE_MAP_POSITIVE_X, mip, format,
          w, h, 0, format, type, data[0]);
glTexImage2D(GL_TEXTURE_CUBE_MAP_NEGATIVE_X, mip, format,
          w, h, 0, format, type, data[1]);
glTexImage2D(GL_TEXTURE_CUBE_MAP_POSITIVE_Y, mip, format,
          w, h, 0, format, type, data[2]);
glTexImage2D(GL_TEXTURE_CUBE_MAP_NEGATIVE_Y, mip, format,
          w, h, 0, format, type, data[3]);
glTexImage2D(GL_TEXTURE_CUBE_MAP_POSITIVE_Z, mip, format,
          w, h, 0, format, type, data[4]);
glTexImage2D(GL_TEXTURE_CUBE_MAP_NEGATIVE_Z, mip, format,
          w, h, 0, format, type, data[5]);
```

Note that, for the first time, we're using a texture target other than GL_TEXTURE_2D. This can be a bit confusing because the function call name still has the 2D suffix. It helps to think of each face as being 2D, although the texture object itself is not.

The enumerants for the six faces have contiguous values, so it's more common to upload the faces of a cube map using a loop. For an example of this, see Example 8-8, which creates and populates a complete mipmapped cube map.

Example 8-8. CreateCubemap function

```
GLuint CreateCubemap(GLvoid** faceData, int size, GLenum format, GLenum type)
{
    GLuint textureObject;
    glGenTextures(1, &textureObject);
    glBindTexture(GL_TEXTURE_CUBE_MAP, textureObject);
    for (int f = 0; f < 6; ++f) {
        GLenum face = GL_TEXTURE_CUBE_MAP_POSITIVE_X + f;
        glTexImage2D(face, 0, format, size, size, 0, format, type, faceData[f]);
    }
    glTexParameteri(GL_TEXTURE_CUBE_MAP,
                    GL_TEXTURE_MIN_FILTER,
                    GL_LINEAR_MIPMAP_LINEAR);
    glTexParameteri(GL_TEXTURE_CUBE_MAP, GL_TEXTURE_MAG_FILTER, GL_LINEAR);
    glGenerateMipmap(GL_TEXTURE_CUBE_MAP);
    return textureObject;
}
```

Example 8-8 is part of the rendering engine in a sample app in this book's downloadable source code (see "How to Contact Us" on page xvii).

In Example 8-8, the passed-in **size** parameter is the width (or height) of each cube map face. Cube map faces must be square. Additionally, on the iPhone, they must have a size that's a power-of-two.

Example 8-9 shows the vertex shader that can be used for cube map reflection.

Example 8-9. Vertex shader (cube map sample)

```
attribute vec4 Position;
attribute vec3 Normal;

uniform mat4 Projection;
uniform mat4 Modelview;
uniform mat3 Model;
uniform vec3  EyePosition;

varying vec3 ReflectDir;

void main(void)
{
    gl_Position = Projection * Modelview * Position;

    // Compute eye direction in object space:
    mediump vec3 eyeDir = normalize(Position.xyz - EyePosition);
```

```
    // Reflect eye direction over normal and transform to world space:
    ReflectDir = Model * reflect(eyeDir, Normal);
}
```

Newly introduced in Example 8-9 is GLSL's built-in `reflect` function, which is defined like this:

```
float reflect(float I, float N)
{
    return I - 2.0 * dot(N, I) * N;
}
```

N is the surface normal; I is the *incident vector*, which is the vector that strikes the surface at the point of interest (see Figure 8-8).

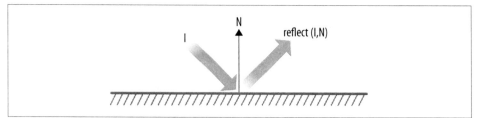

Figure 8-8. The GLSL "reflect" function

 Cube maps can also be used for refraction, which is useful for creating glass or other transparent media. GLSL provides a `refract` function to help with this.

The fragment shader for our cube mapping example is fairly simple; see Example 8-10.

Example 8-10. Fragment shader (cube map sample)

```
varying mediump vec3 ReflectDir;

uniform samplerCube Sampler;

void main(void)
{
    gl_FragColor = textureCube(Sampler, ReflectDir);
}
```

Newly introduced in Example 8-10 is a new uniform type called `samplerCube`. Full-blown desktop OpenGL has many sampler types, but the only two sampler types supported on the iPhone are `samplerCube` and `sampler2D`. Remember, when setting a sampler from within your application, set it to the stage index, not the texture handle!

The sampler function in Example 8-10 is also new: `textureCube` differs from `texture2D` in that it takes a `vec3` texture coordinate rather than a `vec2`. You can think of it as a direction vector emanating from the center of a cube. OpenGL finds which of the three components have the largest magnitude and uses that to determine which face to sample from.

A common gotcha with cube maps is incorrect face orientation. I find that the best way to test for this issue is to render a sphere with a simplified version of the vertex shader that does not perform true reflection:

```
//ReflectDir = Model * reflect(eyeDir, Normal);
ReflectDir = Model * Position.xyz; // Test the face orientation.
```

Using this technique, you'll easily notice seams if one of your cube map faces needs to be flipped, as shown on the left in Figure 8-9. Note that only five faces are visible at a time, so I suggest testing with a negated Position vector as well.

Figure 8-9. From left to right: incorrect face orientation, corrected faces, corrected faces with reflection

Render to Cube Map

Instead of using a presupplied cube map texture, it's possible to generate a cube map texture in real time from the 3D scene itself. This can be done by rerendering the scene six different times, each time using a different model-view matrix. Recall the function call that attached an FBO to a texture, first presented in "A Super Simple Sample App for Supersampling" on page 239:

```
GLenum attachment = GL_COLOR_ATTACHMENT0;
GLenum textureTarget = GL_TEXTURE_2D;
GLuint textureHandle = myTextureObject;
GLint mipmapLevel = 0;
glFramebufferTexture2D(GL_FRAMEBUFFER, attachment,
                       textureTarget, textureHandle, mipmapLevel);
```

The textureTarget parameter is not limited to GL_TEXTURE_2D; it can be any of the six face enumerants (GL_TEXTURE_CUBE_MAP_POSITIVE_X and so on). See Example 8-11 for a high-level overview of a render method that draws a 3D scene into a cube map. (This code is hypothetical, not used in any samples in the book's downloadable source code.)

Example 8-11. Rendering to a cube map

```
glBindFramebuffer(GL_FRAMEBUFFER, fboHandle);
glViewport(0, 0, fboWidth, fboHeight);

for (face = 0; face < 6; face++) {

    // Change the FBO attachment to the current face:
    GLenum textureTarget = GL_TEXTURE_CUBE_MAP_POSITIVE_X + face;
    glFramebufferTexture2D(GL_FRAMEBUFFER, GL_COLOR_ATTACHMENT0,
                           textureTarget, textureHandle, 0);

    // Set the model-view matrix to point toward the current face:
    ...

    // Render the scene:
    ...
}
```

 Rendering to a cube map texture is supported only in iPhone OS 3.1 and newer.

Anisotropic Filtering: Textures on Steroids

An issue with standard bilinear texture filtering is that it samples the texture using the same offsets, regardless of how the primitive is oriented on the screen. Bilinear filtering samples the texture four times across a 2×2 square of texels; mipmapped filtering makes a total of eight samples (2×2 on one mipmap level, 2×2 on another). The fact that these methods sample across a uniform 2×2 square can be a bit of a liability.

For example, consider a textured primitive viewed at a sharp angle, such as the grassy ground plane in the Holodeck sample from Chapter 6. The grass looks blurry, even though the texture is quite clear. Figure 8-10 shows a zoomed-in screenshot of this.

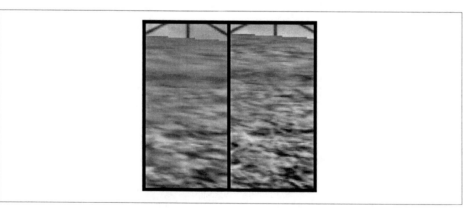

Figure 8-10. Isotropic versus anisotropic filtering

A special type of filtering scheme called *anisotropic filtering* can alleviate blurriness with near edge-on primitives. Anisotropic filtering dynamically adjusts its sampling distribution depending on the orientation of the surface. *Anisotropic* is a rather intimidating word, so it helps to break it down. Traditional bilinear filtering is *isotropic*, meaning "uniform in all dimensions"; *iso* is Greek for "equal," and *tropos* means "direction" in this context.

Go with the Grain

Anisotropic can also describe a lighting model that simulates a surface with directional grain, such as satin or brushed metal. David Banks developed this technique in a 1994 SIGGRAPH paper. My favorite example can be found in the uniforms worn by the main characters in *The Incredibles*.

Anisotropic texturing is made available via the GL_EXT_texture_filter_anisotropic extension. Strangely, at the time of this writing, this extension is available only on older iPhones. I strongly suggest checking for support at runtime before making use of it. Flip back to "Dealing with Size Constraints" on page 204 to see how to check for extensions at runtime.

 Even if your device does not support the anisotropic extension, it's possible to achieve the same effect in a fragment shader that leverages derivatives (discussed in "Smoothing and Derivatives" on page 301).

The anisotropic texturing extension adds a new enumerant for passing in to glTexParameter:

```
glTexParameterf(GL_TEXTURE_2D, GL_TEXTURE_MAX_ANISOTROPY_EXT, 2.0f);
```

The GL_TEXTURE_MAX_ANISOTROPY_EXT constant sets the maximum degree of anisotropy; the higher the number, the more texture lookups are performed. Currently, Apple devices that support this extension have a maximum value of 2.0, but you should query it at runtime, as shown in Example 8-12.

Example 8-12. Enabling anisotropic filtering

```
GLfloat maxAniso;
glGetFloatv(GL_MAX_TEXTURE_MAX_ANISOTROPY_EXT, &maxAniso);
glTexParameterf(GL_TEXTURE_2D, GL_TEXTURE_MAX_ANISOTROPY_EXT, maxAniso);
glTexParameteri(GL_TEXTURE_2D,
                GL_TEXTURE_MIN_FILTER,
                GL_LINEAR_MIPMAP_LINEAR);
glTexParameteri(GL_TEXTURE_2D, GL_TEXTURE_MAG_FILTER, GL_LINEAR);
```

For highest quality, you'll want to use this anisotropic filtering in concert with mip-mapping. Take care with this extension; the additional texture lookups can incur a loss in performance.

Image-Processing Example: Bloom

Whenever I watch a classic *Star Trek* episode from the 1960s, I always get a good laugh when a beautiful female (human or otherwise) speaks into the camera; the image invariably becomes soft and glowy, as though viewers need help in understanding just how feminine she really is. *Light blooming* (often called *bloom* for short) is a way of letting bright portions of the scene bleed into surrounding areas, serving to exaggerate the brightness of those areas. See Figure 8-11 for an example of light blooming.

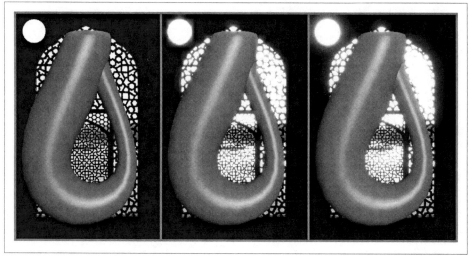

Figure 8-11. Original image, crude bloom, and Gaussian bloom

For any postprocessing effect, the usual strategy is to render the scene into an FBO then draw a full-screen quad to the screen with the FBO attached to a texture. When drawing the full-screen quad, a special fragment shader is employed to achieve the effect.

I just described a single-pass process, but for many image-processing techniques (including bloom), a single pass is inefficient. To see why this is true, consider the halo around the white circle in the upper left of Figure 8-11; if the halo extends two or three pixels away from the boundary of the original circle, the pixel shader would need to sample the source texture over an area of 5×5 pixels, requiring a total of 25 texture lookups (see Figure 8-12). This would cause a huge performance hit.

There are several tricks we can use to avoid a huge number of texture lookups. One trick is downsampling the original FBO into smaller textures. In fact, a simple (but crude) bloom effect can be achieved by filtering out the low-brightness regions,

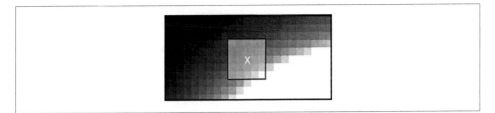

Figure 8-12. 5×5 filtering area

successively downsampling into smaller FBOs, and then accumulating the results. Example 8-13 illustrates this process using pseudocode.

Example 8-13. Algorithm for "crude bloom"

```
// 3D Rendering:
Set the render target to 320x480 FBO A.
Render 3D scene.

// High-Pass Filter:
Set the render target to 320x480 FBO B.
Bind FBO A as a texture.
Draw full-screen quad using a fragment shader that removes low-brightness regions.

// Downsample to one-half size:
Set the render target to 160x240 FBO C.
Bind FBO B as a texture.
Draw full-screen quad.

// Downsample to one-quarter size:
Set the render target to 80x120 FBO D.
Bind FBO C as a texture.
Draw full-screen quad.

// Accumulate the results:
Set the render target to the screen.
Bind FBO A as a texture.
Draw full-screen quad.
Enable additive blending.
Bind FBO B as a texture.
Draw full-screen quad.
Bind FBO C as a texture.
Draw full-screen quad.
Bind FBO D as a texture.
Draw full-screen quad.
```

This procedure is almost possible without the use of shaders; the main difficulty lies in the high-pass filter step. There are a couple ways around this; if you have a priori knowledge of the bright objects in your scene, simply render those objects directly into the FBO. Otherwise, you may be able to use texture combiners (covered at the beginning of this chapter) to subtract the low-brightness regions and then multiply the result back to its original intensity.

The main issue with the procedure outlined in Example 8-13 is that it's using nothing more than OpenGL's native facilities for bilinear filtering. OpenGL's bilinear filter is also known as a *box filter*, aptly named since it produces rather boxy results, as shown in Figure 8-13.

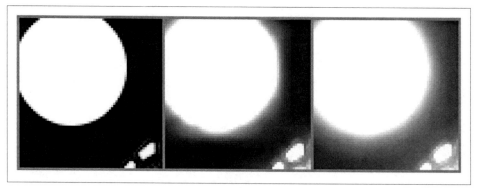

Figure 8-13. Zoom on the original image, crude bloom, and Gaussian bloom

A much higher-quality filter is the *Gaussian filter*, which gets its name from a function often used in statistics. It's also known as the *bell curve*; see Figure 8-14.

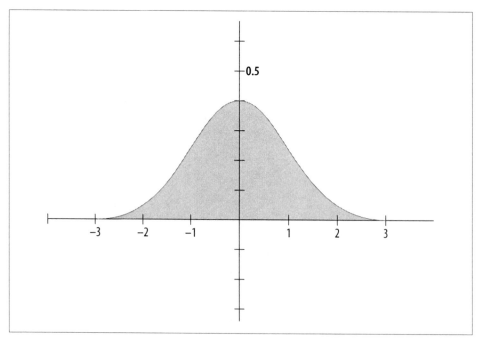

Figure 8-14. Gaussian function

Much like the box filter, the Gaussian filter samples the texture over the square region surrounding the point of interest. The difference lies in how the texel colors are averaged; the Gaussian filter uses a weighted average where the weights correspond to points along the bell curve.

The Gaussian filter has a property called *separability*, which means it can be split into two passes: a horizontal pass then a vertical one. So, for a 5×5 region of texels, we don't need 25 lookups; instead, we can make five lookups in a horizontal pass then another five lookups in a vertical pass. The complete process is illustrated in Figure 8-15. The labels below each image tell you which framebuffer objects are being rendered to. Note that the B_0–B_3 set of FBOs are "ping-ponged" (yes, this term is used in graphics literature) to save memory, meaning that they're rendered to more than once.

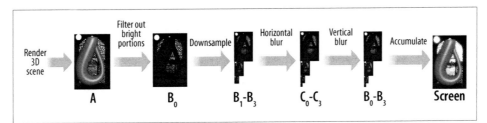

Figure 8-15. Gaussian bloom with 10 FBOs

Yet another trick to reduce texture lookups is to sample somewhere other than at the texel centers. This exploits OpenGL's bilinear filtering capabilities. See Figure 8-16 for an example of how five texture lookups can be reduced to three.

Figure 8-16. Five samples versus three samples

A bit of math proves that the five-lookup and three-lookup cases are equivalent if you use the correct off-center texture coordinates for the three-lookup case. First, give the row of texel colors names **A** through **E**, where **C** is the center of the filter. The weighted average from the five-lookup case can then be expressed as shown in Equation 8-1.

Equation 8-1. Weighted average over five texels

$(A + 4{}^*B + 6{}^*C + 4{}^*D + E) / 16 = A/16 + B{}^*4/16 + C{}^*6/16 + D{}^*4/16 + E/16$

For the three-lookup case, give the names **F** and **G** to the colors resulting from the off-center lookups. Equation 8-2 shows the weighted average.

Equation 8-2. Weighted average over three texels

$(5{*}F + 6{*}C + 5{*}G) / 16 = F{*}5/16 + C{*}6/16 + G{*}5/16$

The texture coordinate for **F** is chosen such that A contributes one-fifth of its color and **B** contributes four-fifths. The **G** coordinate follows the same scheme. This can be expressed like this:

$F = (A + 4{*}B) / 5 = A/5 + B{*}4/5G = (E + 4{*}D) / 5 = E/5 + D{*}4/5$

Substituting **F** and **G** in Equation 8-2 yields the following:

$(A/5 + B{*}4/5){*}5/16 + C{*}6/16 + (E/5 + D{*}4/5){*}5/16$

This is equivalent to Equation 8-1, which shows that three carefully chosen texture lookups can provide a good sample distribution over a 5-pixel area.

Better Performance with a Hybrid Approach

Full-blown Gaussian bloom may bog down your frame rate, even when using the sampling tricks that we discussed. In practice, I find that performing the blurring passes only on the smaller images provides big gains in performance with relatively little loss in quality.

Sample Code for Gaussian Bloom

Enough theory, let's code this puppy. Example 8-14 shows the fragment shader used for high-pass filtering.

Example 8-14. High-pass filter fragment shader

```
varying mediump vec2 TextureCoord;

uniform sampler2D Sampler;
uniform mediump float Threshold;

const mediump vec3 Perception = vec3(0.299, 0.587, 0.114);

void main(void)
{
    mediump vec3 color = texture2D(Sampler, TextureCoord).xyz;
    mediump float luminance = dot(Perception, color);
    gl_FragColor = (luminance > Threshold) ? vec4(color, 1) : vec4(0);
}
```

Of interest in Example 8-14 is how we evaluate the perceived brightness of a given color. The human eye responds differently to different color components, so it's not correct to simply take the "length" of the color vector.

Next let's take a look at the fragment shader that's used for Gaussian blur. Remember, it has only three lookups! See Example 8-15.

Example 8-15. Blur fragment shader

```
varying mediump vec2 TextureCoord;

uniform sampler2D Sampler;
uniform mediump float Coefficients[3];
uniform mediump vec2 Offset;

void main(void)
{
    mediump vec3 A = Coefficients[0]
      * texture2D(Sampler, TextureCoord - Offset).xyz;
    mediump vec3 B = Coefficients[1]
      * texture2D(Sampler, TextureCoord).xyz;
    mediump vec3 C = Coefficients[2]
      * texture2D(Sampler, TextureCoord + Offset).xyz;
    mediump vec3 color = A + B + C;
    gl_FragColor = vec4(color, 1);
}
```

By having the application code supply `Offset` in the form of a `vec2` uniform, we can use the same shader for both the horizontal and vertical passes. Speaking of application code, check out Example 8-16. The `Optimize` boolean turns on hybrid Gaussian/crude rendering; set it to false for a higher-quality blur at a reduced frame rate.

Example 8-16. Rendering engine (bloom sample)

```
const int OffscreenCount = 5;
const bool Optimize = true;

struct Framebuffers {
    GLuint Onscreen;
    GLuint Scene;
    GLuint OffscreenLeft[OffscreenCount];
    GLuint OffscreenRight[OffscreenCount];
};

struct Renderbuffers {
    GLuint Onscreen;
    GLuint OffscreenLeft[OffscreenCount];
    GLuint OffscreenRight[OffscreenCount];
    GLuint SceneColor;
    GLuint SceneDepth;
};

struct Textures {
    GLuint TombWindow;
    GLuint Sun;
    GLuint Scene;
    GLuint OffscreenLeft[OffscreenCount];
    GLuint OffscreenRight[OffscreenCount];
```

```
};

...

GLuint RenderingEngine::CreateFboTexture(int w, int h) const
{
    GLuint texture;
    glGenTextures(1, &texture);
    glBindTexture(GL_TEXTURE_2D, texture);
    glTexParameteri(GL_TEXTURE_2D, GL_TEXTURE_MIN_FILTER, GL_LINEAR);
    glTexParameteri(GL_TEXTURE_2D, GL_TEXTURE_MAG_FILTER, GL_LINEAR);
    glTexParameteri(GL_TEXTURE_2D, GL_TEXTURE_WRAP_S, GL_CLAMP_TO_EDGE);
    glTexParameteri(GL_TEXTURE_2D, GL_TEXTURE_WRAP_T, GL_CLAMP_TO_EDGE);
    glTexImage2D(GL_TEXTURE_2D, 0, GL_RGBA, w, h,
                 0, GL_RGBA, GL_UNSIGNED_BYTE, 0);
    glFramebufferTexture2D(GL_FRAMEBUFFER,
                           GL_COLOR_ATTACHMENT0,
                           GL_TEXTURE_2D,
                           texture,
                           0);
    return texture;
}

void RenderingEngine::Initialize()
{
    // Load the textures:
    ...

    // Create some geometry:
    m_kleinBottle = CreateDrawable(KleinBottle(0.2), VertexFlagsNormals);
    m_quad = CreateDrawable(Quad(2, 2), VertexFlagsTexCoords);

    // Extract width and height from the color buffer:
    glGetRenderbufferParameteriv(GL_RENDERBUFFER,
                                 GL_RENDERBUFFER_WIDTH,
                                 &m_size.x);
    glGetRenderbufferParameteriv(GL_RENDERBUFFER,
                                 GL_RENDERBUFFER_HEIGHT,
                                 &m_size.y);

    // Create the onscreen FBO:
    glGenFramebuffers(1, &m_framebuffers.Onscreen);
    glBindFramebuffer(GL_FRAMEBUFFER, m_framebuffers.Onscreen);
    glFramebufferRenderbuffer(GL_FRAMEBUFFER, GL_COLOR_ATTACHMENT0,
                              GL_RENDERBUFFER, m_renderbuffers.Onscreen);
    glBindRenderbuffer(GL_RENDERBUFFER, m_renderbuffers.Onscreen);

    // Create the depth buffer for the full-size offscreen FBO:
    glGenRenderbuffers(1, &m_renderbuffers.SceneDepth);
    glBindRenderbuffer(GL_RENDERBUFFER, m_renderbuffers.SceneDepth);
    glRenderbufferStorage(GL_RENDERBUFFER,
                          GL_DEPTH_COMPONENT16,
                          m_size.x,
                          m_size.y);
    glGenRenderbuffers(1, &m_renderbuffers.SceneColor);
```

```
        glBindRenderbuffer(GL_RENDERBUFFER, m_renderbuffers.SceneColor);
        glRenderbufferStorage(GL_RENDERBUFFER,
                              GL_RGBA8_OES,
                              m_size.x,
                              m_size.y);
        glGenFramebuffers(1, &m_framebuffers.Scene);
        glBindFramebuffer(GL_FRAMEBUFFER, m_framebuffers.Scene);
        glFramebufferRenderbuffer(GL_FRAMEBUFFER, GL_COLOR_ATTACHMENT0,
                                  GL_RENDERBUFFER, m_renderbuffers.SceneColor);
        glFramebufferRenderbuffer(GL_FRAMEBUFFER, GL_DEPTH_ATTACHMENT,
                                  GL_RENDERBUFFER, m_renderbuffers.SceneDepth);
        m_textures.Scene = CreateFboTexture(m_size.x, m_size.y);

        // Create FBOs for the half, quarter, and eighth sizes:
        int w = m_size.x, h = m_size.y;
        for (int i = 0;
             i < OffscreenCount;
             ++i, w >>= 1, h >>= 1)
        {
            glGenRenderbuffers(1, &m_renderbuffers.OffscreenLeft[i]);
            glBindRenderbuffer(GL_RENDERBUFFER,
                               m_renderbuffers.OffscreenLeft[i]);
            glRenderbufferStorage(GL_RENDERBUFFER, GL_RGBA8_OES, w, h);
            glGenFramebuffers(1, &m_framebuffers.OffscreenLeft[i]);
            glBindFramebuffer(GL_FRAMEBUFFER,
                              m_framebuffers.OffscreenLeft[i]);
            glFramebufferRenderbuffer(GL_FRAMEBUFFER,
                                      GL_COLOR_ATTACHMENT0,
                                      GL_RENDERBUFFER,
                                      m_renderbuffers.OffscreenLeft[i]);
            m_textures.OffscreenLeft[i] = CreateFboTexture(w, h);

            glGenRenderbuffers(1, &m_renderbuffers.OffscreenRight[i]);
            glBindRenderbuffer(GL_RENDERBUFFER,
                               m_renderbuffers.OffscreenRight[i]);
            glRenderbufferStorage(GL_RENDERBUFFER, GL_RGBA8_OES, w, h);
            glGenFramebuffers(1, &m_framebuffers.OffscreenRight[i]);
            glBindFramebuffer(GL_FRAMEBUFFER,
                              m_framebuffers.OffscreenRight[i]);
            glFramebufferRenderbuffer(GL_FRAMEBUFFER,
                                      GL_COLOR_ATTACHMENT0,
                                      GL_RENDERBUFFER,
                                      m_renderbuffers.OffscreenRight[i]);
            m_textures.OffscreenRight[i] = CreateFboTexture(w, h);
        }

        ...
}

void RenderingEngine::Render(float theta) const
{
    glViewport(0, 0, m_size.x, m_size.y);
    glEnable(GL_DEPTH_TEST);
```

```
// Set the render target to the full-size offscreen buffer:
glBindTexture(GL_TEXTURE_2D, m_textures.TombWindow);
glBindFramebuffer(GL_FRAMEBUFFER, m_framebuffers.Scene);
glBindRenderbuffer(GL_RENDERBUFFER, m_renderbuffers.SceneColor);

// Blit the background texture:
glUseProgram(m_blitting.Program);
glUniform1f(m_blitting.Uniforms.Threshold, 0);
glDepthFunc(GL_ALWAYS);
RenderDrawable(m_quad, m_blitting);

// Draw the sun:
...

// Set the light position:
glUseProgram(m_lighting.Program);
vec4 lightPosition(0.25, 0.25, 1, 0);
glUniform3fv(m_lighting.Uniforms.LightPosition, 1,
             lightPosition.Pointer());

// Set the model-view transform:
const float distance = 10;
const vec3 target(0, -0.15, 0);
const vec3 up(0, 1, 0);
const vec3 eye = vec3(0, 0, distance);
const mat4 view = mat4::LookAt(eye, target, up);
const mat4 model = mat4::RotateY(theta * 180.0f / 3.14f);
const mat4 modelview = model * view;
glUniformMatrix4fv(m_lighting.Uniforms.Modelview,
                   1, 0, modelview.Pointer());

// Set the normal matrix:
mat3 normalMatrix = modelview.ToMat3();
glUniformMatrix3fv(m_lighting.Uniforms.NormalMatrix,
                   1, 0, normalMatrix.Pointer());

// Render the Klein bottle:
glDepthFunc(GL_LESS);
glEnableVertexAttribArray(m_lighting.Attributes.Normal);
RenderDrawable(m_kleinBottle, m_lighting);

// Set up the high-pass filter:
glUseProgram(m_highPass.Program);
glUniform1f(m_highPass.Uniforms.Threshold, 0.85);
glDisable(GL_DEPTH_TEST);

// Downsample the rendered scene:
int w = m_size.x, h = m_size.y;
for (int i = 0; i < OffscreenCount; ++i, w >>= 1, h >>= 1) {
    glViewport(0, 0, w, h);
    glBindFramebuffer(GL_FRAMEBUFFER, m_framebuffers.OffscreenLeft[i]);
    glBindRenderbuffer(GL_RENDERBUFFER,
                       m_renderbuffers.OffscreenLeft[i]);
    glBindTexture(GL_TEXTURE_2D, i ? m_textures.OffscreenLeft[i - 1] :
```

```
                                        m_textures.Scene);
    RenderDrawable(m_quad, m_blitting);
    glUseProgram(m_blitting.Program);
}

// Set up for Gaussian blur:
float kernel[3] = { 5.0f / 16.0f, 6 / 16.0f, 5 / 16.0f };
glUseProgram(m_gaussian.Program);
glUniform1fv(m_gaussian.Uniforms.Coefficients, 3, kernel);

// Perform the horizontal blurring pass:
w = m_size.x; h = m_size.y;
for (int i = 0; i < OffscreenCount; ++i, w >>= 1, h >>= 1) {
    if (Optimize && i < 2)
        continue;
    float offset = 1.2f / (float) w;
    glUniform2f(m_gaussian.Uniforms.Offset, offset, 0);
    glViewport(0, 0, w, h);
    glBindFramebuffer(GL_FRAMEBUFFER,
                    m_framebuffers.OffscreenRight[i]);
    glBindRenderbuffer(GL_RENDERBUFFER,
                    m_renderbuffers.OffscreenRight[i]);
    glBindTexture(GL_TEXTURE_2D, m_textures.OffscreenLeft[i]);
    RenderDrawable(m_quad, m_gaussian);
}

// Perform the vertical blurring pass:
w = m_size.x; h = m_size.y;
for (int i = 0; i < OffscreenCount; ++i, w >>= 1, h >>= 1) {
    if (Optimize && i < 2)
        continue;
    float offset = 1.2f / (float) h;
    glUniform2f(m_gaussian.Uniforms.Offset, 0, offset);
    glViewport(0, 0, w, h);
    glBindFramebuffer(GL_FRAMEBUFFER, m_framebuffers.OffscreenLeft[i]);
    glBindRenderbuffer(GL_RENDERBUFFER, m_renderbuffers.OffscreenLeft[i]);
    glBindTexture(GL_TEXTURE_2D, m_textures.OffscreenRight[i]);
    RenderDrawable(m_quad, m_gaussian);
}

// Blit the full-color buffer onto the screen:
glUseProgram(m_blitting.Program);
glViewport(0, 0, m_size.x, m_size.y);
glDisable(GL_BLEND);
glBindFramebuffer(GL_FRAMEBUFFER, m_framebuffers.Onscreen);
glBindRenderbuffer(GL_RENDERBUFFER, m_renderbuffers.Onscreen);
glBindTexture(GL_TEXTURE_2D, m_textures.Scene);
RenderDrawable(m_quad, m_blitting);

// Accumulate the bloom textures onto the screen:
glBlendFunc(GL_ONE, GL_ONE);
glEnable(GL_BLEND);
for (int i = 1; i < OffscreenCount; ++i) {
    glBindTexture(GL_TEXTURE_2D, m_textures.OffscreenLeft[i]);
    RenderDrawable(m_quad, m_blitting);
```

```
    }
    glDisable(GL_BLEND);
}
```

In Example 8-16, some utility methods and structures are omitted for brevity, since they're similar to what's found in previous samples. As always, you can download the entire source code for this sample from this book's website.

Keep in mind that bloom is only one type of image-processing technique; there are many more techniques that you can achieve with shaders. For example, by skipping the high-pass filter, you can soften the entire image; this could be used as a poor man's anti-aliasing technique.

Also note that image-processing techniques are often applicable outside the world of 3D graphics—you could even use OpenGL to perform a bloom pass on an image captured with the iPhone camera!

Wrapping Up

This chapter picked up the pace a bit, giving a quick overview of some more advanced concepts. I hope you feel encouraged to do some additional reading; computer graphics is a deep field, and there's plenty to learn that's outside the scope of this book.

Many of the effects presented in this chapter are possible only at the cost of a lower frame rate. You'll often come across a trade-off between visual quality and performance, but there are tricks to help with this. In the next chapter, we'll discuss some of these optimization tricks and give you a leg up in your application's performance.

## CHAPTER 9

Optimizing

Act, and you shall have dinner; wait,
and you shall be dinner.

—Klingon proverb

One reason you might be reading this book in the first place is that you don't just want pretty graphics; you want *fast* graphics. Since OpenGL ES gives you the lowest possible level of access to Apple's graphics hardware, it's the ideal API when speed is your primary concern. Many speed-hungry developers use OpenGL even for 2D games for this reason.

Until this point in this book, we've been focusing mostly on the fundamentals of OpenGL or showing how to use it to achieve cool effects. We've mentioned a few performance tips along the way, but we haven't dealt with performance head-on.

Instruments

Of all the performance metrics, your *frame rate* (number of `presentRenderbuffer` calls per second) is the metric that you'll want to measure most often. We presented one way of determining frame rate in Chapter 7, where we rendered an FPS counter on top of the scene. This was convenient and simple, but Apple's Instruments tool (Figure 9-1) can accomplish the same thing, and much more—without requiring you to modify your application! The best part is that it's included in the SDK that you already have.

 As with any performance analysis tool, beware of the Heisenberg effect. In this context, I'm referring to the fact that measuring performance can, in itself, affect performance. This has never been problematic for me, and it's certainly not as bothersome as a Heisenbug (a bug that seems to vanish when you're in the debugger).

Figure 9-1. Instruments

First, be sure that your *Active SDK* (upper-left corner of Xcode) is set to a Device configuration rather than a Simulator configuration. Next, click the Run menu, and select the *Run with Performance Tool* submenu. You should see an option for OpenGL ES (if not, you probably have your SDK set to Simulator).

> Alternatively, you can run Instruments directly from */Developer/Applications/Instruments.app*.

While your application is running, Instruments is constantly updating an EKG-like graph of your frame rate and various other metrics you may be interested in. Try clicking the information icon in the OpenGL ES panel on the left, and then click the *Configure* button. This allows you to pick and choose from a slew of performance metrics.

Instruments is a great tool for many aspects of performance analysis, not just OpenGL. I find that it's particularly useful for detecting memory leaks. The documentation for Instruments is available on the iPhone developer site. I encourage you to read up on it and give it a whirl, even if you're not experiencing any obvious performance issues.

Understand the CPU/GPU Split

Don't forget that the bottleneck of your application may be on the CPU side rather than in the graphics processing unit (GPU). You can determine this by diving into your rendering code and commenting out all the OpenGL function calls. Rerun your app with Instruments, and observe the frame rate; if it's unchanged, then the bottleneck is on the CPU. Dealing with such bottlenecks is beyond the scope of this book, but Instruments can help you track them down. Keep in mind that some types of CPU work (such as transforming vertices) can be moved to the GPU through clever usage of OpenGL.

Vertex Submission: Above and Beyond VBOs

The manner in which you submit vertex data to OpenGL ES can have a huge impact on performance. The most obvious tip is something I mentioned early in this book: use vertex buffer objects whenever possible. They eliminate costly memory transfers. VBOs don't help as much with older devices, but using them is a good habit to get into.

Batch, Batch, Batch

VBO usage is just the tip of the iceberg. Another best practice that you'll hear a lot about is *draw call batching*. The idea is simple: try to render as much as possible in as few draw calls as possible. Consider how you'd go about drawing a human head. Perhaps your initial code does something like Example 9-1.

Example 9-1. Highly unoptimized OpenGL ES sequence

```
glBindTexture(...);  // Bind the skin texture.
glDrawArrays(...);   // Render the head.
glDrawArrays(...);   // Render the nose.
glLoadMatrixfv(...); // Shift the model-view to the left side.
glDrawArrays(...);   // Render the left ear.

glBindTexture(...);  // Bind the eyeball texture.
glDrawArrays(...);   // Render the left eye.
glLoadMatrixfv(...); // Shift the model-view to the right side.

glBindTexture(...);  // Bind the skin texture.
glDrawArrays(...);   // Render the right ear.

glBindTexture(...);  // Bind the eyeball texture.
glDrawArrays(...);   // Render the right eye.
glLoadMatrixfv(...); // Shift the model-view to the center.

glBindTexture(...);  // Bind the lips texture.
glDrawArrays(...);   // Render the lips.
```

Right off the bat, you should notice that the head and nose can be "batched" into a single VBO. You can also do a bit of rearranging to reduce the number of texture binding operations. Example 9-2 shows the result after this tuning.

Example 9-2. OpenGL ES sequence after initial tuning

```
glBindTexture(...);  // Bind the skin texture.
glDrawArrays(...);   // Render the head and nose.
glLoadMatrixfv(...); // Shift the model-view to the left side.
```

```
glDrawArrays(...);   // Render the left ear.
glLoadMatrixfv(...); // Shift the model-view to the right side.
glDrawArrays(...);   // Render the right ear.

glBindTexture(...);  // Bind the eyeball texture.
glLoadMatrixfv(...); // Shift the model-view to the left side.
glDrawArrays(...);   // Render the left eye.
glLoadMatrixfv(...); // Shift the model-view to the left side.
glDrawArrays(...);   // Render the right eye.
glLoadMatrixfv(...); // Shift the model-view to the center.

glBindTexture(...);  // Bind the lips texture.
glDrawArrays(...);   // Render the lips.
```

Try combing through the code again to see whether anything can be eliminated. Sure, you might be saving a little bit of memory by using a single VBO to represent the ear, but suppose it's a rather small VBO. If you add two instances of the ear geometry to your existing "head and nose" VBO, you can eliminate the need for changing the model-view matrix, plus you can use fewer draw calls. Similar guidance applies to the eyeballs. Example 9-3 shows the result.

Example 9-3. OpenGL ES sequence after second pass of tuning

```
glBindTexture(...);  // Bind the skin texture.
glDrawArrays(...);   // Render the head and nose and ears.

glBindTexture(...);  // Bind the eyeball texture.
glDrawArrays(...);   // Render both eyes.

glBindTexture(...);  // Bind the lips texture.
glDrawArrays(...);   // Render the lips.
```

You're not done yet. Remember texture atlases, first presented in "Animation with Sprite Sheets" on page 306? By tweaking your texture coordinates and combining the skin texture with the eye and lip textures, you can reduce the rendering code to only two lines:

```
glBindTexture(...);  // Bind the atlas texture.
glDrawArrays(...);   // Render the head and nose and ears and eyes and lips.
```

 Pixomatic's ZBrush application is a favorite with artists for generating texture atlases.

OK, I admit this example was rather contrived. Rarely does production code make linear sequences of OpenGL calls as I've done in these examples. Real-world code is usually organized into subroutines, with plenty of stuff going on between the draw calls. But, the same principles apply. From the GPU's perspective, your application is merely a linear sequence of OpenGL calls. If you think about your code in this distilled manner, potential optimizations can be easier to spot.

Interleaved Vertex Attributes

You might hear the term *interleaved data* being thrown around in regard to OpenGL optimizations. It is indeed a good practice, but it's actually nothing special. In fact, every sample in this book has been using interleaved data (for a diagram, flip back to Figure 1-8 in Chapter 1). Using our C++ vector library, much of this book's sample code declares a plain old data (POD) structure representing a vertex, like this:

```
struct Vertex {
    vec3 Position;
    vec3 Normal;
    vec2 TexCoord;
};
```

When we create the VBO, we populate it with an array of **Vertex** objects. When it comes time to render the geometry, we usually do something like Example 9-4.

Example 9-4. Using interleaved attributes

```
glBindBuffer(...);
GLsizei stride = sizeof(Vertex);

// ES 1.1
glVertexPointer(3, GL_FLOAT, stride, 0);
glNormalPointer(GL_FLOAT, stride, offsetof(Vertex, Normal));
glTexCoordPointer(2, GL_FLOAT, stride, offsetof(Vertex, TexCoord));

// ES 2.0
glVertexAttribPointer(positionAttrib, 3, GL_FLOAT, GL_FALSE, stride, 0);
glVertexAttribPointer(normalAttrib, 3, GL_FALSE,
                      GL_FALSE, stride, offsetof(Vertex, Normal));
glVertexAttribPointer(texCoordAttrib, 2, GL_FLOAT,
                      GL_FALSE, stride, offsetof(Vertex, TexCoord));
```

OpenGL does not require you to arrange VBOs in the previous manner. For example, consider a small VBO with only three vertices. Instead of arranging it like this:

```
Position-Normal-TexCoord-Position-Normal-TexCoord-Position-Normal-TexCoord
```

you could lay it out it like this:

```
Position-Position-Position-Normal-Normal-Normal-TexCoord-TexCoord-TexCoord
```

This is perfectly acceptable (but not advised); Example 9-5 shows the way you'd submit it to OpenGL.

Example 9-5. Unoptimal vertex layout

```
glBindBuffer(...);

// ES 1.1
glVertexPointer(3, GL_FLOAT, sizeof(vec3), 0);
glNormalPointer(GL_FLOAT, sizeof(vec3), sizeof(vec3) * VertexCount);
glTexCoordPointer(2, GL_FLOAT, sizeof(vec2),
                  2 * sizeof(vec3) * VertexCount);

// ES 2.0
glVertexAttribPointer(positionAttrib, 3, GL_FLOAT,
                      GL_FALSE, sizeof(vec3), 0);
glVertexAttribPointer(normalAttrib, 3, GL_FALSE,
                      GL_FALSE, sizeof(vec3),
                      sizeof(vec3) * VertexCount);
glVertexAttribPointer(texCoordAttrib, 2, GL_FLOAT,
                      GL_FALSE, sizeof(vec2),
                      2 * sizeof(vec3) * VertexCount);
```

When you submit vertex data in this manner, you're forcing the driver to reorder the data to make it amenable to the GPU.

Optimize Your Vertex Format

One aspect of vertex layout you might be wondering about is the ordering of attributes. With OpenGL ES 2.0 and newer Apple devices, the order has little or no impact on performance (assuming you're using interleaved data). On first- and second-generation iPhones, Apple recommends the following order:

1. Position
2. Normal
3. Color
4. Texture coordinate (first stage)
5. Texture coordinate (second stage)
6. Point size
7. Bone weight
8. Bone index

You might be wondering about the two "bone" attributes—stay tuned, well discuss them later in the chapter.

Another way of optimizing your vertex format is shrinking the size of the attribute types. In this book, we've been a bit sloppy by using 32-bit floats for just about everything. Don't forget there are other types you can use. For example, floating point is often overkill for color, since colors usually don't need as much precision as other attributes.

```
// ES 1.1
// Lazy iPhone developer:
glColorPointer(4, GL_FLOAT, sizeof(vertex), offset);

// Rock Star iPhone developer!
glColorPointer(4, GL_UNSIGNED_BYTE, sizeof(vertex), offset);

// ES 2.0
// Lazy:
glVertexAttribPointer(color, 4, GL_FLOAT, GL_FALSE, stride, offset);

// Rock star!
glVertexAttribPointer(color, 4, GL_UNSIGNED_BYTE,
                      GL_FALSE, stride, offset);
```

 Don't use GL_FIXED. Because of the iPhone's architecture, fixed-point numbers actually require *more* processing than floating-point numbers. Fixed-point is available only to comply with the Khronos specification.

Apple recommends aligning vertex attributes in memory according to their native alignment. For example, a 4-byte float should be aligned on a 4-byte boundary. Sometimes you can deal with this by adding padding to your vertex format:

```
struct Vertex {
    vec3 Position;
    unsigned char Luminance;
    unsigned char Alpha;
    unsigned short Padding;
};
```

Use the Best Topology and Indexing

Apple's general advice (at the time of this writing) is to prefer GL_TRIANGLE_STRIP over GL_TRIANGLES. Strips require fewer vertices but usually at the cost of more draw calls. Sometimes you can reduce the number of draw calls by introducing degenerate triangles into your vertex buffer.

Strips versus separate triangles, indexed versus nonindexed; these all have trade-offs. You'll find that many developers have strong opinions, and you're welcome to review all the endless debates on the forums. In the end, experimentation is the only reliable way to determine the best tessellation strategy for your unique situation.

Imagination Technologies provides code for converting lists into strips. Look for *PVRTTriStrip.cpp* in the OpenGL ES 1.1 version of the PowerVR SDK (first discussed in "Texture Compression with PVRTC" on page 191). It also provides a sample app to show it off (*Demos/OptimizeMesh*).

Lighting Optimizations

If your app has highly tessellated geometry (lots of tiny triangles), then lighting can negatively impact performance. The following sections discuss ways to optimize lighting. Use your time wisely; don't bother with these optimizations without first testing if you're *fill rate bound*. Applications that are fill rate bound have their bottleneck in the rasterizer, and lighting optimizations don't help much in those cases—unless, of course, the app is doing per-pixel lighting!

There's a simple test you can use to determine whether you're fill rate bound. Try modifying the parameters to `glViewport` to shrink your viewport to a small size. If this causes a significant increase in your frame rate, you're probably fill rate bound.

If you discover that you're neither fill rate bound nor CPU bound, the first thing to consider is simplifying your geometry. This means rendering a coarser scene using larger, fewer triangles. If you find you can't do this without a huge loss in visual quality, consider one of the optimizations in the following sections.

 If you're CPU bound, try turning off Thumb mode; it enables a special ARM instruction set that can slow you down. Turn it off in Xcode by switching to a Device configuration and going to Project→Edit Project Settings→Build Tab→Show All Settings, and uncheck the "Compile for Thumb" option under the *Code Generation* heading.

Object-Space Lighting

We briefly mentioned object-space lighting in "Bump Mapping and DOT3 Lighting" on page 335; to summarize, in certain circumstances, surface normals don't need transformation when the light source is infinitely distant. This principle can be applied under OpenGL ES 1.1 (in which case the driver makes the optimization for you) or in OpenGL ES 2.0 (in which case you can make this optimization in your shader).

To specify an infinite light source, set the **W** component of your light position to zero. But what are those "certain circumstances" that we mentioned? Specifically, your model-view matrix cannot have non-uniform scale (scale that's not the same for all three axes). To review the logic behind this, flip back to "Normal Transforms Aren't Normal" on page 131.

DOT3 Lighting Revisited

If per-vertex lighting under OpenGL ES 1.1 causes performance issues with complex geometry or if it's producing unattractive results with coarse geometry, I recommend that you consider DOT3 lighting. This technique leverages the texturing hardware to perform a crude version of per-pixel lighting. Refer to "Normal Mapping with OpenGL ES 1.1" on page 343 for more information.

Baked Lighting

The best way to speed up your lighting calculations is to not perform them at all! Scenes with light sources that don't move can be prelit, or "baked in." This can be accomplished by performing some offline processing to create a grayscale texture (also called a *light map*). This technique is especially useful when used in conjunction with multitexturing.

As an added benefit, baked lighting can be used to create a much higher-quality effect than standard OpenGL lighting. For example, by using a raytracing tool, you can account for the ambient light in the scene, producing beautiful soft shadows (see Figure 9-2). One popular offline tool for this is xNormal, developed by Santiago Orgaz.

Figure 9-2. Ambient occlusion (courtesy of Malcolm Kesson)

Texturing Optimizations

If your frame rate soars when you try disabling texturing, take a look at the following list:

- Don't use textures that are any larger than necessary. This is especially true when porting a desktop game; the iPhone's small screen usually means that you can use smaller textures.
- Older devices have 24MB of texture memory; don't exceed this. Newer devices have unified memory, so it's less of a concern.
- Use a compressed or low-precision format if possible.
- Use texture atlases to reduce the number of bind calls.

Another tip: it won't help with frame rate, but your load time might be improved by converting your image files into a "raw" format like PVRTC or even into a C-array header file. You can do either of these using `PVRTexTool` ("The PowerVR SDK and Low-Precision Textures" on page 198).

Culling and Clipping

Avoid telling OpenGL to render things that aren't visible anyway. Sounds easy, right? In practice, this guideline can be more difficult to follow than you might think.

Polygon Winding

Consider something simple: an OpenGL scene with a spinning, opaque sphere. All the triangles on the "front" of the sphere (the ones that face that camera) are visible, but the ones in the back are not. OpenGL doesn't need to process the vertices on the back of the sphere. In the case of OpenGL ES 2.0, we'd like to skip running a vertex shader on back-facing triangles; with OpenGL ES 1.1, we'd like to skip transform and lighting operations on those triangles. Unfortunately, the graphics processor doesn't know that those triangles are occluded until after it performs the rasterization step in the graphics pipeline.

So, we'd like to tell OpenGL to skip the back-facing vertices. Ideally we could do this without any CPU overhead, so changing the VBO at each frame is out of the question.

How can we know ahead of time that a triangle is back-facing? Consider a single layer of triangles in the sphere; see Figure 9-3. Note that the triangles have consistent "winding"; triangles that wind clockwise are back-facing, while triangles that wind counterclockwise are front-facing.

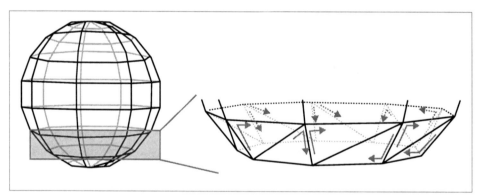

Figure 9-3. Triangle winding

OpenGL can quickly determine whether a given triangle goes clockwise or counterclockwise. Behind the scenes, the GPU can take the cross product of two edges in screen space; if the resulting sign is positive, the triangle is front-facing; otherwise, it's back-facing.

Face culling is enabled like so:

```
glEnable(GL_CULL_FACE);
```

You can also configure OpenGL to define which winding direction is the front:

```
glFrontFace(GL_CW);  // front faces go clockwise
glFrontFace(GL_CCW); // front faces go counterclockwise (default)
```

Depending on how your object is tessellated, you may need to play with this setting.

Use culling with caution; you won't always want it to be enabled! It's mostly useful for opaque, enclosed objects. For example, a ribbon shape would disappear if you tried to view it from the back.

As an aside, face culling is useful for much more than just performance optimizations. For example, developers have come up with tricks that use face culling in conjunction with the stencil buffer to perform CSG operations (composite solid geometry). This allows you to render shapes that are defined from the intersections of other shapes. It's cool stuff, but we don't go into it in detail in this book.

User Clip Planes

User clip planes provide another way of culling away unnecessary portions of a 3D scene, and they're often useful outside the context of performance optimization. Here's how you enable a clip plane with OpenGL ES 1.1:

```
void EnableClipPlane(vec3 normal, float offset)
{
    glEnable(GL_CLIP_PLANE0);
    GLfloat planeCoefficients[] = {normal.x, normal.y, normal.z, offset};
    glClipPlanef(GL_CLIP_PLANE0, planeCoefficients);
}
```

Alas, with OpenGL ES 2.0 this feature doesn't exist. Let's hope for an extension!

The coefficients passed into `glClipPlanef` define the plane equation; see Equation 9-1.

Equation 9-1. Implicit plane equation

$$Ax + By + Cz + D = 0$$

One way of thinking about Equation 9-1 is interpreting A, B, and C as the components to the plane's normal vector, and D as the distance from the origin. The direction of the normal determines which half of the scene to cull away.

Older Apple devices support only one clip plane, but newer devices support six simultaneous planes. The number of supported planes can be determined like so:

```
GLint maxPlanes;
glGetIntegerv(GL_MAX_CLIP_PLANES, &maxPlanes);
```

To use multiple clip planes, simply add a zero-based index to the `GL_CLIP_PLANE0` constant:

```
void EnableClipPlane(int clipPlaneIndex, vec3 normal, float offset)
{
    glEnable(GL_CLIP_PLANE0 + clipPlaneIndex);
    GLfloat planeCoefficients[] = {normal.x, normal.y, normal.z, offset};
    glClipPlanef(GL_CLIP_PLANE0 + clipPlaneIndex, planeCoefficients);
}
```

This is consistent with working with multiple light sources, which requires you to add a light index to the GL_LIGHT0 constant.

CPU-Based Clipping

Unlike the goofy toy applications in this book, real-world applications often have huge, sprawling worlds that users can explore. Ideally, you'd give OpenGL only the portions of the world that are within the viewing frustum, but at first glance this would be incredibly expensive. The CPU would need to crawl through every triangle in the world to determine its visibility!

The way to solve this problem is to use a *bounding volume hierarchy* (BVH), a tree structure for facilitating fast intersection testing. Typically the root node of a BVH corresponds to the entire scene, while leaf nodes correspond to single triangles, or small batches of triangles.

A thorough discussion of BVHs is beyond the scope of this book, but volumes have been written on the subject, and you should be able to find plenty of information. You can find an excellent overview in *Real-Time Rendering* (AK Peters) by Möller, Haines, and Hoffman.

Shader Performance

I'll keep this section brief; GLSL is a programming language much like any other, and you can apply the same algorithmic optimizations that can be found in more general-purpose programming books. Having said that, there are certain aspects of GPU programming that are important to understand.

Conditionals

Shaders are executed on a *single-instruction, multiple-data architecture* (SIMD). The GPU has many, many execution units, and they're usually arranged into blocks, where all units with a block share the same program counter. This has huge implications. Consider an if-else conditional in a block of SIMD units, where the condition can vary across units:

```
if (condition) {

  // Regardless of 'condition', this block always gets executed...

} else {
```

```
        // ...and this block gets executed too!

    }
```

How on Earth could this work and still produce correct results? The secret lies in the processor's ability to ignore its own output. If the conditional is false, the processor's execution unit temporarily disables all writes to its register bank but executes instructions anyway. Since register writes are disabled, the instructions have no effect.

So, conditionals are usually much more expensive on SIMD architectures than on traditional architectures, especially if the conditional is different from one pixel (or vertex) to the next.

Conditionals based solely on uniforms or constants aren't nearly as expensive. Having said that, you may want to try splitting up shaders that have many conditionals like this and let your application choose which one to execute. Another potential optimization is the inverse: combine multiple shaders to reduce the overhead of switching between them. As always, there's a trade-off, and experimentation is often the only way to determine the best course of action. Again, I won't try to give any hard and fast rules, since devices and drivers may change in the future.

Fragment Killing

One GLSL instruction we haven't discussed in this book is the kill instruction, available only within fragment shaders. This instruction allows you to return early and leave the framebuffer unaffected. While useful for certain effects, it's generally inadvisable to use this instruction on Apple devices. (The same is true for alpha testing, first discussed in "Blending Caveats" on page 226.)

Keep in mind that alpha blending can often be used to achieve the same effect that you're trying to achieve with kill and at potentially lower cost to performance.

Texture Lookups Can Hurt!

Every time you access a texture from within a fragment shader, the hardware may be applying a filtering operation. This can be expensive. If your fragment shader makes tons of texture lookups, think of ways to reduce them, just like we did for the bloom sample in the previous chapter.

Optimizing Animation with Vertex Skinning

Typically, *blending* refers to color blending, discussed in Chapter 6. *Vertex blending* (also known as *vertex skinning*) is an entirely different kind of blending, although it too leverages linear interpolation.

First, a disclaimer, this is a chapter on optimization, and yes, vertex skinning is an optimization—but only when performed on the GPU. Generally speaking, vertex skinning is more of a technique than an optimization. Put simply, it makes it easy to animate "rounded" joints in your model.

For example, let's go back to the stick figure demo, originally presented in "Rendering Anti-Aliased Lines with Textures" on page 252. Figure 9-4 shows a comparison of the stick figure with and without vertex skinning. (Usually skinning is applied to 3D models, so this is a rather contrived case.) Notice how the elbows and knees have curves rather than sharp angles.

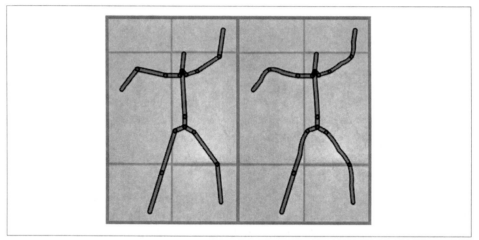

Figure 9-4. Unskinned versus skinned stick figure

The main idea behind GPU-based skinning is that you need not change your vertex buffer during animation; the only data that gets sent to the GPU is a new list of model-view matrices.

Yes, you heard that right: a *list* of model-view matrices! So far, we've been dealing with only one model-view at a time; with vertex skinning, you give the GPU a list of model-views for only one draw call. Because there are several matrices, it follows that each vertex now has several post-transformed positions. Those post-transformed positions get blended together to form the final position. Don't worry if this isn't clear yet; you'll have a deeper understanding after we go over some example code.

Skinning requires you to include additional vertex attributes in your vertex buffer. Each vertex is now bundled with a set of *bone indices* and *bone weights*. Bone indices tell OpenGL which model-view matrices to apply; bone weights are the interpolation constants. Just like the rest of the vertex buffer, bone weights and indices are set up only once and remain static during the animation.

The best part of vertex skinning is that you can apply it with both OpenGL ES 2.0 (via the vertex shader) or OpenGL ES 1.1 (via an iPhone-supported extension). Much like

I did with bump mapping, I'll cover the OpenGL ES 2.0 method first, since it'll help you understand what's going on behind the scenes.

Skinning: Common Code

Much of the prep work required for vertex skinning will be the same for both OpenGL ES 1.1 and OpenGL ES 2.0. To achieve the curvy lines in our stick figure, we'll need to tessellate each limb shape into multiple slices. Figure 9-5 depicts an idealized elbow joint; note that the vertices in each vertical slice have the same blend weights.

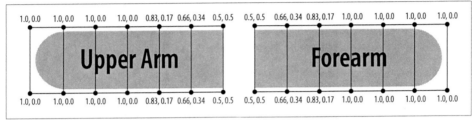

Figure 9-5. Blend weights

In Figure 9-5, the upper arm will be rigid on the left and curvy as it approaches the forearm. Conversely, the forearm will curve on the left and straighten out closer to the hand.

Let's define some structures for the rendering engine, again leveraging the vector library in the appendix:

```
struct Vertex { ❶
    vec3 Position;
    float Padding0;
    vec2 TexCoord;
    vec2 BoneWeights;
    unsigned short BoneIndices;
    unsigned short Padding1;
};

typedef std::vector<Vertex> VertexList;
typedef std::vector<GLushort> IndexList;
typedef std::vector<mat4> MatrixList;

struct Skeleton { ❷
    IndexList Indices;
    VertexList Vertices;
};

struct SkinnedFigure { ❸
    GLuint IndexBuffer;
    GLuint VertexBuffer;
    MatrixList Matrices;
};
```

❶ The Vertex structure is a POD type that defines the layout of the vertex buffer.

❷ The Skeleton structure encapsulates a relatively small set of points that make up an animated "stick figure." We won't be sending these points to OpenGL: it's for internal purposes only, as you'll see.

❸ The SkinnedFigure structure encapsulates the data that we'll send to OpenGL. It contains handles for the static VBOs and a list of matrices that we'll update at every frame.

Given a Skeleton object, computing a list of model-view matrices is a bit tricky; see Example 9-6. This computes a sequence of matrices for the joints along a single limb.

Example 9-6. Generation of bones matrices

```
void ComputeMatrices(const Skeleton& skeleton, MatrixList& matrices)
{
    mat4 modelview = mat4::LookAt(Eye, Target, Up);❶

    float x = 0;
    IndexList::const_iterator lineIndex = skeleton.Indices.begin();
    for (int boneIndex = 0; boneIndex < BoneCount; ++boneIndex) {

        // Compute the length, orientation, and midpoint of this bone:
        float length;
        vec3 orientation, midpoint;
        {
            vec3 a = skeleton.Vertices[*lineIndex++].Position;
            vec3 b = skeleton.Vertices[*lineIndex++].Position;
            length = (b - a).Length();
            orientation = (b - a) / length;
            midpoint = (a + b) * 0.5f;
        }

        // Find the endpoints of the "unflexed" bone
        // that sits at the origin:
        vec3 a(0, 0, 0);
        vec3 b(length, 0, 0);
        if (StickFigureBones[boneIndex].IsBlended) {
            a.x += x;
            b.x += x;
        }
        x = b.x;

        // Compute the matrix that transforms the
        // unflexed bone to its current state:
        vec3 A = orientation;
        vec3 B = vec3(-A.y, A.x, 0);
        vec3 C = A.Cross(B);
        mat3 basis(A, B, C); ❷
        vec3 T = (a + b) * 0.5;
        mat4 rotation = mat4::Translate(-T) * mat4(basis);❸
        mat4 translation = mat4::Translate(midpoint);❹
        matrices[boneIndex] = rotation * translation * modelview;❺
```

```
    }
}
```

❶ Compute the primary model-view, which will be multiplied with each bone-specific transform.

❷ Fill the columns of a change-of-basis matrix; to review the math behind this, flip back to "Another Foray into Linear Algebra" on page 337.

❸ Translate the bone to the origin, and then rotate it around the origin.

❹ Translate the bone to its current position.

❺ Combine the primary model-view with the rotation and translation matrices to form the final bone matrix.

Skinning with OpenGL ES 2.0

Example 9-7 shows the vertex shader for skinning; this lies at the heart of the technique.

Example 9-7. Vertex shader for vertex skinning

```
const int BoneCount = 17;

attribute vec4 Position;
attribute vec2 TextureCoordIn;
attribute vec2 BoneWeights;
attribute vec2 BoneIndices;

uniform mat4 Projection;
uniform mat4 Modelview[BoneCount];

varying vec2 TextureCoord;

void main(void)
{
    vec4 p0 = Modelview[int(BoneIndices.x)] * Position;
    vec4 p1 = Modelview[int(BoneIndices.y)] * Position;
    vec4 p = p0 * BoneWeights.x + p1 * BoneWeights.y;
    gl_Position = Projection * p;
    TextureCoord = TextureCoordIn;
}
```

Note that we're applying only two bones at a time for this demo. By modifying the shader, you could potentially blend between three or more bones. This can be useful for situations that go beyond the classic elbow example, such as soft-body animation. Imagine a wibbly-wobbly blob that lurches around the screen; it could be rendered using a network of several "bones" that meet up at its center.

The fragment shader for the stick figure demo is incredibly simple; see Example 9-8. As you can see, all the real work for skinning is on the vertex shader side of things.

Example 9-8. Fragment shader for vertex skinning

```
varying mediump vec2 TextureCoord;
uniform sampler2D Sampler;

void main(void)
{
    gl_FragColor = texture2D(Sampler, TextureCoord);
}
```

The ES 2.0 rendering code is fairly straightforward; see Example 9-9.

Example 9-9. ES 2.0 Render method for vertex skinning

```
GLsizei stride = sizeof(Vertex);
mat4 projection = mat4::Ortho(-1, 1, -1.5, 1.5, -100, 100);

// Draw background:
...

// Render the stick figure:
glUseProgram(m_skinning.Program);

glUniformMatrix4fv(m_skinning.Uniforms.Projection, 1,
                   GL_FALSE, projection.Pointer());

glUniformMatrix4fv(m_skinning.Uniforms.Modelview,
                   m_skinnedFigure.Matrices.size(),
                   GL_FALSE,
                   m_skinnedFigure.Matrices[0].Pointer());

glBindTexture(GL_TEXTURE_2D, m_textures.Circle);
glEnable(GL_BLEND);
glBlendFunc(GL_SRC_ALPHA, GL_ONE_MINUS_SRC_ALPHA);

glEnableVertexAttribArray(m_skinning.Attributes.Position);
glEnableVertexAttribArray(m_skinning.Attributes.TexCoord);
glEnableVertexAttribArray(m_skinning.Attributes.BoneWeights);
glEnableVertexAttribArray(m_skinning.Attributes.BoneIndices);

glBindBuffer(GL_ELEMENT_ARRAY_BUFFER, m_skinnedFigure.IndexBuffer);
glBindBuffer(GL_ARRAY_BUFFER, m_skinnedFigure.VertexBuffer);

glVertexAttribPointer(m_skinning.Attributes.BoneWeights, 2,
                      GL_FLOAT, GL_FALSE, stride,
                      _offsetof(Vertex, BoneWeights));
glVertexAttribPointer(m_skinning.Attributes.BoneIndices, 2,
                      GL_UNSIGNED_BYTE, GL_FALSE, stride,
                      _offsetof(Vertex, BoneIndices));
glVertexAttribPointer(m_skinning.Attributes.Position, 3,
                      GL_FLOAT, GL_FALSE, stride,
                      _offsetof(Vertex, Position));
glVertexAttribPointer(m_skinning.Attributes.TexCoord, 2,
                      GL_FLOAT, GL_FALSE, stride,
                      _offsetof(Vertex, TexCoord));
```

```
size_t indicesPerBone = 12 + 6 * (NumDivisions + 1);
int indexCount = BoneCount * indicesPerBone;
glDrawElements(GL_TRIANGLES, indexCount, GL_UNSIGNED_SHORT, 0);
```

This is the largest number of attributes we've ever enabled; as you can see, it can be quite a chore to set them all up. One thing I find helpful is creating my own variant of the offsetof macro, useful for passing a byte offset to glVertexAttribPointer. Here's how I define it:

```
#define _offsetof(TYPE, MEMBER) (GLvoid*) (offsetof(TYPE, MEMBER))
```

The compiler will complain if you use offsetof on a type that it doesn't consider to be a POD type. This is mostly done just to conform to the ISO C++ standard; in practice, it's usually safe to use offsetof on simple non-POD types. You can turn off the warning by adding -Wno-invalid-offsetof to the gcc command line. (To add gcc command-line arguments in Xcode, right-click the source file, and choose *Get Info*.)

Skinning with OpenGL ES 1.1

All Apple devices at the time of this writing support the GL_OES_matrix_palette extension under OpenGL ES 1.1. As you'll soon see, it works in a manner quite similar to the OpenGL ES 2.0 method previously discussed. The tricky part is that it imposes limits on the number of so-called vertex units and palette matrices.

Each *vertex unit* performs a single bone transformation. In the simple stick figure example, we need only two vertex units for each joint, so this isn't much of a problem.

Palette matrices are simply another term for bone matrices. We need 17 matrices for our stick figure example, so a limitation might complicate matters.

Here's how you can determine how many vertex units and palette matrices are supported:

```
int numUnits;
glGetIntegerv(GL_MAX_VERTEX_UNITS_OES, &numUnits);

int maxMatrices;
glGetIntegerv(GL_MAX_PALETTE_MATRICES_OES, &maxMatrices);
```

Table 9-1 shows the limits for current Apple devices at the time of this writing.

Table 9-1. Matrix palette limitations

Apple device	Vertex units	Palette matrices
First-generation iPhone and iPod touch	3	9
iPhone 3G and 3GS	4	11
iPhone Simulator	4	11

Uh oh, we need 17 matrices, but at most only 11 are supported! Fret not; we can simply split the rendering pass into two draw calls. That's not too shoddy! Moreover, since `glDrawElements` allows us to pass in an offset, we can still store the entire stick figure in only one VBO.

Let's get down to the details. Since OpenGL ES 1.1 doesn't have uniform variables, it supplies an alternate way of handing bone matrices over to the GPU. It works like this:

```
glEnable(GL_MATRIX_PALETTE_OES);
glMatrixMode(GL_MATRIX_PALETTE_OES);
for (int boneIndex = 0; boneIndex < boneCount; ++boneIndex) {
    glCurrentPaletteMatrixOES(boneIndex);
    glLoadMatrixf(modelviews[boneIndex].Pointer());
}
```

That was pretty straightforward! When you enable `GL_MATRIX_PALETTE_OES`, you're telling OpenGL to ignore the standard model-view and instead use the model-views that get specified while the matrix mode is set to `GL_MATRIX_PALETTE_OES`.

We also need a way to give OpenGL the blend weights and bone indices. That is simple enough:

```
glEnableClientState(GL_WEIGHT_ARRAY_OES);
glEnableClientState(GL_MATRIX_INDEX_ARRAY_OES);

glMatrixIndexPointerOES(2, GL_UNSIGNED_BYTE, stride,
                        _offsetof(Vertex, BoneIndices));
glWeightPointerOES(2, GL_FLOAT, stride, _offsetof(Vertex, BoneWeights));
```

We're now ready to write some rendering code, taking into account that the number of supported matrix palettes might be less than the number of bones in our model. Check out Example 9-10 to see how we "cycle" the available matrix slots; further explanation follows the listing.

Example 9-10. ES 1.1 Render method for vertex skinning

```
const SkinnedFigure& figure = m_skinnedFigure;

// Set up for skinned rendering:
glMatrixMode(GL_MATRIX_PALETTE_OES);
glEnableClientState(GL_WEIGHT_ARRAY_OES);
glEnableClientState(GL_MATRIX_INDEX_ARRAY_OES);

glBindBuffer(GL_ELEMENT_ARRAY_BUFFER, figure.IndexBuffer);
glBindBuffer(GL_ARRAY_BUFFER, figure.VertexBuffer);

glMatrixIndexPointerOES(2, GL_UNSIGNED_BYTE, stride,
                        _offsetof(Vertex, BoneIndices));
glWeightPointerOES(2, GL_FLOAT, stride, _offsetof(Vertex, BoneWeights));
glVertexPointer(3, GL_FLOAT, stride, _offsetof(Vertex, Position));
glTexCoordPointer(2, GL_FLOAT, stride, _offsetof(Vertex, TexCoord));
```

```
// Make several rendering passes if need be,
// depending on the maximum bone count:
int startBoneIndex = 0;
while (startBoneIndex < BoneCount - 1) {

    int endBoneIndex = min(BoneCount, startBoneIndex + m_maxBoneCount);

    for (int boneIndex = startBoneIndex;
         boneIndex < endBoneIndex;
         ++boneIndex)
    {

        int slotIndex;

        // All passes beyond the first pass are offset by one.
        if (startBoneIndex > 0)
            slotIndex = (boneIndex + 1) % m_maxBoneCount;
        else
            slotIndex = boneIndex % m_maxBoneCount;

        glCurrentPaletteMatrixOES(slotIndex);
        mat4 modelview = figure.Matrices[boneIndex];
        glLoadMatrixf(modelview.Pointer());
    }

    size_t indicesPerBone = 12 + 6 * (NumDivisions + 1);
    int startIndex = startBoneIndex * indicesPerBone;
    int boneCount = endBoneIndex - startBoneIndex;

    const GLvoid* byteOffset = (const GLvoid*) (startIndex * 2);
    int indexCount = boneCount * indicesPerBone;
    glDrawElements(GL_TRIANGLES, indexCount,
                   GL_UNSIGNED_SHORT, byteOffset);

    startBoneIndex = endBoneIndex - 1;
}
```

Under our system, if the model has 17 bones and the hardware supports 11 bones, vertices affected by the 12th matrix should have an index of 1 rather than 11; see Figure 9-6 for a depiction of how this works.

| Pass 1: | 0 | 1 | 2 | 3 | 4 | 5 | 6 | 7 | 8 | 9 | 10 |
| Pass 2: | 10 | 11 | 12 | 13 | 14 | 15 | 16 | | | | |

Figure 9-6. Rendering a 17-bone system on 11-bone hardware

Unfortunately, our system breaks down if at least one vertex needs to be affected by two bones that "span" the two passes, but this rarely occurs in practice.

Generating Weights and Indices

The limitation on available matrix palettes also needs to be taken into account when annotating the vertices with their respective matrix indices. Example 9-11 shows how our system generates the blend weights and indices for a single limb. This procedure can be used for both the ES 1.1-based method and the shader-based method; in this book's sample code, I placed it in a base class that's shared by both rendering engines.

Example 9-11. Generation of bone weights and indices

```
for (int j = 0; j < NumSlices; ++j) {

    GLushort index0 = floor(blendWeight);
    GLushort index1 = ceil(blendWeight);
    index1 = index1 < BoneCount ? index1 : index0;

    int i0 = index0 % maxBoneCount;
    int i1 = index1 % maxBoneCount;

    // All passes beyond the first pass are offset by one.
    if (index0 >= maxBoneCount || index1 >= maxBoneCount) {
        i0++;
        i1++;
    }

    destVertex->BoneIndices = i1 | (i0 << 8);
    destVertex->BoneWeights.x = blendWeight - index0;
    destVertex->BoneWeights.y = 1.0f - destVertex->BoneWeights.x;
    destVertex++;

    destVertex->BoneIndices = i1 | (i0 << 8);
    destVertex->BoneWeights.x = blendWeight - index0;
    destVertex->BoneWeights.y = 1.0f - destVertex->BoneWeights.x;
    destVertex++;

    blendWeight += (j < NumSlices / 2) ? delta0 : delta1;
}
```

In Example 9-11, the delta0 and delta1 variables are the increments used for each half of limb; refer to Table 9-2 and flip back to Figure 9-5 to see how this works.

Table 9-2. Bone weight increments

Limb	Increment
First half of upper arm	0
Second half of upper arm	0.166
First half of forearm	0.166
Second half of forearm	0

For simplicity, we're using a linear falloff of bone weights here, but I encourage you to try other variations. Bone weight distribution is a bit of a black art.

That's it for the skinning demo! As always, you can find the complete sample code on this book's website. You might also want to check out the 3D skinning demo included in the PowerVR SDK.

Watch Out for Pinching

Before you get too excited, I should warn you that vertex skinning isn't a magic elixir. An issue called *pinching* has caused many a late night for animators and developers. Pinching is a side effect of interpolation that causes severely angled joints to become distorted (Figure 9-7).

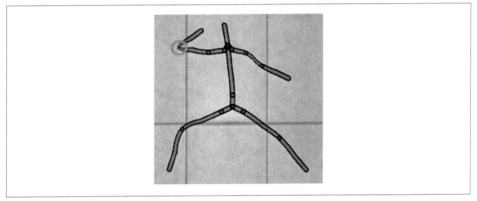

Figure 9-7. Pinching

If you're using OpenGL ES 2.0 and pinching is causing headaches, you should research a technique called *dual quaternion skinning*, developed by Ladislav Kavan and others.

Further Reading

The list of optimizations in this chapter is by no means complete. Apple's "OpenGL ES Programming Guide" document, available from the iPhone developer site, has an excellent list of up-to-date advice. Imagination Technologies publishes a similar document that's worth a look.

Since we're at the end of this book, I'd also like to point out a couple resources for adding to your general OpenGL skills. *OpenGL Shading Language* (Addison-Wesley Professional) by Randi Rost provides a tight focus on shader development. Although this book was written for desktop GLSL, the shading language for ES is so similar to standard GLSL that almost everything in Randi's book can be applied to OpenGL ES as well.

The official specification documents for OpenGL ES are available as PDFs at the Khronos website:

http://www.khronos.org/registry/gles/

The OpenGL specs are incredibly detailed and unambiguous. I find them to be a handy reference, but they're not exactly ideal for casual armchair reading. For a more web-friendly reference, check out the HTML man pages at Khronos:

http://www.khronos.org/opengles/sdk/docs/man/

In the end, one of the best ways to learn is to play—write some 3D iPhone apps from the ground up, and enjoy yourself!

C++ Vector Library

A decent vector library is useful in any 3D graphics application but doubly so when you're using OpenGL ES 2.0, since it doesn't provide functions for matrix math on its own. Review "Vector Beautification with C++" on page 66 for an overview of the library listed in this appendix. In brief, it's template-based C++, and it's composed solely of three simple header files. The library defines a set of types that are named after GLSL's vector types.

Disclaimer Regarding Performance

This code herein is designed for readability and ease of use. It does not attempt to leverage the ARM's special instructions for squeezing out maximum performance from your CPU.

First- and second-generation iPhones and iPod touches have dedicated hardware called the *VFP unit*, which can help with vector math. The iPhone 3GS has an extended instruction set for these operations called *NEON*. If you're interested in using these special instruction sets, I suggest taking a look at the math portion of the excellent *oolong* library, available here:

> *http://code.google.com/p/oolongengine*

The gcc compiler may be able to generate some vector-oriented ARM instructions when maximum optimizations are enabled, but there are no guarantees. In Xcode, select Project→Edit Project Settings, go to the Build tab, select Show All Settings, and look for the Optimization Level option under the *Code Generation* heading. Don't assume anything until you look at the generated assembly code.

Vector.hpp

```cpp
#pragma once
#include <cmath>

const float Pi = 4 * std::atan(1.0f);
const float TwoPi = 2 * Pi;

template <typename T>
struct Vector2 {
    Vector2() {}
    Vector2(T x, T y) : x(x), y(y) {}
    T Dot(const Vector2& v) const
    {
        return x * v.x + y * v.y;
    }
    Vector2 operator+(const Vector2& v) const
    {
        return Vector2(x + v.x, y + v.y);
    }
    Vector2 operator-(const Vector2& v) const
    {
        return Vector2(x - v.x, y - v.y);
    }
    void operator+=(const Vector2& v)
    {
        *this = Vector2(x + v.x, y + v.y);
    }
    void operator-=(const Vector2& v)
    {
        *this = Vector2(x - v.x, y - v.y);
    }
    Vector2 operator/(float s) const
    {
        return Vector2(x / s, y / s);
    }
    Vector2 operator*(float s) const
    {
        return Vector2(x * s, y * s);
    }
    void operator/=(float s)
    {
        *this = Vector2(x / s, y / s);
    }
    void operator*=(float s)
    {
        *this = Vector2(x * s, y * s);
    }
    void Normalize()
    {
        float s = 1.0f / Length();
        x *= s;
        y *= s;
    }
    Vector2 Normalized() const
```

```cpp
    {
        Vector2 v = *this;
        v.Normalize();
        return v;
    }
    T LengthSquared() const
    {
        return x * x + y * y;
    }
    T Length() const
    {
        return sqrt(LengthSquared());
    }
    const T* Pointer() const
    {
        return &x;
    }
    operator Vector2<float>() const
    {
        return Vector2<float>(x, y);
    }
    bool operator==(const Vector2& v) const
    {
        return x == v.x && y == v.y;
    }
    Vector2 Lerp(float t, const Vector2& v) const
    {
        return Vector2(x * (1 - t) + v.x * t,
                       y * (1 - t) + v.y * t);
    }
    template <typename P>
    P* Write(P* pData)
    {
        Vector2* pVector = (Vector2*) pData;
        *pVector++ = *this;
        return (P*) pVector;
    }
    T x;
    T y;
};

template <typename T>
struct Vector3 {
    Vector3() {}
    Vector3(T x, T y, T z) : x(x), y(y), z(z) {}
    T Length()
    {
        return std::sqrt(x * x + y * y + z * z);
    }
    void Normalize()
    {
        float s = 1.0f / Length();
        x *= s;
        y *= s;
        z *= s;
```

```cpp
}
Vector3 Normalized() const
{
    Vector3 v = *this;
    v.Normalize();
    return v;
}
Vector3 Cross(const Vector3& v) const
{
    return Vector3(y * v.z - z * v.y,
                   z * v.x - x * v.z,
                   x * v.y - y * v.x);
}
T Dot(const Vector3& v) const
{
    return x * v.x + y * v.y + z * v.z;
}
Vector3 operator+(const Vector3& v) const
{
    return Vector3(x + v.x, y + v.y,  z + v.z);
}
void operator+=(const Vector3& v)
{
    x += v.x;
    y += v.y;
    z += v.z;
}
void operator-=(const Vector3& v)
{
    x -= v.x;
    y -= v.y;
    z -= v.z;
}
void operator/=(T s)
{
    x /= s;
    y /= s;
    z /= s;
}
Vector3 operator-(const Vector3& v) const
{
    return Vector3(x - v.x, y - v.y,  z - v.z);
}
Vector3 operator-() const
{
    return Vector3(-x, -y, -z);
}
Vector3 operator*(T s) const
{
    return Vector3(x * s, y * s, z * s);
}
Vector3 operator/(T s) const
{
    return Vector3(x / s, y / s, z / s);
}
```

```cpp
    bool operator==(const Vector3& v) const
    {
        return x == v.x && y == v.y && z == v.z;
    }
    Vector3 Lerp(float t, const Vector3& v) const
    {
        return Vector3(x * (1 - t) + v.x * t,
                       y * (1 - t) + v.y * t,
                       z * (1 - t) + v.z * t);
    }
    const T* Pointer() const
    {
        return &x;
    }
    template <typename P>
    P* Write(P* pData)
    {
        Vector3<T>* pVector = (Vector3<T>*) pData;
        *pVector++ = *this;
        return (P*) pVector;
    }
    T x;
    T y;
    T z;
};

template <typename T>
struct Vector4 {
    Vector4() {}
    Vector4(T x, T y, T z, T w) : x(x), y(y), z(z), w(w) {}
    Vector4(const Vector3<T>& v, T w) : x(v.x), y(v.y), z(v.z), w(w) {}
    T Dot(const Vector4& v) const
    {
        return x * v.x + y * v.y + z * v.z + w * v.w;
    }
    Vector4 Lerp(float t, const Vector4& v) const
    {
        return Vector4(x * (1 - t) + v.x * t,
                       y * (1 - t) + v.y * t,
                       z * (1 - t) + v.z * t,
                       w * (1 - t) + v.w * t);
    }
    const T* Pointer() const
    {
        return &x;
    }
    T x;
    T y;
    T z;
    T w;
};

typedef Vector2<bool> bvec2;

typedef Vector2<int> ivec2;
```

```cpp
typedef Vector3<int> ivec3;
typedef Vector4<int> ivec4;

typedef Vector2<float> vec2;
typedef Vector3<float> vec3;
typedef Vector4<float> vec4;
```

Matrix.hpp

```cpp
#pragma once
#include "Vector.hpp"

template <typename T>
struct Matrix2 {
    Matrix2()
    {
        x.x = 1; x.y = 0;
        y.x = 0; y.y = 1;
    }
    Matrix2(const T* m)
    {
        x.x = m[0]; x.y = m[1];
        y.x = m[2]; y.y = m[3];
    }
    vec2 x;
    vec2 y;
};

template <typename T>
struct Matrix3 {
    Matrix3()
    {
        x.x = 1; x.y = 0; x.z = 0;
        y.x = 0; y.y = 1; y.z = 0;
        z.x = 0; z.y = 0; z.z = 1;
    }
    Matrix3(const T* m)
    {
        x.x = m[0]; x.y = m[1]; x.z = m[2];
        y.x = m[3]; y.y = m[4]; y.z = m[5];
        z.x = m[6]; z.y = m[7]; z.z = m[8];
    }
    Matrix3(vec3 x, vec3 y, vec3 z) : x(x), y(y), z(z)
    {
    }
    Matrix3 Transposed() const
    {
        Matrix3 m;
        m.x.x = x.x; m.x.y = y.x; m.x.z = z.x;
        m.y.x = x.y; m.y.y = y.y; m.y.z = z.y;
        m.z.x = x.z; m.z.y = y.z; m.z.z = z.z;
        return m;
    }
    const T* Pointer() const
```

```cpp
    {
        return &x.x;
    }
    vec3 x;
    vec3 y;
    vec3 z;
};

template <typename T>
struct Matrix4 {
    Matrix4()
    {
        x.x = 1; x.y = 0; x.z = 0; x.w = 0;
        y.x = 0; y.y = 1; y.z = 0; y.w = 0;
        z.x = 0; z.y = 0; z.z = 1; z.w = 0;
        w.x = 0; w.y = 0; w.z = 0; w.w = 1;
    }
    Matrix4(const Matrix3<T>& m)
    {
        x.x = m.x.x; x.y = m.x.y; x.z = m.x.z; x.w = 0;
        y.x = m.y.x; y.y = m.y.y; y.z = m.y.z; y.w = 0;
        z.x = m.z.x; z.y = m.z.y; z.z = m.z.z; z.w = 0;
        w.x = 0; w.y = 0; w.z = 0; w.w = 1;
    }
    Matrix4(const T* m)
    {
        x.x = m[0];  x.y = m[1];  x.z = m[2];  x.w = m[3];
        y.x = m[4];  y.y = m[5];  y.z = m[6];  y.w = m[7];
        z.x = m[8];  z.y = m[9];  z.z = m[10]; z.w = m[11];
        w.x = m[12]; w.y = m[13]; w.z = m[14]; w.w = m[15];
    }
    Matrix4 operator * (const Matrix4& b) const
    {
        Matrix4 m;
        m.x.x = x.x * b.x.x + x.y * b.y.x + x.z * b.z.x + x.w * b.w.x;
        m.x.y = x.x * b.x.y + x.y * b.y.y + x.z * b.z.y + x.w * b.w.y;
        m.x.z = x.x * b.x.z + x.y * b.y.z + x.z * b.z.z + x.w * b.w.z;
        m.x.w = x.x * b.x.w + x.y * b.y.w + x.z * b.z.w + x.w * b.w.w;
        m.y.x = y.x * b.x.x + y.y * b.y.x + y.z * b.z.x + y.w * b.w.x;
        m.y.y = y.x * b.x.y + y.y * b.y.y + y.z * b.z.y + y.w * b.w.y;
        m.y.z = y.x * b.x.z + y.y * b.y.z + y.z * b.z.z + y.w * b.w.z;
        m.y.w = y.x * b.x.w + y.y * b.y.w + y.z * b.z.w + y.w * b.w.w;
        m.z.x = z.x * b.x.x + z.y * b.y.x + z.z * b.z.x + z.w * b.w.x;
        m.z.y = z.x * b.x.y + z.y * b.y.y + z.z * b.z.y + z.w * b.w.y;
        m.z.z = z.x * b.x.z + z.y * b.y.z + z.z * b.z.z + z.w * b.w.z;
        m.z.w = z.x * b.x.w + z.y * b.y.w + z.z * b.z.w + z.w * b.w.w;
        m.w.x = w.x * b.x.x + w.y * b.y.x + w.z * b.z.x + w.w * b.w.x;
        m.w.y = w.x * b.x.y + w.y * b.y.y + w.z * b.z.y + w.w * b.w.y;
        m.w.z = w.x * b.x.z + w.y * b.y.z + w.z * b.z.z + w.w * b.w.z;
        m.w.w = w.x * b.x.w + w.y * b.y.w + w.z * b.z.w + w.w * b.w.w;
        return m;
    }
    Vector4<T> operator * (const Vector4<T>& b) const
    {
        Vector4<T> v;
```

```cpp
        v.x = x.x * b.x + x.y * b.y + x.z * b.z + x.w * b.w;
        v.y = y.x * b.x + y.y * b.y + y.z * b.z + y.w * b.w;
        v.z = z.x * b.x + z.y * b.y + z.z * b.z + z.w * b.w;
        v.w = w.x * b.x + w.y * b.y + w.z * b.z + w.w * b.w;
        return v;
    }
    Matrix4& operator *= (const Matrix4& b)
    {
        Matrix4 m = *this * b;
        return (*this = m);
    }
    Matrix4 Transposed() const
    {
        Matrix4 m;
        m.x.x = x.x; m.x.y = y.x; m.x.z = z.x; m.x.w = w.x;
        m.y.x = x.y; m.y.y = y.y; m.y.z = z.y; m.y.w = w.y;
        m.z.x = x.z; m.z.y = y.z; m.z.z = z.z; m.z.w = w.z;
        m.w.x = x.w; m.w.y = y.w; m.w.z = z.w; m.w.w = w.w;
        return m;
    }
    Matrix3<T> ToMat3() const
    {
        Matrix3<T> m;
        m.x.x = x.x; m.y.x = y.x; m.z.x = z.x;
        m.x.y = x.y; m.y.y = y.y; m.z.y = z.y;
        m.x.z = x.z; m.y.z = y.z; m.z.z = z.z;
        return m;
    }
    const T* Pointer() const
    {
        return &x.x;
    }
    static Matrix4<T> Identity()
    {
        return Matrix4();
    }
    static Matrix4<T> Translate(const Vector3<T>& v)
    {
        Matrix4 m;
        m.x.x = 1; m.x.y = 0; m.x.z = 0; m.x.w = 0;
        m.y.x = 0; m.y.y = 1; m.y.z = 0; m.y.w = 0;
        m.z.x = 0; m.z.y = 0; m.z.z = 1; m.z.w = 0;
        m.w.x = v.x; m.w.y = v.y; m.w.z = v.z; m.w.w = 1;
        return m;
    }
    static Matrix4<T> Translate(T x, T y, T z)
    {
        Matrix4 m;
        m.x.x = 1; m.x.y = 0; m.x.z = 0; m.x.w = 0;
        m.y.x = 0; m.y.y = 1; m.y.z = 0; m.y.w = 0;
        m.z.x = 0; m.z.y = 0; m.z.z = 1; m.z.w = 0;
        m.w.x = x; m.w.y = y; m.w.z = z; m.w.w = 1;
        return m;
    }
    static Matrix4<T> Scale(T s)
```

```
{
    Matrix4 m;
    m.x.x = s; m.x.y = 0; m.x.z = 0; m.x.w = 0;
    m.y.x = 0; m.y.y = s; m.y.z = 0; m.y.w = 0;
    m.z.x = 0; m.z.y = 0; m.z.z = s; m.z.w = 0;
    m.w.x = 0; m.w.y = 0; m.w.z = 0; m.w.w = 1;
    return m;
}
static Matrix4<T> Scale(T x, T y, T z)
{
    Matrix4 m;
    m.x.x = x; m.x.y = 0; m.x.z = 0; m.x.w = 0;
    m.y.x = 0; m.y.y = y; m.y.z = 0; m.y.w = 0;
    m.z.x = 0; m.z.y = 0; m.z.z = z; m.z.w = 0;
    m.w.x = 0; m.w.y = 0; m.w.z = 0; m.w.w = 1;
    return m;
}
static Matrix4<T> Rotate(T degrees)
{
    T radians = degrees * 3.14159f / 180.0f;
    T s = std::sin(radians);
    T c = std::cos(radians);

    Matrix4 m = Identity();
    m.x.x =  c; m.x.y = s;
    m.y.x = -s; m.y.y = c;
    return m;
}
static Matrix4<T> Rotate(T degrees, const vec3& axis)
{
    T radians = degrees * 3.14159f / 180.0f;
    T s = std::sin(radians);
    T c = std::cos(radians);

    Matrix4 m = Identity();
    m.x.x = c + (1 - c) * axis.x * axis.x;
    m.x.y = (1 - c) * axis.x * axis.y - axis.z * s;
    m.x.z = (1 - c) * axis.x * axis.z + axis.y * s;
    m.y.x = (1 - c) * axis.x * axis.y + axis.z * s;
    m.y.y = c + (1 - c) * axis.y * axis.y;
    m.y.z = (1 - c) * axis.y * axis.z - axis.x * s;
    m.z.x = (1 - c) * axis.y * axis.z - axis.y * s;
    m.z.y = (1 - c) * axis.y * axis.z + axis.x * s;
    m.z.z = c + (1 - c) * axis.z * axis.z;
    return m;
}
static Matrix4<T> Ortho(T left, T right, T bottom, T top, T near, T far)
{
    T a = 2.0f / (right - left);
    T b = 2.0f / (top - bottom);
    T c = -2.0f / (far - near);
    T tx = (right + left) / (right - left);
    T ty = (top + bottom) / (top - bottom);
    T tz = (far + near) / (far - near);
    Matrix4 m;
```

```cpp
        m.x.x = a; m.x.y = 0; m.x.z = 0; m.x.w = tx;
        m.y.x = 0; m.y.y = b; m.y.z = 0; m.y.w = ty;
        m.z.x = 0; m.z.y = 0; m.z.z = c; m.z.w = tz;
        m.w.x = 0; m.w.y = 0; m.w.z = 0; m.w.w = 1;
        return m;
    }
    static Matrix4<T> Frustum(T left, T right, T bottom, T top, T near, T far)
    {
        T a = 2 * near / (right - left);
        T b = 2 * near / (top - bottom);
        T c = (right + left) / (right - left);
        T d = (top + bottom) / (top - bottom);
        T e = - (far + near) / (far - near);
        T f = -2 * far * near / (far - near);
        Matrix4 m;
        m.x.x = a; m.x.y = 0; m.x.z = 0; m.x.w = 0;
        m.y.x = 0; m.y.y = b; m.y.z = 0; m.y.w = 0;
        m.z.x = c; m.z.y = d; m.z.z = e; m.z.w = -1;
        m.w.x = 0; m.w.y = 0; m.w.z = f; m.w.w = 1;
        return m;
    }
    static Matrix4<T> LookAt(const Vector3<T>& eye,
                             const Vector3<T>& target,
                             const Vector3<T>& up)
    {
        Vector3<T> z = (eye - target).Normalized();
        Vector3<T> x = up.Cross(z).Normalized();
        Vector3<T> y = z.Cross(x).Normalized();

        Matrix4<T> m;
        m.x = Vector4<T>(x, 0);
        m.y = Vector4<T>(y, 0);
        m.z = Vector4<T>(z, 0);
        m.w = Vector4<T>(0, 0, 0, 1);

        Vector4<T> eyePrime = m * Vector4<T>(-eye, 1);
        m = m.Transposed();
        m.w = eyePrime;

        return m;
    }
    vec4 x;
    vec4 y;
    vec4 z;
    vec4 w;
};

typedef Matrix2<float> mat2;
typedef Matrix3<float> mat3;
typedef Matrix4<float> mat4;
```

Quaternion.hpp

```cpp
#pragma once
#include "Matrix.hpp"

template <typename T>
struct QuaternionT {
    T x;
    T y;
    T z;
    T w;

    QuaternionT();
    QuaternionT(T x, T y, T z, T w);

    QuaternionT<T> Slerp(T mu, const QuaternionT<T>& q) const;
    QuaternionT<T> Rotated(const QuaternionT<T>& b) const;
    QuaternionT<T> Scaled(T scale) const;
    T Dot(const QuaternionT<T>& q) const;
    Matrix3<T> ToMatrix() const;
    Vector4<T> ToVector() const;
    QuaternionT<T> operator-(const QuaternionT<T>& q) const;
    QuaternionT<T> operator+(const QuaternionT<T>& q) const;
    bool operator==(const QuaternionT<T>& q) const;
    bool operator!=(const QuaternionT<T>& q) const;

    void Normalize();
    void Rotate(const QuaternionT<T>& q);

    static QuaternionT<T> CreateFromVectors(const Vector3<T>& v0, const Vector3<T>& v1);
    static QuaternionT<T> CreateFromAxisAngle(const Vector3<T>& axis, float radians);
};

template <typename T>
inline QuaternionT<T>::QuaternionT() : x(0), y(0), z(0), w(1)
{
}

template <typename T>
inline QuaternionT<T>::QuaternionT(T x, T y, T z, T w) : x(x), y(y), z(z), w(w)
{
}

// Ken Shoemake's famous method.
template <typename T>
inline QuaternionT<T> QuaternionT<T>::Slerp(T t, const QuaternionT<T>& v1) const
{
    const T epsilon = 0.0005f;
    T dot = Dot(v1);

    if (dot > 1 - epsilon) {
        QuaternionT<T> result = v1 + (*this - v1).Scaled(t);
        result.Normalize();
        return result;
    }
```

```
        if (dot < 0)
            dot = 0;

        if (dot > 1)
            dot = 1;

        T theta0 = std::acos(dot);
        T theta = theta0 * t;

        QuaternionT<T> v2 = (v1 - Scaled(dot));
        v2.Normalize();

        QuaternionT<T> q = Scaled(std::cos(theta)) + v2.Scaled(std::sin(theta));
        q.Normalize();
        return q;
}

template <typename T>
inline QuaternionT<T> QuaternionT<T>::Rotated(const QuaternionT<T>& b) const
{
    QuaternionT<T> q;
    q.w = w * b.w - x * b.x - y * b.y - z * b.z;
    q.x = w * b.x + x * b.w + y * b.z - z * b.y;
    q.y = w * b.y + y * b.w + z * b.x - x * b.z;
    q.z = w * b.z + z * b.w + x * b.y - y * b.x;
    q.Normalize();
    return q;
}

template <typename T>
inline QuaternionT<T> QuaternionT<T>::Scaled(T s) const
{
    return QuaternionT<T>(x * s, y * s, z * s, w * s);
}

template <typename T>
inline T QuaternionT<T>::Dot(const QuaternionT<T>& q) const
{
    return x * q.x + y * q.y + z * q.z + w * q.w;
}

template <typename T>
inline Matrix3<T> QuaternionT<T>::ToMatrix() const
{
    const T s = 2;
    T xs, ys, zs;
    T wx, wy, wz;
    T xx, xy, xz;
    T yy, yz, zz;
    xs = x * s;  ys = y * s;  zs = z * s;
    wx = w * xs; wy = w * ys; wz = w * zs;
    xx = x * xs; xy = x * ys; xz = x * zs;
    yy = y * ys; yz = y * zs; zz = z * zs;
    Matrix3<T> m;
```

```
    m.x.x = 1 - (yy + zz); m.y.x = xy - wz;  m.z.x = xz + wy;
    m.x.y = xy + wz; m.y.y = 1 - (xx + zz); m.z.y = yz - wx;
    m.x.z = xz - wy; m.y.z = yz + wx;  m.z.z = 1 - (xx + yy);
    return m;
}

template <typename T>
inline Vector4<T> QuaternionT<T>::ToVector() const
{
    return Vector4<T>(x, y, z, w);
}

template <typename T>
QuaternionT<T> QuaternionT<T>::operator-(const QuaternionT<T>& q) const
{
    return QuaternionT<T>(x - q.x, y - q.y, z - q.z, w - q.w);
}

template <typename T>
QuaternionT<T> QuaternionT<T>::operator+(const QuaternionT<T>& q) const
{
    return QuaternionT<T>(x + q.x, y + q.y, z + q.z, w + q.w);
}

template <typename T>
bool QuaternionT<T>::operator==(const QuaternionT<T>& q) const
{
    return x == q.x && y == q.y && z == q.z && w == q.w;
}

template <typename T>
bool QuaternionT<T>::operator!=(const QuaternionT<T>& q) const
{
    return !(*this == q);
}

// Compute the quaternion that rotates from a to b, avoiding numerical instability.
// Taken from "The Shortest Arc Quaternion" by Stan Melax in "Game Programming Gems."
template <typename T>
inline QuaternionT<T> QuaternionT<T>::CreateFromVectors(const Vector3<T>& v0,
    const Vector3<T>& v1)
{
    if (v0 == -v1)
        return QuaternionT<T>::CreateFromAxisAngle(vec3(1, 0, 0), Pi);

    Vector3<T> c = v0.Cross(v1);
    T d = v0.Dot(v1);
    T s = std::sqrt((1 + d) * 2);

    QuaternionT<T> q;
    q.x = c.x / s;
    q.y = c.y / s;
    q.z = c.z / s;
    q.w = s / 2.0f;
    return q;
```

```
}

template <typename T>
inline QuaternionT<T>  QuaternionT<T>::CreateFromAxisAngle(const Vector3<T>& axis,
    float radians)
{
    QuaternionT<T> q;
    q.w = std::cos(radians / 2);
    q.x = q.y = q.z = std::sin(radians / 2);
    q.x *= axis.x;
    q.y *= axis.y;
    q.z *= axis.z;
    return q;
}

template <typename T>
inline void QuaternionT<T>::Normalize()
{
    *this = Scaled(1 / std::sqrt(Dot(*this)));
}

template <typename T>
inline void QuaternionT<T>::Rotate(const QuaternionT<T>& q2)
{
    QuaternionT<T> q;
    QuaternionT<T>& q1 = *this;

    q.w = q1.w * q2.w - q1.x * q2.x - q1.y * q2.y - q1.z * q2.z;
    q.x = q1.w * q2.x + q1.x * q2.w + q1.y * q2.z - q1.z * q2.y;
    q.y = q1.w * q2.y + q1.y * q2.w + q1.z * q2.x - q1.x * q2.z;
    q.z = q1.w * q2.z + q1.z * q2.w + q1.x * q2.y - q1.y * q2.x;

    q.Normalize();
    *this = q;
}

typedef QuaternionT<float> Quaternion;
```

Index

Symbols

+ (plus sign), denoting class methods in Objective-C, 15
- (minus sign), denoting instance methods in Objective-C, 15
2D rendering in OpenGL ES, 281
4D coordinates, 48
@ (at sign), prefixing Objective-C keywords, 13
@end keyword, 13
@interface keyword, 13
@property keyword, 19
@synthesize keyword, 19
{ } (curly braces), enclosing data fields in class declarations, 14

A

accelerometer support, adding to Holodeck (example), 269–272
  in GLView class, 269–272
  phi as function of acceleration, 272
AccelerometerGraph example, iPhone developer site, 269
accessor methods, defining, 19
additive blending, 322
alloc-init pattern in Objective-C, 17, 20
alpha, 221
  ensuring color contains, 222
  premultiplied, 224
  setting for buttons in Holodeck HUD (example), 266
  tweaking uniformly across entire texture, 229
alpha combiners, 332

arithmetic operations used for, 334
alpha testing, 226
  using with distance fields in ES 1.1, 300
altitude, 257
ambient lighting, 135
  ambient occlusion, 373
  in OpenGL, 136
animations, 64–66
  animating rotation with quaternions, 65
  Core Animation framework, 2
  heads-up display (HUD), 264
  interpolation techniques, 64
  texture coordinates, 181
  transition animation in wireframe viewer, 115–117
  using sprite sheets, 307
  vertex skinning, 377, 379–381
    generating weights and indices, 386
    OpenGL ES 1.1, 383–385
    OpenGL ES 2.0, 381–383
    problems with pinching, 387
anisotropic filtering, 352
anti-aliasing, 221
  rendering anti-aliased lines with textures, 252–256
  using offscreen FBOs, 239–252
    jittering, 247–252
    supersampling, 239–247
Apple
  iPhone developer site, 5
  OpenGL ES Programming Guide, 387
Apple Macintosh, transitioning to, 3
application delegate, 19–21
ApplicationEngine class, 104
  consuming IResourceManager from, 161

We'd like to hear your suggestions for improving our indexes. Send email to *index@oreilly.com*.

(see also shaders)
built-in variables, 147
gl_FragColor variable, 145
OES_standard_derivatives extension, 303
precision qualifiers, 146
texture lookups and performance, 377
frame rate, 282, 365
framebuffer objects (FBOs), 17
anti-aliasing tricks with offscreen FBOs,
239–252
jittering, 247–252
supersampling, 239–247
attaching stencil buffer, 231
Gaussian bloom with ten FBOs, 357
gl_FragColor variable, 147
image postprocessing effects, 354
initializing, 27
promotion to core API in OpenGL ES 2.0,
39
setting up in HelloCone (example), 71
setup code in HelloCone (example), 119
simulating stencil buffer with framebuffer
alpha, 236–239
frameworks
defined, 12
referencing 3.1 (or greater) version of SDK,
36
frustum for field of view, 60, 122
function suffixes in OpenGL ES, 52
fwidth function, 303

G

game logic, separation from rendering engine,
10
Gaussian bloom, 354, 356
example code, 358–364
Gaussian filter, 356
gcc compiler, 389
generic attribute, 47
geometry
loading from OBJ files, 157–163
implementing ISurface, 162
managing resource files, 159–162
gl*Pointer functions, 96
glActiveTexture function, 310
glAlphaFunc function, 226
glBindBuffer function, 95
glBindRenderbuffer function, 123
glBlendColor function, 223

glBlendEquation function, 227
glBlendEquationSeparate function, 227
glBlendFunc function, 222
adjusting to handle premultiplied alpha,
224
sfactor and dfactor arguments, 223
glBufferData function, 95
glBufferSubData function, 95
glCheckFramebufferStatus function, 244
glClear command, 77
glClearDepthf function, 124
glClipPlanef function, 375
glColor4f function, 92
adjusting vertex color, 229
glColorMask function, 234
glCompressedTexImage2D function, 197
glDeleteBuffers function, 175
glDepthFunc function, 124
glDepthMask function, 234
glDepthRangef function, 50
glDrawArrays function, 28, 89
glDrawElements function, 89, 92
indices parameter, 97
glDrawTexOES function, 293–295, 309
glFramebufferTexture2D function, 243
glFrustumf command, 60
glGenBuffers function, 95
glGenerateMipmap function, 187
glGetError function, 244
glLightfv function, 142
glLightModelf function, 144
glMaterialf function, 140
glMaterialfv function, 140
glMatrixMode function, 59, 384
glOrthof function, 28
orthographic projection, 60
glow effect, 306
glPointSize function, 324
glPolygonOffset function, 156
glPushMatrix and glPopMatrix methods, 30
glRotatef function, 58
glRotatef method, 30
glScalef function, 55, 85
GLSL (OpenGL Shading Language), 34
resources for further information, 387
storage qualifiers, 145
translating lighting pseudocode to, 148
glStencilFunc function, 233
glStencilOp function, 233

generating glyphs texture, 285–288
installing Python modules, 285
modules for imaging manipulation, 285

Q

quadratic easing equations, 64
Quartz
    generating and transforming OpenGL
        textures, 201–204
    linking in library with OpenGL library, 12
    scaling textures to POT, 206
Quartz 2D rendering engine, 1
Quaternion.hpp file, 67
quaternions, 65
    handling trackball-like behavior, 108
    rotation state in HelloCone (example), 69
    use in HelloCone (example), 71

R

reflect function, 350
reflection with stencil buffer, 230–236
    rendering disk to stencil only, 232–234
    rendering disk with front-to-back blending,
        236
    rendering real object, 236
    rending reflected object with stencil testing,
        235
reflections with cube maps, 347–352
    rendering to cube map, 351
reflective surfaces, creating, 329
Render method
    implementing for HelloCone (example), 77
    for vertex skinning, 382, 384
renderbuffers, 17
rendering engine
    augmented reality Holodeck (example)
        modifying to support camera underlay,
            278
    bloom (example), 359–364
    bump mapping example, ES 2.0, 342
    changing implementation for OpenGL 2.0
        application, 37–42
    declaration in HelloCone (example), 69–71
    defining and consuming interface, 22–25
    enabling textures in ES 1.1, 172–175
    enabling textures in ES 2.0, 175–179
    formats for textures, 190–191
    handling device orientation, 29–31

implementing, 26–29
passing resource manager to during
    construction, 169
Quartz texture loading code, 202
Render method for HelloCone (example),
    77
separation from application engine, 10
with shaders in HelloCone (example), 78
    Render method, 79
resource files
    image file for grid cell in ModelViewer
        texturing, 166
    managing, 159–162
ResourceManager class, 160
    adding PVRTC support, 195
    creating and passing to rendering engine
        during construction, 169
    format for textures, 189
    low-precision uncompressed texture
        formats, 199
    with PNG loading, 168
    Quartz generation of texture, 203
    Quartz texture loading code, 202
    texture scaling to power-of-two, 206–208
RGB combiners, 332
    list of arithmetic operations used for, 333
    <operand> arguments, 334
RGB, reason for using, 136
right-hand rule (cross product), 130
rotation
    animating, 31–33
    animating with quaternions, 65
    responding to changes in device orientation,
        29
    smooth, in three dimensions, 75
    trackball rotation in wireframe viewer, 106–
        108
rotation transform, 56
row vectors, 53

S

samplerCube type, 350
sampling, 165
    supersampling, 239–247
    tweaking for mipmaps levels, 186
scale transform, 55
    for model matrix, 55
SDK references, changing, 36
shaders, 34–42, 34

normal transforms, 131
OBJ file with vertex normals, 158
in OpenGL ES, 128
in per-pixel lighting fragment shader, 154
transformation by shaders from tangent to object space, 337

T

tab bar, creating for wireframe viewer, 111–114
tangent plane, 129
tangent space, 337
support for computing tangent in ParametricSurface, 339
target parameter for binding buffered data, 95
tessellation, 73
cone tessellation, indexed, 91
lighting and, 152
parametric surfaces, 100
texels, 165
text rendering, 281–307
crisper text with distance fields, 295–307
adding effects with fragment shaders, 300
generating distance fields with Python, 297–300
outline, flow, and shadow effects, 304–307
smoothing and derivatives, 301–304
using in ES 1.1 with alpha testing, 300
drawing FPS counter, 282–293
generating glyphs texture with Python, 284–288
rendering FPS text, 288–293
simple text layout algorithm, 284
simplifying with glDrawTexOES, 293–295
texture combiners, 329, 332–335
GL_DOT3_RGB, 343
texture coordinate attribute, 47
texture environments, 330
texture lookups
anisotropic filtering, 353
limiting number of, 354–358
shader performance and, 377
texture2D function, 177
textureCube function, 351
textures, 165–179

adding to ModelViewer (example), 165–179
generating texture coordinates, 169–172
rendering engine (ES 1.1), 172–175
rendering engine (ES 2.0), 175–179
alpha, 225
anisotropic filtering, 352
compression with PVRTC, 191–198
creating with the camera, 208–219
rendering image implementation, 214–219
enabling mipmapping in ModelViewer (example), 186
fighting aliasing with filtering, 181
formats and types, 187–191
loading formats, 188–191
generating and transforming OpenGL textures with Quartz, 201–204
generating glyphs texture with Python, 284–288
improving quality and performance with mipmaps, 184–186
line anti-aliasing with, 252–256
low-precision, and PowerVR SDK, 198–201
multitexturing, 309
normal maps, 335
reducing binding operations, 367
representing distance fields in, 296
shifting color with per-vertex color, 229
size constraints, 204–208
scaling to POT, 206–208
sprite sheets, 307
texture combiners in OpenGL ES 1.1, 332–335
texture coordinates, 180
texture environments in OpenGL ES 1.1, 330–332
texturing optimizations, 373
texturetool, 192
encoding argument, 192
explanation of parameters, 192
making automatic step in Xcode build process, 193
third-order texture filtering, 296
toon shading, 154
Touch, 1
touch points, 83

About the Author

Philip Rideout has been a fanatic of real-time graphics programming for over a decade. He has held positions at several pioneering graphics companies, including Intergraph, 3Dlabs, and NVIDIA. Philip currently works at Medical Simulation Corporation in Denver, where he develops new ways to visualize the inside of the human body.

Colophon

The insect on the cover of *iPhone 3D Programming* is a grasshopper (insects of the suborder *Caelifera*). To date, there have been over 11,000 different species discovered, about 660 of which are found in North America. They thrive in all kinds of habitats, including the rainforest, grasslands, and deserts.

Grasshoppers have short antennae, wings, and large back legs that allow them to jump nearly 20 times their body length. Their legs also help produce the familiar chirping sound grasshoppers are known for when they rub against the insect's abdomen.

Several species of grasshopper are categorized as locusts, due to their habit of swarming. These swarms come about when locusts are overcrowded. All grasshoppers feed on grass and other live plant matter, consuming roughly 16 times their weight each day. Most species are green or brown so they can camouflage themselves from predators, although more colorful grasshoppers can be found in tropical climates. If picked up or otherwise threatened, grasshoppers will spit out a brownish liquid known colloquially as "tobacco juice."

Grasshoppers are the only kosher insects—Leviticus 11:21–22 forbids the consumption of any flying insect with legs, except for the locust. A locust swarm was also one of the biblical plagues of Egypt.

The cover image is from the Dover Pictorial Archive. The cover font is Adobe ITC Garamond. The text font is Linotype Birka; the heading font is Adobe Myriad Condensed; and the code font is LucasFont's TheSansMonoCondensed.

CPSIA information can be obtained at www.ICGtesting.com
Printed in the USA
BVOW060534190612

293070BV00007B/2/P